The Eagle Has Eyes

LATINOS IN THE UNITED STATES SERIES

The Eagle Has Eyes

THE FBI SURVEILLANCE OF CÉSAR ESTRADA CHÁVEZ
OF THE UNITED FARM WORKERS UNION
OF AMERICA, 1965–1975

José Angel Gutiérrez

Michigan State University Press • *East Lansing*

⊗ The paper used in this publication meets the minimum requirements
of ANSI/NISO Z39.48–1992 (R 1997) (Permanence of Paper).

Michigan State University Press
East Lansing, Michigan 48823-5245

Printed and bound in the United States of America.

28 27 26 25 24 23 22 21 20 19   1 2 3 4 5 6 7 8 9 10

LIBRARY OF CONGRESS CATALOGING-IN-PUBLICATION DATA
Names: Gutierrez, Jose Angel, author.
Title: The eagle has eyes : the FBI surveillance of César Estrada Chávez
of the United Farm Workers Union of America, 1965–1975 / Jose Angel Gutierrez.
Description: East Lansing : Michigan State University Press, [2019] | Series: Latinos
in the United States | Includes bibliographical references and index.
Identifiers: LCCN 2018020123| ISBN 9781611863079 (pbk. : alk. paper)
| ISBN 9781609175863 (pdf) | ISBN 9781628953503 (epub) | ISBN 9781628963502 (kindle)
Subjects: LCSH: Chávez, César, 1927–1993. | United Farm Workers. | United States. Federal Bureau of
Investigation. | Domestic intelligence—United States—History—20th century. | Labor unions—Political
activity—United States—History. | Civil rights—United States—History—20th century. | United States—
Politics and government—20th century.
Classification: LCC HD6509.C48 G88 2019 | DDC 331.88/13092—dc23
LC record available at https://lccn.loc.gov/2018020123

Book and cover design by Charlie Sharp, Sharp Desígns, East Lansing, MI
Cover art is "Huelga," 1970s, The United Farm Worker (UFW) Collection: Poster & Graphics, #31870.
Walter P. Reuther Library, Archives of Labor and Urban Affairs, Wayne State University.

Michigan State University Press is a member of the Green Press Initiative and is
committed to developing and encouraging ecologically responsible publishing
practices. For more information about the Green Press Initiative and the use of
recycled paper in book publishing, please visit *www.greenpressinitiative.org*.

Visit Michigan State University Press at *www.msupress.org*

To all of us who have been the target of surveillance by local, state, and federal governments (U.S. and Mexico) over the years. To those who have not escaped that vigilance, entrapment, character assassination, dragnets, and have been or still are incarcerated or in exile. And to those among us, the fortunate ones, who have remained unindicted, not convicted, and unjailed for any length of time.

I can only imagine what greater successes at fundamental social change we could have achieved but for the counterintelligence operations of governments that viewed us as subversives because we opposed their governance, their policies, and only sought a better quality of life. They used the "people's" resources illegally to enhance their police power and thwart our every move.

To my wife, Natalia Verjat, and our blended children, Adrian, Tozi Aide, Olin Roldan, Avina Cristal, Lina Maria, Andrea Lucia, Clavel Amariz, Ian Scott, Nadia Gabrielle, Alan Jude, and Mara Isabella. Thank you all for putting up with me: the piles of books, FBI files in boxes everywhere, my daily grumpiness, and not paying enough attention to your needs and wants during the years of research and manuscript production.

To the Next Generation of Activists, including my most recent grandchildren, Analee Lynne Rotolo and Lucia Luna Price: Be prudent with internet connectivity; watch out for the hegemonic power of technology over your lives; learn new tactics and strategies to protect your privacy; and cope with your paranoia. They *are* watching and listening to you.

Contents

Acknowledgments

I AM MOST GRATEFUL TO ALL WHO HAVE HELPED ME GATHER DOCUMENTS dating back to 1976 and the Free Ramsey Muñiz campaign, which led us to the Freedom of Information Act (FOIA). We found a treasure trove of redacted FBI documents, but documents nonetheless, on ourselves and the Chicano Movement. And more documents with the Internal Revenue Service (IRS), which audited me every year in the 1970s while I served as board president of the Crystal City Independent School District; later as county judge for Zavala County, Texas; and founder and national president of the Raza Unida Party. I thank them because I learned then that there were intelligence agencies in existence other than the Federal Bureau of Investigation (FBI) and the Central Intelligence Agency (CIA), such as the IRS and the NSA, for example.

Over the years, many others have shared their documents with me, beginning with Harry Ring (now deceased), longtime writer and activist with the Socialist Workers Party (SWP). Their case against the FBI for release of withheld documents remains the longest litigated battle by citizens suing their government for spying on them, thirty-five years. There were many others.

Mauricio Mazon provided copies of military intelligence files on the West Coast military and the police, state and local, from San Diego to Los Angeles. Rodolfo Acuña shared his Red Squad file, aka Los Angeles Police Intelligence Unit, collected by an informant in his classes at California State University-Northridge. Ernesto Vigil, Richard Romero, and John Haro, all high-level members of the Crusade for Justice in Denver, have given me many records on that organization, themselves, and its leader Rodolfo "Corky" Gonzales. An anonymous source gave me the files gathered and held by the Mexican government on my activities during the years I maintained relations with various Mexican presidents and other influential people in Mexico. Yolanda Garza and Walter Birdwell let me copy their FBI files; both were active in the Mexican American Youth Organization in the Houston area. Reies Lopez Tijerina, one of the "Four Horsemen of the Chicano Movement," as Matt Meier and Feliciano Rivera (later Ribera) termed us, let me copy his FBI file.

I also thank the graduate students in my classes and conference attendees who sat in on my lectures and presentations utilizing these documents over the years. They posed questions and analyzed content with different lenses that have made my own views and interpretations clearer. On more than one occasion they saw things in the files I missed.

My deep gratitude goes to Rubén Martinez, director of the Julian Samora Research Institute at Michigan State University, who took an interest in my work and did some fine editing of the draft manuscript. He afforded me time and resources to spend writing this book. I also thank Ernesto Vigil for his work and views on the subject. I dare say he is the most knowledgeable scholar on the surveillance of Chicanos, Mexicans, and Native Americans. And, thank you Bonnie Cobb for your careful copyediting and Michigan State University Press for publishing my analysis of these documents.

Foreword

Rubén Martinez

CÉSAR E. CHÁVEZ WAS A REMARKABLE MAN. LIKE FEW OTHERS, HE ROSE from poverty to have great political influence on the American consciousness and the nation's institutions. He led the building of a powerful farmworker organization, the United Farm Workers of America (UFW), influenced statewide elections in California, and directly challenged the power of federal agencies, local law-enforcement officials, and decisions by the courts. The younger generations of Americans may know about his nonviolent ideology, the nationwide boycotts of nonunion grapes and lettuce, his hunger strikes, and the 340-mile march from Delano to Sacramento, California, in 1966. Those who are older may remember Chávez breaking bread with Senator Robert Kennedy to end a 25-day fast in 1968. They are not likely, however, to know about the struggles with the growers in California and Texas; the repeated violence against him, union members, and supporters who joined him on the front lines; and the bitter struggle with the Teamsters Union. And, least known of all is how the Federal Bureau of Investigation (FBI), the nation's most powerful internal security and law enforcement agency, tracked and monitored Chávez's movements and the union's activities, all the while taking a hands-off approach toward the perpetrators of violence against the union's leadership, members, and followers.

Given Chávez's influence, it is little wonder that surveillance of him by the Federal Bureau of Investigation may seem to some, or perhaps to many, as both reasonable and appropriate, especially given that the unionization struggles of farm workers had a long history of industrial strife and violent opposition, especially in California. Violence, for example, was commonplace against Filipino farm workers attempting to organize labor unions in California in the 1930s, when numerous agricultural strikes occurred. In 1933, the Cannery and Agricultural Workers Industrial Union (CAWIU) organized several strikes in the agricultural fields of California, gaining partial wage increases for striking farm workers. This was a period of intense labor organizing throughout the country that culminated in passage of the National Labor Relations Act (NLRA), also known as the Wagner Act, in 1935. The act gave labor the right to organize workers and form unions to bargain collectively with employers, but it excluded agricultural and domestic workers from its protections.

In the late 1940s and 1950s, Dr. Ernesto Galarza attempted to organize farm workers in California, but growers used *braceros*, Mexican guest workers, to break strikes and quash organizing. It was not until the Bracero Program came to an end in 1964 that Filipino and Chicano farm workers were able to organize themselves in pursuit of collective bargaining rights and better wages and working conditions. On September 16, 1965 (Mexican Independence Day), leading a fledgling labor association (National Farm Workers Association), Chávez joined striking Filipinos (Agricultural Workers Organizing Committee) in what became known as the Delano Grape Strike, which became a turning point in the unionization struggles of farm workers in California. That strike set in motion the enormous gains made by farm workers over the next ten years, leading to passage of the Agricultural Labor Relations Act in California in 1975. Chávez gained national prominence through the struggles of farm workers against growers and the Teamsters, but he also endured violence and threats to himself and his family.

The domination of ethno-racial minority groups in this country has involved and continues to involve the most powerful institutions in society, beginning with the military and law enforcement and ending with institutionalized propaganda that yields compliance. While the concept of "institutional racism" pushes us to examine how the dominant group maintains and perpetuates the subordination of classes and minority groups through the control and use of government agencies at all levels, few studies have been conducted that shed light on how domination occurs through the day-to-day activities of societal institutions. José Angel Gutiérrez has made a major contribution to our understanding, as he has done throughout his life as an activist and a public intellectual, of how institutional power in the form of national law enforcement is organized and exercised against the poor and those viewed as threats to the powerful in society. This time he has done so by focusing on the FBI and how it diminished Chávez's influence in improving the lives of farm workers.

This volume, based primarily on the documents made public at the FBI's Vault (available online) and those the author received through Freedom of Information Act requests, provides a glimpse into the violence endured by Chávez and the UFW during the period from 1965 to 1978. It also provides insight into the FBI directors' stances toward Chávez and the union, and their unwillingness to investigate the violations of civil rights by local law-enforcement officials. The task undertaken by Gutiérrez was an enormous one, as the files released by the FBI on Chávez were highly disorganized, requiring as a first step both time and resoluteness to organize them. Next, analysis of the documents required a broader understanding of the period and of Chávez's aims and activities in order to produce a meaningful account of how the FBI's activities influenced his efforts to improve the lives of farm workers. Gutiérrez's account is informed by his experiences as a leader of the Mexican American Youth Organization and the electoral-power thread of the Chicano Movement (roughly 1965 to 1980). This account of the FBI's surveillance of Chávez's agricultural-labor organizing work was done with redacted documents that constituted an enormous puzzle demanding knowledge not only of the period but also, at least at a rudimentary level, of the FBI's organizational and internal communications structures and processes, its language, and its codes.

The product of Gutiérrez's intellectual labor reflects dedication, courage, and vast knowledge of the Chicano Movement, the Civil Rights Movement, and dominant group institutions. The volume is the result of "slow research" that yields enormous insight, in this case, into the FBI's hidden role in agricultural-labor struggles. By focusing on Chávez, it is the first of its kind in an emergent scholarly subfield that demands the systematic study of the nation's law enforcement agencies and their activities surveilling and undermining leaders of organized civil- and human-rights struggles in Latino communities across the country. Those types of activities continue today, such as the FBI investigating Standing Rock activists opposing the Dakota Access Pipeline as terrorists, using live feeds and infiltrating their ranks.

What Gutiérrez's work does is point us, as critical scholars during a time when higher education is under siege by America's Republican Party, to the examination of the changing forms of social control in the American social order, which has evolved from a social democratic to a neoliberal order over the past forty years. This includes the latest forms of technology and the most sophisticated communications network, the internet, which the dominant classes use to achieve high levels of ideological domination and government control—today represented by the regressive political agenda of President Donald Trump. Beyond the audio/video recording devices of yesteryear, surveillance today is aided by drones, facial recognition technology, multiple tracking devices, and other tools of the "technology of power." Ironically, even as the FBI seems to reject Trump as a capable president, it continues to engage in many tactics, expanded following 9/11 by the Patriot Act, to contain organized challenges to today's plutocracy. Indeed, there are many indicators that Trump would prefer an expanded, more intensive, and more secretive system of social control in American society.

Preface

THE FEDERAL BUREAU OF INVESTIGATION (FBI), AND ITS "G-MEN," HAS
been among the most revered institutions in American society. J. Edgar
Hoover, the FBI director, headed the list of America's top cops during the administrations of eight presidents and seventeen attorney generals. In 1934,
shortly after the apprehension and shooting of John Dillinger by FBI agent
Melvin Purvis, Hoover ensured that all credit for FBI work, particularly in
apprehending criminals, went to him. The following year he created the
Crime Records Section, with Louis B. Nichols as head of that section. Nichols was an aficionado of public relations and a consummate networking
practitioner. He set out over the next twenty years to massage the national
data of "crimes" to reflect the FBI's success at crime fighting.[1] More importantly, the duo of Hoover and Nichols made sure the 1935 movie *G-Men*,
by Warner Brothers, cast Hoover and the FBI men in heroic light. Nichols
saw to it that Hoover always made front-page material, beginning with the
apprehensions of Kate "Ma" Barker, with her Thompson machine gun and
its 100-round circular drum, and Alvin "Creepy" Karpis, bank robber and

murderer of policemen, later that year. For this latter event, Hoover flew into New Orleans to be present as if he had made the arrest.[2]

Hoover, from his first appointment as Director, was the first to conduct surveillance operations without authority from his superiors on persons in opposition to administrations' politics, programs, domestic policies, and foreign affairs. He continued to do so to the day he died. His successors have not discontinued many of these practices and programs despite congressional oversight and mandates to cease such operations.[3] The American public, it seems, is more concerned about safety and security as guaranteed by the FBI than a trouncing of civil rights by that same FBI. Yet, not many Americans can name the components of the United States intelligence community beyond the Federal Bureau of Investigation (FBI), the Central Intelligence Agency (CIA), and perhaps the National Security Agency (NSA). Most Americans cannot tell you what these agencies do for our national security, notwithstanding the daily media reports on these agencies. And, all these agencies within the umbrella of overseeing national security as part of the U.S. intelligence community have in many instances since 9/11 increased, enhanced, expanded, devised, created, and implemented new methods of surveillance to disrupt, destroy, and eliminate opposition to U.S. policy, particularly foreign-policy objectives, and in some cases domestic-policy objectives in place to stop homegrown "terrorists."[4]

Once again, in 2016 the FBI was the subject of distrust and disgust, scrutiny and suspicion, and concern and circumspection not only by the American people but by other components of the United States intelligence community. The impact of the role played by the director of the Federal Bureau of Investigation, James Comey, in the 2016 presidential election will be the subject of continued investigation and debate for years to come. Why did he release a press statement of a new FBI investigation into more emails found on another server that were allegedly sent by Hillary Clinton, the Democratic presidential candidate, with days remaining to Election Day? And, why did he again release another press statement on the eve of Election Day that the investigation revealed no federal crime? These actions were a very public display of how politicized the FBI has become. Comey did not continue in his job under the new Trump administration; he was fired on May 9, 2017. He had a ten-year appointment lasting to 2023.[5] The dismissal is now the focus of one of several congressional investigations and that of the appointed special prosecutor Robert Mueller, himself an ex-FBI director.

This period, 2015-2016, is the third time in FBI history the agency has come under severe criticism and investigation. The last time was after the post-9/11 attack by terrorists in New York. Why did the FBI's intelligence-gathering procedures fail to warn about this attack? The first critical time the FBI was investigated by Congress was during the post-Watergate era, stemming from the burglary of an FBI field office in Media, Pennsylvania.[6] The American public was horrified to learn that since the 1930s the FBI had been conducting illegal break-ins, telephone taps, harassment, disruption of legitimate First Amendment rights, and basically conducting more surveillance of persons for their political beliefs and actions rather than apprehending criminals.

The surveillance of César Chávez was just one of the many FBI actions of surveillance of activists and dissenters in the twentieth century. Since the inception of the Bureau of Investigation and its progeny, the FBI, presidents, and U.S. attorney generals have permitted and encouraged the agency to conduct surveillance on dissidents and suspected subversives. From Franklin D. Roosevelt to Truman, Eisenhower, Johnson, Kennedy, and Nixon, all relied on Hoover to harass and disrupt any anti-government group and its leadership. Nothing was put into writing authorizing such illegal and unconstitutional activity by presidents or attorney generals. All of them involved over the decades, however, knew Hoover was knee-deep into busting civil rights activists and not as preoccupied with apprehending criminals.[7] William C. Sullivan, a top FBI administrator in charge of domestic intelligence during many years with Hoover, writes in his tell-all book:

> As far as I am concerned, we might as well not engage in intelligence
> unless we also engage in counterintelligence. One is the right arm, the
> other the left. They work together. Actually, these counterintelligence pro-
> grams were nothing new; I remember sending out anonymous letters and
> phone calls back in 1941, and we'd been using most of the same disruptive

techniques sporadically from field office to field office as long as I've been an FBI man. In 1956, under Assistant Director Belmont, five years before I came in to take over the Domestic Intelligence Division, the decision was made to incorporate all counter intelligence operations into one program directed against the Communist Party. I merely redirected the use of those techniques toward investigating the Klan.[8]

Admittedly, not a single report in the declassified Chavez file is specifically marked in the subject heading as a COINTELPRO (counterintelligence program), leading some scholars to infer that Mexicans and their progeny of Mexican ancestry, Chicanos, were never under FBI or government surveillance. My files have various code names for identifying the material ranging from Internal Security-Spanish American to Communist Infiltration, or COMINFIL, and New Left, certainly all COINTELPROs. The code "Mexican American Militancy" has been found in documents by others, indicating a link to the huge COINTELPRO operations the FBI had going at the same time aimed at other Mexican American groups and leaders.[9] The first FBI COINTELPRO operation was directed at the American Communist Party in 1956, and the second in August 1960 against the Puerto Ricans striving for independence.[10] Jo Thomas of the *New York Times* wrote about this FBI harassment of Puerto Ricans on the island, in New York, New Jersey, and elsewhere in the country.[11] The first COINTELPRO operation that targeted Mexicans and Mexican Americans discovered during my research on FBI surveillance was the Border Coverage Program, or BOCOV by its code name. This FBI program was aimed specifically at Mexican and Mexican American organizations along the U.S. Mexico border to prevent their association and collaboration on mutual interests.[12]

The methods and tactics utilized against Chávez parallel those outlined in three "smoking gun" memos issued to special agents in charge (SACs) across the country by the FBI Director. "Smoking gun" is a prosecutor's term for having incontrovertible evidence to convict an accused person of the crime in question (e.g., the accused arrested with the gun still smoking from the firing of bullets into the victim). These memos were the first time the Director wrote out the specific orders to his agents on the goals and targets of the COINTELPRO for African Americans—namely, the Black Panthers and the youth of Student Non-Violent Coordinating Committee (SNCC). The targets were coded "Black Nationalist-Hate Groups" under the rubric of "Internal Security"—just like the first reports filed on various Mexican American groups and persons, including Chávez. And as FBI Assistant Director William Sullivan writes, he just used the instructions for one counterintelligence operation on another—all the same. The first Hoover "smoking gun" memo was issued on August 25, 1967, then expanded and clarified with much specificity in memos of February 29 and March 4, 1968.[13]

These memos clearly state the purpose of the new Black Nationalist Hate COINTELPRO: "to expose, disrupt, misdirect, discredit, or otherwise neutralize the activities of black nationalist, hate-type organizations and groupings, their leadership, spokesmen, membership, and supporters, and to counter their propensity for violence and civil disorder." These specific instructions were followed by the field offices, SAC, and other agents investigating Chávez, per the declassified FBI documents analyzed in subsequent chapters. The March 4th memo expanded the counterintelligence program designed to neutralize militant black nationalist groups from twenty-three to forty-one field offices to cover the great majority of black nationalist activity in this country. This memo has underscored this instruction: "PERSONAL ATTENTION FOR ALL THE FOLLOWING SACS." For clarification purposes the FBI Director listed under "Goals" the five specific activities his agents should undertake to neutralize the targets. In summary fashion:

> For maximum effectiveness of the Counterintelligence Program, and to prevent wasted effort, long-range goals are being set. 1. Prevent the COALITION of black militant nationalist groups ... 2. Prevent the RISE OF A "MESSIAH" who could unify, and electrify, the militant black nationalist movement ... 3. Prevent VIOLENCE on the part of black nationalist groups ... 4. Prevent militant black nationalist groups and leaders from gaining RESPECTABILITY, by discrediting them in three separate segments of the community ... the responsible Negro community ... the white

community ... to "liberals" who have vestiges of sympathy for militant black nationalist [*sic*] simply because they are Negroes ... 5. A final goal should be to prevent the long-range GROWTH of militant, black nationalist organizations, especially among the youth" [capitalization in the original memo].[14]

I ask the reader to substitute the words "Chávez and UFW" for black nationalist, and "Chicano" or "Mexican" for Negro in the text of these COINTELPRO memos. It is very doubtful that any SAC, field agent, and FBI informant, particularly in the Southwest and major urban centers with large concentrations of people of Mexican ancestry, would make the distinction that the goals and specific instructions for each goal were to be applied only to black nationalists and organizations and not to Chicano militants and their organizations in their field office cities, such as Chicago, Denver, Los Angeles, San Antonio, and Albuquerque. Assistant Director Sullivan of the FBI's Domestic Intelligence Division did not, and had not done so since 1941 by his own admission. Counterintelligence was part and parcel of intelligence/surveillance. Moreover, a cursory reading of the Chavez file documents reveals the use by local police and the FBI of the very tactics listed and emphasized in the COINTELPRO memos. In the 1960s all dissenting groups—black, white, brown, yellow—were viewed by the FBI as constituting the New Left, the target of another COINTELPRO.

The Declassified FBI File

The FBI declassified the extensive file on Césario Estrada Chávez, aka César Chávez, in the late 1990s.[15] Richard Steven Street first analyzed these documents, after extensive newspaper coverage of their existence, in an article for the *Southern California Quarterly* in 1996.[16] In this pioneering work on the FBI surveillance of Chávez, he concluded:

What becomes abundantly clear in Chavez's FBI file is that after Hoover's men wrapped-up their spying, bound up their foot-thick dossier, cross-referenced and indexed their material, and analyzed hundreds of reports, they came up empty. They found nothing in Chavez. No communist leanings stained his reputation. No ugly incidents detracted from his reputation. No misappropriation of funds marred his union administration. No extramarital affairs undermined his reputation as a family man. No subversive activities cast suspicion on the movement he championed. In all of his actions, and in all of his associations, Chavez never displayed even one iota of disloyalty. All that the FBI was able to show through its spying was a man with a single-minded devotion to farm workers and ever-present vigilance against those who would harm his cause with their self-serving ideology and petty politics.[17]

Street, like many of the secondary sources published prior to 1996, was effusive in praise of César and ignored the FBI files. Perhaps if Street were to rewrite his conclusions now after the spate of critical books on Chávez, make a closer examination of the content in the files, and review books available on the dark side of the U.S. government's abuse, repression, and illegal activity, he might retract his words. For example, Mike Yates, in a review of a critical book on Chávez, writes, "Most accounts of UFW history speculate that something happened to Chavez after the lost initiative, and he somehow went off the deep end. Certainly, bizarre and ugly things began to happen."[18]

Indeed, if Chávez did go over the deep end after the defeat of Proposition 22 in California in 1974, were the "bizarre and ugly things" early manifestations of emotional and mental instability? Chávez had won and lost other electoral battles before; why was this one so life-changing? What other factors or events may have caused him to change his character and behavior? The declassified FBI files may offer new clues. The FBI files released to the public account for nearly a decade of monitoring Chávez and his union activities. These declassified FBI files on Chávez consist of seven parts arranged into seventeen packets beginning with a document dated October 8, 1965. They end with a document dated August 1, 1975. The notes on my methodology and research are in appendix 1.

The surveillance of Chávez continued well past 1975 until his death in

1993. I have other FBI files on Chávez that are not posted on The Vault, the FBI website, including some dated December 2, 1977, and February 4, 1982 (see appendices 2B and C). Obviously, the FBI files released to the public are what the FBI wanted made public regarding 1965 to 1975; but by no means are they the entire set of FBI files on Chávez or the union.

Regardless of the surveillance time frame, does not the sustained and ubiquitous presence of police agents—local, state, federal—and their informants take a toll on the subject under surveillance? How about those around the subject? Is paranoia due to the surveillance a normal state of mental affairs for the target, family, and core staff? If Chávez was not found to be a criminal by the FBI, as Street concludes, perhaps the surveillance was not intended for that purpose. Could it have been for strictly political purposes? This would be an illegal activity on the part of the FBI, would it not? Would not ignoring, derailing, suspending, ending, and not authorizing investigations by the FBI, and the U.S. attorney's failure to prosecute not be obstruction of justice?

This book is about the government surveillance by the FBI of César Estrada Chávez, a migrant farm worker who founded the first successful labor union for seasonal agricultural workers in the United States. The fundamental question is why the surveillance? If Chávez was simply trying to form a labor union, how was that subversive or a threat to national security? And, if answers can be found to that fundamental question in the files, then why did the U.S. government and the FBI thwart that goal and destroy the Chávez persona? The files will reveal some answers.

Prior Scholarship

No further scholarly study of these documents has ensued since Street published his article. For that matter, not much scholarly work has been done on the government surveillance of Chicano groups, organizations, and leaders.[19] These FBI documents—2,085 pages—are my primary sources of information, despite the documents being heavily redacted, disorganized in the released format, and not the entire file.[20] On appeal, I was able to wrest

63 more pages dated 1988-1989. Chávez was the best known Chicano leader of the 1960s. He generated much interest as a research subject for academics and journalists. The body of knowledge and information on Chávez in secondary sources is extensive.[21] I rely on these for the construction of narrative to accompany the analysis of FBI documents. In other words, what Chávez was doing according to the secondary sources will help me ground the primary-source documents in the file around specific dates, events, and activities to determine the scope and nature of governmental intrusion into Chávez's organizing of Filipino, Mexican, African American, Anglo, and Chicano farm workers, primarily in California, then Texas and Arizona, plus a few other locations such as Ohio, Wisconsin, Florida, Oregon, and Washington.[22]

In 1976, while finishing my doctoral work at the University of Texas at Austin, I began a serious study of government surveillance of Chicanos and Mexicanos. With each request, new doors of inquiry opened, and I systematically continued to make several Freedom of Information Act (FOIA) requests over the years to the present time. I never had the money to finance litigation nor the assistance of pro bono attorneys to sue the intelligence agencies, primarily the FBI and the CIA, to turn over redacted or missing documents, and reexamine their reasons for redacting huge portions of material. The FBI files have large gaps in reporting on a target of interest such as César E. Chávez that are unexplained and unexplainable without court orders. I have acquired and reviewed so many files that I can generalize that the FBI has probably surveilled every Chicano leader and organization since the 1930s—perhaps earlier, but those first records were either not kept, had been destroyed, or were lost in some warehouse or basement. And, letters of inquiry and proposals have been submitted without success to the major foundations and other related funding sources. It seems that government surveillance is a topic of interest to the public and scholars, but not the surveillance of Chicano leaders or their organizations. No program or department of any university has made the gathering of these documents a major research agenda, and neither have any Chicano or Latino studies programs or departments.[23]

FBI Surveillance of Others

There are files dating to the 1940s, during which time the FBI did a national survey of where the Mexican-origin population resided, complete with names of organizations, officers, and addresses. The FBI also targeted as a matter of course many, if not all, African American leaders and organizations from the early 1920s as well.[24] Japanese Americans came under surveillance with President Franklin Delano Roosevelt's Executive Order 9066. Over 110,000 Japanese Americans and permanent residents were rounded up and held in detention centers for most of the period of war with Japan.[25] The U.S. Supreme Court upheld the constitutionality of such an order in *Korematsu v. United States*, 323 U.S. 214 (1944).[26] These surveys of Mexican and Japanese communities were very much like the post-9/11 FBI survey of Arab Americans living in the United States. The Anti-Terrorism and Effective Death Penalty Act of 1996 specifically targeted persons from Iraq, Iran, and Libya residing in the United States.[27] Are COINTELPROs continuing into the twenty-first century?[28]

With passage of the USA Patriot Act and the National Security Entry-Exit Registration System (NSEERS) after 9/11, Arab Americans and permanent residents from twenty Arab/Muslim countries were targeted for registration; it did not matter that the prime candidates for registration, 63 percent of them, were young Christian males over the age of sixteen, according to James Zogby's poll from the late 1990s.[29]

In April 2015, perhaps since 2003, the FBI began operating a fleet of spy planes over U.S. cities in eleven states and the District of Columbia. This operation is a huge leap into collecting metadata and placing all persons in an area under surveillance for unknown reasons or no reason at all. The FBI utilized no less than thirteen fake companies registered to post office boxes in Bristow, Virginia, and another box shared with the Department of Justice. These 115 or more 182T Cessna Skylanes were used for video surveillance and cell-site simulation. Video footage assists in vehicle description and registration data, facial recognition of occupants, and even vehicle destinations. The cell-site simulation tricks cellphones on the ground, regardless of being on or off, into sending their signals to the airplane instead of a cell tower. Such a practice, termed "cell-site simulation," reveals personal data and other subscriber information about the cellphone owner/user to the FBI airplanes, plus the video feed.[30]

First Glimpse of FBI Abuse

In January 1971, the FBI office raid in Media, Pennsylvania, the Citizens' Commission to Investigate the FBI, and three months later, the literature generated by Daniel Ellsberg's release of the Pentagon Papers in March was the most useful exposé of the FBI since its founding.[31] Recent developments in government surveillance of citizens and residents in general, and intelligence metadata-gathering by electronic means by the United States have renewed interest in this field. For example, in Chávez's day, an actual boots-on-the-ground type of surveillance was necessary and aided by phone taps, break-ins, and other illegal practices and agency abuses. Today, the power of technology, the internet, has given way to the technology of power, metadata collection of personal information that makes possible huge databases or "Big Data." "Dataveillance," as some scholars like Roger Clarke call it, is the new name of the government's activity of "watching," listening, gathering, analyzing, disseminating, storing, and utilizing the information gleaned.[32] The intelligence agencies mine the data from the internet and other electronic devices to gather information on individuals at will. Government agencies now wait for "self-reporting" by individuals rather than seeking out persons for physical observation. Self-reporting is done by monitoring the use of electronic devices such as postings on social media, emails sent and received, credit card purchases, GPS devices on vehicles (personal or rental), toll permit stickers, passports, and phone calls, for example. The current whistle-blowers such as Bradley Manning (now Chelsea Elizabeth), with the help of Julian Assange of WikiLeaks, and Edward Snowden are contemporary examples of private action to expose *ultra vires* acts by public agencies.[33] The National Security Agency is under high scrutiny by Congress and civil libertarians for its massive collection of personal records obtained from servers, internet providers, and host server companies, as well as telephone service providers.[34]

These recent revelations of continual U.S. government abuses of individual civil liberties—namely, the right to privacy—make the study of the FBI role in preventing Chávez from reaching success sooner even more important. From this look back in time, we can glean lessons of what the government can do once again, perhaps already is doing to some if not many U.S. citizens and residents, as in the case of the FBI Cessna spy planes. The FBI documents will also reveal the methods, tactics, scope, initiatives, and actions utilized by the agency against Chávez. This information is useful to contrast with the rise and failure of recent activists, such as the Occupy Wall Street movement that collapsed almost as soon as it began, perhaps because of the violent police actions taken in city after city to remove the protesters. Analyzing the Chávez documents will also be useful in making the case for renewed efforts at reform by these rogue agencies that have operated outside the law while making the case that civilians need to follow the rule of law.

The overall importance of this type of study is also to focus on the issue of formulating limits on the nation-state and its police power. Ultimately, the question post-9/11 is what rights to privacy must the citizenry of a democratic society forego for security? Is the constant reframing of a post-9/11 terrorist threat era a ruse driven primarily by the U.S. executive branch to push for a permanent state of war that requires primacy for vigilance of its citizens and foreigners over the erosion of civil liberties?

Why the Surveillance?

What were the fundamental reasons for the FBI monitoring and intervening in the Chávez movement to organize farm workers? In the early 1950s, the John Birch Society was in full operation against any and all enemies of the United States, including Mexicans in the United States. John Burma, in his book of 1954, presented five reasons for the discrimination against Mexican Americans. First, color of skin; second, their poverty; third, a belief that their culture was different and deficient; fourth, that they were predominantly Catholic in a Protestant United States; and lastly, that they spoke Spanish in public places to offend, exclude, insult, and talk about whites.[35] Are these reasons for the discrimination also the foundation for FBI suspicion of disloyalty and evidence of anti-Mexican sentiments and bias?

There could be other reasons. Was it because Chávez was a pacifist during the Vietnam era? Was it because the United States is a capitalist system and diametrically opposed to labor unionization drives in any sector? Was it because Chávez was a devout Catholic, a papist with strong allies within the organized Church? Was it because Chávez was an environmentalist warning the public about pesticides and herbicides that poisoned not only farm workers but also consumers? Was it because he was a Democrat in a California dominated by Republican presidents such as Richard Nixon and Ronald Reagan, and governors such as George Deukmejian (1983-1991) and Pete Wilson (1991-1999)? Was it simply that he was a Chicano of Mexican ancestry? Or because Chicanos should not be leaders of labor unions?

Was the reason for the surveillance because Chávez not only was developing a labor union but also an effective political machine with which to elect Democrats supportive of his politics? Was he seeking political and economic power to challenge economic and political elites in California and the nation? Was the intelligence gathering a manifestation of anti-Catholic sentiments among FBI agents and the director? Hoover had great affinity with the hierarchy of the U.S. Catholic Church for their shared anti-Communism, according to Steve Rosswurm; not so among the Mormon and Protestant FBI agents.[36] Are the roots of this religious hostility against Catholics by U.S. Protestants to be found in the break with the pope by Henry VIII dating to the sixteenth century? Was the Catholic global empire built by the Spanish in the New World during those times a final determinant of open warfare between the two European powers? In hindsight, we can respond affirmatively. The Spanish accused the British of having perpetuated the black legend of Spanish cruelty toward natives in the Americas and previously in the Netherlands. The English view also included the Spanish as the model of racial impurity based on skin color and religion, while they reserved whiteness as the symbol of purity and goodness and, more importantly, Christianity for themselves. If the Spanish were the low rung on the ladder of God's chosen children, then the Mexicans and their Chicano progeny did not even get onto a rung.

Was the basis for the surveillance economic or environmental? That California became a huge agricultural engine after the Depression and into the 1950s and 1960s is a foregone conclusion. After water was piped into the central arid regions of California, agriculture boomed. And, agricultural interests relied on stoop labor from every ethnic group they could find to labor in their fields. Sam Kushner in *Long Road to Delano* details these eras in California's agribusiness.[37] Del Monte Corporation, based in California, became the agribusiness model not only in the United States but also in Latin America.[38] Specifically, this was the case in the fruit and vegetable industry, from dried and fresh fruits and vegetables to wineries and emerging food processors such as the California Packing Corporation, which became Del Monte. DiGiorgio and Gallo, also based in California, became the name brands for American wine and an integral part of the national economy.[39] The Chávez labor strikes in California and national consumer boycotts of grapes, wine, lettuce, other produce, and specific growers crippled this national economic engine. Adding the charge that California growers were contaminating the nation's food supply with chemicals made Chávez the slayer of the Jolly Green Giant. As president, both Nixon and Reagan sided with the growers against Chávez and used their presidential powers, including control of the FBI and other federal agencies such as the Immigration and Naturalization Service (INS), to break strikes, cross picket lines, and seek to halt the unionization of field hands. On the flip side, as Chávez signed more growers to contracts, his economic power grew exponentially. He could not only provide his union members with benefits but also invest monies in more international consumer education programs, domestic voter registration, citizenship drives, and get-out-the-vote campaigns. Conventional wisdom in California particularly was that Chávez both elected Jerry Brown as governor and handed the presidential primary victory to Robert F. Kennedy (RFK) in 1968. Chávez was Mr. National Democrat, even nominating RFK for president during the Democratic National Convention that year. During the early years of the Raza Unida Party (RUP) in the 1970s, upon my invitation, Chávez campaigned for RUP candidates in nonpartisan elections in Texas cities and school districts.[40]

The answer to "why the surveillance" is found in all these plausible and possible reasons because Chávez did all those things.

Are Persons of Mexican Ancestry the Historic Enemy of the U.S. Government?

In the early 1800s, the people of Mexican ancestry and the scores of Native American tribes, dating to early battles over their lands in what is now the Southwest and West, were perceived by whites as the historical enemies of the United States. Native Americans were subjected to genocide, and those that survived were removed to military-supervised "reservations" to live out their lives. Surveillance of Mexicans and their progeny in the United States has been in place since the first violent encounters dating to the movement for independence by Texas in the 1830s, increasing in scope and intensity by 1846, and the advent of the U.S. invasion of Mexico. With that successful land grab from Mexico, the United States perpetrated acts of aggression against Spain in a quest to take more of its possessions: Florida, Cuba, Puerto Rico, Dominican Republic, and the Philippines. Between 1848 and 1851, the United States financially and militarily backed attempts by Narciso López to take Cuba from Spain.[41] Quarrels with Canada in the 1870s over boundaries and fisheries led the United States to conduct military reconnaissance (Army) and establish a Military Information Division (MID). The U.S. Navy had already established within its command an intelligence-gathering division on information about foreign countries, friend or foe, and neighbors north and south. When rebellion resurfaced in Cuba against Spain, the United States declared neutrality but supported Cuban exiles such as General Calixto García. He was unsuccessful in dislodging Cuba from Spain in La Guerra Grande (1868-78) and La Guerra Chiquita (1879-80). In 1895, Calixto García was at it again, organizing support in New York City for yet another invasion. U.S. designs on making Cuba a colony originated with Thomas Jefferson. During Grover Cleveland's term, MID spies were sent to Cuba; Andrew Rowan was the principal figure. By 1898 the United States had declared war on Spain, which resulted in a vast gain of lands in the Caribbean and Pacific.[42] The new sovereign not only changed flags and boundaries, it looked the other way as the private property of those who "lost" the war literally lost their private landholdings and homeland. They became strangers in their own land—the Other.

Shortly after the war when military occupation was totally complete, the U.S. War Department, precursor to the current Department of Defense, ordered the Joint Army and Navy Board in 1920 to prepare war plans for every country in the world, coded by color. These plans were updated in 1939 and became known as the five Rainbow Plans based on a U.S. war waged on multiple fronts. The plan for Mexico was coded Green and implemented during the latter stages of the Mexican Revolution, which began November 20, 1910, and lasted until normalcy reigned in the late 1920s.[43] The first permanent police and military action institutionalized along the U.S.-Mexico border (not Canada) was the Border Patrol in 1924.[44] The militarization of the U.S.-Mexico border has continued unabated into the twentieth and twenty-first centuries—first, with the implementation of low-intensity warfare in the area, and second, with the implementation of Operation Gatekeeper in 1994 by President Bill Clinton. And third, the building of a physical barrier, a fence, between the two countries in 2006 by President George W. Bush.[45]

President Barack Obama has been referred to as the "Deporter-in-Chief" by immigrant advocates because during his years in office more Mexicans were deported, over 3 million, than in all prior years combined, regardless of administration, dating to the 1950s. During the Eisenhower years, when Operation Wetback was implemented in the mid-1950s, the INS deported millions of Mexicans as well. President Trump was threatening in 2017 not only to build a bigger physical wall between the United States and Mexico but also to deport all immigrants without papers, particularly Mexicans, from the United States. The new Department of Homeland Security Customs and Border Protection agency has increased its roundups and deportation activity since January 1, 2017.

Racism has been made part and parcel of U.S. armed intervention in the affairs of other peoples and their countries in Latin America, the Caribbean, and Pacific islands. Robert J. Rosenbaum posits that

> the victors can use their win as evidence that the losers are a benighted, backward people who will benefit by the change in the long run ... A third attitude takes the speed of conquest as proof that the defeated are a cowardly and inferior branch of humankind, patently unfit for self-determination and prosperity in God's chosen land. Anglos expressed all three, often simultaneously, to justify and explain U.S. expansion into the Southwest.[46]

Arnoldo De León, in *They Called Them Greasers: Anglo Attitudes toward Mexicans in Texas, 1821–1900*, states:

> The evidence is heavy that Anglos perceived the physical contrasts of Mexicans as indicating mental and temperamental weaknesses. Moreover, my findings square with recent scholarship which argues that racism originated either in the Western psyche, in capitalist social development, or in religion, and that native peoples in the path of white civilization have historically been either exterminated or reduced to a hereditary caste because of the peculiar strain of that racism.[47]

The animus between Mexicans and whites has long roots.[48] In the United Kingdom, the British viewed the Spanish with contempt, and after the defeat of the Spanish Armada as inferior to other Europeans. Both Spaniards and British brought with them the doctrine of Pax Dominus to the New World, conquests to justify taking land from the indigenous tribes as ordained by God. Once settled into their role as empire builders in the Americas, the British, now calling themselves American Anglo-Saxons, turned to the Spanish holdings and those of their newly independent progeny, Mexico, the nearest enemy to their goal of One America, north to south, east to west, in this hemisphere. Joseph Smith in *The Spanish-American War* refers to the gradual whittling away of Spanish possessions in North America as the "Laws of Gravitation," taken from a House document penned by Secretary of State John Quincy Adams on April 28, 1823.

The United States acquired the Louisiana Territory when Napoleon had his brother, Joseph, whom he installed as king of Spain, sell the land to Thomas Jefferson in 1803, hoping to curry favor with the Americans against the British. This was followed by the taking of Florida in 1819, and finally in 1836 by the insurrection fomented by southern whites in Mexican Texas/ Coahuila.[49] The hostile attitudes formed as a result of taking Texas, and later adopting Manifest Destiny as the political slogan of the white racial frame are well developed in Arnoldo De Léon's work and in Reginald Horsman, *Race and Manifest Destiny*.[50] Although Mexicans were considered "white" racially because of the slim thread of Spanish genetic lineage some three hundred years previously during Spanish colonization of the Americas, North and South, the Mexican-ancestry group had never been treated or afforded the privileges of being classified racially as white.

The White Baptism

In 1940, the U.S. Census Bureau made the white racial designation for Mexicans official government policy and regulation. School officials continued the practice of segregation of Mexican-origin children in the public schools across the country, not because they were of "Mexican" race, but because the children lacked sufficient English language skills. A spate of court cases filed decades before *Brown v. Board of Education* by Mexican Americans became useful precedents in that case.[51]

The contradictions in U.S. racial policy regarding Mexicans as white are juxtaposed in two court cases: one in California in 1946, and the other in Texas in 1952. The California case involved a Mexican American woman, Andrea Perez, seeking to marry an African American man, Sylvester Davis. She was considered racially white. The couple was denied a marriage license because in that state, miscegenation laws prohibited whites marrying nonwhites, and Davis was black. The California Supreme Court ruled in their favor and struck down the ban; this case was a precedent for the U.S. Supreme Court nineteen years later in ending all miscegenation laws in the *Loving* case.[52] Interestingly, Texas never passed miscegenation laws because too many white males took up with Native American women, Mexican women, black women, and mixtures of these categories to acquire and hold title to land when it was under Mexican rule.

In Texas, the case of Pete Hernandez against the state is illustrative of the racial classification of Mexicans as white, but not being considered white enough by Anglos in jury selection. Hernandez had murdered another Mexican American. He was tried by an all-Anglo, male jury. The defense proved that no Mexican American had ever been considered for jury service despite being white. Blacks and women, even white women, were excluded by law from serving on a jury. The U.S. Supreme Court ruled that Mexican Americans, despite being classified white for racial purposes, were not treated equally as white; therefore, this group constituted a class apart and could seek constitutional protection from discrimination in the future.[53]

In 1977, the Office of Management and Budget (OMB) reopened the door to the racial classification of Mexicans and other Latinos by providing four racial categories for Hispanics to choose from: White, Black, Asian, and Native American. It also created only one ethnic category with a new U.S. government-imposed ethnic group label: Hispanic.

The Door to Governmental Transparency Cracks Opens

Recent aphoristic statements by former CIA and NSA director General Michael Hayden ("We kill people based on metadata"), during a debate with David Cole at Johns Hopkins University over the collection of metadata by the NSA, took me back in time to 1976.[54] That year was the apogee of the electoral gains made by the Raza Unida Party (RUP) in Texas, and the beginning of the lifetime incarceration of its candidate for governor in 1974, Ramsey Muñiz. He jumped bail while awaiting trial on various drug-related charges, and when apprehended declared his innocence alleging a frame-up by the DEA and FBI. As national party chair of the RUP, and with the help of Armando Gutierrez—now deceased, but then a tenure-track assistant professor of government at the University of Texas-Austin—I began a long, drawn-out ordeal trying to get documents under the Freedom of Information Act. We sought records held by the FBI on Ramsey, the RUP, and Chicano Movement activists of the time such as Reies Lopez Tijerina from New Mexico, Rodolfo "Corky" Gonzales from Colorado, César E. Chávez from California, and me.[55] My principal question then was, and still is today, "Why the surveillance on the leadership of the Chicano Movement?" Is engaging in a social movement a federal crime? Is the building of an electoral power base in the Southwest a federal crime? Or was it that the adherents of the Chicano Movement and these leaders, en masse, were vocal in their public opposition to national policies such as the administration of the War on Poverty and the war in Vietnam, for example?

The FBI and other documents obtained began to offer clues in their content, albeit heavily redacted but nonetheless indicating scope, methods, time periods, locations, use of informants, and names of personnel in the surveillance loop within the FBI. The most startling find was the sharing of files by the FBI with other intelligence agencies, known as "cross-fertilization," and the White House. It seemed everyone in the executive branch was aware and approved of the surveillance. Was the surveillance directed by the president or was it directed by the FBI director? Who wags the tail on the dog? Who wagged it then? They know, and try to keep their illegal activities secret. Those of us unaware and ignorant of this government activity, and those in opposition to federal government policies and politics became easy targets for surveillance. Not so much those who are also inside the government, such as members of Congress and the judiciary.

The Cannikin Papers

On January 22, 1973, the Supreme Court of the United States (SCOTUS) heard a case filed by a member of Congress, Patsy T. Mink (D-Hawaii) et al. against the Environmental Protection Agency et al., seeking to obtain from the executive branch information concerning effects of nuclear testing on the island of Amchitka done in 1971. The island is a National Wildlife Refuge created by Executive Order 1733 by President William Howard Taft on March

3, 1913. More importantly, it is 1,400 miles southwest of Anchorage—a part of the Aleutian chain of islands off Alaska's coast, but only 700 miles from Russia. Japan and Canada were also very concerned about these nuclear tests, closer to their nations than was mainland United States, and voiced their objections. The case, while it involves both environmental and foreign policy, became known as the "Mink case," filed originally as an FOIA request under the 1966 law by thirty-one members of Congress. Release of information was declined on national-security grounds, and on another amazingly novel assertion that the president had the sole and absolute right to protect data from disclosure by the FOIA's list of exemptions. The case was first heard by the District Court for the District of Columbia, which ruled against them. On appeal, the case won some concessions and lost on other issues. Central to the victory at the appellate level was that henceforth, responses to FOIA requests had to have the exemption claimed by the government specifically enumerated section by section, and not applied to entire documents or files. Furthermore, the plaintiffs won another victory in that *in camera* inspections of documents would occur at the trial court's discretion, and not be an absolute denial of inspection based on a single affidavit filed by the president's office. The government sought *certiorari* of the case before SCOTUS, which was granted, and held that the executive branch could withhold information, and could do so without need for *in camera* inspection. The case, while it reduced the power of both the legislative and judicial branches of government over the executive branch, and disclosure and transparency to a mere passive role, did bring about some favorable changes.[56]

Non-Disclosure Continues Even on the Texas Rangers (Not the Baseball Team!)

Dozens of FOIA requests were made in the 1970s with little result, including a local request to the Texas Department of Public Safety on the Texas Rangers, trying to find answers to a number of questions.[57] Without money and human resources to pursue appeals much less litigation, I settled for what documents were released to me from various intelligence agencies on Chicano leaders and organizations dating back to the 1920s through the 1990s.[58] Others also requested files, particularly from the FBI, and some of us have shared and exchanged documents.[59] By 1986, I had published my first article on the surveillance of Chicano leaders and groups, and had uncovered an unreported, much less admitted, FBI COINTELPRO operation by the code name of BOCOV, for Border Coverage Program. This program consisted of counterintelligence operations conducted in Mexico and the U.S.-Mexico borderlands to divide and disrupt activities between Chicanos and Mexicans, namely, building alliances and coalitions.[60] Mauricio Mazon two years previously had published his work on the Zoot Suit Riots in Southern California utilizing FBI and military intelligence documents shared with him by Rodolfo Acuña, professor emeritus of Chicano studies at California State University at Northridge.[61] The burning question as to why the surveillance occurred continued to beg for an answer.

Hispanic FBI Agents Sue over Discrimination

Much to my surprise and that of others, the national media reported on a federal class-action suit filed by Hispanic agents against their employer, the FBI, in the Western District of Texas in January 1987.[62] These FBI agents, a total of 311 Hispanic agents among the ranks of 9,000 non-Hispanic FBI agents, alleged discrimination in assignments, promotions, and unfair disciplinary actions. In some cases, according to the news reports, it was for speaking Spanish. Some sixty agents testified in the two-week trial and put forth some damaging testimony against their white, mostly Mormon counterparts known as the "Mormon Mafia." No Hispanic was a special agent in charge (SAC) of a major U.S. field office, only in Puerto Rico. They were assigned low positions in major offices along the U.S.-Mexico border the FBI higher-ups called the "Taco Circuit." The lead plaintiff was Bernardo Matias "Matt" Perez, then forty-eight, who sought $5 million in damages and a change in the way the FBI treated Hispanic agents and other employees. A year later, they won their case. In a 95-page ruling, the judge found that the FBI had discriminated racially against Hispanics and ordered then FBI director William Sessions to make some immediate changes in the treatment of Hispanic agents. By 2012, however, out of the 12,000 FBI agents only 7.1 percent were Hispanics.[63]

After the disturbances in Ferguson, Missouri, forced the FBI to look into local police misconduct in the treatment of African American residents in that city, the FBI's lack of diversity among its agent staff came into question again. In 2015, FBI Director James Comey revealed that only 915, or 6.8 percent, of 13,455 FBI agents were Hispanics. The percentages had dropped from three years prior. Only 2.8 percent were special agents, and only one was an assistant director at the top level in Washington, DC, headquarters on March 12, 2015, according to the *Washington Post*.[64]

Some Literature on the Subject of Surveillance

The documents obtained revealed lawful actions by Chicano activists that did not justify the constant monitoring. Regrettably, this meager body of knowledge about Chicano leaders and organizations is the extent of research utilizing FBI and other intelligence agencies' files during the Chicano Movement. The published works on the FBI and its activities during the Hoover years completely ignore any mention, citation, listing, or reference to surveillance of Chicanos. The ignoring of this community and its leadership in the annals of FBI abuse by major scholars is tantamount to erasing our history of struggle against great odds, including against the U.S. government. But for the work of Ernesto Vigil, Mauricio Mazon, and mine in this area of research and study, we would have no history, no body of knowledge in academe of this government surveillance. Most recently, David Correia published an article and subsequent book that incorporated some FBI documents in his narrative, probably from Tijerina's deposit at the Zimmerman Library at the University of New Mexico.[65]

Organization of the Book

These issues and questions will be paramount in the analyses of the documents spread over eight chapters utilizing FBI files and secondary sources.
Chapter 1 will present mini-biographies of César E. Chávez, the FBI target,
and Hoover, one of the architects of oppression. This is the story of "CC,"
César Chávez: who he was, from migrant to *pachuco*; why he became important to farm workers, Catholics, Chicanos, consumers, and recognized
the world over. The narrative will trace his early formative years, military
service, marriage, and first major non-agricultural job with the Community
Service Organization (CSO). I will describe aspects of J. Edgar Hoover as one
of the architects of oppression in making the United States a police state, by
tracing his career, training, and the radical right-wing currents promoting
the Palmer Raids, Red Scares, McCarthyism, the John Birch Society, and
Hoover's early forays into creating indexes for all types of targets to spy
on. The Hoover COINTELPRO operations as the crux of his police state—or
Seat of Government, as he signed his correspondence—will be examined.
Chapter 2 will feature an examination of how Chávez and his coleaders
Dolores Huerta, Gil Padilla, Antonio Orendain, and Philip Vera Cruz built the
UFW union, and first drew FBI attention as allegations were made in 1965 of
their Communist affiliations.[66] Chávez's early successes, which prompted
copycats in other states that wanted affiliation with his union, are the
content of chapter 3. He rejected affiliation with other startups in Texas,
Arizona, Florida, Ohio, and Wisconsin, not wanting to dilute the efforts
in California, or with any other union insisting on an independent union
of farm workers, then changed his mind in the cases of Arizona and, for a
short time, Texas. Chávez also resisted becoming a Chicano leader despite
pleas from Chicano groups and organizations nationally. He did participate
with other Chicano groups in their events, activities, and conferences, but
rejected any leadership mantle. Chapters 4 through 8 will examine the FBI
files by years from 1969 to 1975. These narratives will also detail the Johnson,
Nixon, Ford, and Reagan roles in opposing Chávez when mentioned in the
documents and the Teamsters' role as competitors in the fields. Operation
Hoodwink, another of Hoover's COINTELPRO operations, and local police

and Teamster violence against the farm workers will be detailed in chapter 7. The last chapter covers the unraveling of César Chávez to the end of FBI documents in 1975. The epilogue will summarize the methods, scope, activities, tactics, and outcomes of the FBI surveillance with conclusions on their impact on Chávez and the union. The epilogue will also review the changing nature of U.S. intelligence operations post-9/11 to the current state of permanent war and recent governmental abuses of the rights of citizens and residents. Central to this portion of the narrative is what I term the "technology of power," or how those in power are using technology not to improve our quality of life but to oppress our every effort at improving our lives that they disagree with or dislike. The work also contains appendices: methodology and research, some select FBI documents and an explanation of FOIA exemptions, and a list of FBI directors, presidents, and U.S. attorney generals. A bibliography of sources is also provided as well as an index.

A copy of the entire FBI declassified file used in preparation of this manuscript is on deposit with the Julian Samora Research Institute at Michigan State University and can be downloaded at https://vault.fbi.gov; search for César Chávez. Another copy, but not arranged in chronological order, is at the University of Texas Benson Latin American Collection in Austin, Texas, under my name, as are the rest of my personal papers.

Onomasticon

ABBREVIATIONS AND ACRONYMS OF FREQUENTLY USED TERMS, NAMES, codes, numbers, locations, titles, and agencies related to the subject of this book and appearing in documents utilized. It is not an exhaustive list, and more recent publications will contain modified entries for old ones and new ones, and deletions of those not in use.[1]

AAG is the Assistant Attorney General of the U.S., also sometimes referred to as the **AUSA**.

AD is Assistant Director of the FBI.

ADEX is the Administrative Index initiated in 1971 to avoid destruction of information when the Emergency Detention Act was repealed. Incorporated names from the Agitator Index, Security Index, and Reserve Index. It was kept at FBI headquarters and 29 field offices of the time, computerized in 1972, and allegedly discontinued in January 1976.

ADIC is an Assistant Director in Charge of a huge FBI field office such as Los Angeles and New York. **SAC**s are under an **ADIC** in these offices.

Agent, also referred to as **SA** for Special Agent, is a member of the investigative and administrative staff, not clerks, located in a field office.

AG is United States Attorney General.

Agitator Index or **ADEX** or **AI** was formerly the Rabble Rouser Index and changed names in March 1968.

Airtel is an internal FBI communication term for a message sent typically from a field office to the Director or Washington FBI office.

AKA or **aka** or **a/k/a/** is for "also known as"; an alias or nickname or code name.

AQ is the FBI Albuquerque field office.

Aztlan is the name for the Southwest in the Nahuatl language of the Meshicas/Aztecs, meaning "land in the north," referring to that part of present-day United States.

B. is informal language used by field agents and others to refer to the **FBI** or **Bureau.**

BIA is the United States Bureau of Indian Affairs.

BLM is the United States Bureau of Land Management.

Block Stamp is found at the bottom right corner of the front page of most FBI documents indicating which FBI office it is filed in, and date of handling by clerks. The clerks will check off appropriate words: searched, serialized, filed, or indexed.

BOCOV is an FBI operation along the U.S.-Mexico border under various other COINTELPROs from 1961; Operation Border Coverage. Purpose was to prevent and disrupt contact and relationships between U.S. persons (namely, Mexican Americans, aka Chicanos) and Mexicans in Mexico.

BOP is the Federal Bureau of Prisons.

BUDED is Bureau deadline.

BUFIL or **BUFILE** is the FBI's term for Bureau File located in Washington, DC, FBI headquarters, not the Washington, DC, field office, the **WFO.**

Bureau is for the FBI headquarters but often used in general for the **FBI.**

Caption is the subject matter title or name for the FBI file. All documents have a caption or reference to a caption, most certainly the original copy of a document and filed under that subject heading or caption.

Case File or **Main File** is name or caption or designation of a file where all relevant material is placed for that subject.

Case Number or **Classification Number** is the assigned number in the classification scheme used by the FBI to distinguish and categorize files. In the late 1960s into the 1970s when the Alianza was most viable, the FBI had 210 classification numbers.[2] From time to time, new numbers are added or changes are made to descriptions of categories.

Chicano is the ethnic self-descriptor of the activist generation among the U.S. population of Mexican ancestry that emerged after World War II.

Chicano Movement is the civil rights era, roughly between the end of World War II and the Gulf War, late 1940s to early 1980s, propelled by the political generation of activists of Mexican ancestry who called themselves Chicanos.

CHIP is the California Highway Patrol or state police.

Classified Information is material or information that is deemed to require protection from unauthorized disclosure. See Executive Order 12065. Before 1975, the FBI did not classify material not intended to be disseminated to other agencies; pre-1975 information now is designated exempt from disclosure under (b)(1), the national security exemption.

Clubs are FBI locations, not in or near FBI field offices, where electronic surveillance is monitored.

COINTELPRO stands for counterintelligence programs, which were numerous FBI operations aimed at disruption, character assassination, neutralizing, destroying, immobilizing, and other dirty tricks undertaken against groups and individuals. Taken from military operations for domestic use, the FBI targeted groups and individuals beginning in 1956 and allegedly discontinued in 1971. Still, COINTELPRO-style tactics by the FBI have continued post-1971.

Communist is a term used by the FBI since the 1920s and defined broadly to mean persons that adhere to the principles of the Communist Party USA (**CPUSA**) and other groups such as the Socialist Workers Party (SWP), Progressive Labor Party (PLP), and other such groups. It also was sometimes defined to mean an occult force of influence that can enter anywhere, and infiltrate groups and thinking of individuals.

Communist Index was the list of names of known Communists in the U.S. kept by the FBI since 1948. In 1956, the list was expanded to include persons associated with other groups beyond those listed above in "Communist." In 1960, the name was changed to **Reserve Index**.

Confidential Informant or **CI** or **CS** is a person that provides information to the FBI. Other names are **snitch, informant, source**, and **PSI** for "person supplying information."

CPLC is for United States Court of Private Land Claims.

DEA is the Drug Enforcement Administration, branch of DOJ, established in July 1973.

Declassify or **Declassified** is to remove the security classifications such as top secret, confidential, secret.

DETCOM is FBI code for Detention of Communists. In 1969, this was replaced with **PAP** for Priority Apprehension Program to include all persons/subjects on **SI** whose apprehension is tabbed a high priority.

DID is the Domestic Intelligence Division of the FBI; during the Tijerina years of first surveillance, William Sullivan was the director of this division for Hoover; then Mark Felt.

DOB is date of birth.

DOJ is United States Department of Justice.

"Do Not File" files are documents kept out of the Central Records System.

ELSUR is electronic surveillance aka a "Bug." Also referred to as **MISUR** for microphone surveillance.

ELSUR INDEX is the list of names in a card file started in 1960 that were the subject of, overheard in, or mentioned in an electronic surveillance activity.

EP is the FBI office in El Paso, Texas.

FAFCS is the new name the Alianza took after DA Sanchez sought to compel Tijerina to turn over the membership lists. It stands for Federal Alliance of Free City States (Alianza Federal de Pueblos Libres).

FBI is the Federal Bureau of Investigation.

FBI HQ is the FBI's main headquarters.

FDs are forms used by the FBI to designate documents to be used for a specific purpose. For example, **FD-4** is a Routing Slip; **FD-73** is an

Automobile Record Form; **FD-330** is an Itinerary Form; and **FD 340** is for a "1A Envelope."[3]

Field Office is the main FBI office in a state and city (cities). There are also **Resident Agencies** and **Liaison Offices,** also named **Legats.**[4]

File Number is a three-part series of numbers for an FBI file. The first numbers, say 100, before the dash (-) is the classification number for domestic security, the type of case it is. The second set of numbers between the dashes (-) are the individual case number, and it is sequential as in 1022 being the one-thousand-twenty-second investigation in that office. The last set of numbers are the serial or document number as in 32 being the thirty-second document in that specific investigation. Hence, 100-1022-32 means domestic security, the 1022nd such investigation out of that office, and it is document 32 in that file on that subject. Not all documents are serialized, and more than one file can exist on any given person or group or event. There were 210 classification numbers in 1968.

FOIA is the Freedom of Information Act. Also referred to as **FOI/PA** for Freedom of Information and Privacy Act (1974).

Four Horsemen is the term made popular by historians of the era, Matt Meier and Feliciano Rivera, during the Chicano Movement for the four principal leaders by region: César Chávez in California, Rodolfo "Corky" Gonzales in Colorado, Reies Lopez Tijerina in New Mexico, and this author, José Angel Gutiérrez, in Texas.

GAO is the Government Accounting Office.

GIP or **Ghetto Informant Program** begun in October 1967 to recruit informants for the FBI to monitor activity in ethnoracial groups such as Puerto Ricans, African Americans, Chicanos, and Native Americans. Allegedly ended in July 1973, but the FBI still recruits and maintains informants. In the previous year, 1972, the FBI had 7,500 such "Ghetto Informants."

G-men is the nickname for FBI agents.

HUMINT is human intelligence, referring to source of information or the process of intelligence gathering, and/or analysis is from a person.

Huston Plan first drafted in 1970 by Tom Huston, aide to President Nixon, on renewed and expanded domestic surveillance activity after Hoover ended his COINTELPRO operations. Huston Plan was partially disapproved by President Nixon; it continued until July 1973.

IDIU is the Interdivisional Information Unit; changed to Interdivisional Intelligence Unit, then Civil Disturbance Unit (**CDU**), and placed organizationally under the Civil Disturbance Group (**CDG**) first established in July 1969 to monitor and coordinate **DOJ** intelligence on civil disturbances.

IEC is for Intelligence Evaluation Committee, a group within the Justice Department in 1970; partially carried out parts of the Huston Plan and coordinated with **NSA** and **CIA** their involvement in domestic intelligence until July 1973.

IES is the staff of the Intelligence Evaluation Committee, established January 1971; prepared studies and evaluations issued by the **IEC** and terminated July 1973.

IGRS was within the Internal Revenue Service (**IRS**), which operated from May 1973 to January 1975. Duties were to gather political intelligence information on individuals and companies of interest to them—465,442 files at one time during this period and made available to the FBI.

INLET is for FBI intelligence letter for the President. Began in November 1969 until December 1972 and was routed to the President, Vice President, and Attorney General containing consolidated intelligence information. SACs and field offices would mark documents with "INLET" when the content of their transmission contained derogatory information on prominent people.

INS is the Immigration and Naturalization Service in existence in the late 1960s to post-9/11 when name changed to Immigration Control and Enforcement Agency (**ICE**) and became part of the new Homeland Security Administration.

IRS is for the Internal Revenue Service.

IS is for Internal Security. **IS-1, IS-2, IS-3** are the sections within the Internal Security Branch of the FBI: 1 is **Extremists,** 2 is **Subversives,** and 3 is **Research.**

IS-C is Internal Security-Communist.

JUNE mail is a system begun in June 1949 to keep electronic surveillance information, surreptitious photographs, microphone surveillance, telephone taps, and records on burglaries carried out by the FBI separate from other documents. They are kept separate in a subfile labeled JUNE.

LHM is a letterhead memorandum sent from a field office to the Director or Washington FBI office comprised of a cover letter and a detailed report covering a period of time and disseminated to other FBI offices and other agencies.

Liaison Office or **Legat** is the FBI office attached to the U.S. Embassy in another country; assists domestic investigations by providing liaison in other countries. They are also referred to as **Legal Attaché(s)**.

Liaison Program was, perhaps still is, the mandate to each field office to contact, visit, and create goodwill with all airlines, banks, military and defense entities, hotels, schools and universities, stockbrokers, truck companies, news media, hotels, federal agencies, and civic organizations at least once every six months. Purpose was to ensure the FBI would receive information from these sources when requested.

Limited Investigation is a type of domestic security investigation to determine need for a full investigation. Lasts only 90 days unless extended by FBI HQ.

LUPE is the name of La Union del Pueblo Entero, Spanish for "the union is for the entire community," a group formed by the UFW to perform investigations and provide services.

MPD is the Metropolitan Police Department for Washington, DC. It is not to be confused with the Capitol Police with jurisdiction over federal buildings and properties.

NARA is National Archives and Records Administration, Washington, DC.

NISO, sometimes also **NIS,** for Naval Investigative Service or Naval Investigative Service Office.

Nitel is an internal FBI communication sent typically from a field office to the Director or Washington FBI office after "normal" working hours, meaning in the evening into the night.

NSA is the National Security Agency; is exempt by statute from FOIA.

OC is for files marked **Official and Confidential** that Hoover kept in his office on special targets. Also, **PC** or **PF** were for files **Personal and Confidential** and **Personal Folder** also kept by the Director.

OEO is Office of Economic Opportunity aka War on Poverty.

OO is Office of Origin, as in **EP** for El Paso. Only in **FBI HQ** do each of the 210 classifications used in 1968 have a O or a OO placed in front of the file drawer. For example, 136 is the classification for the American Legion Contact program. This program began in the 1940s and assumed Legionnaires were unpaid sources for the FBI on domestic security matters in their communities. The 136-O, in this case, is used for complaints and miscellaneous nonspecific data relating to this classification The OO is used to house policies and procedures that pertain to that classification.

POB is place of birth.

POCAM is the FBI's code name for the Poor People's Campaign held in Washington, DC, summer of 1968.

POTUS is President of the United States.

RABBLE ROUSER INDEX was established in August 1967 by Hoover to identify and list individuals with propensity to foment violence or racial discord. Changed name to Agitator Index in March 1968. In 1970 the list contained 1,131 names.

RACIAL MATTER was FBI investigations of ethnoracial groups, including white hate groups.

RC is for Resurrection City, the name given to the location of the Poor People's Campaign. It is also referred to as Tent City because the residents temporarily stayed in tents.

RCSO is the Riverside County Sheriff's Office.

Rebulet means reference to a bureau letter.

Relet (date) is reference to a letter of (date).

Resident Agency or **RA** is the suboffice of the FBI in a state or territory comprised of 1 to 35 agents who report to the main FBI office in that state or territory. **RA** could also be the **Resident Agent**.

Routing Block is stamp on upper right corner of FBI document that lists names of top officials. Those checked are the persons who are supposed to view the document.

RUC is for Referred Upon Completion meaning investigative work is done and sending matter back to office of origin.

RUP is the name of the political party La Raza Unida Party.

SA is **Special Agent**, regular staff in a field office. **SA** could also be the San Antonio FBI office.

SAC is **Special Agent in Charge**, person leading a local or field FBI office.

SCLC is for Southern Christian Leadership Conference; umbrella organization for Rev. Martin Luther King, Jr.

SCOTUS is Supreme Court of the United States.

SDS is Students for a Democratic Society, an organization of radical, counterculture, white youth.

SI is for Security Index.

Six-Way Search is the process to use in checking a name utilizing six variations of the name, e.g., Jose Angel Gutierrez, Jose A. Gutierrez, J. Angel Gutierrez, J. Gutierrez, J. A. Gutierrez, and Jose Gutierrez.

SNCC is for Student Non-Violent Coordinating Committee, organization of black youth.

SOG is Hoover's self-description of his **FBI HQ** office as the **Seat of Government**.

Special Agent is any FBI agent.

SRA is Senior Resident Agent.

Squad is a component of a field office. Average number of agents in a field office is 126 in the late 1960s and early 1970s, divided into eight squads. Larger FBI offices have more agents and larger squads. The **Field Supervisor** is the agent in charge of a squad. Squad 47 in New York had over 60 agents in 1978.

STAT is U.S. Statutes.

Subfile is a subdivision of a main file and can be lettered or numbered and usually contains newspaper clippings, prosecution summaries, and handwritten notes.

Subj. is the subject or the target.

SuBULET is an instruction to submit a **BULET**.

Sulet is instruction to submit letter on the particular matter listed or in question.

SuRep is submit report.

T-(number) is a confidential informant or source, as in **T-1 or T-5**, who is temporary and applies to that informant that one time only. The same number, therefore, can appear multiple times, but it may not be the same informant.

Teletype is an urgent communication typically from a field office to the Director or Washington FBI office before the advent of internet and reliance on telegraphing messages.

TESUR is telephone surveillance, a wiretap.

TGP is theft of government property.

TOPLEV is for top level of the FBI.

TS is for top secret.

UACB means "Unless advised to the contrary by the Bureau."

UFWOC was the early name for the United Farm Workers Organizing Committee, later to become the **UFW**. It was also known after merger as **UFW AFL-CIO.**

UNSUB is an unknown subject.

US is for United Slaves, organization founded by Ron Karenga for black nationalists/activists; faculty member at California State University Long Beach. It could also be for the United States.

USA is not just for the United States of America; could also be reference to a U.S. Attorney of the U.S. Attorney General's staff in a given area/city. Advise to read context to make the determination.

USC is for United States Code, federal laws, or could be United States Court.

USDC is United States District Court, the lowest and local federal court in a jurisdiction.

VISTA is a War on Poverty-era program named Volunteers in Service to America.

WDC is the FBI abbreviation for Washington, DC.

WFO is the FBI's Washington Field Office.

Chronology of Key Events

May 10, 1924: John Edgar Hoover was named Director of the Bureau of Investigation by President Calvin Coolidge.

March 31, 1927: Césario Estrada Chávez was born to Librado Chávez and Juana Estrada near Yuma, Arizona, on the plot of land (118.58 acres) his grandfather, Césario "Papa Chayo" Chávez, homesteaded with his wife, Dorotea "Mama Tella." Upon entering the first grade, Césario's name was changed to César by his English-speaking teacher.

April 10, 1930: Dolores Fernandez was born to Alicia Chávez Fernandez in New Mexico but raised in Stockton, California. When she married her second husband, Ventura Huerta, Dolores kept the name Huerta. Later, she and César's brother Richard lived together; they had four children.

August 29, 1937: Foreclosure on the Chávez land and property for nonpayment of $4,080.80 in property taxes occurred.

February 6, 1939: Auction of the family land took place and Librado was the highest bidder at $2,300, but was unable to obtain the money. In a second round of bidding, the land went for $1,750; again, Librado could not borrow money to bid. The Chávez family turned to seasonal agricultural labor in California.

1942: César quit school and worked full-time to help the family make ends meet after his father was injured in a car accident.

1943: Manuel Chávez, César's cousin, joined the Navy.

1944: César joined the Navy.

1944: César, dressed in civilian clothes, was arrested by Delano police for defying the segregated seating arrangement of a theater and sitting with Anglos. He refused to move and was taken to jail.

1946: Discharged from the Navy and resumed migrant labor with his family.

November 1946: Richard Milhous Nixon, Republican, elected to represent the 12th district in California.

1948: Chávez married Helen Fabela, also a migrant farm laborer. They began a large family: Fernando (1949), Silvia (1950), Linda (1951), Eloise (1952), Anna (1953), Paul (1957), Elizabeth (1958), and Anthony (1958). His younger brother by two years, Richard Chávez, had married the previous year, and sister Rita, older sister by two years, also married in 1948.

1952: Chávez and Helen relocated to the Sal Si Puedes barrio in San Jose, California. He began reading labor history, Gandhi, St. Francis of Assisi, and papal encyclicals provided by a Catholic priest, Donald McDonnel. Fred Ross Sr., working with the Community Service Organization (CSO), met and recruited César that spring as an organizer.

1954: Leroy Galyen was elected sheriff in Kern County, California; former captain in the California Highway Patrol.

1958: César expanded the work of the CSO as an organizer and was reassigned from Madera to Oxnard, California, where he faced the reality of the Bracero Program. Oxnard had the largest Bracero camp in the nation.

December 1958: Robert Welch formed the John Birch Society in Indianapolis, Indiana, now headquartered in Appleton, Wisconsin.

March 31, 1962: César resigned from the CSO and relocated to Delano. He and others formed the National Farm Workers Association (NFWA).

September 30, 1962: The NFWA held its first convention in Fresno, California. Chávez was elected president.

November 22, 1963: President John F. Kennedy was assassinated, and Vice President Lyndon B. Johnson assumed the presidency.

Winter 1964: The Farm Worker Press was founded with $200 to buy a typesetting machine and layout table.

1964: NFWA reported membership of 1,000; the first edition of *El Malcriado* was published as the official organ of the association by Farm Worker Press.

September 8, 1965: Grape strike began in Delano, California, initiated by Filipinos.

September 16, 1965: Chávez's association joined the Filipino Agricultural Workers Organizing Committee (AWOC), which was on strike against grape growers in Delano. The strike lasted for five years. The boycott began against Schenley Vineyards Corporation, DiGiorgio Fruit Corporation, S&W Fine Foods, and TreeSweet Corporation.

March 17, 1966: Chávez began the 340-mile march to Sacramento. During the march the Filipino group agreed to merge with Chávez into the United Farm Workers Organizing Committee (UFWOC).

April 10, 1966: Chávez arrived at the California state capitol with 10,000 supporters. During the march, Schenley Vineyards Corporation signed a contract with the NFWA.

June 1, 1966: Eugene Nelson, as lead organizer of the Independent Workers Association (ITA), called for a strike against eight major growers in the Rio Grande Valley of Texas.

June 8, 1966: The ITA voted to join the NFWA of César Chávez.

July 4, 1966: Texas farm workers went on strike and began a march to the capitol in Austin, Texas.

September 15, 1966: The White House asked the FBI to investigate Chávez, who was being considered for a position at the White House.

1966: Wisconsin workers in Wautoma, led by Jesus, Manuel, and Chacho Salas, settled out-migrants from Crystal City, Texas, went on strike, and formed Obreros Unidos de Wisconsin. They sought affiliation with Chávez.

1967: UFWOC on strike against Giumarra Vineyards Corporation, the largest table-grape grower in California; shortly thereafter against all

California table-grape growers. DiGiorgio Fruit Company signed a contract with UFWOC. Chávez bought forty acres at La Paz, California, and relocated the union and staff away from city center Delano to that site.

June 1, 1967: Texas Rangers Capt. Alfred Y. Allee and Fred Dawson severely beat Magdaleno Dimas and Benito Rodriguez in Starr County, Texas.

1967: Ohio workers in and around Toledo, Ohio, led by Baldemar Velasquez and the Duran extended family, settled out-migrants from Crystal City, Texas, went on strike against tomato growers. They sought affiliation with Chávez.

1968: Roger Ailes was hired to aid presidential candidate Nixon in the campaign as media advisor; twenty-six years later became head of Fox News in early 1996. Ailes died on May 18, 2017, in Palm Beach, Florida.

February 14, 1968: Chávez began a 25-day fast to stop the violence taking place on the picket lines. Sen. Robert F. Kennedy attended mass with Chávez. Rev. Martin Luther King, Jr. sent messages of support.

February 29, 1968: The National Advisory Commission on Civil Disorders, aka the Kerner Commission, issued its report on the violence of 1967 in major urban centers.

March 11, 1968: Chávez ended the 25-day fast.

March 24, 1968: Chávez called for a global boycott of California grapes.

April 16, 1969: Chávez presented testimony before the Subcommittee on Labor of the Senate Committee on Labor and Public Welfare hearing held in Delano. The other two hearings were in Sacramento and San Francisco. Senator Robert F. Kennedy was the only senator to attend the Delano hearing.

April 17, 1969: Chávez began 340-mile march to Sacramento. During the march, Sidney Korshak, lawyer for the owner of Schenley, called Chávez to sign a contract with the union. Chávez traveled to Beverly Hills to sign and returned to the march.

May 10, 1969: Boycott Day Proclamation issued by Chávez was read before the beginning of a 100-mile march from the California Central Valley area to the Mexican border to protest the hiring by growers of Mexican nationals without proper visas as strikebreakers.

May 29, 1970: More than twenty table-grape growers signed contracts with Chávez.

Summer 1970: The Teamsters Union began to sign contracts with growers in the Salinas Valley area. Chávez called a strike and boycott against lettuce growers.

December 10, 1970: Chávez disobeyed a court order enjoining him from boycotting the lettuce crop from Bud Antle Company. He was jailed. Prominent visitors Ethel Kennedy and Coretta Scott King came to visit him while in jail.

February 5, 1971: Chávez spoke on the capitol steps in Austin, Texas, in support of the Economy Furniture strikers and urged supporters to boycott lettuce and Montgomery Ward's stores for buying the scab furniture from Economy.

1971: Chávez signed a jurisdictional pact with the Teamsters to get out of organizing farm laborers but not the warehouse personnel.

July 1971: Agents from the U.S. Bureau of Alcohol, Tobacco, and Firearms alerted Jerry Cohen, Chávez lawyer, that there was an assassination contract out on Chávez.

December 1971: Jimmy Hoffa was paroled by President Richard Nixon.

1971–1972: Chávez union membership swelled to 80,000. The union became the United Farm Workers of America, AFL-CIO (UFW) after joining the larger federation.

May 2, 1972: John Edgar Hoover, FBI Director, died after 48 years in office.

May 10, 1972: Chávez began a three-and-a-half-week fast to protest Arizona law that prohibited secondary boycotts, and to promote the recall of Governor Jack Williams.

June 4, 1972: Chávez ended his fast related to Arizona issues.

January 1972: Nan Freeman, a volunteer on the picket line against Talisman Sugar Plant, was crushed to death while on a picket line near Belle Grande, Florida.

1973: Linda Chávez, César's daughter, was assigned to work the boycott effort in Detroit, Michigan. Arturo Rodriguez, a graduate student at the University of Michigan, joined the boycott and married Linda a year later. Arturo is president of the UFW in 2018.

January 1973: Teamsters reneged on the jurisdictional pact and signed contracts with lettuce growers, which included pay raises and annual increases.

March 1973: Jerry Cohen, Chávez's lawyer, met with "Fred Schwartz," an alias used by Jerome Joseph Ducote. He offered to sell union records taken from a break-in of the UFW Delano office for $35,000. The Justice Department halted the investigation underway by the FBI.

1973: Manuel Chávez, cousin to César, was accused of violence against undocumented workers attempting to cross the Arizona border with Mexico.

April 6, 1973: The Bishop's Committee on Farm Labor of the Catholic Church, led by George Higgins, sided with Chávez against the Teamsters and made public their letter.

Summer 1973: Growers did not renew contracts with Chávez and opted instead for signing with the Teamsters union. Chávez called for another grape strike; violence ensued, resulting in two deaths and dozens hurt from Teamster violence. Chávez called off the strike and called for a second boycott of grapes.

July 5, 1973: Acting FBI Director William Ruckelshaus refused request by Chávez and members of Congress to investigate Teamster violence against the farm workers.

July 15, 1973: Chávez began a 36-day fast.

August 21, 1973: Chávez ended fast due to deteriorating health. Major public figures joined him and a crowd of 8,000 for a mass attended by his mother, Juana, then 96 years old, Rev. Jesse Jackson, Ethel Kennedy and some of her children, Martin Sheen, Edward James Olmos, and state assemblyman Tom Hayden.

September 21, 1973: The UFW held its first convention, with 346 delegates representing 60,000 farm workers.

August 14, 1973: Farm worker Nagi Daifullah, a picket captain, was severely beaten by Gilbert Cooper, a Fresno County deputy sheriff. Nagi died a few days later.

August 17, 1973: Juan de la Cruz was shot from a speeding pickup while picketing near Arvin, California. The shooter was acquitted years later of any wrongdoing.

December 12, 1973: The Colegio César Chávez was formally dedicated in Mt. Angel, Oregon.

May 16, 1974: Chávez visited the Colegio César Chávez in Mt. Angel, Oregon—his third visit to Oregon, having previously visited Hubbard, Salem, and Portland.

May 20, 1974: The U.S. Supreme Court vacated the 1967 convictions of strikers in the Rio Grande Valley and held that state authorities and Texas Ranger Capt. Alfred Y. Allee violated the workers' civil rights. See *Allee v. Medrano*, 416 U.S. 802 (1974).

August 9, 1974: President Richard M. Nixon resigned from the presidency.

September 26, 1974: Chávez met with Pope Paul VI at the Vatican.

1974: Chávez received the Martin Luther King Nonviolent Peace Award from Coretta Scott King in Atlanta, Georgia.

April 14, 1975: Clyde Tolson, longtime partner to J. Edgar Hoover and the number two man in the FBI for as long as Hoover was Director, died.

November 1975: With Chávez's support and work in getting out the vote, Jerry Brown, Democrat, was elected governor of California.

1975: Jacques E. Levy published *Cesar Chavez: Autobiography of La Causa* (New York: W.W. Norton and Co.); reissued in 2007 by the University of Minnesota in Minneapolis, MN.

1975: The California Labor Relations Act (CLRA), the first state to protect farm labor organizing by legislation in the nation, was signed. Chávez marched across and through the Imperial and San Joaquin Valleys to promote support for union elections under the protection of the CLRA. Chávez won a protracted battle banning the use of the short hoe, *el cortito*, in thinning weeds in the fields.

July 14, 1976: Chávez nominated Jerry Brown as a Democratic presidential candidate during the Democratic National Convention.

June 4, 1979: Fernando Chávez, son of César and Helen, passed his bar exam and became a practicing attorney in California.

1979: Chávez was the keynote speaker at the first convention of the Farm Labor Organizing Committee (FLOC) in Ohio led by Baldemar Velasquez.

February 10, 1979: Rufino Contreras was murdered in a lettuce field on the Mario Saikhon ranch—fourth person to die during a UFW strike in the Imperial Valley of California.

February 25, 1979: Chávez spoke to the Texas Organizing Convocation in

Pharr, Texas, and invoked the memory of Rufino Contreras.

July 31, 1979: Chávez began another march from Salinas to San Francisco for support against lettuce growers and called for a boycott against major subsidiaries of United Brands such as Chiquita Bananas, A&W Root Beer, Morrell Meats, and Sun Harvest.

September 1979: Sun Harvest signed a contract with the UFW.

1983–1990: George Deukmejian, Republican, was elected governor and promptly shut down enforcement of the CLRA. Thousands of farm workers covered under the law lost jobs and were blacklisted.

1983: Chávez joined FLOC leader Baldemar Velasquez in his 580-mile march from Ohio to Camden, New Jersey, headquarters for Campbell Soup Company, hoping to bring the company to the negotiating table.

September 1983: Rene Lopez, UFW representative, was shot and killed by either Donato Estrada or Dietmar Ashmann while trying to negotiate a contract with Ralph Sikkema, a dairy-farm operator near Fresno, California. Estrada was convicted of manslaughter and received a six-month prison term while Ashmann, the dairy-farm owner's brother-in-law, was acquitted.

1984: Chávez called for a third grape boycott and introduced a new campaign against pesticides used by growers to produce the nation's fruits and vegetables.

September 1984: Chávez addressed the 7th Annual UFW Constitutional Convention. Also speaking to the union delegates was Willie Brown, Speaker of the California State Assembly.

August 5, 1985: Juan Chavoya died from pesticide poisoning while working in the fields in San Diego County, California.

October 25, 1985: Chávez addressed the Los Angeles County Chicano Employee Association.

December 1985: Colegio César Chávez, Mt. Angel, Oregon, closed its doors due to foreclosure by HUD.

1986: The Immigration Reform and Control Act was passed, which made hiring undocumented persons a crime.

1987: Chávez produced *The Wrath of Grapes*, a movie graphically depicting birth defects, cancer growths, and pesticide poisoning among farm workers and consumers.

1987: Jerome Joseph Ducote, who admitted to the FBI that he possessed UFW documents taken from the Delano union office, died of a heart attack.

1987: Chávez spoke to the workers of the Santa Cruz Valley Pecan Company in Arizona.

July 16, 1988: Chávez began another 36-day fast to dramatize the issue of harmful pesticides.

August 21, 1988: Chávez ended his 36-day fast.

1988: Dolores Huerta was severely beaten by San Francisco police while protesting President George H. W. Bush.

1991: City of San Francisco settled out of court for $825,000 with Dolores Huerta for the police brutality inflicted on her while protesting a visit to the city by President George H. W. Bush.

December 14, 1991: Chávez's mother, Juana Estrada, age 99, died in San Jose, California.

Spring 1992: Chávez led walkouts from the vineyards in Coachella and San Joaquin Valleys. Wine growers signed new contracts with the UFW that included a pay hike for farm workers—the first in eight years.

September 27, 1992: Fred Ross Sr., age 82, died in San Rafael, California.

April 23, 1993: Chávez died in his sleep at age 66 while engaged in a fast and defending a UFW court case in Arizona. No autopsy ordered or done by the family.

April 29, 1993: Chávez's funeral procession involving 35,000 persons went from Delano to La Paz in Keene, California.

August 1994: President Bill Clinton posthumously awarded César E. Chávez the Presidential Medal of Freedom, the highest civilian award in the United States, by presenting the medal in a White House ceremony to Helen Fabela Chávez.

1996: The documentary on the history of the UFW, *The Fight in the Fields*, was released nationally.

1997: The companion book to the UFW documentary bearing the same title was published by Harvest Books, an imprint of Harcourt Brace & Co.

May 30, 1999: Manuel Chávez, cousin to César Chávez, who did many "off the books" jobs for César, mainly along the border in Arizona, died at age 73.

October 8, 2000: Linda Chávez, daughter of César and Helen, wife of Arturo Rodriguez, the UFW president, died at age 49.

May 1, 2002: Monsignor George Higgins, "the labor movement's parish priest," died.

April 2003: The U.S. Postal Service issued a 37-cent postage stamp with César E. Chávez as the image.

January 23, 2005: Jessica Govea died. She was a UFW volunteer with her father, Juan. A UFW member since age 19, boycott coordinator for Canada in 1968, national board member in 1977, and diagnosed with cancer in 1993. Ironically, she raised and pressed the issue of pesticide poisoning of farm workers.

2010: U.S. Census Bureau reported the population as 1,929 for a newly incorporated city in Hidalgo County, Texas, named César Chávez.

March 25, 2011: Anthony Chávez, son of César and Helen Chávez, filed suit against his brother Paul for wrongful termination after 32 years of work with the National Farm Workers Service Center (NFWSC) as executive vice president. Paul was the president of the NFWSC, the Cesar Chavez Foundation, and Radio Campesina Network. See #5-1500-CV-273196 in Kern County Superior Court.

April 25, 2012: Benny E. "Chingon" Tapia, Chávez's oldest and main bodyguard, died.

May 5, 2012: The U.S. Navy launched the ship named USNS *Cesar Chavez*.

May 29, 2012: Dolores Huerta was presented with the Presidential Medal of Freedom by President Barack Obama.

July 27, 2011: Richard Chávez died at age 81, brother to César and longtime partner of Dolores Huerta.

October 8, 2012: President Barack Obama designated La Paz in Keene, California, a National Monument under the care and control of the National Park Service.

March 28, 2014: Filmmaker Diego Luna premiered the movie *César Chávez*, a commercial venture featuring well-recognized stars.

April 12, 2016: Antonio Orendain, cofounder with César Chávez and others of what became the UFW, and later leader of the Texas Farm Workers Union, died.

June 6, 2016: Helen Fabela, César Chávez's wife, died at age 88.

March 6, 2017: "Dolores-the Movie" was commercially screened in ten cities. Directed by Peter Bratt.

August 28, 2018: Teresa Romero was elected President of the UFW.

Note: See www.ufw.org/research/history/ufw-history/ for their own listing of important dates.

The Target and the Architects of Oppression

CÉSARIO ESTRADA CHÁVEZ, ON March 31, 1927, could have been born into a caste system in India and that would explain why he was a migrant laborer, married another migrant worker, lived in poverty most of his life, and was unable to provide the necessities of life for his wife and eight children. Instead he was born near Yuma, Arizona, and forced into a caste system in the United States of America, where most persons of Mexican ancestry have been relegated, since the loss of their homelands, to the lower rungs of a stratified white society.[1]

This history of violence and exploitation by whites against Mexicans —primarily by those who entered Mexico illegally—dates to the 1820s in Texas/Coahuila. Mexicans in possession of the northern limits of Mexico in 1821 numbered 473,718.[2] In 1848 Mexico was forced by the United States to sign a treaty ending the invasion by whites from the United States. The Treaty of Guadalupe Hidalgo made foreigners out of Mexicans and indigenous tribes who had been on the land for centuries. The United States paid Mexico the paltry sum of $14 million for what are now the Southwestern states. By the 1850 census of the population, the first enumeration of persons in the newly acquired lands, nearly half a million Mexicans became U.S. citizens, and generations later, a dispossessed minority. The number of Mexicans dropped to a population range somewhere between 86,000 and 116,000. This dramatic loss of population was offset by white in-migration in the Southwestern states, just as had been the case in Texas/Coahuila.

The Gold Rush brought many whites, some 80,000 by 1849, to the area between Sacramento and Lake Tahoe, particularly along the "rio de los Americanos," as it became known after January 1948 when gold was first found. The U.S. war on Mexico, white in-migration in search of gold, and Abraham Lincoln's proposals and policies that usurped millions upon millions of acres of land in what previously were native and Mexican lands created the loss of homeland for both natives and Mexicans. Among Lincoln's policies in the 1860s were the Homestead Act and the building of the Transcontinental Railroad. By the time whites moved west for free land to homestead and the rail line was completed, railroad companies owned 22 million acres of land in California alone, and another 126 million acres were in the hands of "a few thousand people."[3] The newcomers proceeded to continue the violence against Mexicans in the West and Southwest. Lynching became common practice as well as vigilantism, mob violence, and massacres.[4] The best-known of such massacres occurred in Porvenir, Texas, on January 28, 1918, at the hands of Texas Rangers Captain J. M. Fox and his men, accompanied by the U.S. Army. The Rangers killed 15 unarmed men and boys over the age of sixteen. The remaining 140 survivors of the tiny hamlet—women, children, and a few old men—hurriedly gathered the bodies of their loved ones, crossed into Mexico to bury them in a mass grave, then fled into the brush, other parts of Mexico, and to San Antonio, away from Porvenir, braving the winter cold without any of their possessions. All they owned, built, and tended—crops and livestock—was left behind. Within days, the U.S. Army returned to burn every structure in Porvenir.

This type of Mexican removal of survivors became a common practice.[5] The bodies of these victims remain entombed in a mass grave just yards from U.S. soil in Mexico to this day. On January 18, 2018, a hundred years later, a protest was held on the capitol steps in Austin to remember this atrocious massacre.

The Chávez Clan: Grandparents and Parents

Chávez's grandfather, Césario, fled Chihuahua, Mexico, during the 1880s at the apogee of Porfirio Diaz's dictatorship. As Chávez recalled, his grandfather was indentured to one of the largest *hacendados*, the Terrazas, and was to be conscripted into the Diaz army when he fled to El Paso, Texas. Later, he brought over Chávez's grandmother and their fourteen children; his father, Librado, was two years of age when they crossed the border into the United States in 1888.[6]

The grandparents eventually acquired one hundred acres in the North Gila Valley near the Colorado River and Laguna Dam. The Chávezes created a middle-class existence with property, a business, and sufficient income for his family, now consisting of fifteen children. Papa Chayo and Mama Tella, César's grandparents, turned over operation of the family farm to Librado, César's father, as most of the other grown children moved away. When Librado married Juana Estrada in 1924, he was thirty-eight years of age, hardly a young man, and she was thirty-two. He bought more land and continued to work his plot as well as the family farm. The couple was entrepreneurial and ambitious, operating a pool hall, grocery store, and automobile repair shop on their land. César's favorite hangout after completing his chores was the pool hall, which served him well when he first began seeking union recruits at pool halls in Delano. In 1932, Librado and Juana began to be cash-short due to much credit extended to family, friends, and poor people in general who were their customers. Bills did not get paid, including property taxes, and wholesalers couldn't be paid, so their stock room and supplies dwindled. They sold the businesses and moved back to the family farm with Papa Chayo and Mama Tella. In 1933, a severe drought shriveled the Colorado River and Laguna Dam; this dried up the canals with which to irrigate the crops. Again, cash was short, and little produce to sell caused them to fall behind on bill payments, including property taxes and water district assessments. The Chávez family, Librado and Juana with five kids in tow, became migrant farm laborers working the fields in California near Oxnard at starvation wages.

The reserve labor pool of agricultural workers like them from Texas, Arkansas, Oklahoma, and Arizona drove the wages down and made work scarce. They went on to Brawley to pick cotton. Penniless, they returned to Yuma to obtain a loan to rescue the family farm from foreclosure. Librado was not successful. The neighbor who had sold some of the land to the Chávezes bought it back for a pittance. The lawyer who prepared the Chávezes in their fight against foreclosure took the remaining land, also at a pittance. Both ultimately took the Chávez homestead and property at public auction. Chávez was eleven when he witnessed the sheriff serving his father with the final notice of eviction. As they made plans to return to migrant field labor, the family watched the bulldozers raze their home, corrals, chicken coops, and cover up the irrigation canals. When they lived on the farm, they felt empowered by the freedom to roam the land; buy, sell, eat the livestock; swim in the canals; and sleep in uncrowded rooms with thick adobe walls that kept the home cool in the summer and warm in the winter. Now it was all gone but for the memories. In time the land would become part of Bruce Church Incorporated, a giant vegetable company, which Chávez would battle until his death.[7]

The Chávez family migrated back to Brawley, California, and spent the next few years traveling north of Sacramento and down to the Imperial Valley for jobs in the fields in between. While they were picking plums in the Santa Clara Valley when César was twelve, a union organizer came to talk to the migrant families. He was a white man talking about a strike to force growers to pay more money for the picking of the crops. Many migrants listened and agreed to strike. Within days the strike was broken by replacement labor brought in to pick the plums. According to Jean M. Pitrone, "Librado Chavez joined every union that recruited members from among migrant farm workers, even though each union was soon destroyed by the powerful growers and by the timidity of the workers, fearful of losing their jobs—no matter how poorly paid the jobs were."[8] By the time César was fifteen, the family finally settled in the Chicano barrio of San Jose, California, and lived in a rented house, not a labor camp or under a tree or bridge. They continued working the fields in the surrounding area, but at least they had a base to call home. There he met a lovely girl named Helen Fabela, also from a migrant family, who was to become his wife.

César: A Push Out or Drop Out?

César did not finish high school, opting instead to work in the fields and help his family. Segregated schools in the Southwest, just like in the case of blacks in the South, were the norm.[9] The public schools at that time, as today, had as the primary mission of public education to socialize all children into the Anglo way of life and heritage—one size fits all. Césario became César—pronounced in English as either "Say Sar" or "See Sar." The Anglo model and size did not fit César, and like many Latino children to this day, he opted for dropping out of school after attending some thirty-six different schools. The only jobs he learned as a field hand were the actual labor, translator, and advocate for his father, Librado, in negotiating terms of the field work. The pay was miserable, as were the working conditions—no fresh water, no toilets, no respite from the heat or cold or wind or rain, no protection from pesticides and fertilizers, backbreaking work, especially when using *el cortito*, the short-handled hoe.[10] And, there was no recourse.

Organized labor was not interested in forming a union of farm workers after the Wheatland incident in 1913 and Corcoran strike in 1933. The growers were not interested in negotiating with farm laborers. The Wheatland, California, incident involved the International Workers of the World (IWW) organizers Herman Suhr and Blackie Ford. Hundreds of migrant workers had been lured to the Durst Brothers farm in Wheatland by the prospects of a job. "That summer there were 10 unemployed men for every job," writes Ronald B. Taylor in *Chavez and the Farm Workers*. The workers "were earning $1 a day, or less." When Durst rejected their demands and called police to

remove them from his land, a riot ensued leaving one deputy and two workers dead. A couple of workers plus Suhr and Ford were tried for murder. Suhr
and Ford were convicted and given a life sentence; the workers were acquitted.[11] The ugly scenario repeated itself during the 1933 cotton strike in
Corcoran, California. In this strike, involving thousands of cotton pickers,
mostly of Mexican ancestry, the growers from October 9 to 18 evicted thousands of families from their farms for striking. The workers' demand was $1
for every 100 pounds of cotton. The evening of the 18th, deputies fired on the
crowd holding a rally; three workers were killed by police, and many more
were wounded. The organizers, Pat Chambers and Caroline Decker, were
arrested along with seventeen others on vagrancy charges, with fourteen
eventually being tried. The organizers and six others were convicted and
sentenced to varying prison terms. From that day on, only the Federation of
Labor showed any interest in unionizing farm workers.[12] The situation was
so bad that state and federal authorities stepped in and ordered the strike
over and forced the growers to pay 75 cents per 100 pounds.[13]

Chávez's Early Anti-Mexican Sentiments: *Braceros*

The United States government opened the door during World War II for
Mexican labor to enter the USA for agricultural-related jobs through the
Bracero Program of 1942. *Braceros* (roughly meaning strong arms) were
needed in agriculture, primarily, and later other jobs in fisheries, railroads,
and forestry. Allegedly, it was an emergency measure aimed to help the U.S.
war effort by supplying cheap labor to replenish the agricultural labor that
left for the war. The program continued until 1964 and was expanded to
cover employment in agriculture, forestry, railroads, and fisheries. During
the twenty-two-year span of the "emergency measure," 4.5 million Mexican
laborers came to work in U.S. jobs as "guest workers." A prime target in 1947
to organize workers and strike was the giant DiGiorgio Corporation, which
owned 33 square miles of land in the San Joaquin Valley. Their ranch in
Arvin, California, in Kern County alone was 11,000 acres of land. The strike
failed miserably within five months. An activist and scholar, labor organizer

Ernesto Galarza pressed for workers' rights and launched a career of labor organizing and opposition to the exploitation of *braceros*.[14]

The Bracero Program became an addiction for the vested agribusiness, forestry, railroad, and fishery interests in the United States. Regardless of partisan affiliation, president after president continued and extended the program. Calls for "immigration reform" by these same interests and others in the service and hotel industries have sought to legislatively incorporate some aspect of this type of "guest worker" program during the 1970s through 2017. While working in the fields during these turbulent times of failed strikes and imprisoned union organizers, César Chávez learned there were three main enemies: the growers, the labor contractors, and Mexican workers, whom he saw as strikebreakers.

The Making of a Labor Leader

The Chávez family remained migrant workers into the next decade. César, however, tired of migrant labor in 1944, when he joined the navy in service of his country.

> Neither my mother nor my dad wanted me to go, but I joined up anyway. It was wartime. I suppose my views were pretty much the views of most members of a minority group. They really don't want to serve, but they feel this awesome power above them that's forcing them to do it. I had little choice, either get drafted or sign up. Since I wanted even less to go into the army, I enlisted in the navy when I was still seventeen.[15]

Chávez did not like military service, where he experienced more discrimination and maltreatment. During his years in the navy, his job assignment was as a deck hand on small boats. Fortunately, he did not see combat and returned home safely. Prior to his actual discharge in 1948, he returned home on leave for 72 hours to see his fiancée, Helen. He was promptly jailed for refusing to give up his seat in the white section of the segregated Delano movie house. He was not wearing his sailor uniform. For having taken seats in the Anglo side of the movie house, they were quickly removed. Mexicans were to sit at the opposite side of the theater. Unable to cite him with a specific offense, the police chief let him go with a stern warning to let things be and not cause any more trouble.[16]

While he served in the military the requisite amount of time and was honorably discharged, he did not avail himself of benefits afforded veterans upon discharge. The Servicemen's Readjustment Act of 1944 (P.L. 78-346) was available and could have been utilized for a home or business loan, educational programs, and even unemployment compensation. César, like many other Chicanos being honorably discharged, was not informed while processing out that he was entitled to those benefits. He chose to return to what he knew, the fields of California, and to Helen Fabela, his wife to be. They married a year later and resumed migrant labor picking grapes and cotton. That is what César and Helen both knew how to do.[17] Eventually, César joined his brother Richard in Crescent City, California, near the border with Oregon for jobs with a lumber company. This experience eventually helped him land a job in a lumber mill back in San Jose, California.

Helen had given birth to three kids by then, and they settled into a tiny house in the same Chicano barrio of San Jose where his family resided, aptly named Sal Si Puedes (Get out if you can).[18] Always practicing Catholics, the Chávezes began helping the local priest, Donald McDonnell, by accompanying him to nearby labor camps housing Mexican *braceros*. McDonnell, with César at his side, listened to tales of the never-ending train of abuse and exploitation narrated by the men. Basically, the Bracero Program was a third-party contract between the Mexican government, the U.S. government, and the grower, not the *bracero*. Hence, when a *bracero* was injured, he was replaced without care or compensation; when they got sick they had to self-medicate as there was no health insurance for them under the program. When it rained, they did not work but were still charged for their daily meals, and they slept in unventilated barracks without indoor plumbing. The grower was free of all liability and duty to *braceros*; his contract was with the U.S. government to hire an agreed number of Mexican laborers.

Many *braceros* discovered they owed the grower money before the end of their contractual term and could not and would not pay.[19] Many jumped their contracts and made their way into the barrios of major cities in California and across the nation. The growers and the U.S. and Mexican governments couldn't care less if *braceros* jumped the contract; there were many more available.

President Eisenhower's Operation Wetback was the institutionalization of this rent-and-deport-the-slave program. The Bracero Program continued to bring in Mexican workers, who continued to jump their contracts and settle out in Mexican American communities across the land. Eisenhower's administration during the 1950s would hunt down these jumpers and deport them.[20] The growers continued to get plenty of cheap labor at the same time that anti-immigrant forces were placated by these dragnets and deportations. Chávez, like Galarza, was among those who viewed the Mexican guest workers as an impediment to unionizing the workers, and not as potential union members. The scapegoating of undocumented workers from Mexico by Chávez was constant from the early beginnings of the National Farm Workers Association, United Farm Workers Organizing Committee, and the United Farm Workers of America. On May 20, 1974, Chávez's anti-Mexican-labor bias was made official policy. He instructed all UFW entities from Florida to Arizona to California to keep the "illegals out of California" by setting up what became known as the "wet line."[21]

Becoming a Labor Leader with a Catholic Religious Base

Chávez's religious training got a head start from Mama Tella, who was literate in both Spanish and Latin. On many an evening, she would relate stories of saints, virgins, and other Catholic icons to her grandchildren, all of whom lived on the family farm. César was among the grandchildren who were exempted from catechism classes by the area priest when it came time for them to do their First Communion because of their knowledge of the commandments, saints, and religious rituals, including the parishioners' responses in Latin during Mass. Chávez also learned compassion and the true meaning of "love thy neighbor" from his mother, Juana, who always urged her children to let her know which of their friends' family members needed food. At times, she would invite the homeless and the hungry to eat dinner with the family. César had to deliver plates of food to many a destitute family or person on several occasions, but in particular on October 16, saint's day for Eduvigis, a Polish duchess who gave away her worldly possessions to the poor when she became a Christian. César stated to Jacques E. Levy, his biographer, that his religious training led him closer to the Catholic Church and its teachings. These teachings from parents and church doctrine became his marching orders: "I have read what Christ said when he was here. He was very clear in what he meant, and he knew exactly what he was after. He was extremely radical, and he was for social change. For me the base must be faith."[22]

Frank Bardacke believes this was the root cause for Chávez's use of the slogan "la causa" (the cause) in his farm worker organizing and making the song "De Colores," taken from the *cursillo* movement within the church, as the union fight song, and the Virgen de Guadalupe his union's standard bearer. *La causa* was the substitute for his Catholicism; it became the religion of his work in farm labor organizing.[23]

In 1951, Chávez was introduced to Fred Ross, his mentor in organizing, by his parish priest, Donald McDonnell. McDonnell took Chávez to labor camps, and César got to witness the priest demand access to the camp and the migrants. This priest also provided Chávez with more substance by explaining the teachings of Saint Paul and Francis of Assisi. More importantly, McDonnell introduced Chávez to papal encyclicals on labor, beginning with Pope Leo XVIII's letter on the condition of labor dating to 1891, and Pope John XXIII's 1961 encyclical on Christianity and Social Progress. According to Marco G. Prouty, two more encyclicals followed in 1965 and 1971 that "seemed to speak directly to *la causa*."[24] Pope Paul VI's Call to Action supported labor's right to organize. Chávez had his marching orders on which to base his faith; he found his cause. And, Fred Ross, the Industrial Areas Foundation man on the West Coast, recruited Chávez into the new organizing effort among Mexican Americans, the Community Service Organization. Chávez and Helen, and later Dolores Huerta, all received training in Chicago on the Saul Alinsky methods, tactics, and strategies for organizing grassroots working-class people.[25]

Starting the Farm Workers Union

The Mexican American population was rapidly becoming urbanized by the 1960s, but in the 1940s the majority were still residing in small rural American towns, predominantly across the Southwest. Chávez thought while he worked for the Community Service Organization (CSO) that he would convince the membership and board of directors of the need to unionize farm workers in small rural communities. Chávez rose from new hire to director of the CSO in a matter of years. He was earning $150 a week in salary. The CSO had an urban focus; the leadership understood demographic projections making the Mexican American people an urban community. After years of laboring in emerging urban barrios registering voters, conducting citizenship classes, and protesting discrimination and employment conditions on behalf of the CSO, Chávez offered the board of directors to forfeit his salary for a year while he organized farm workers. He gave the board an ultimatum in March 1962; the board turned down his recommendation to unionize farm workers. He resigned, taking Dolores Huerta with him, and within months Gil Padilla, also working for CSO, joined them. Six months later, Chávez convened the first National Farm Workers Association (NFWA) convention in Fresno, California. He worked tirelessly organizing farm workers over the next three years. During the interim he turned down job offers from the Agricultural Workers Organizing Committee (AWOC), an affiliate of the AFL-CIO. He refused the offer from Sargent Shriver to head oversight of the Peace Corps in Latin American countries.[26] According to Philip Vera Cruz, the Filipino leader along with Larry Itliong, another Filipino, Dolores Huerta joined them in the AWOC and she helped pull Chávez into their circle; eventually both groups, the Filipinos and Chávez, merged.[27]

In 1965, symbolically on Mexican Independence Day, September 16, Chávez joined forces with the AWOC in their strike against grape growers, which lasted until 1970. The following year, in 1966, Chávez began three of his most famous tactics—long marches, boycotts, and fasts. He issued the Plan de Delano and began walking from Delano to Sacramento in hopes of meeting with the governor by Easter Sunday. He was disappointed.

Governor Edmund Brown, a Democrat, chose to party with Frank Sinatra in Palm Springs over those holidays and not listen to sad stories from these striking migrant laborers. Chávez called on Chicano activists and other supporters across the nation to boycott grapes. And, in an unprecedented step, Chávez pushed to internationalize the farm worker cause via the boycott of grapes in Europe and those sent to the U.S. military forces warring in Vietnam.

Chávez fasted twenty-five days in February and March 1968 to protest grower and local police violence against farm workers, and to renew his call for nonviolence in the fields. Thousands of farm workers were arrested weekly by local police for picketing fields and grocery stores; hundreds were beaten during these arrests. The thousands arrested, including Chávez himself, were tried and found guilty of minor misdemeanors; dozens were shot, maimed, hurt, and mutilated; and some died. Legal defense costs, including bail and court fees, mounted into an unexpected expense for the fledging union. Those arrested were financially hurt and emotionally broken; they feared police brutality. The summer of 1973, two union members were killed: Juan de la Cruz and Nagi Daifullah. This brutality took its toll on individual farm workers and their families. Chávez and his family were horrified at the violence directed at them as well. Chávez surrounded himself with bodyguards and guard dogs for his and his family's protection.

Being the Labor Leader

With a few contracts under his union label by the end of the 1960s, Chávez had to turn to the actual administration and management of the contracts and their terms. He became a bifurcated leader—one central to the Chicano Movement and the other the union boss who had to approve even the most minor of expenses, such as buying tires. He did not fare well at either over time. The union began to enjoy record membership numbers into the early 1970s, then dues dropped from 50,000 members to 6,000. Then, by the 1980s the union collapsed completely. How this story unfolded is summarized in this quote by Bardacke:

No one has told it yet, despite the appearance of a fair number of books about the union. The early ones were mostly hagiography, tales of how the wise and saintly Cesar Chavez miraculously built the UFW. More recent works blame Chavez for the union's fall, citing his "personal demons" and his periodic purges of the UFW staff, especially the dismissal of his highly skilled top aides. In almost all accounts, the history of the union is essentially a story of Cesar Chavez and his staff, in which farm workers provide little more than background color as either the beneficiaries of his genius or the victims of his faults.[28]

Chicanos tired of his refusal to lead other Chicano endeavors and concerns.[29] Other fledging unionization efforts in Texas, Ohio, Florida, Wisconsin, Washington, and Oregon refused to keep sending money and support to California at the expense of their needs. Moreover, Chávez made it clear he was going to establish the union in California first; all others had to wait. They didn't. Texas, Ohio, Florida, Washington, and Oregon farm workers formed their own unions. Some met with limited success; Wisconsin simply fizzled out.

His union membership and inner core found it difficult to maneuver around his micromanagement style and acerbic lifestyle. Chávez insisted on farm worker committees to be the base of the union. He vehemently opposed formation of union locals. While he was soft-spoken at times, he would often yell, scream, and shout at office staff and volunteers. He demanded all union organizers and staff, single or married, live on the starvation-scale weekly wage of $5 plus room and board.

Chávez had to develop new skills to become the head of his union. Recruiting volunteers to help with organizing boycotts, strikes, and services administration from among the Chicano, white, black, and Filipino youthful activists depended on campus speaking engagements. Union business greatly reduced his travel to college campuses and Chicano groups' conventions. Youthful, middle-class, non-farm-worker volunteers, predominantly Anglos, accepted the low weekly wage and long hours with few resources; they could always go back home or to college where they came from. Farm workers, however, refused that extreme poverty wage and did not want to work for the union. They had trouble enough making the monthly dues payment with or without work. Training farm-worker union members to run their own union was next to impossible. They wanted a better than $5 a week wage and full benefits; no more farm work for them. They lacked the formal education to perform the simplest of tasks such as budgeting, running a health clinic, credit union, union hiring hall, and food pantry, not to mention the law department, finance, and contract compliance and accountability.

Unbecoming the Union Leader

Recent scholarship on Chávez is not as flattering as were the first books. Pawel, Garcia, and Prouty are among the recent critics of how Chávez failed to lead the union he so desperately wanted to build, and why. According to these sources, from the mid-1970s until his death Chávez became more and more isolated from everyone, physically moving from the Delano office to Forty Acres on the edge of town, then to La Paz, a commune-like existence in the mountains, away from the union offices in Delano. He tried to initiate a cult-like training program to make faithful followers out of volunteers and staff. Purges, reassignments, and resignations became the norm in the last two decades of his life, particularly beginning in 1977, which coincided with Helen Chávez leaving her husband, suspecting infidelity.[30] Matt Garcia chronicles how Chávez and Dolores Huerta entered a power struggle with loyalists such as Marshall Ganz, Jerry Cohen, Chris Hartmire, Jim Drake, and Eliseo Medina over union strategy.

The third and fourth faces of the original farm workers movement besides Chávez and Huerta were Gilbert Padilla and Antonio Orendain.[31] Both left the union opposing Chávez's lack of adherence to democratic processes in conducting union business—Orendain in 1974 and Padilla in October 1980. The original Filipino leadership also quit and left. Philip Vera Cruz, another UFW founder, vehemently opposed Chávez's travel to the Philippines to be feted by dictator Ferdinand Marcos in 1977. He resigned over that issue that year. Upon resignation, he was asked to sign a loyalty pledge and to not criticize Chávez or the union in his writings.[32] The founding pair, Chávez and Huerta, wanted to focus on the institutionalization of gains by creating a community at La Paz up in the mountains away from the fields. To further institutionalize this "community," Chávez called for celebrating union events such as the founding of the union, the death of martyrs, his birthday, and playing Synanon's "The Game." This was alleged to be a therapeutic session involving residents of La Paz and the inner core leadership. The Game was nothing more than a confrontational session at which participants expressed their innermost opinions and beliefs about others.[33]

The following year, 1978, Chávez prevailed on the board to dismantle the legal department. More importantly, he ended the boycotts of Gallo wine, grapes, and lettuce. In effect, these decisions ended strategies that had brought the mightiest of growers to the negotiating table. The decision to remove veteran lawyers, headed by Jerry Cohen, and replace them with rookie first-year law graduates was devastating to successful litigation.[34] Moreover, by ending the boycott strategy, all networks of volunteers and staff, national and international, soon disappeared. It would be next to impossible to revive such a field operation in case of need. And need was around the corner.

Union dues reached their peak of almost $3 million in 1982 and dropped precipitously to $1 million by 1985 with only seventy-five contracts. By 1988 the union had invested dues monies in eighteen other nonunion ventures; some were nonprofit, like the school and credit union, while others were strictly commercial. Chávez and his children became housing developers. They utilized nonunion labor for housing construction, enraging his trade union brethren as well as all other supporters of union labor. The Chávez-run Martin Luther King, Jr. Fund became the Cesar Chavez Foundation in 1989 with $8 million in principal corpus. Grant-making became a subsidy for UFW related enterprises, but none in direct services to farm workers.[35] And, the Cesar Chavez Foundation opened three major offices, two in California and one in Arizona, to market UFW products and Chávez memorabilia.

Democratic Party Politics Takes Center Stage

According to Simone Cinotto, the Gallo family contributed heavily in 1968 to Democratic U.S. Senator Alan Cranston for special favors in Congress, namely, obtaining corporate tax breaks. Between 1986 and 1996, the Gallo empire also gave $274,000 in contributions to Republican U.S. Senator Robert Dole and an additional $705,000 in contributions to foundations connected to him.[36] Chávez felt he had to match these political contributions with union money and volunteer labor in California and at the national level. He began to build and run a statewide political organization in addition to the union and the community at La Paz. The UFW efforts on behalf of Robert Kennedy's presidential run paid off handsomely in that other Democrats curried favor with Chávez for his endorsement and support in getting voters to the polls. But Kennedy was assassinated, and Ronald Reagan remained in Sacramento as governor until he moved into the White House as president. Chávez's first and last major electoral victory was to elect Jerry Brown to the governorship in 1978. After that the Chávez touch was lost and buried with Proposition 22, and when Republican George Deukmejian won in 1983 and remained in office until 1991 only to be followed by another Republican in Sacramento—Pete Wilson until 1999—there was a decade and a half plus of anti-farm-worker policies and benefits for California's agribusiness interests. Not once did Chávez think of organizing and fielding candidates to take local government positions in school districts, cities, counties, community colleges, and legislative seats. Yet, then and now, most eligible Latino voters reside and vote in these local governmental units. He opted for a top-down strategy at the national and state levels over a bottom-up movement to have farm workers control local government. At the very least, he could have controlled and contained the police violence against farm workers if local government had been on his side.

The End

Chávez spent himself trying to form a labor union of farm workers, and died in his sleep on April 23, 1993, near his birthplace in Yuma, Arizona. He had just passed the age of 66. He was in Yuma as a witness in a trial over the economic loss to growers the UFW boycott had caused; the union's liability was the fundamental concern. Chávez was on trial, not the growers. In the first case, the UFW was found liable for $5.4 million in damages.[37] In a subsequent case, Bruce Church, Inc. sought $9.7 million in damages and were awarded $2.9 million. He lost this case. After his death, however, the appellate courts reversed the money judgment amounts. Later, in March 29, 1996, the UFW reached a historic settlement and five-year contract with Bruce Church, Inc., ending all labor charges and lawsuits against each other.[38] It is plausible to assume Chávez died in the middle of these legal battles from a broken spirit. It is equally plausible to assume Chávez died from the harassment by police at all levels, constant fear of continual assassination threats and attempts, animus from growers and Republicans at all levels, and the crumbling of the UFW from within from self-inflicted wounds he often caused himself. Those around him in the late 1980s and early 1990s had not lived or shared his dream of building a union, much less a movement. For the most part, the *veteranos* and *veteranas* of the UFW had resigned, been purged, been fired, or taken leaves of absence never to return to *la causa* of the 1960s as they knew it. We will never know. We will also never know the exact cause of his death; there was no autopsy.

The Architects of Oppression

Events surrounding J. Edgar Hoover's last day, May 2, 1972, will also remain mysterious and secret. There are conflicting versions of the discovery that Hoover had died in the night, and without autopsy no one will ever know the cause of death.[39] His inner circle, household staff and office staff, closed many doors to openness, transparency, information, and verification of facts and circumstances such that we may never know the truth about many aspects of Hoover's death and life.[40] Anthony Summers writes, "The Hoover who preached stern moral sermons to Americans secretly practiced homosexuality—even transvestitism."[41] Richard Hack maintains an opposite view; he offers contradictory evidence in his book.[42] Curt Gentry, another of Hoover's unofficial biographers, does not take a clear position on the subject but does make repeated mention of the "rumors" and "jokes" about Hoover's unmanliness and the exacting "revenge" he took on those who called him a "fairy" or "queer."[43] Athan Theoharis produces actual FBI documents from the "secret files" on those homosexual allegations in his book.[44] Richard Powers provides more in-depth information about Hoover's private life and relationships with his immediate subordinates in the FBI. Specifically, he implies that Hoover's first assistant, T. Frank Baughman, dating to the Palmer Raids era, was involved with him in more than just a working relationship. He writes: "In 1928 . . . Hoover promoted more head-quarters staff ahead of his old friend. Hoover had lost interest in Baughman. (And, obviously, Baughman, who got married at about that time, had less time for Hoover.) Clyde Tolson had taken Baughman's place."[45]

And, Lyndon B. Johnson, Robert F. Kennedy, and Richard Nixon, to name a few, are credited by Darwin Porter with inflammatory comments on Hoover's sexual proclivities. Lyndon B. Johnson: "America is in the grip of two homosexual lovers, and there's not a god damn thing I can do about it . . . They've got enough on me to bring down my presidency." Robert F. Kennedy: "J. Edna is the kind of guy who has to squat to pee. Any day now, I expect him to show up to work wearing one of Jackie's Dior creations." Richard M. Nixon on news of Hoover's death: "Jesus Christ! That old cock-sucker!"[46] Marc Aronson calls Hoover's homosexual relationship with Clyde Tolson the second secret in his book. He refutes the allegations that Hoover dressed in women's clothing and engaged in homosexual orgies.[47]

Anthony Summers claims that Hoover's body was found that morning by Annie Fields, the black housekeeper, as does Mark Felt in his book.[48] Curt Gentry, however, writes that Hoover's body was found by James Anderson, whose duties for nearly forty years had included being the Director's driver, gardener, errand boy, and man Friday. Anderson was a black man. Hoover's racist beliefs did not permit black agents in the FBI Academy or as special agents, and those he had inherited from the days of the Bureau of Investigation he promptly terminated along with the handful of white women agents. Blacks could open doors, drive his car, and wait for his beck and call—that's all.

Anderson reportedly found Hoover's seminude, cold body early in the morning and immediately notified Hoover's personal physician and former deputy director Clyde Tolson. Despite the fact that Tolson no longer had any responsibilities or authority within the FBI, he had been Hoover's companion for decades and was the number two man in the organization. They rode to work together, ate lunch and dinner together daily, vacationed together, worked together as Director and Assistant Director—numbers one and two—and Tolson, as designated beneficiary, inherited the bulk of the Hoover estate.[49] The couple is buried side by side in a Washington, DC, cemetery.

Anderson then called Helen Gandy with the news of the Director's death and relayed the Tolson instructions. One of those instructions was to remove and destroy files. Hoover's secret files were not kept in his office; most were with Gandy in her office, and in the basement of the Department of Justice building. Gandy and Tolson were Hoover's closest confidants; Tolson was inseparable from Hoover even when the Director took vacations.[50] According to Richard Hack, "Rumors of a homosexual relationship between the two men refused to die despite repeated denials." And, Hack maintains that Hoover kept eighteen file cabinets marked "Obscene" full of pornographic material, a stock of pornographic movies, and even some lurid literature in his desk.[51] Shortly after learning of Hoover's death, President Nixon ordered Assistant Attorney General Patrick Gray III to retrieve Hoover's secret files at once and deliver them to the White House. Gray did as instructed, only to be lied to by Assistant to the Director John Mohr, who claimed that no such files existed.[52]

Anthony Summers has more lurid and shocking details in his book on Hoover's secret life. Summers, a noted investigative reporter for the British Broadcasting Corporation (BBC), journalist, and author of several books, writes in the prologue and first two chapters of *Official and Confidential* that Hoover not only was a closet homosexual and transvestite but also a purveyor of prurient material to presidents and members of Congress; unethically voracious for gifts from the rich and famous; appropriator of federal property, particularly FBI facilities and supplies for his personal use; primary saboteur of the Warren Commission's investigation into the Kennedy assassination; and he had ignored warnings about the attack on

Pearl Harbor.[53] If these disclosures were not enough, he concludes that Hoover was a troubled youth, son of a mentally ill father (Dickerson Naylor Hoover), most demanding mother (Annie Marie Scheitlin, aka "Nanny"), and grandson of a dogmatic Calvinist preacher (John Hitz).[54]

Little Hoover

Bible reading was a nightly affair at the Hoover household. On Sunday afternoons, the Hitz grandparents would visit; they lived across Seward Square at 414 while the Hoovers lived at 413. Young Edgar would sit and listen to his grandfather's Bible reading and his admonitions against sinners, "the fate of drunks, and heathens—two characteristics Hitz routinely credited to blacks."[55] Young Edgar lived in a controlled white world with limited exposure to blacks as servants in the household and as laborers in Washington, DC. Segregation kept blacks away from whites in church, school, work, and play. There was no exposure to Spanish-speaking people but for an occasional mention in the print media about Puerto Ricans in New York.

Hoover was considered the "runt of the litter" and a late bloomer; he stuttered as a child. He found a cure for this malady, a machine-gun, staccato, rapid talk. The cure was to talk not slower but faster. Practicing alone in his room (his young nieces sometimes surreptitiously listening), he learned to talk rapidly and—except in moments of great stress—overcame the problem. A court reporter acting as transcriber for Hoover quit in frustration because he was speaking at a 400-word per minute rate, exceeding her 200-word per minute capacity. Hoover took up debating while in junior high to overcome his fear of speaking before a group of people, according to Curt Gentry.[56]

Hoover was also a little man, never growing to average height or weight for white men of the 1930s. He suffered from a Napoleon complex. In debate, his physical size did not matter. By speaking rapidly, his opponent or listener did not have a chance to get a word in edgewise and he could dominate a conversation. As Director of the FBI, this was his customary approach to all face-to-face encounters. Hoover did all the talking, first and fast, then you were dismissed. He kept his personal physical information vague. His public relations department would respond to such queries with "The director is just a shade under six feet tall." He elevated the space behind his desk to appear larger to his guest, avoided standing next to tall people, and rarely promoted tall agents to work near his office.[57]

Hoover also had an early penchant for monitoring people and meticulous record-keeping. He began a diary at age eleven and published a two-page mimeographed "newspaper" for his neighborhood, *Weekly Review*, which he sold for a penny. In his weekly he also advertised delivery services of groceries, messages, and packages for ten cents without regard for distance. He acquired and perpetuated the nickname "Speed" for his promptness in deliveries. His speed was acquired from participating in track sports; the football coach had turned him down because he was a runt. His disciplined approach to tasks developed in him an affinity for regimen, predictability, order, and regulation, according to Richard Hack.[58]

The Troubled Youth

Hack's research into the life of J. Edgar Hoover confirmed that young Edgar grew into convoluted manhood after a conflicted and rigid upbringing under the stern tutelage of his mother. With profoundly radical events taking place around the world, particularly the first revolutions of the twentieth century in Mexico then Russia, his home world began to collapse. His father suffered a complete nervous breakdown and entered a massive depressive state requiring commitment. There he remained until mid-1912 when he was composed enough to work part-time. He never returned to his prior self. Because of good scholastic achievement Hoover became the valedictorian of his graduating class. He rose to become captain of his cadet corps his senior year. At graduation, he was accompanied by his parents to the ceremony and dance. His dance card, which he preserved until death, was blank; he danced with no one.

Because of his academic record, a full scholarship was offered to Hoover by the University of Virginia Law School, but his family were without means to pay for his room and board. The affordable choice for the study of law was the night program at George Washington University in D.C. He took a job at the Library of Congress, where he learned the system of cataloging books, a skill that served him well in his next job.

No Enlistment but Deferment

The hysteria surrounding the discovery of the infamous Zimmermann telegram on January 16, 1917, prompted President Woodrow Wilson to begin regular public harangues against Eastern European immigrants, but not those from Western Europe. He railed against the easterners time and again, according to Stanley Cohen, describing them as "creatures of passion, disloyalty, and anarchy" that did not belong in "America."[59] Wilson was reviving the virulent strain of American nativism dating to the mid-1850s and the Know Nothing Party movement. The German menace and the Red Scare were not in Hoover's world, but were rapidly approaching. None of these events moved Hoover to enlist in the military or wait to be drafted into World War I.[60] Hoover buried himself in his law books and studies, oblivious to the need for men in uniform to make the world safe for democracy. He completed law school with a master's in law in 1917 and passed the District of Columbia bar on July 26 of that same year.

Special Agent Hoover: The Beginnings of a Career

Rather than practice law, Attorney Hoover hired on as a low-level clerk in charge of maintaining the filing system at the Department of Justice. In that position, he was exempt from induction into military service. He worked seven days a week, often until midnight, at his job indexing files and keeping names of men and women he considered "low vermin" and "subversives." From this early work, Hoover developed the Subversive Index for the Bureau of Investigation. After his father died in 1921, Hoover's life revolved around his job and caring for his mother, who was bedridden the last three years of her life. He never married and remained living in the family home with his mother until she died in 1938.[61] He was forty-three years of age.

Hoover learned new prejudices, anti-immigrant bigotry, and anti-Communist ideology during his first years at the Bureau of Investigation. Ackerman, quoting William Sullivan, part of Hoover's top leadership at the FBI, stated that the Director "didn't like the British, didn't care for the French, hated the Dutch, and couldn't stand the Australians."[62] Fortunately for Hoover, the attorney general developed a program to rid the United States of radicals and potentially subversive immigrants flowing in great numbers into the country.[63] This was a clarion call for Hoover; he was up for the job. The massive manhunts and subsequent deportations in many cases became known as the Palmer Raids—for the AG's name, Alexander Mitchell Palmer—which were conducted during 1919-1920. Hoover had been promoted to head the newly created General Intelligence Division of the bureau and actively worked to implement the Palmer Raids. Implement he did, and with enthusiasm. As Hoover dug into his formidable and growing index card file on potential subversives and radicals, topping 100,000 names, the first raids were conducted in twelve cities, leading to 650 arrests in New York alone that resulted in 43 deportations. By January 2, 1920, Hoover's team was ready to extend the dragnet to thirty cities in twenty-three states, leading to the arrest of over 3,000 persons.[64] By 1921, Hoover had a collection of 450,000 persons on his list; many were not immigrants, much less radicals. His net now was being cast to include those with dissenting views to those of Hoover, and of course the White House. Among the names in his index card file were those of Felix Frankfurter, law professor who became justice of the Supreme Court; Marcus Garvey, the noted African American separatist leader; Jane Addams, the most celebrated pacifist; Robert La Follette, a progressive U.S. senator from Wisconsin; Roger Baldwin, the civil libertarian; and sitting Supreme Court Justice Louis Brandeis.[65]

The October Revolution in Russia provided new fodder for Hoover's cannon. During congressional testimony before the Fish Committee, authorized to investigate Communist propaganda in the United States, Hoover stated, according to Theoharis, "that self-preservation of the Nation is the first law of patriotic duty."[66] So much for "government of the people, by the people, and for the people," or the First Amendment guaranteeing free speech, the right to assembly, and the right to petition for redress of grievances.[67] This expansive reach into propaganda coming from the Red Menace provided Hoover with new tools: break-ins, burglaries, wiretaps, and more preventive surveillance to gather the evidence of propaganda. With evidence in hand, Hoover created a new thesis of subversion, that of class and racial hatred, which cast the poor against the rich, and white against nonwhite.[68]

President Roosevelt Opens the Doors to the Architects of Oppression

Hoover took advantage of a meeting in 1936 with President Roosevelt, who wanted the Federal Bureau of Investigation (FBI) to investigate Communism and fascism. Hoover focused his investigation on domestic groups to find this developing un-American subversion. Given the absence of a record of the details of the actual Roosevelt instruction, Athan Theoharis posits that Hoover took this presidential interest and converted it into a decades-long deception of Congress and his bosses, the various U.S. attorney generals. AG Stone, as a condition of making Hoover the Director of the Bureau of Investigation, extracted from Hoover a commitment not to use the bureau for investigating domestic political groups and persons. Despite the verbal pledge, this is exactly what Hoover set out to do again, just as he had done unilaterally and in secret dating to 1924. Hoover promptly ordered his field agents to "have investigations made of the subversive activities in this country, including communism and fascism."[69] In December 1941, Hoover began FBI operations in Mexico and other international stations.[70] This initial program and presidential illegal "order" were the foundation for subsequent forays into *ultra vires* acts by subsequent presidents, willingly and often initiated by the FBI Director and approved by compliant attorney generals. Presidents seek running mates, make Cabinet appointments, and plan to place many other appointees to high-level positions to help implement the chief executive's agenda, both foreign and domestic. Many of these selections are based on political expediency to placate special interests; reward financial donors, particularly in the naming of ambassadors; and win favor with prior electoral sectors or future votes. This expediency leads to institutional mistrust from within the White House toward the occupiers of Cabinet positions, the military generals, and other such high-ranking officials. It isn't so much distrust of doing the best they can in the job as it is of not doing the president's bidding, legal or otherwise. Often the president seeks out those closer to him in the White House to do what his other appointees in buildings across Washington, DC, and the nation are supposed to do. In other words, presidents have, metaphorically speaking, the right hand doing what the left hand is also doing. The duality of staff within the parameters of the White House chain of command and the job responsibilities of Cabinet members and other staff causes conflict and unnecessary competition.[71]

Over the decades, the executive branch has created more dual offices within the White House that challenge the primacy of Cabinet positions such as the State Department in foreign affairs and the Department of Justice in domestic affairs. The most obvious competition and conflict is found with the National Security Council that meets in the White House and the seventeen other intelligence agencies, plus the Joint Chiefs of Staff headquartered in the Pentagon. Each president since Eisenhower has created a competitive arm to existing Cabinet positions, as outlined by Barry Rubin in his book *Secrets of State: The State Department and the Struggle over U.S. Foreign Policy.*[72] And, every president has a different style of receiving, digesting, interpreting information and briefings, and governing, which in turn become his political messages to the people. Much of the content and competition between those charged with providing the information to the president, such as intelligence briefings, are components left untold, unreported, and secret.[73] For example, "Johnson reveled in reading 'the same kinds of dirt on his foreign counterparts that he enjoyed from J. Edgar Hoover on his domestic counterparts,' Gates says."[74] President Donald Trump has added a new level of political oversight of his Cabinet members and White House staff by naming special advisors, unpaid, most of whom are family members, rich friends, and business associates that report directly to him.[75]

Foreign Affairs for the FBI: The Case of John S. Service

The reemergence of the Ku Klux Klan in the late 1940s together with the McCarthy era added to Hoover's phobia of foreigners and un-American elements, e.g., minorities. During the *"Amerasia* affair" of June 6, 1945, Hoover continued to practice his skills at ordering break-ins and framing innocent persons as Communists. John S. Service, a career foreign service officer, was stationed in China. While visiting the United States, Service briefed Philip Jaffe, the editor of a journal, and loaned him a few pages of government documents on activities in the Communist stronghold of Yenan. He was arrested by the FBI for espionage based on thirteen illegal entries into Jaffe's office. The documents pilfered contained no sensitive or classified information tied to John S. Service, but what Hoover feared was that the content would support the critics of the president's China policy toward Chiang Kai-shek. Service's policy recommendations were to not align U.S. interests with Chiang as he was headed for defeat by Mao Tse-tung. He recommended neutrality toward Mao Tse-tung. Service was exonerated of espionage in the remaining years of the 1940s until the red-baiting by U.S. Senator Joseph McCarthy of the 1950s again took up his case for review. The Loyalty Security Board on six occasions found no evidence of disloyalty by Service, but McCarthy pressed his insinuations and accused him of being a Communist sympathizer inside the State Department. McCarthy cast reasonable doubt on Service's loyalty to the United States. The State Department fired him on December 13, 1951. Service sued Secretary of State John Foster Dulles. When the case finally reached the Supreme Court, they ruled in his favor unanimously. Hoover had created a culture of anti-Communism within the agency and its personnel to the point of ideological paranoia. After the court case, Hoover's men had been exposed for their wrongdoing.[76] Yet, they paid no price for their illegal activity. There was no oversight of the FBI in place at that time within the Department of Justice, the White House, or Congress.

Noted biographer James Cross Giblin turned his energies toward a work on Joe McCarthy due to a past incident that plagued him for years. His college professor had refused to discuss Marx, Marxism, or Communism in his class on world philosophies because he was afraid of losing his job again. Reportedly he had lost his job the previous year based on accusations that he was a Communist and was spreading Communist ideas with his teaching. Giblin felt shortchanged and never forgot the incident. Those ugly memories triggered an insatiable curiosity about McCarthy the man. Giblin, needing to satisfy that curiosity, produced a biography on the man.[77]

In October 22 and 23, 1957, Hoover held a conference on Internal Security-Espionage "at the Seat of Government." As early as the mid-1950s, Hoover began referring to his FBI office as the Seat of Government, not the president's Oval Office and not the White House. During this conference, it was suggested and agreed upon to place an informant "into the position of being selected by the CPUSA as a courier between the Party in this country and the Soviet Union." This was the birth of CG 5824-S, aka "Solo," the person who would infiltrate the Communist Party USA (CPUSA) and feed the FBI the most confidential information and communication between the Soviets and domestic Communists.[78] In a memorandum dated August 30, 1957, from A. H. Belmont to L. V. Boardman, both near the top of the FBI hierarchy, the background of this espionage move was detailed:

> We have been trying for sometime [*sic*] to produce direct evidence of the fact that the Communist Party, USA (CPUSA), follows orders and takes direction from the Communist Party, Soviet Union (CP-SU). If we are able to develop such evidence, it would not only strengthen our case against the CPUSA but would enhance tremendously the Bureau's prestige as an intelligence agency.

Hoover and two of his successors kept the existence and identity of Solo from the president, secretary of state, and CIA until 1975. Adding fuel to the fire of red-baiting and distorted white nativism and racism was the emergence of the John Birch Society in 1958. The "Birchers" introduced "un-Americanism" as a euphemism for any dissent or view they disagreed with.[79] The society was also the precursor to the rise of domestic white terrorists, the extreme Right in the late 1970s, that viewed government as the source of all evil and a hotbed of un-American politicians, appointees, and civil service employees. Hoover came to share the John Birch Society's view that dissenters and protestors were subversives and un-American, or had the potential to become such.

Hoover's narrow and rigid views on what constituted "American" and "Americanism" were supported by his racist foundation built during childhood. As a child, he had no power to affect any change or situation; his mother was in complete charge of all affairs. As Director, Hoover had the power of his position; command of his office personnel, which grew with each budget year; his international reach, with agents in embassies and consular offices abroad; and, more importantly, the investigations commissioned and dossiers kept on influential members of Congress and the executive branch. He was a powerful man, willing to use his power to affect the change he desired and willed, or prevent from happening what he disliked, including prompt dismissal of agents over trivial matters. He was a tyrant. Often, he clashed with members of Congress, presidents, attorney generals, State Department and Defense secretaries, and generals in the military over his methods, actions, programs, and analyses. He won most battles and stayed in the war for forty-eight long years as Director, and a total of fifty-three years with the Department of Justice, until he died. President Lyndon Johnson waived his mandatory retirement at age seventy for unexplained reasons. President Nixon may have called him the night prior to his death to demand he resign, according to various sources. Nixon had tried before to no avail.[80] Ronald Kessler posits that Hoover had "dirt" on just about every member of Congress, did not hesitate to "blackmail" them and presidents with such dirt, and "wiretapped" everyone he despised, particularly "celebrities," to learn of their sexual exploits.[81]

Presidents and Attorney Generals as Architects of Oppression with Hoover

Morton H. Halperin was the deputy assistant secretary of defense and senior staff member of the National Security Council when Henry Kissinger was secretary of state and suspected him, among others, of leaking national security information to the press. Kissinger, with Nixon's approval, ordered comprehensive surveillance of Halperin and others, which derailed their careers as public servants, and in the case of Halperin, his marriage.[82] Later, Halperin, Jerry J. Berman, Robert J. Borosage, and Christine Marwick founded the Center for National Security Studies and published a first book on some agencies in the U.S. intelligence community and their domestic spying. Among these agencies was the FBI, who had, according to these investigators, the support and knowledge of men from presidents to Cabinet secretaries to White House staff who said nothing, much less curb these abuses. They write:

> Parts of the FBI's vendetta were carried out with the knowledge, if not approval, of men in high political office who claimed to be [Rev. Martin Luther] King's allies and supporters. President Kennedy and Johnson, Attorneys General Robert Kennedy and Nicholas Katzenbach, Assistant Attorney General Burke Marshall, and Special Assistant to the President, Bill Moyers all knew of some of the bureau's activities. None of these men approved of the vendetta, but their failure to act gave Hoover free rein long after there was even a minimum pretext for continuing any kind of inquiry into King's activities. They must share the responsibility and blame for Hoover's actions.[83]

When Franklin Delano Roosevelt died and Harry Truman became president, Hoover quickly moved into action against him because he felt Truman hated him. Hoover told his top associate directors, Tolson, Nichols, and Hotell,

> We've got to dig deep to get the dirt on this pig farmer from Missouri. I think Truman will try to slice us down to size. I hear he wants an intelligence agency spanning the globe. I want that agency to be under the FBI. I see a few battles along the way, but ultimately, we'll win this war with Truman.[84]

President Truman prevailed, and Hoover did not win his turf war over intelligence with the creation of the Central Intelligence Agency (CIA) in

1947. The CIA wasted no time in competing with the FBI on domestic surveillance in the United States, contrary to their charter. That competition for intelligence turf began the rivalry that not just permeated the FBI and CIA then, but has persisted to this day in the entire intelligence community, which has grown to no less than nineteen agencies.[85]

Francis Biddle, the U.S. attorney general under President Franklin D. Roosevelt, had direct supervision over the FBI; nevertheless, Hoover began surveillance of his boss. The Biddle file was then used by Hoover when Harry Truman assumed the presidency. On July 1, 1945, the president fired Biddle and replaced him with Tom Clark as attorney general. Hoover could not have been more elated with that appointment because, as Hoover said, "The fucker will more or less rubber stamp anything I want to do." And, Clark is reported to later have said,

> I didn't bother to read Hoover's secret memos. If he wiretapped people, I figured he knew what he was doing. I handed his memos over to my assistant. He wrote several times about queers in the State Department. So what? Queers can show up everywhere, even as captains of football teams. In America, it's possible for a queer to become director of the FBI. Hey, don't quote me on that.[86]

More on Nixon and Hoover

Hoover had enjoyed a close working relationship with Nixon, as congressman and later as vice president. During an occasion when Nixon was vice president, Hoover dropped a bombshell in his laudatory remarks on behalf of Nixon during the 1954 graduation exercises at the FBI National Academy. He told the crowd Nixon had applied to become a special agent of the FBI in 1937. His application was reviewed and he had been interviewed by Clyde Tolson, who found him unfit because he was "not aggressive enough to be an FBI man."[87] In 1969, the news media discovered this tidbit of news and jumped on that revelation like ticks on a dog. Why did Nixon not become an FBI agent if he had been accepted into the ranks of G-men? It took a lot of explaining by both Nixon and Hoover as to what had happened, and both had different versions.[88]

In a reciprocal arrangement between the two, Hoover and Nixon, despite bumps on the political road they hit from time to time since Nixon was a congressman, they kept each other supplied with information deemed important to both in their respective jobs. Unbeknown to Nixon, his FBI application file grew larger by the year as Hoover monitored his political career while in and out of office. Hoover's practice was to begin surveillance on anyone who showed promise of attaining political power, mainly new members of Congress. Nixon had an extramarital affair with a possible Chinese spy, Marianna Liu, which Hoover monitored closely.[89] Of more interest to Hoover during the Nixon vice-presidency and presidency was his forty-four-year relationship with Charles "Bebe" Rebozo, a known homosexual from Miami. As early as 1936, Hoover had begun collecting information on gays and originated the Sex Deviates Program and File (105-34074). While the number 105 refers to foreign counterintelligence, Hoover thought the surveillance belonged there because gays in government could be used by foreign agents as spies. David K. Johnson called this period the Lavender Scare.[90] In 1950 Hoover used that file material to get gays fired from government service.[91] While president, Nixon made as many as fifty trips to Key Biscayne and built what became known as the Florida White House. As Lyndon B. Johnson put it, "I don't know how anyone could make love to Nixon, but if there's one person on earth who can stomach the fucker, it's that Cuban faggot, Rebozo, down there in Miami."[92]

Nixon and Hoover's Relationship

John Ehrlichman, in his book on Nixon, *Witness to Power*, reveals that Nixon and Hoover maintained a relationship of sharing information that began after Nixon lost the presidential election of 1960 until he won the presidency in 1968.[93] That relationship was cultivated because "Hoover had bet on Nixon's return to office as the surest way to stay in power. Hoover and Nixon had kept in touch during all these years Nixon was out of office. Rose

Mary Woods had been Hoover's Nixon contact for exchange of information and advice between them." And Cartha DeLoach and Lou Nichols had been Nixon's Hoover contacts and in charge of looking after Nixon when traveling abroad. Hoover used the legal attachés at various U.S. embassies abroad for that mission. Once in the Oval Office, Nixon began to create a wall of separation between them; first, Bob Haldeman, as chief of staff, was the go-to person if Hoover wanted to see Nixon. John Ehrlichman, the counsel to the president, then became the liaison. Nixon began to lose confidence in the FBI's ability to neutralize his political enemies and stop violence in the country. Ehrlichman was told by Nixon that rather than call on the FBI to investigate and gather intelligence on specific targets of Nixon's choice, he should find another source. He turned to his staffer Jack Caulfield, formerly with the New York Police Department, who "was able to secure far better data for the President from NYPD than we could get from Hoover."

Hoover retaliated. When he no longer had direct access to the president, Hoover reached Nixon via John Mitchell and Rose Mary Woods with an alarming discovery of a homosexual coterie consisting of Ehrlichman, Haldeman, and Dwight Chapin, the appointments secretary in the White House. These three men had worked for Nixon, on and off, for nearly ten years. The news that Nixon was surrounded by these gay men was going to be publicized by Jack Anderson. Mark Felt, sent by Hoover at Nixon's request for an internal investigation, interrogated Ehrlichman under oath and recorded by a stenographer. No such story was ever published, but Ehrlichman wondered if Hoover may have had a part in contriving the accusations.

Hoover had a specific method to obtain information with which to garner support for his goals, according to Ehrlichman, who witnessed the process during a dinner at Hoover's home for Nixon, Mitchell, and him. Ehrlichman termed the Hoover process as "trolling subjects" before guests to get "reactions to FBI activity." Hoover told Nixon of his unsuccessful attempts to bug the new Russian Embassy being built in D.C., and of other black-bag jobs and late-night entries at other embassies. The Russians only permitted Russian workers to build the facility, Hoover told Nixon, Mitchell, and Ehrlichman. If only Nixon could insist to the Russians that American workers be included in the mix, he could pose FBI agents as such and bug the building. "Nixon promised to see what he could do about 'the little shits at State.'" Not only had Nixon and Mitchell, the U.S. attorney general and Hoover's superior, acquiesced to illegal surveillance practices, but they had also provided insight as to Nixon's antagonistic views of the State Department. Hoover interpreted the promise to get State to push for Russian contracts for American workers in that construction as an opening for more FBI surveillance opportunities. More importantly, Nixon approved of illegal surveillance. During another Hoover-Nixon face-to-face meeting in the Oval Office, witnessed by Ehrlichman and Mitchell, there was a discussion of increasing FBI work against organized crime. Hoover, rather than refuse the order, turned the tables on Mitchell and the president by citing statistics on cases pending trial nationwide: "Over 400 cases waited in New York City alone." The problem, according to Hoover, was the lack of prosecutors. "No reason for more FBI activity until the backlog was cleaned up." Mitchell, who would have had better statistics on organized crime cases pending, opined that Hoover didn't want to be involved. He feared "his agents might be bribed if they worked 'O.C.' files." Nixon agreed. "Nixon said, 'He kept the bureau out of drugs, the riots and organized crime.'" Other topics broached during conversations between Nixon and Hoover that Ehrlichman memorialized in his book included the wrath expressed by Hoover against Mike Wallace for airing a documentary on the Black Panthers; the funding of antiwar groups, the Students for a Democratic Society, and the Panthers by Communists; and the "half dozen Senate jackals who are behind it. The Senate is out of touch with the country." Nixon grew estranged from Hoover and wanted to replace him because he was not diligent enough in finding the leak behind the theft of the "Pentagon Papers." Nixon wanted more surveillance. Hoover refused.[94]

Nixon was scheduled to fire Hoover in the fall of 1971. He had Ehrlichman draft a memo with talking points Nixon was to use in telling Hoover his days were over. But Nixon not only backed off at the scheduled breakfast meeting between the two, but also agreed to increase the FBI's program of adding legal attachés to U.S. embassies worldwide. Hoover got permission to increase his overseas force by about 20 percent, with new offices in Manila, Rio de Janeiro, the Dominican Republic, Australia, Malaysia, and India.

Hoover used these new hires to bolster congressional and business support for the FBI from among U.S. visitors to those countries. His FBI men as legal attachés also, in addition to other "legal matters," would escort visitors' wives, arrange for shopping and dinners, act as tour guides, and arrange for purchases to be sent home. During the Johnson administration, Hoover used his legal attaché in Costa Rica to monitor the activities of U.S. Ambassador Raymond Telles in 1965, among the first Mexican Americans named by President Kennedy to such posts. The FBI hit pay dirt on allegations of bribe money paid to the ambassador and the activities of the ambassador's wife. The allegations were that she frequently drank too much and left social events in the company of other males and not her husband. The Telles FBI file is #161-383-34.

Interestingly, Ehrlichman does not mention either Chávez and the farm-worker grape strike, or the Nixon-ordered Huston Plan, perhaps because he and Haldeman were fired by Nixon on April 30, 1973, during the heat of Teamster violence in California.[95] The Huston Plan was named after Nixon aide Tom Huston, who drafted the memo for the president at Bob Haldeman's request. The purpose of the plan was to intensify the program of domestic surveillance without judicial oversight (search warrants, telephone taps), much less congressional approval.[96]

Nixon: The Voice of Agribusiness in California

Hoover had specific attitudes and notions about nonwhite people and women in general that were institutionalized in the FBI culture. Agents learned to share, emulate, and voice similar views because the Director was notorious for his pettiness, revenge, and sanctions toward those who deviated from his norms for agents. Promotions hinged on how much Hoover liked the person being considered and the lack of demerits in their personnel file. The rule for years was no women and no blacks and no Chicanos in the FBI as agents.[97] A dialogue between AG Robert Kennedy and Hoover is illustrative. Hoover recalled during a *Time* magazine interview an exchange with his superior, according to the DOJ organizational chart.

My differences with Bobby were very unfortunate. His father was one of my closest friends. He wanted me to lower our qualifications, and to hire more Negro agents ... I said, 'Bobby, that's not going to be done as long as I am director of this Bureau.' He said, 'I don't think you are being cooperative.' And I said, 'Why don't you get a new director?' I went over to see President Johnson and he told me to 'stick to your guns.'"

Regarding Mexicans and Puerto Ricans, Hoover had this to say on protecting the president:

We cooperate with the Secret Service on presidential trips abroad. You never have to bother about a President being shot by Puerto Ricans or Mexicans. They don't shoot very straight. But if they come at you with a knife, beware.[98]

The FBI did hire agents of Mexican and other Latino ancestries over time, but continued to discriminate against them in hiring, promotions, assignments, and pay scales, according to the 1988 class-action lawsuit filed by Special Agent Bernardo "Matt" Perez in El Paso. He accused the "Mormon Mafia" within the bureau of being Hoover's chosen group of agents, hired as the perfect G-men—married, white, male, with no vices, caused no trouble, no divorces, no homosexuals, and no loyalty question—that perpetuated Hoover's anti-Hispanic culture, which led to discrimination. The court agreed with Perez's contentions of class discrimination against Hispanics. There were 255 or so other Hispanic agents in the class action finally decided on September 11, 1988.[99]

In the 1970s Nixon's plumbers, Ellsberg's psychiatrist break-in, and Morton Halpern's telephone tapping would become repeat scenarios of the *Amerasia* Affair.[100] Not all presidents were as compulsive and seemingly paranoid as Nixon—certainly not John F. Kennedy, despite the dangerously deteriorated relations with Russia over the Cuban Revolution and subsequent Bay of Pigs fiasco. Lyndon B. Johnson was not compulsive or paranoid, just overbearing and manipulative, as the volumes on his life by Robert Caro reveal.[101] These same years plus the Johnson vice-presidential and presidential years were also examined in Robert Dallek's two volumes on the man.[102] Kennedy and Johnson shared the beginning of the FBI surveillance of César Chávez, according to the released files. The first page of the declassified FBI file is dated October 8, 1965. Under his brother as president, Robert Kennedy was Hoover's boss, the U.S. attorney general until September 3, 1964, when he resigned to seek the New York U.S. Senate seat. Kennedy as AG approved wiretaps and surveillance by the FBI. Lyndon Johnson, as president, named Tom Clark as his AG, and they approved by default the continued surveillance of Chávez and the UFW in the mid-1960s into the Nixon years.

Hoover's "Commonist" of 1965

CHÁVEZ WAS JUST ANOTHER "COM-
monist," as Hoover pronounced
the word. Hoover got his G-men to
promptly investigate Chávez when
the telephone call that triggered the
preliminary investigation came into
the Washington FBI office.[1] Hoover
had been promoted from mere indexing clerk when he was hired into
the Bureau of Investigation (BI) into director of the newly created Anti-
Radical Division with the BI. He was twenty-four years of age. As director,
he used the Deportation Act of 1918 to order BI agents to round up persons
on his index card file. Hoover had a list of 60,000 such persons to arrest,
detain, and investigate, with a view to obtaining deportation cases. Nine out
of ten were "not citizens of the United States."[2] In the late summer of 1919,
the Communist Party and the Communist Labor Party were formed in the
United States. The combination of noncitizen immigrants and Communist

Party sympathizers and members became the perfect recipe for Hoover's reign of terror on working men and women, organized labor, and "Communists." "On December 27, 1919, secret orders were issued by the Justice Department to district chiefs. The orders revealed that the "date fixed for the arrests of the COMMUNISTS is Friday evening, January 2, 1920."[3] That day, "in a series of dramatic raids more than 4,000 persons were arrested in 33 cities."[4] The raids and arrests continued until the 1924 presidential election in which the Democrats were turned out of office and the Republicans won. Labor unions had been crushed by the Democrats. The capitalist class under two successive Republican administrations became the ruling elite of the United States. During this period, Hoover disavowed the raids as being his job but not his program; that belonged to discredited Attorney General A. Mitchell Palmer.[5] But Hoover embraced anti-Communism as his passion for life.

FDR's Carte Blanche to Hoover

On August 24, 1936, Hoover met with the president and was told by FDR that he wanted systematic intelligence about "subversive activities in the United States, particularly Fascism and Communism." The next day Hoover once again met with FDR and Secretary of State Cordell Hull because Hoover had insisted on being requested to conduct general intelligence investigations by the State Department. Hull reportedly gave him the "go-ahead" in front of the president.[6] Hoover used this verbal authority from the president and secretary of state and Executive Order 8840 until he died to investigate anyone he suspected of being a subversive or under Communist influence. Immediately after these meetings, Hoover initiated the COMINFIL program at the FBI.[7] Hoover claimed to know about Communism in depth. He had read some of the basic documents of the ideology, but would not correct his pronunciation of the word when it was uttered correctly by others.

The Call on César E. Chávez

The telephone call on October 6, 1965, was to Cartha "Deke" DeLoach, one of Hoover's assistant directors, but handled by M. A. Jones.[8] The caller asked to speak to an FBI agent about the information he had on César Chávez. The caller was contacted the very same day. The person (name deleted in file) claimed that César Chávez, the executive director of the National Farm Workers Association, had received a money grant of $267,887 from the Office of Economic Opportunity. Chávez, this person feared, possibly had a subversive background. By the second paragraph of this first letterhead memorandum (LHM), the caller was outed as being male. "He allegedly said Chavez had sought a job with the Peace Corps in 1961 but had been rejected." The caller "stated that reportedly [LINE REDACTED] has a file on Chavez allegedly showing a communist background." The caller had already checked with the House Committee on Un-American Activities and the Civil Service Commission for any record of Chávez; neither had records. This LHM also referred to another telephone call: "On October 7, 1965, [NAME REDACTED] contacted SA [NAME REDACTED]and stated there were several other individuals involved with the National Farm Workers Association who allegedly have subversive backgrounds" (p.1). With this call, the FBI opened file #100-67449 on César Estrada Chávez and placed it under "Communist Infiltration of the National Farm Workers Association Delano, California." It was a foregone conclusion based on what today would be Trump-termed "alternative facts."[9]

The next day, the same or another caller contacted the FBI's special agent to report more names involved with the National Farm Workers Association who "allegedly have subversive backgrounds." Among them was that of Larry Itliong, an organizer with the Agricultural Workers Organizing Committee (AWOC) dating to 1959.[10] He alerted the special agent that "local authorities [REDACTED] have information about them. Said he has been told that a recent issue of 'The Worker' or some other communist publication carried a picture of 'Delores' [*sic*] Huerta." Also implicated was the California Migrant Ministry. This person remained unidentified because the FBI redacted his name utilizing exemption (b)(7)(c).[11] A handwritten notation on the bottom right of page 3 of this memorandum indicates a close working relationship with a member of Congress and his top assistant: "Handled 10-12-65 with Geo. Baker, Adm. Asst. to Cong. Hagen," and was initialed by "DMB/1." From the days of the Corcoran Cotton strike in the San Joaquin Valley of California in 1933, Congressman Hagen represented that region; the local economy was dependent on agriculture. The congressman was a friend of the agricultural interests and not of migrant labor.[12] William Sullivan, Hoover's number three man in the FBI hierarchy until 1971, reveals the connection Hoover established and maintained with members of Congress:

> There were two ways we could help senators and congressmen: we could give them useful information and we would cater to their needs, big or small. We gave them information on their opponents, of course, and thanks to the FBI network of field offices which blanketed the country we were sometimes able to tell an incumbent who was planning to run against him before his own people knew. We dealt in more personal information, too. If a senator heard about a son's drug problem from us before the story got into the papers, he'd be mighty grateful. It was unlikely that that senator would ever stand up in the senate to criticize the FBI. In fact, if the FBI was being criticized he'd probably get up and defend it. It gave Hoover his leverage.[13]

FBI incompetence jumps from the last page of this first set of documents under the caption "INFORMATION IN BUFILES": that references an earlier document (not included in the declassified files) dated October 19, 1965, from a redacted source "asking if we can identify Cesar E. Chavez, a Mexican male, 35 to 38 years of age, who was an applicant for Peace Corps Director in 1962 and is Director of the National Farm Workers Association in Delano." On June 3, 1965, a redacted source mentioned in this first file "requested the Attorney General for any information indicating communists or subversive affiliations on the part of Chavez."

Strangely, FBI files declassified and released to the public on Chávez do not go back into the 1950s; if there are any, they have not been made part of the declassified documents available online. Chávez recalled that when Adlai Stevenson challenged Eisenhower for the presidency in 1952, he signed a protest petition circulated by the Community Service Organization (CSO) against the Republican Central Committee in California for harassment of Mexican Americans wanting to register to vote. Within days, his foreman and coworkers at the lumberyard where he worked turned away from him. Finally, the FBI came to interrogate him at work and drove him away to face the members of the Republican committee he had complained about. Chávez claims he faced them squarely with facts, and that the FBI told the Republicans to stop harassing Mexican Americans.[14] From that day on, Chávez frequently had to answer the accusatory question "Are you a Communist?"

Hoover wanted to know from the SAC, Los Angeles in 1965 about César Chávez and six others identified by name in an Airtel dated October 11, 1965.[15] Apparently, the White House sometime prior to 1965 had requested the FBI conduct a special inquiry on César Chávez and furnished partial background on him.[16] The Hoover Airtel included an address in Delano, his position with the National Farm Workers Association, and a physical description with an age range of "approximately 37 to 39 years of age." Hoover stated Chávez was being considered for a staff position at the White House. The White House wanted this information within two weeks.[17] There has been little to no indication or information about this aspect of Chávez's career aspirations to include a stint for the White House in some capacity—not from the Levy biography or most secondary sources. The only reference to Chávez possibly taking the Peace Corps position with the Kennedy administration was in 1961. Ignacio Garcia notes that Chávez had been involved with the 1960 Viva Kennedy Clubs movement in California.[18] Julie Leininger Pycior adds more information in her book on Mexican Americans and Lyndon B. Johnson.[19] Chávez was also involved with the Viva Johnson campaign of 1964. Joining other Mexican Americans in protesting Johnson's early reticence in making appointments they sought to high positions, several Mexican American leaders from across the country began demanding a White House conference on Mexican Americans be held, like the regularly held conferences on blacks. The other sore point between

Mexican Americans and Johnson was the virtual exclusion of Chicanos at the top levels of the War on Poverty program, with only token regional and local appointments such as Rodolfo "Corky" Gonzales in Denver, Colorado. Vicente Ximenes was the only Mexican American in the White House, along with Louis Martin, the only black in the White House; both pressed for such a gathering of Mexican American leaders and the president. Johnson acquiesced. For the first time in the history of the United States, Chicano leaders were invited to discuss their concerns and issues at a preliminary meeting at the White House in March 1965.[20] This first and only meeting was successful in listening to Chicano leaders from across the country, but failed in getting a White House conference on their concerns. David S. North, aide to President Johnson, sent a memorandum to Califano on December 23, 1966, indicating that two of three names being considered as part of the advisory committee for the national conference "have name check problems."[21] The two names were César Chávez and Rudolph [sic] Gonzales. North writes: "I have not seen the files, but gather that the objections to the first two are related to their militancy and to the fact that Chavez has had the help of some extreme left wingers in his grape strike."[22] The more important portion of this memorandum is found in the third paragraph. It reads in its entirety, "As you may recall, we started a full field on Chavez, with this in mind, but called it off at his request. He probably won't accept, anyway, and we would like to use [Ralph] Guzman if he does not."

Implicit in this language is that Chávez was aware of the full field investigation and took himself out of any further consideration for any job, committee membership, or role of any sort with Johnson. He was also aware he had been under surveillance and monitoring by the FBI for some time, and that is probably why he asked to be taken off any list by the White House. Employers do ask for a criminal record on a prospective employee, as does the federal government. Incomplete FBI records too often prevent an applicant from obtaining employment. Chávez may have been alert to this problem and taken himself out of consideration, or he may not have wanted to be part of any presidential administration; he was building a farm worker union.[23]

A week later, the SAC, Los Angeles via Airtel dated October 11 to the

Director, FBI adds more names provided to that office by a redacted source "indicating various individuals associated with the National Farm Workers Association have communist backgrounds." The names were César Chávez; Dave Havens of the California Migrant Ministry; Larry Itliong and Ben Gines, organizers for Agricultural Workers Organizing Committee; Pete Manuel and Marcello Tansi, union leaders in Delano; and Delores [sic] Huerta, secretary of the association. At the close of this Airtel, the Los Angeles FBI office is charged with the task of determining what, if any, information they have indicating subversive affiliations on the part of the named SAC: "Los Angeles should exercise discretion in this inquiry since each of the named individuals reportedly is involved in a current strike against grape growers in the Delano area, and under no circumstances should your contact imply an FBI interest in this labor activity."

By the following week of October 15, M. A. Jones informed DeLoach in a memorandum that "Chavez has a 'clean' background."[24] And, he corrects the information on the Huerta photograph as appearing in the *People's World* and not *The Worker*. More startling is the revelation contained in this memorandum that a redacted source asked Chávez about the photo. Chávez was most forthcoming with information as to who took the photo and her role in the NFWA. Chávez and the NFWA had an informant with close access to Chávez who reported regularly to the FBI. The redacted source also provided more detailed information on Wendy Pangburn Goepel and her role with the OEO grant. Apparently, the FBI had a file on her because she "was considering attending the 8th World Youth Festival in Helsinki, Finland, in 1962 along with other Stanford University students." But the investigation into "Miss Goepel" ended because "there is no indication that she did attend." The FBI report noted that Harvey Richards, the photographer of the Dolores Huerta photo, and his wife were both brought before the HUAC in 1957 because they had been members of the Communist Party in the 1940s. Richards invoked his Fifth Amendment rights when questioned by HUAC members, and "Richards' wife was identified . . . as a Communist Party member from 1943 to 1951 by Dorothy Jeffers." Again, this memorandum contains a handwritten notation at bottom right of page 2 that the subject matter has been "Handled with Congressman Hagen's office."

Hoover sent a follow-up Airtel to the same offices, plus San Francisco and Denver, with enclosures that referenced Airtels of October 11, 15, and 18 of 1965 that already had classified the Chávez matter under the label "Communist Infiltration of the National Farm Workers Association, Delano, California." Hoover was spreading the word about Chávez and the United Farm Workers Association (UFWA) internally within the FBI and nationally to many field offices.

By October 20, 1965, Hoover had made up his mind on Chávez and reclassified him and the UFWA as "IS-C" in the first of many letterhead memorandums (LHMs) to come.[25] Besides several names listed along with Chávez's was the notice that "CHAVEZ publishes and sells a paper called 'El Malcriado,' described as the voice of the farm worker, and the official voice of the NFQWA. This paper sells for 10 [cents] a copy."[26] Further along in the LHM is the notice that "At the present time, CHAVEZ sells automobile tires at the NFWA location at 102 Albany Street, Delano." And, "CHAVEZ has recently been cited for not having a business license, and is due to appear in the Delano Justice Court in the near future to show cause why he should not be penalized for operating a business without having a city license." Oddly, the FBI is concerned with Chávez operating a business without a license, but not concerned with local police arresting lawful pickets during a lawful strike the following week.

For the next decade, the FBI would view Chávez and the UFWA and its successor, the United Farm Workers Union (UFW), as Communists. The name Delores was changed to Dolores Clara, and her surname was changed from Huerta to Head, and later corrected again by October 25. The Los Angeles office notes on the last page that he also copied the teletype to "One Hundred Fifteenth INTC, United States Army, Region Two, Bakersfield, advised of above. LHM follows."

The LHM followed on October 25, 1965, accompanying an Airtel from the SAC, San Francisco to the Director, FBI. The Airtel, however, was focused solely on information on Dolores Huerta. The LHM traced her recent work history to the Community Service Organization in Stockton, and her divorce from Ventura Huerta in 1961; more importantly, they claimed that "they had no knowledge that Dolores Huerta was involved in any Communist

Party activities in the Stockton area." Again, the informant's identity was redacted under exemptions "B7c & d," and twenty-five pages of this set of documents were withheld entirely under exemptions "b7C & b7D."

Chávez, despite the FBI field agents, informants, and sources' written statements to Washington that he was not a subversive or Communist, continued to have constant surveillance because he was FBI classified as Internal Security-C for Communist. The FBI under Johnson and Nixon shadowed Chávez continuing to seek that evidence. Ronald Reagan as governor of California regularly attacked Chávez as a Communist who posed a danger to the American people. In Donald Trump fashion, Reagan warned that "the loud-mouth Chavez must be punished." As president, Reagan continued the verbal assault and directives to the FBI for dirt on Chávez.[27]

Cross-Fertilization of the Chávez/NFWA Files

The first full 13-page report cited above, which was prepared by a redacted source, marked "Confidential," and sent to unnamed sources on October 20, 1965, contains a final disclaimer paragraph on the last page: "This document contains neither recommendations nor conclusions of the FBI. It is the property of the FBI and is loaned to your agency; it and its content are not to be distributed outside your agency." The substantive part of this lengthy report is the history it provides not only on the Agricultural Workers Organizing Committee, the Filipino effort, but also the NFWA and its leadership. Chávez's brother Richard is brought into surveillance focus along with detailed information on the persons identified in the Airtel of October 11. The sources relied on to make the report repeatedly assert on every page after each name that they are not aware of any subversive activities on the part of any of the persons mentioned. Beginning on page 9, the report reviews the content of the *People's World* (PW) as a West Coast Communist newspaper. The information from the *PW* is attested as being reliable and obtained from sources that have furnished information in the past. Of particular importance is the mention of an article in the newspaper that Chávez was assaulted by farmers during the strike in the vineyards of the Delano-Earlimart area that started September 8 with pay-raise demands. The report quotes the article: "Cesar Chavez (leader of the FWA) was roughed up by some farmers while the police stood by and watched and only moved in when they knocked him to the ground." Apparently, not sufficient grounds for the FBI to investigate this assault or to admonish the local police to prevent violence rather than watch it happen.

Agustin "Augie" Lira, age nineteen at the time, witnessed police and grower violence against pickets when he first volunteered to help Chávez and the farm workers. He recalled that the emotions he experienced during this first fight were conflictive; he was afraid of the violence, but he was empowered by the nonviolent response on the part of the picketers. Augie was to become a principal in the Teatro Campesino, formed in 1965.[28]

This FBI notice of violence against farm workers and Chávez, issued to other agencies by the FBI itself, shows a shameless disregard for the rule of law, and possible violation of the law by failing to enforce federal law against those committing these assaults. Ignoring the incidents reported, and reporting on the violence that continued to be committed by growers became the practice of the FBI and its parent agency, the Department of Justice. The FBI stopped work on its mission to investigate federal crimes, and its agenda became that of becoming overt accomplices as observers.

On page 10 of the confidential report, the source provides information on a division between the FWA (his acronym for NFWA) and the Mexican American Political Association (MAPA) over *bracero* labor. Chávez is reported to have picketed the MAPA convention held in Fresno for supporting the recruitment of farm workers by the California State Department of Employment and the federal Department of Labor. According to the report, Dolores Huerta addressed MAPA on this issue during their convention and chastised them for not understanding that the practice of bringing Mexican labor into California was to further slave labor. Chávez was to make this issue a paramount goal of his union building drive. He was determined to stop the importation of Mexican labor into the United States. The union's newspaper, *El Malcriado*, regularly attacked Mexican labor, documented and undocumented, as enemies of the farm worker union, using strident racist language referring to these laborers as wetbacks and illegals.[29] The UFWOC from its inception collaborated with the immigration authorities, namely, the U.S. Border Patrol, by informing on the presence in the fields of undocumented labor, and on many occasions supplied lists of names to the Border Patrol for deportation enforcement.[30]

Following this confidential report of October 20, 1965, the Los Angeles FBI office began using "URGENT" teletypes to post informational reports of NFWA activity indicating that informants were now in place to report on daily activity by Chávez, its leaders, and membership. Despite the actual knowledge that neither Chávez nor its leadership were Communists or under Communist influence, the FBI, local field offices and Washington HQ, continued to title their reports, communications, memorandums, Airtels, and other related notices with the caption "Communist Infiltration of the National Farm Workers Association, Delano, California, IS-C."

Pickets Arrested

The October 20 teletype informed that forty-four pickets had been arrested in Delano on the 19th after being warned that they were in an unlawful assembly. The pickets were booked after arrest and jailed in the Bakersfield, California, site of the Kern County jail. They made bail, but not before the police learned from "some of those arrested" that more pickets were "expected to arrive in Delano from San Francisco, Berkeley and Los Angeles, California, tonight and tomorrow, will make themselves subject to additional arrest this weekend." The teletype ends with ominous wording and report of cross-fertilization to the U.S. Army: "Law enforcement officials in area fully cognizant of situation, and state it is not possible to predict potential of situation at present. [REDACTED], Resident Agent, One Hundred Fifteenth INTC, United States Army, Region Two, Bakersfield, advised of above. LHM follows. P END."

SAC, Los Angeles in turn filed its own Airtel on October 25, which revealed FBI methods regarding the pickets arrested. Los Angeles had reviewed its files for any record on any of the arrested persons and found none. The SAC, Los Angeles, however, cross-fertilized both the memorandum of the

20th and the teletype of the 22nd, as noted on bottom left of the Airtel with the date of October 25, 1965, sent to the Director, FBI as follows: "3-Bureau, 2-Albuquerque, 2-Cincinnati, 2-Pittsburgh, 2-San Francisco, 2-Los Angeles." It requested all offices receiving copies "to review the names of the arrested individuals residing in their area for any subversive information. If such information is developed, advise the Bureau and office of origin in form suitable for dissemination." The FBI withheld from my FOIA (also not found in the declassified file from The Vault) twenty-five pages of information related to this LHM under exemptions "b7c and b7d." See appendix 2 for a list of exemptions with explanation. Probably, it is the list of names of those arrested on October 19. Not listed, but mentioned in the text, is "One copy of the LHM is designated for 115th INTC, Region II, U.S. Army, Pasadena, California." Apparently, the U.S. Army had intelligence operations in Bakersfield and Pasadena, California, and both were on ready alert from the FBI on NFWA activity. A subsequent Airtel from SAC, San Francisco to the Director, FBI dated November 8, 1965, makes mention of the October 25, 1965, Airtel but erroneously dates the arrests of pickets as October 19, 1960. And, dated the same day and marked Confidential, the San Francisco office provides additional information on those persons arrested from their files, but the material is redacted. There is a stamped notation at bottom left: "COPIES DE-STROYED," with the numbers "333 FEB 9 1971" below the stamped lettering.

The declassified files for the year 1965 end abruptly with a final LHM dated November 8, 1965, which provides some background information in the files of FBI, San Francisco on some picketers arrested back on the 19th of October.

Watching and Walking with Chávez

The FBI reporting on Chávez the following year began January 21, 1966, with an Airtel from the SAC, Los Angeles to the Director, FBI listing by name the sources or informants utilized in the LHM from October 25 and November 8 of the previous year. Apparently, the Director wanted to know who supplied the information on Chávez as well as the Student Non-violent Coordinating

Committee (SNCC) and the Congress of Racial Equality (CORE).[31] Both organizations' members were seen by informants, the press, and FBI agents to have participated in support activities for Chávez and the NFWA. The first LHM of the year, dated January 21, 1966, however, made reference to four redacted sources under exemptions B1 and B7D providing information on January 11.[32] And, the LHM (p.2) identified the NFWA staff member by name and location of residence. In the case of Harvey Richards, who took Dolores Huerta's photograph holding the poster reading "HUELGA," his car was described as "a 1965 Oldsmobile station wagon, California license S75763." The bulk of the LHM is dedicated to the effects of the grape strike, funding for the strike and picket lines, and the volunteer organizations arriving to support Chávez in Delano and surrounding counties and volunteering for the national boycott—among them SNCC, CORE, Du Bois Clubs, and the Students for a Democratic Society (SDS). The FBI had classified the first three organizations as subversive and black nationalist in their range of COINTELPRO operations, while SDS was targeted by the FBI under a separate COINTELPRO, classified as NEW LEFT. Walter Reuther of the United Auto Workers was quoted as pledging $5,000 a month to NFWA with $10,000 expected in December 1965 (p.2). There is no indication from the FBI in 1966 if the money pledged in 1965 arrived. The LHM noted that César Chávez had been "arrested by the Tulare County, California Sheriff's Office during November 1965, for illegal use of a loud speaker, has pled innocent, but the case is still pending ... and he is presently out on $110 bail." Chávez was using the loudspeaker from an airplane circling grape vineyards (pp.3–4). If it were not serious to have Chávez in a county jail with hostile sheriff's deputies and the FBI looking the other way from any abuses against farm workers, the arrest would be hilarious material for a comedian's skit.

From these documents, no increased picketing activity, which the local police and FBI had been so alarmed about on October 20, 1965, ever materialized. The cross-fertilization of packets of FBI information, including name checks on those arrested, proved useless and unnecessary. Moreover, involving the INTC of the U.S. Army in Pasadena and Bakersfield made the entire month-long hysteria by the FBI an extremely paranoid episode. The same forty pickets arrested the previous year continued their picketing in Delano and Tulare County.

The FBI Los Angeles office's LHM enumerated, "Sixty three civic and church organizations have protested the actions of the National Farm Workers Association (NFWA), but the NFWA seems to issue only ultimatums rather than make any reasonable attempts to resolve the problems that exist between farm owners and the union, or to reach any solution to the problem at hand" (p.1). Further editorializing on the NFWA's unreasonableness, the FBI document returns to their comfortable paranoia: "The future will bring mass picketing of all agricultural areas in the San Joaquin Valley and other California locations, in the opinion of the source" (p.1).

In this same narrative report, the Director is informed that Dolores Huerta "was in Los Angeles, California, attempting to set up an NFWA office there. It is also believed that she is and will be in the near future instrumental in organizing boycotts of grapes, grape products, and labor recruiting in California, and possibly other agricultural localities in nearby states." More importantly, the Director is advised of additional financial support coming from the Mexican American Political Association (MAPA) of California (p.4). And, it was noted that the *Los Angeles Times* of December 22, 1965, carried a photograph of Hollywood actor and TV personality Steve Allen joining the picket line at a grocery store in Encino, California (p.7).

True to past practices and rigid form regarding the finding of Communist influence within the UFWA demanded by Hoover, the LHM report resurrects Wendy Goepel and Harvey Richards as being on the scene once again. It adds a new name: "James Lynn Drake, a white male, born December 25, 1937 . . . and who is supposedly a minister of the Congregational Church in Visalia and part of the California Migrant Ministry since 1962" (p.2). The FBI could have done a quick name check by calling the church in Visalia and asking for Drake's credentials as a minister; this would have removed him from "supposedly a minister" to ordained minister of the United Church of Christ.[33] The narrative in the LHM is quick to point out that at one time SDS decried "authoritarian movements both of Communism and the domestic Right," but by 1965 had amended the preamble of their constitution to eliminate those words. And, it was noted in paragraphs on the SDS that "The SDS is opposed to present American foreign policy in Vietnam" (p.3).[34]

These tidbits of information were much appreciated by President Lyndon B. Johnson. Hoover had his residence across Thirtieth Place from Johnson, Lady Bird, and the girls for several years. Neither a neighborly friendship nor a professional relationship developed over all those years; LBJ's main contact had been Cartha "Deke" DeLoach since his Senate years. In 1965 DeLoach was assistant FBI director responsible for all investigative activities of the Bureau. President LBJ had installed a private line in DeLoach's bedroom and the White House for when the president wanted instant FBI information on anybody and anything. DeLoach also prepared "Air Force One Specials": packets for the president placed in the presidential airplane that consisted of background information on any person coming to the White House, the Texas ranch, any event, any protest, and any political meeting lest LBJ be embarrassed by not knowing what Hoover knew.[35] Lyndon, as vice president, disapproved of wiretaps and other electronic surveillance. He opposed Robert Kennedy's wiretapping of Martin Luther King while attorney general, despised the reports of their content, but was impressed by what they revealed. President Johnson ordered the commissioner of the Internal Revenue Service to stop the use of microphones, taps, or any other hidden devices, legal or illegal, or be fired.[36] By 1967, during his State of the Union address, President Johnson went public with his opposition to such practices: "We should outlaw all wiretapping—public and private wherever it occurs, except when the security of this nation itself is at stake—and only then with the strictest governmental safeguards."[37] The president, despite his disdain for the lurid details of sexual escapades Hoover uncovered, enjoyed the reading and sometimes the photos accompanying the reports. He had a sense of humor about the content.

The NFWA and Bill Esher's *El Malcriado* staff also had a great sense of humor about the FBI surveillance. The LHM of January 21, 1966, reposts the announcement of a $1,000 reward:

> *El Malcriado* will pay a cash reward of $1,000 for information leading to the arrest and conviction of any person or persons referring to the National

Farm Workers Association, its leaders and officers, or *El Malcriado* and its representatives as 'communists' or 'communist-led,' 'inspired' or any similar statements. Such references are false and illegal, and we intend to punish anyone saying these things to the full extent of the law."

Perhaps Esher and Chávez wanted someone to point to the FBI and charge them for such a continual violation by slander and red-baiting, and collect this reward. The FBI found more open source material in *El Malcriado*, for example, on the success of the NFWA credit union, which reportedly increased its assets from $37 in November 1963 to $28,000, and membership to two thousand dues-paying families by print time of issue no. 26 (p.7).

From time to time, the FBI would receive telegrams and letters addressed to Hoover asking for evidence or support for a suspicion the sender had about a person—such as Wendy Goepel or Luis Valdez or Larry Itliong—being Communist, as was the case in late February 1966.[38] A standard reply from Hoover would be sent acknowledging receipt of such telegrams or letters but declining to respond given the confidential nature of the FBI's investigative role and DOJ regulations.[39] However, the FBI promptly would look in their files to see if the "Correspondent is not identifiable in the Bufiles." In other words, the FBI would initiate a file under the person's name.

The Seat of Government

On March 8, 1966, the Director learned that several U.S. senators had scheduled hearings in the San Joaquin Valley of California for March 14th in Sacramento, 15th in Visalia, and the 16th in Delano. It included both Kennedys—Robert of New York and Ted of Massachusetts. Granted, both were U.S. senators, but only one was a member of the Subcommittee on Migratory Farm Labor. The Airtel also reported that Senator George Murphy, also a member of the subcommittee, would be attending. An aide to Murphy had called the FBI resident agent in Visalia, California, for a status report on the farm workers' strike so he could better interrogate the witnesses coming before the hearings set out over three days in three different California locations. In clear language, the Airtel message assured the Director that protocol had been followed when dealing with a member of Congress. Only the FBI Director at the Seat of Government or the appropriate liaison would have those conversations. Only Hoover and his top staff could lead the "orchestra" of Congress and no one else, certainly not a resident agent:

> In accordance with existing Bureau instructions, [REDACTED] was advised that the disclosure of any information which the Bureau might possess could only be effected through appropriate liaison at the Seat of Government. [REDACTED] then stated that contact would be had by Senator MURPHY with appropriate officials at the Seat of Government.[40]

"Ceasar [sic] Chavez President of NFWA, publicaly [sic] stated that the NFWA only received $1,000.00 . . . Chavez had called Reuther, a 'four-flusher,' because of his failure to support the NFWA with funds as previously promised."[41] In a redacted portion of this same report, the Director was advised that the House Un-American Activities Committee (HUAC) had been requested by an unidentified source to investigate the NFWA in Delano. The Director was informed that the state equivalent of the HUAC was already in Delano conducting a preliminary investigation, as if to spur him on to get HUAC in the mix and not be outflanked by Californians.

While Chávez made plans to attend the subcommittee hearings and testify, he also prepared for his "Peregrinacion" March to Sacramento. The FBI called it the *Terigrinacion* Route—exposing their limited Spanish-language interpreting and translating skills. The local FBI agents and their informants knew well before Hoover of the impending march. Hoover, however, did not get his teletype until March 14 with all the details: final destination with arrival date, numbers of marchers involved, and preparations underway by local police, the state highway patrol in four counties along the route, and the U.S. Army Region Two in Pasadena.[42]

More Airtels and reports followed upon the news that Chávez was about to march to Sacramento about the time of the hearings. SAC, Los Angeles expanded the net for cross-fertilization to include Chicago and the U.S.

Secret Service.[43] Chicago was requested to "check indices on PAUL BOOTH." In San Francisco, the alert was to "Check indices on DONNA SUE HABER," and FBI offices "AT BAKERSFIELD, VISALIA, FRESNO AND MERCED, CALIFORNIA: Will alert local police departments and other law enforcement agencies of details instant march and alert confidential sources to report any pertinent information immediately."[44]

The terse and direct wording of these instructions does not indicate what would be considered standard police procedures when handling a march of this sort. For example, there is no mention of public safety, emergency vehicle preparation in case of illness or accident involving bystanders or marchers, and there is no concern for weather conditions. The instructions seem to be a call for police preparedness for the worst and full military alert to confidential sources to report everything and anything. Oddly, the Los Angeles FBI referenced an open source article taken from *Newsweek* about the march that mentioned CORE to be the sponsor. "Source One … personally asked Donna Sue Haber, Office Secretary for the National Farm Workers Association (NFWA), if such a march was being organized." Haber reportedly denied any knowledge of the march, as did "other officials of NFWA." The report continues with information about the upcoming U.S. Senate Subcommittee hearings on March 14th in Sacramento, Visalia on the 15th, and Delano on the 16th at the local high school auditorium. Paul Booth was identified as being the director of SDS from Chicago and had been at the NFWA office in Delano "for the past several days." The report repeats the SDS preamble and subsequent amendment deleting their opposition to "Communism and the domestic Right." On page 3 of this LHM, after a redacted paragraph and opening sentence, the actual itinerary for the march, "which would start at 9:00 AM on March 17, 1966," was listed day by day with "Location of Each Stop" and "Cities to Pass Through." On the entry for "Days of March 15 & 16," at "Location of Each Stop" for "Modesto," the parenthetical note is indicative of deep surveillance by the FBI sources as to the planning by the NFWA; it is also another indication of FBI paranoia: "(will pick up large number here to continue on to Sacramento)" (p.3).

Robert Kennedy and the Migrant Labor Hearings in California

As the freshman U.S. senator from New York, Robert Kennedy was given a seat on the Migratory Labor Subcommittee of the Senate Labor Committee in 1965. Hearings in California on that topic were set by Senator Harrison Williams Jr. for the following year. Senator Williams had put in motion for congressional approval a comprehensive farm-labor reform package that would include farm workers in the National Labor Relations Act (NLRA). The package also included "farm workers within the federal minimum wage protections to include $1.15 an hour, 10 cents an hour less than other workers" and "no overtime pay."[45] Kennedy supported the Williams farm-labor reform package, but did not want to go to these hearings. He was convinced by staffer Peter Edelman to do so. Chávez testified before the committee meeting in Delano and was passionate, forceful, and powerful. Kennedy was impressed with this fellow Catholic and nonviolent disciple of Gandhi and sought him out during a break to talk with him about his union efforts.

At the Delano hearing, Senator Kennedy confronted Kern County Sheriff Leroy Galyen about his 1965 edict prohibiting pickets and strikers from shouting from the roadside. If they did, they would face disturbing-the-peace charges. Sheriff Galyen specifically prohibited the shouting of the word *huelga* (strike) in Spanish. Helen Chávez, César's wife, was not only arrested by the sheriff for doing so but also jailed. The word-for-word confrontation between Kennedy and Sheriff Galyen has been memorialized in various documentaries and books.[46]

This event began a bond between the senator and the farm worker leader that lasted until Kennedy was assassinated in 1968. This relationship and the hearings greatly boosted Chávez's social and political capital. The march to Sacramento received wide national publicity because of the hearings and Kennedy's open support of Chávez and his union. Regardless, the Williams farm-labor reform package was defeated in Congress. To this day, the farm workers are not included in the NLRA provisions that afford protections to covered workers.[47]

Terigrinacion Becomes *Peregrinacion*

The name of the march erroneously written in prior notices, "Terigrina-cion," is corrected in ink to read "Peregrinacion," which is Spanish for pilgrimage. According to this LHM, "The line of march as set forth above was furnished to [REDACTED] Region II, 115th INTC, U.S. Army, Pasadena, by SA [REDACTED] at 2:45PM, March 14th, 1966"—indicating a very close collaborative relationship between the Los Angeles FBI and the U.S. Army intelligence unit based in Pasadena, California (p.4). Copies of this report were also forwarded to the U.S. Secret Service, indicating a developing relationship with this other intelligence agency with direct responsibilities to the Office of the President and White House.

Scurrilous Add-on Material

The remaining two pages of the report are titled "APPENDIX" and contain a lengthy description of a black organization, the "W.E.B. DU BOIS CLUB OF SAN FRANCISCO aka Du Bois Youth Group, San Francisco Du Bois Club, San Francisco Du BOIs Youth Group, Student-Labor Alliance." The description is taken from a 1963 source that reported on the first general meeting of the organization in San Francisco. The "APPENDIX CONTINUED" with information "that W.E.B. Du Bois joined the Communist Party after applying for admission on October 1, 1961." The source supplying this information to the FBI was very aware of the operations of the local Du Bois Club: "On May 10, 1963, the source informed that the 'San Francisco News & World Report,' although written and edited by members of the Club, is run off on a mimeograph machine located in the office of the 'People's World'" and that the Club "has no permanent headquarters but the majority of its general meetings are held on Sunday afternoon at 307 Page Street, Apartment 3, San Francisco, California." The relevance or connection to the march or NFWA is not mentioned in this appendix.

They Start Walking to Sacramento

César Chávez recalls the inception of the march from Delano to Sacramento this way:

> The march was barely underway when we had a confrontation with the Delano police. After we left the Union office in the southwest corner of Delano, we planned to march east on Garces and then north on Main Street through Delano. But the chief of police refused. He brought out his officers, about thirty men, who locked arms right across Garces to prevent us from marching through. I was at the head of the march ... We marched right up to the police line and stopped. 'We'll stay here if it takes a year,' we said, 'but we're going to march right through the city ... After about three hours, the chief reluctantly gave in, and we marched along the side of the street on through Delano.[48]

The FBI report of the same date had another version of the start of the march. Los Angeles FBI informed Hoover that just as the march began in Delano, they changed route from what they originally had stated, "taking a route north of the downtown section of Delano."[49] After discussions with local police, who acquiesced, the marchers were permitted to go through downtown on Main Street even though "no city parade permit had been requested or issued." The (redacted) source reported the marchers were peaceful and orderly. The marchers "carried NFWA official flags and 'Huelga' signs, sang, and shouted 'Huelga,'" and were described as numbering "approximately 100 persons ... including men, women and small children. About seventy-five percent of the marchers were Mexican-Americans or Filipinos and the remainder Anglo-Caucasians, with two or three Negroes" (p.2). No mention is made in the FBI reports of the large banner of the iconic and revered Catholic figure the Virgen de Guadalupe, front and center of the march, or of the numerous clergy of all denominations also accompanying the marchers. "Religious symbols were nearly always present at his meetings, marches, and fasts. Chavez linked his religious devotion and his labor activism."[50] Luis Leon terms this duality of the Chávez persona as religious politics—a "living civil religion that speaks to the idiom of public Christianity while redefining Americanism."[51] Not all the marchers and union supporters, particularly staff, agreed with Chávez and his use of religious icons and public pronouncements of doing penance by walking to demonstrate their faith. Among those dissenting were members of his Jewish legal team; the many youthful volunteers, who were mainly of various Protestant denominations; Protestant Mexican Americans and Mexicans; and the Filipinos, also affiliated with AWOC. The Filipinos, like most of AWOC staff and membership, were on strike and in the boycott because it was a trade union issue, not a religious exercise.[52]

It appears from the plain reading of these documents that Chávez's Catholicism and total commitment to pacifism and nonviolence were well known to all but the FBI.[53] The report closed with the good news to the perhaps incredulous FBI and other police and military units on alert "that no incidents or arrests had occurred thus far."

The March and the First Contract

By the time the marchers had reached Ducor and passed Richgrove en route to Terra Bella on March 17, the SAC, Los Angeles, by Airtel to the Director, FBI, was sending information indicating the deletion of CORE as a sponsor of the march as previously reported. More importantly, this Airtel notice expanded cross-fertilization to include two new federal intelligence agencies: the Office of Naval Intelligence (ONI) and the Office of Special Investigations for the U.S. Air Force (OSI). The report again states, as in prior notices, that the highway patrol, county sheriffs, and local police departments "along the line of march have been alerted." And as previously noted, the safety, well-being, and emergency preparedness of bystanders and marchers are ignored. Instead, the closing line of this message reads: "Incidents and arrests, if any, will be followed and reported in form suitable for dissemination." Perhaps it was the concern for violence, not on the part of growers and white extremists but on the part of nonviolent marchers en route to the California state capitol to meet with their governor, that caused the FBI to alert other FBI field offices, federal military agencies, and state, county, and local police units.

The next Airtel from SAC, Los Angeles on the march was not filed until March 28, ten days into the Peregrinacion, if the FBI is to be believed, and contained two oddly numbered pages titled APPENDIX, as was previously done with the March 14th report. The Airtel contained information previously reported but for one item stating that the next stop would be "AT MERCED, CALIFORNIA," indicating perhaps that the march was on schedule. The two-page appendix may be a case of misplacing and releasing incorrect FOIA information, because it contains information about the Du Bois Club being formed in Central Los Angeles with names of the principal actors behind the organizing and leadership.

In the narrative of the three-page document about the march, Los Angeles FBI reports on a series of problems with food, rest stops, change of route and march plans, and housing. It also alerts the undisclosed recipients of the report to the additional numbers of marchers joining the march in Salinas, Merced, Turlock, and Modesto. The report, based on these growing numbers of marchers, predicted a mass of 1,500 marchers arriving in Stockton. Interestingly, the report specifically mentions that "The marchers have a field kitchen for emergencies, as well as chemical toilets, and they are in possession of a car equipped with a two-way car radio, bearing the call number KFZ-478, as well as a car with a radio telephone, the number of which is not known." Had the FBI coordinated with the NSA, all the transmissions over these phones would have been made available to them for monitoring the conversations. That is what the NSA does primarily—and maybe it did.

On April 1st, the marchers were refused a permit to hold a rally at Graceada Park in Modesto, California. The grantor of the land to the city for a park restricted the use "for cultural purposes and if otherwise used property would revert to estate of donor." One must wonder if cookouts, family reunions, sporting games, birthday parties, love making, beer and soda drinking are cultural purposes. According to local police, a rally for marchers demanding fair wages and working conditions was political and not cultural. Nevertheless, "TERRY CANNON who identified himself as a member of the Student Committee for Non-Violent Action [*sic*], Berkeley, California . . . was present in Graceada Park and at the rally." The rally was held despite the denial of a city permit, with no arrests according to this report. Either the FBI report is wrong on both counts—permit required and rally held—or the local police and every other police and military entity looked the other way. Regardless, the marchers went from Graceada Park to the auditorium of the Cannery Workers Local 748 in Modesto for another rally that evening. "After attending church on the morning of April 2, 1966, the marchers continued in route to San Joaquin County, California. On the 4th of April, the marchers held rallies at St. Linus' Catholic Church and in Washington Park across the street from St. Mary's Catholic Church." The Airtel dated April 5, 1966, from SAC, Los Angeles to Director, FBI alerted Washington FBI "that General DWIGHT D. EISENHOWER is presently residing at El Dorado Country Club, Palm Desert, California," and "The foregoing was orally furnished to U.S. Secret Service, Los Angeles, and Region II, U.S. Army, Pasadena by SA [REDACTED] on 4/5/66." Perhaps this is the justification for Secret Service surveillance of anyone coming near one of the ex-presidents and presidents residing in California during these years, and not vigilance over protesting farm workers.

Meanwhile at FBI, Chicago

The FBI routinely relies on open source material for their information gathering on persons, activities, organizations, events, and places. This was the case with the FBI, Chicago office, which read with alarm in the *Chicago Sun Times* that "more than 250 persons paraded on the near west side of Chicago in a demonstration of support for migrant farm laborers on strike in Delano, California." They had been organized by a committee named Chicago Citizens' Committee to Aid Delano Farm Workers. A two-page LHM with more details on the demonstration was promptly sent to FBI headquarters.[54] The name "Chicago Citizens' Committee to Aid Delano Farm Workers was unfamiliar to him [REDACTED SOURCE] but it would appear that the name was being utilized only about the April 3, 1966 parade" (p.2).

To be sure, FBI, Chicago was not asleep at the wheel, and this new Chicago Citizens' Committee was in fact subversive and Communist; the LHM was sent "to the United States Attorney, United States Secret Service and 113th INTC Group, Region 1, all Chicago, Illinois" (p.2).This is the first FBI document on Chávez cross-fertilized to include the U.S. attorney (USA).The USA oversees prosecutions of federal crimes investigated by the FBI.Apparently, somewhere in missing FBI files is the determination made by the FBI that Chávez and the farm workers union and those that support them, such as this Chicago group, are not only Communists and threats to internal security but also engaged now in criminal conduct at the federal level.

Back on the March

Marchers and Chávez when in Fresno, California, apparently "met briefly with Mayor Floyd H. Hyde on the steps of the City Hall," according to the report accompanying the Airtel of April 5, 1966.This report makes mention of the Riverside County Committee in Support of the Delano Grape Strikers led by Joe Aguilar, a member of the Riverside City College Board of Trustees, organizing a protest parade due to the governor's refusal to meet the marchers in Sacramento. Other members of this committee are identified in the report as being Arthur Jurado, Dr. Eugene Cota-Robles, and student Douglas Boyes.The report in the second to last paragraph states the typical FBI practice: "The records of the Los Angeles Office of the Federal Bureau of Investigation contain no information identifiable with the members of the Riverside County Committee in Support of the Delano Grape Strikes."[55]

An Airtel on April 7 and report sent by SAC, San Francisco to the Director, FBI and other undisclosed recipients contained an unusual dissemination pattern to include the three military branches—Army, Navy, and Air Force. It also appears to be the passing of reporting responsibility from the Los Angeles FBI office to the San Francisco FBI office because the marchers are within days of reaching the state capitol in Sacramento. However, SAC, Los Angeles is not completely passing the baton to San Francisco, because Los Angeles sent an OO (Office of Origin) Airtel the next day to the Director, FBI claiming turf. It reads as follows: "LEAD LOS ANGELES AT RIVERSIDE AND PALM SPRINGS, CALIFORNIA: Will maintain contact with local law enforcement agencies and will report any arrests or incidents that might occur as a result of this march in a form suitable for dissemination."[56]

A new NFWA leader was identified in the Los Angeles FBI report of April 8, 1966. His name, Gilbert Padilla, is not redacted, indicating no concern under any exemption of the Freedom of Information Act (FOIA) and, more importantly, the Privacy Act (PA) about printing his name and title in the report. The FBI was casting a broad and wide net over all persons involved with Chávez and the farm workers union by supplying names indicating FBI files were being started on them and by those receiving cross-fertilized FBI reports. Padilla, according to the report, "advised the local Palm Springs newspaper ... the new route and the choice of the park ... was made necessary when Reverend Thomas J. Flahive, Pastor of the Lady of Guadalupe Catholic Church refused use of church grounds. He said marchers will gather at Hardy Park in Palm Springs at 2:00 p.m. Sunday, April 10, 1966." A redacted source at the bottom of the cover page indicates that no permit is needed "since they intend to march on the sidewalk which will not obstruct traffic."[57] Mention is made that Governor Edmund G. Brown would not meet the marchers on Easter Sunday because he was spending time with Frank Sinatra at his Tamarisk Country Club home, also in Palm Springs. The report continues, however, with information that the governor changed his mind and would meet them in Sacramento. The April 7th report has the marchers arriving in West Sacramento on the 9th and "to see the Governor on Easter Sunday, April 10, 1966" (p.2).

The First Contract with Schenley Industries, Inc.

Oddly, the FBI field agents covering the march reported on many subjects yet were unaware of what Chávez was doing during the pilgrimage: where he slept, where he disappeared to at night, why he was limping and using a cane. Or so it seems from lack of documents on these questions. He was limping because he had sores on his feet from walking in a new pair of shoes. He had never marched that far before, much less in new shoes.[58] He slept in motel rooms along the way obtained in others' names and was secretly driven there late at night. He disappeared often—once to Stockton, and another time to Los Angeles to negotiate a contract on April 3.[59] Chávez recalled Gilbert Padilla telling him he had an urgent telephone call from Sidney Korshak. Chávez refused the call, not knowing Korshak was Schenley's lawyer. Padilla then told him Korshak's message was about Schenley wanting to sign a contract with the union and stop the boycott of their products and grape harvesting on their fields. Korshak called again within minutes and repeated that Schenley wanted to sign a contract. Chávez hung up on him. Korshak called again. This time Chávez interrogated Korshak to his satisfaction and agreed to meet the next day in Beverly Hills. Secretly, Chávez left the marching group, and with Wayne Chris Hartmire driving all night arrived by dawn to negotiate the first contract with Schenley Industries at Korshak's upscale suite of offices.[60] Korshak had been of FBI interest for some time, given his reputation as a mob lawyer and attorney for the Teamsters Union. His brother, Marshall, was a major political player in Chicago and Illinois politics, having served as city treasurer, state senator, and state revenue director; together they had a law firm in the city.[61]

The arrival of the 1,500 striking marchers in Sacramento on Easter Sunday, April 10, after twenty-five days of walking the three hundred miles, could not have been better staged. The crowd, including marchers, was estimated at ten thousand persons; the speakers were emotional, and Chávez delivered the crowning blow for victory by announcing the Schenley contract, which included a thirty-five-cent-an-hour, across-the-board wage increase.[62]

While the FBI field agents were monitoring Chávez and the marchers and learning from the speeches that Schenley had signed a union contract with the NFWA, Hoover received a Schenley letterhead communication.[63] The letter disavows any approval of any agreement between the company and the NFWA. Specifically mentioned is the attorney for Schenley, Sidney Korshak, as not representing the company, and the signer states, "I have never met Sidney Korshak who is well known to the Bureau." J. Edgar Hoover initials a personal note at bottom right of this letter, "Let me have summary on Union & Korshak." At top right of the letter is the typical stamp of routing the correspondence or transmission with names of the top echelon of FBI officers. This letter has six top officers checked off, including Tolson, No. 2 in the Bureau, DeLoach, No. 3, Robert Wick (Crime Records), Alex Rosen (Investigations), and William Sullivan, No. 4 (Domestic Intelligence); any one of them or several could have been assigned the full field and ongoing investigation of Chávez and the NFWA.

The Director's response to this letter, dated April 15, 1966, was addressed to [REDACTED], but the salutation is to "Dear Nick," and is more informative as to who was in the loop to apprise the Director of the "Union" and Korshak. Copies of the Hoover response to Nick were forwarded only to De Loach, Wick, Rosen, Sullivan, and "1-Mr. Morrell" (sent with cover memo), who was not listed in the stamp with names previously mentioned. Additionally, a "NOTE: See Jones to Wick memorandum dated 4-14-66 captioned National Farm Workers Association" is located at the bottom of the response. Obviously, these notations were added later to the copy of the original letter sent to Nick.[64] The FBI, however, withheld seven pages of this file under exemption (b)(7)(c).

At the Beverly Hills meeting with Korshak, three unions were present, much to the chagrin of Chávez: AFL-CIO represented by Bill Kircher, a Teamsters representative, and Chávez representing the NFWA. The Teamsters agreed to have NFWA sign the contract, and Kircher was satisfied by having been a part of the negotiations and signing the preliminary agreement as a witness. Chávez left the meeting with an agreement that would be reduced to writing within ninety days. Beyond an immediate pay raise of thirty-five cents an hour, the agreement also called for a checkoff for the Credit Union, hiring hall, and union recognition. Chávez, in return, would call off the boycott only against Schenley.[65] The boycott energy was now directed toward DiGiorgio, S&W Food, and TreeSweet.

News of the contract with Schenley made the Sacramento arrival even more of a triumph for Chávez. So much so that when Governor Brown changed his mind and wanted to meet them, Chávez and the marchers spurned him. They had already met with Lt. Governor Glenn Anderson a few days previously and presented him with the legislative package they wanted passed and signed into law. Chávez the political operative was becoming an electoral powerhouse as well.

"Three days after the march ended on Easter Sunday," Chávez told Levy,

> we started all-out picketing at DiGiorgio ... while they were picketing at Sierra Vista, a DiGiorgio guard had threatened Ida Cousino with a gun, and another DiGiorgio employee knocked her down. Someone struck Manuel Rosas on the head as he went to her aid. It took thirteen stiches to close his wound. Then our people were arrested. DiGiorgio ... were more mature than other growers, they spent their time gathering information, getting police to do their dirty work, and filing suits against us. Finally, on May 20, they obtained a court order restricting the number of pickets.[66]

The FBI had a radically different view of future events and tactics by the NFWA members. On April 25, 1966, the Los Angeles FBI office submitted a three-page report on information received by a source that the NFWA was planning on discrediting law enforcement agencies by forcing police to arrest them, then claim and file civil rights violations with the DOJ. The report also repeated information from an open source, the *Los Angeles Times*, that Chávez and DiGiorgio were engaged in talks leading to an election by workers to be represented by a union. Pickets in Sierra Vista called Chávez in Fresno, where he was negotiating with DiGiorgio officials about being targeted by DiGiorgio guards. Chávez broke off negotiations and immediately wired AG Nicholas B. Katzenbach about the assault on Rosas. "If the officers had arrested the offender (a company security guard) and disarmed him, we would not have had this near-tragedy. We are tired of having to do battle with growers and their allies, the police."[67]

Los Angeles FBI reported on June 15, 1966, that as of May 12 they had information from (redacted) in Bakersfield, California, citing an open source, *Scope*, a publication of the National Student Association, where Chávez was recruiting college students across the country to spend the summer in Delano for work in the San Joaquin Valley on behalf of the union.[68] The report reiterates the prediction "that NFWA will continue to inject civil rights into their activities, which will include accusations of police brutality and civil rights violations against law enforcement agencies."

The most damaging content with regard to Hoover's FBI relentless pursuit of "Commonists" everywhere, particularly within the NFWA, was contained in the July 13, 1996, memorandum from SAC, Los Angeles to Washington FBI. It contains the most clear and unequivocal statement negating the rationale and continued practice of placing the Chavez file under COMINFIL and classifying the investigation as IS-C. It reads, "The files of the Los Angeles Office contain no pertinent subversive information concerning DOLORES HUERTA, Vice President of the National Farm Workers Association (NFWA), other than the fact that SAM KUSHNER, editor of "The People's World" (PW), has been in touch with her on several occasions." Media sources seek out people that make news and are in the news; that is their job regardless of the ideological orientation of the owners or responsible parties for the publication. The report continues: "Files of the Los Angeles Office indicate little, if any, effort to actually infiltrate the NFWA. Discussions at various CP meetings have been numerous concerning the Delano Grape Strikers and all members have been urged to help the strikers on the picket lines, and if not there, to help by giving them food and clothing." In closing, the SAC writes Hoover, "In view of the above, it is not felt that continued investigation concerning the COMINFIL of the NFWA is warranted at this time, and accordingly, Los Angeles is closing this case. Upon receipt of information indicating CP efforts to infiltrate the NFWA, Los Angeles will reopen its case."

Case Closed?

After two years of constant vigilance and monitoring by large numbers of FBI agents, informants, and support staff in field offices and Washington, DC, of the lawful activities of farm workers, their leadership, and supporters in pursuit of a fair wage, safe working conditions, and a union of their choice did the FBI in fact cease to use the "Commonist" bogey man against the NFWA?

COMINFIL "IS-C" Continues

The SAC, Los Angeles was still using the subject line with the old Communist Infiltration line and IS-C classification in another heavily redacted memorandum dated September 13, 1966, to the Director, FBI. The LHM reviewed material previously submitted to Washington FBI on César Chávez and the NFWA. On page 2 of the report, however, a new line of inquiry is revealed on David Phillip Verlin. A full description of the twenty-year-old is included. His parents are Paul and Luba Verlin. Verlin, the father, is noted to belong to Local 26 of the International Longshoremen and Warehousemen Union in Los Angeles. No details or explanation are provided of what relationship, other than being the son of a union man, this has with the NFWA. Similarly, this report has a two-page appendix on the Central Los Angeles Du Bois Club, repeating old information dating to 1963 and Leonard Potash, Paul Rosenstein, Franklin Alexander, and Dorothy Healey, all members, according to an FBI source, of the Southern California District Communist Party (SCDCP). No details or explanation are given as to the inclusion of this material with this report, particularly from the same office that closed the investigative file on the NFWA and Chávez for lack of any evidence of Communist membership, leanings, sympathies, or affiliations.

CHAPTER 3

The UFW Eagle Comes to the Lone Star State, 1966–1968

THE WORDS "GONE TO TEXAS" RE-portedly were used by those who left states in the southeastern part of the United States like Tennessee, Georgia, Kentucky, and Alabama, for example, for Mexican Texas during the years 1820-30. They heard that under the Mexican Colonization Act of 1825, a legally admitted settler who pledged to be loyal to Mexico, become Catholic, and bring no Afri-can slaves could obtain 4,500 acres of land for fifty dollars payable over a six-year period.[1] The flood of Anglo-Americans who entered illegally with no willingness to abide by the terms of colonization fomented a rebellion against Mexico. Not only were they in opposition to the requirements, particularly the loyalty to Mexico, but they also opposed the anti-slavery provision. They wanted to bring slaves to farm the 4,500 acres of land. By 1835 these white migrants, largely Protestant and pro-slavery, who had illegally entered Mexican Texas succeeded in their rebellion. They established the Republic of Texas. Mexico's president and commander in chief, Antonio de Santa Anna, was held prisoner of war by the rebellious Texans at the time he signed the Treaty of Velasco conceding to the rebels large parts of Mexican Texas up to New Mexico and down to the Nueces River.

The debate about whether this sizable land mass should be incorporated into the United States as a state posed difficult issues in Texas and Washington. Should it be a slave state? Should it be two states, one free and the other slaveholding? Finally, the Republic of Texas, as an independent nation, was annexed by congressional resolution and not by treaty, which required a two-thirds consent of the U.S. Senate.[2] Subsequently, in another war with Mexico, the Texas border moved further south to the Rio Grande, where it remains today. Most of the laboring Mexicans stayed and worked for the new Anglo occupiers. Within a decade, by hook or by crook, the landed elite Mexicans were deprived of their land grants, given by Spanish kings, and some fled to Mexico, as did the Seguin and Zaragoza families, who had sided with the Anglo rebels against Mexico. Some fought back—for example, Juan Nepomuceno Cortina, who fought against both the U.S. Army and Texas Rangers and Mexican troops in and around Brownsville, Texas, during 1848-59.[3] To scholars like John R. Chávez, "the lost land has served as a focus for Mexican nationalism in the Southwest."[4]

The Bracero Program

Land and labor has been the foundation on which many a white man, woman, and family became rich in the Southwest, particularly Texas. Other whites obtained riches from the natural resources and the mineral rights never transferred in title or conferred on stolen Mexican land. Mexican labor cleared the borderlands by removing the *chaparrales y nopaleras* (thick mesquite brush and cactus patches) before labor-intensive agriculture could begin. Texas growers have always relied on plentiful, cheap, nonunion

Mexican labor—so much so that they took the first opportunity to institutionalize the Texas version of rent-a-slave, the U.S.-Mexico Bracero Program in 1947.

The program initially publicized as an emergency war measure was
national in scope. California and Texas, however, received more than half
of all *braceros* during the continuation of the program until 1964. Along
the border in Texas, white boss politicians created political machines,
with local Mexican Americans as their voters and low-level officeholders
such as sheriff's deputies, constables, justices of the peace, and city police
officers. These Mexican Americans did the bosses' bidding for decades
until they decided they could be the political bosses. There were several
in the Rio Grande Valley: the Guerras in Starr County, Bravo in Zapata
County, Ximenes in Wilson County, and Laurel in Webb County. Lyndon
Johnson was a direct beneficiary of the political bosses in South Texas as
he made his ascension to U.S. senator. Julie Leininger Pycior details the
role Mexican Americans played in making LBJ senator, vice president, and
president.[5] And, Sheila Allee describes in fascinating detail, as a relative of
Texas Ranger Captain A. Y. Allee, the role the Rangers played in maintaining the status quo in Duval County, home to the political boss of bosses,
George Parr, then his son, Archer Parr.[6]

In California, the agriculturalists took on a different strategy than
Texas regarding Mexican labor. Deborah Cohen in *Braceros* outlines the
California grower strategy this way: They formed grower associations to
collectively fight unionization; growers connected themselves to politicians and police from city hall to the White House; and they promoted
themselves as indispensable to the growth of the state via public-relations
campaigns. Taken together, these components quashed all labor protests
and organizing movements until Chávez with his UFW came along. Texas
growers followed a different strategy to control Mexican labor. The growers
exploited the Mexican workers in a myriad of ways, the most important of
which was to create a surplus labor pool over and above the numbers authorized under the Bracero Program by hiring Mexican labor from across the
river. The El Paso incident of 1948 is illustrative of this surplus labor pool, as
explained by Cohen.[7]

Texas initiated the addiction to undocumented, cheaper Mexican labor that continues to this day. Growers recruited Mexicans seeking work who crossed the border with impunity on their own having heard about the Bracero Program and ex-*braceros* whose term was up or who had jumped their original contract but were remaining within the United States. When public clamor reached its zenith over an "open border" that was allowing too many Mexicans into the U.S., the Border Patrol tightened up. The grower solution was to turn those undocumented and illegal Mexicans over to the Immigration and Naturalization Service (INS), which "deported" them across the border for an instant and returned them as parolees to the growers, particularly to pick cotton. The $2.50 a day wage for workers in the Bracero Program dropped to $1.50. Those hoping for raising the daily wage to $3 were left waiting. The second piece of the Texas grower strategy was to have the U.S. government enforce the Bracero agreement, not Mexico. The program became a three-party arrangement between the Mexican government, U.S. government, and the individual grower, not the worker. If the worker had issues, he could contact his own Mexican government for redress. The United States enforced the terms of the agreement, not wages or benefits. In Texas, farm laborers were paid at maximum fifty cents an hour—a lower wage than that paid the *braceros*. Lastly, Texas had its own private "army" in addition to local and other state law enforcement, the infamous Texas Rangers.[8]

The Texas Rangers

The formation of the Texas Rangers dates to 1823 and the days of illegal Anglo-American settler colonization of Mexican Texas.[9] The job of these men hired by white ranchers was to patrol the range, hence the name Rangers. From Texas Independence to World War I these Rangers had statewide jurisdiction and were charged with keeping the border safe. Safe meant to the Rangers, shoot first and ask questions later.[10] Texas Rangers have been historically used by Texas governors to break strikes under the color of law, among other illegal activities such as suppressing voter turnout in voting precincts with large numbers of voters of Mexican origin.[11]

During the period of 1967 to 1976, the Texas Rangers were very much part of the scene in Starr County, Texas, where striking farm workers struggled to form a union and press for equitable pay and humane working conditions. There are many stories from several perspectives: FBI documents tell one story, the strikers tell another, and the Texas Ranger apologists have yet another.[12] The fact remains that police forces, local and state and national, have had a sustained presence in that part of Texas, usually siding with the agricultural and political interests rather than labor. From 1835 to the present time, the border from Texas to California has been militarized.

Violence combined with blatant white racism against Mexicans, especially during the Bracero Program, were the overarching connections between California, Texas, and the nation. Idaho, for example, was placed off limits to contract for *braceros* by the government of Mexico, as was Texas, specifically because of the racism that fomented violence, discrimination, prejudice, abuse, and exploitation of the Mexican worker. Erasmo Gamboa documented the abuse and exploitation in the Pacific Northwest in his book on the Bracero Program.[13] Dennis Nodin Valdes covers agricultural labor, including *braceros*, in the history of the Great Lakes region.[14]

After some of his early successes in California, Chávez was besieged with requests to come help form locals of his union in other states. Moreover, the union newspaper *El Malcriado* carried the entire text in Spanish and English of El Plan de Delano, which contained a six-point program.[15] Word spread, and calls started coming into Delano asking for help in their areas. In Wautoma, Wisconsin, the Salas brothers, Jesus, Manuel, and Chacho, were organizing cucumber pickers. In Florida, farm workers working in the shadows of Disney World Epcot Center were seeking help from him. In Arizona, Gustavo Gutierrez was asking for help also. In Texas, the melon workers protesting low wages wanted to strike, but were leaderless and split into factions and wanted César to come organize them. In 1966, Chávez finally sent organizers to the Rio Grande Valley of Texas, where farm workers again were trying to strike over better wages and work conditions. Texas was the new president's home state.[16]

Texas Was Key to the White House in 1960

In 1960, Texas gave John F. Kennedy and Lyndon B. Johnson the keys to the White House with a slim margin of victory, 30,000 votes, that pushed them over the top and into the winner's circle of the Electoral College vote needed to win the presidency. Mexican American voters in Texas gave the Kennedy-Johnson ticket 91 percent of their votes. Nationally, the estimated Mexican American vote for the Democrats was 85 percent. A few appointments, as political reward, were forthcoming, but not in any significant numbers. The leadership of the Mexican American community when Johnson assumed the presidency saw his focus turn to African Americans and not them. As proof, they pointed to the 1964 White House Civil Rights Conference to which only African Americans were invited. Again in 1966, LBJ held another White House Civil Rights Conference, inviting only blacks. The most conservative of Mexican American groups, the American G.I. Forum (AGIF), picketed the White House on Easter Sunday, 1966. By May 1966, the president was obliged to invite some Mexican American leaders from the League of United Latin American Citizens (LULAC), Mexican American Political Association (MAPA), and the American G.I. Forum to the White House to soothe and calm the bad feelings. The guests asked that a White House aide be appointed, and a White House Conference on Mexican American Affairs be held. LBJ rejected both requests, but promised to look into a conference in the spring of 1967. The following February 1967, some of the Mexican American leaders were invited again to the White House to begin planning the conference. They met with Johnson's domestic policy advisor, Henry McPherson. The LBJ advisor agreed it was necessary and timely to hold such a conference; he summarized his recommendations in a memo for the president with some analysis. The 1968 presidential election was a year away, and the five southwestern states were crucial to victory provided the Mexican American voters went to the polls to support his candidacy. LBJ was not impressed with the analysis and was incensed that the Mexican Americans wanted to have such a conference in the White House. According to Lisa Bedolla, citing Julie L. Pycior, Johnson tersely and offensively wrote back a note to McPherson that read: "Keep this trash out of the White

House."[17] Lyndon Baines Johnson was not like Nixon, and Texas was not like California, as Chávez soon found out.

The Melon Strike and March to Austin

Chávez, by accepting this new Texas group, would now have two strike fronts because the IWA had called a strike against the major melon growers in the Rio Grande Valley on June 1, 1966.[18] This strike was to last almost two years. Eugene Nelson and Antonio "Tony" Orendain faced the same type of harassment, legal and extralegal, from local police, courts, and politicians as Chávez and the NFWA did in California. Chávez would have to finance these costs stemming from police action against the Texas strikers. Plus, there was a new and vicious element not found in California, the infamous Texas Rangers.

On June 1, 1966, the new IWA leadership formally declared a strike against melon workers in Starr County, Texas. At first picketing, they were promptly arrested and jailed. To save face in a Chávez-like tactic they began a four hundred mile march to the state capitol in Austin. The march generated much publicity and garnered immense support from Chicanos, Catholic and Protestant, and organized labor. The march was led by a Catholic priest, Antonio Gonzales, and a Baptist minister, James Novarro. In every community along the route, the media had ample photo opportunities, which made the coverage more intimate to other Mexican Americans across the state and nation.[19] Governor Edmund Brown Sr. had refused to meet and greet Chávez when he marched on Sacramento. Texas Governor John Connally did the same thing; he refused to meet the striking marchers, with the same negative publicity. Connally drove south from Austin to New Braunfels near San Antonio with the Speaker of the House, Ben Barnes, and the state attorney general, Waggoner Carr, in tow to tell the marchers he would not receive them at the capitol on Labor Day weekend, nor would he support legislation increasing farm worker wages to $1.25 per hour. The arrogance displayed by Connally and Democratic leadership of the era on that issue alienated many Mexican Americans and fired up their militancy in pressing their interests. A crowd estimated at fifteen thousand people gathered to listen to César Chávez and other notable speakers, including farm workers from Rio Grande City, that Labor Day in Austin.[20] The melon harvest ended with not much accomplished by the strikers until 1967.

Mid-1966 the FBI had notice of labor unrest in the Rio Grande Valley of Texas in Starr County, along with names of the organizers in the state who were affiliated with César Chávez in California.[21] Chávez had sent his best men for the job, Eugene Nelson first, and then Antonio "Tony" Orendain, Jim Drake, and Gilbert Padilla later to get them organized and affiliated with the California-based UFWOC.[22] Eugene Nelson had led the organizing of the grape and Schenley boycott around California and was based in Houston, Texas, for that purpose. Orendain was one of Chávez's early supporters and the only Mexican in the inner circle of Chicanos and Filipinos that founded the NFWA. His union organizing work endeared him to Chávez, particularly when Tony worked hand in hand with Manuel Chávez, César's maverick uncle who never espoused nonviolence. Manuel Chávez did all the dirty work for César. Tony had a short radio program in Spanish where he repeated news he gleaned from Mexican newspapers but injected news of the UFW. Besides Chávez, Dolores Huerta, and Luis Valdez of the Teatro Campesino, Tony was well-known up and down the San Joaquin Valley. He rose in the union ranks to become secretary-treasurer of the UFW, and that is when problems began between him and Chávez, according to Miriam Pawel.[23]

Nelson was working in Houston on the Schenley boycott when he learned of the labor strife over melons in the Rio Grande Valley (RGV). He went to see for himself what the situation was. Within days of being in Starr County he decided to organize this group of farm workers into a union while he worked on the grape boycott. And, within days of starting a picket line on the roads leading to the melon fields, he and over a dozen picketers were arrested by the local sheriff and his deputies for disturbing the peace. The bails were more than the maximum fine for such an offense. The purpose was to keep them in jail and off the picket lines while the melons, a highly perishable crop, were picked by others not interested in forming a union, mostly river-crossing Mexican laborers.

The Starr County melon workers called themselves the Independent Workers Association (IWA). They wanted Nelson to make a case to Chávez to quickly affiliate them with Chávez's NFWA. The LHM from SAC, San Antonio, however, utilizing an open source, the *San Antonio News*, was using the divide-and-conquer tactic in reporting that the vice president of IWA, Margil Sanchez, opposed affiliation "until those guys in California clear their names of this communism." The LHM did note that Nelson denied being a Communist or having any knowledge of Communists in their efforts in the Rio Grande Valley (p.2). The LHM reported utilizing another open source, the *Valley Evening Monitor*, that leaders within the Catholic Church were also on opposite sides of the melon strike and workers. The FBI claimed from that newspaper article that the local Monsignor Dan Lanning of Mission, Texas, denounced clergymen from San Antonio "who have taken part in the strike," calling them "'imposters and intruders' and that they 'do not speak for the church.'" On the opposing side and with the strikers was Archbishop Robert Lucey of San Antonio. His spokesman, according to the FBI's LHM information, was Monsignor Charles Grahmann, who stated, "Monsignor Lanning is of the old school that believes priests should sit in the rectory and watch the world go by and not get involved in the social evils of the world" (p.3). SAC, San Antonio in its dissemination of this LHM asked FBI, Houston, and FBI, Los Angeles for any information they might have reflecting subversive activity on the part of Eugene Nelson or Dolores Huerta (p.4).

FBI, San Antonio sent a second LHM on June 28, 1966, reporting another open source article in the *Valley Morning Star*. This report mentioned the financial support Nelson claimed he was getting from the secretary-treasurer of the Texas AFL-CIO, Roy Evans, and of other unions such as the Valley Amalgamated Meat Cutters and Butcher Workmen. Plus, the LHM stated that Nelson had accepted the idea for a march from Rio Grande City to Austin proposed by "Rev. Sherrill Smith and the Rev. K. William Killiam of the San Antonio Diocese, and the Rev. Jack Gist and Rev. Paul Like of the Amarillo Diocese. Roy Evans added his support and suggested that the march should terminate in Austin on Labor Day." As soon as the planners in Rio Grande with the IWA looked at maps and cities along the route, they came up with the logistics that "it would take about a month to cover the distance to Austin." The one in California covered 323 miles and took twenty-five days. The IWA planned on a month to cover the distance and planned that "the march would pass by President Johnson's ranch and be timed to end in Austin on Labor Day" (p.2).

We must assume that conversations were had between Nelson and Chávez on affiliation of the IWA with UFWOC and this march. More importantly, Chávez had sent Antonio Orendain and Gilberto Padilla, more experienced than Nelson, to the South Texas area to help organize this fledgling union. Realizing their hopes for a successful strike were greatly diminished by the arrests, jailings, failure to make bond, and violence at the hands of local police and Texas Rangers who also came into town, Orendain and Padilla echoed Nelson's idea of marching on Austin to rally public opinion to their cause and organize support networks around the state.

A subsequent Airtel from SAC, San Antonio, dated June 29, 1966, attached to a new LHM provided a new name: "LUCIO GALVAN has been active in handling the distribution of food in connection with the strikers." This Airtel contained redacted portions that identify the informants providing information on the activities and plans of the IWA (p.2). The accompanying LHM stated the two informants told FBI, San Antonio the protesters would "march from Rio Grande City, Texas, to the vicinity of San Juan, Texas, on July 4, 1966" (p.1). An URGENT teletype dated July 4, 1966, at 5:42 p.m. from SAC, San Antonio to Director, FBI confirmed that "APPROXIMATELY ONE HUNDRED MARCHERS COMPLETED THE FIRST LEG OF MARCH TO SAN JUAN, TEXAS . . . FROM RIO GRANDE CITY, TEXAS TO SULLIVAN CITY, TEXAS. MARCH TO RESUME TUESDAY, JULY FIVE, NEXT AND CONTINUE TO FRIDAY WHEN MARCHERS EXPECT TO ARRIVE AT SAN JUAN CATHOLIC CHURCH, SAN JUAN, TEXAS, NO INCIDENTS OF VIOLENCE OR DISTURBANCE OF ANY KIND REPORTED TODAY." The next URGENT teletype dated July 6, 1966, from the Director to SAC, San Antonio wanted "the location of the marchers, the number of marchers that have been participating, identity of the leaders and whether any incidents have occurred." SAC, San Antonio reported to Director via teletype dated July 7, 1966, late afternoon that the marchers were now in Mission, Texas, en route to McAllen and then to Edinburg, Texas. "Most of the marchers plan to return to Rio Grande City or Mission,

Texas, to spend the night ... Leader of the march is union organizer Eugene Nelson and he was joined by Reverend James Novarro, Baptist minister from Houston, Texas, and Wendle Scott, McAllen Church of Christ minister. No incidents of any kind have occurred during march up to this point." The next day, July 8, at 7:12 p.m., FBI, San Antonio sent an URGENT teletype to Director reporting that the marchers had reached San Juan at "FIVE FIFTEEN PM. AFTER SPECIAL MASS AND MEETING WITH BISHOP MEDEIROS OF BROWNSVILLE, TEXAS DIOCESE, MARCHERS ARE EXPECTED TO BEGIN RETURNING TO THEIR HOMES IN STARR COUNTY. NO INCIDENTS OR DISTURBANCES REPORTED TODAY AND NO PLANS TO CONTINUE MARCH AFTER TODAY."

A flurry of Airtels and Sulets and LHMs followed from FBI, San Antonio to Director, and FBI, Houston and back from these recipients to FBI, San Antonio. The July 11, 1966, teletype sent "350 PM CST" was to let all others know the march was continuing from San Juan to Weslaco, Elsa, Lyford, and Raymondville, Texas, then Linn, Texas, north to Falfurrias, Texas. The LHM of July 13, 1966, from SAC, Los Angeles to the Director provided information that "EUGENE NELSON is an ex-police reporter and a graduate of Marshall, Ill, 'Handy Institute' [no source]." And, it mentioned that Nelson had written a book, *Huelga*, which was advertised for sale in *El Malcriado*. Regarding Dolores Huerta, the LHM reported, "The files of the Los Angeles Office contain no pertinent subversive information concerning DOLORES HUERTA, Vice President of the National Farm Workers Association (NFWA), other than the fact that SAM KUSHNER, editor of "The Peoples World" (PW), has been in touch with her on several occasions."

The FBI, Los Angeles office must have felt frustrated at the Director's insistence on finding some Communist link or subversive activity on the part of union organizers and leaders of the NFWA. It had been and continued to be a waste of time on their part. The gutsy SAC, Los Angeles closed his LHM of July 13, 1966, with "it is not felt that continued investigation concerning the Cominfil of the NFWA is warranted at this time, and accordingly, Los Angeles is closing this case" (p.2).

FBI, San Antonio did not desist. They kept watching the marchers get to Raymondville and promised to send in a report on "MONDAY, JULY

EIGHTEEN NEXT WHEN SUMMARY OF WEEKEND ACTIVITES WILL BE SUB-MITTED."[24] And they did, with the usual report of no incidents or arrests and where the next stop would be. But not the Airtel dated July 22, 1966, from SAC, Houston to Director, FBI that contained a sleeper paragraph with important leadership changes: "On 7/22/66, EUGENE NELSON, leader of the striking Rio Grande Valley farm laborers and organizer for NFWA, Local No. 2, was reported to have returned suddenly to California, and it was assumed leadership of the march would be taken over by one of the clergymen mentioned above." However, Nelson surfaced again by mention in the Airtel of August 5, 1966, from SAC, Houston to Director, FBI, which reported that about thirty marchers had left Corpus Christi Cathedral the morning of August 2 en route to Gregory, Texas, "headed by EUGENE NELSON, farm labor organizer, and the Rev. JAMES NOVARRO, Southern Baptist minister from Houston, Texas." Hoover gets upset with this notice and replies in Airtel dated August 10, 1966, to SAC, Houston that he has the prior Airtel of August 5th that "a group of approximately 30 marchers left Corpus Christi Cathedral." Then the astonishing declaration by Hoover to the SAC, Houston, "The Bureau is unable to locate any prior correspondence from your office concerning this matter. Promptly furnish the Bureau background information concerning this march and advise whether there are any subversive elements connected with this activity." Hoover must have forgotten his own geographic structure for field offices into divisions, and instructions for field offices to pass on, as if it were a baton, the investigation of a matter if it crossed over into another FBI division. This was the case because SAC, San Antonio reported by Airtel with LHM dated August 5, 1966, that "Activities of the marchers after they entered the Houston Division are not included in this enclosed LHM."

Hoover apparently was satisfied, because no further comment or admonition is found in any subsequent message. An Airtel from SAC, Houston to Director, FBI on August 10, 1966, said that "HIRAM MOON, area Director, UAW, Dallas, Texas, at the Mathis, Texas" rally held on the 6th presented Eugene Nelson with a $1,000 check plus another $1,000 check from "two Corpus Christi locals of the United Steel Workers Union" presented by "PAUL MONTEMAYOR, Staff Representative" of this union. Then, the Airtel lists "the proposed itinerary for the marchers: Leave Mathis, Texas 12:00 noon 8/9/66, arrive ... and will arrive at San Antonio, Texas 8/27/66." These Airtels and subsequent ones began to contain in the "SUBJECT" last line "(SUBVERSIVE CONTROL)." I assume this addition was to placate the director that these "subversive marchers and clergymen" were being monitored for any subversive control measures necessary. And, SAC, Houston adds in his Airtel of August 17, 1966, that "Inasmuch as the marchers are now in San Antonio territory, no further investigation is being conducted by the Houston office, and this case is being placed in an RUC status."

The marchers kept up a very good pace to be past San Antonio and heading now to Austin, according to the Airtel dated September 7, 1966, from SAC, San Antonio to Director, FBI. The Texas governor decided not to wait for the marchers at the capitol building; instead he drove down to New Braunfels and stopped them by the highway:

> On 8/31/66 marchers were met by Governor JOHN CONNALLY, accompanied by Attorney General WAGGONER CARR and House Speaker BEN BARNES (all Texas), near New Braunfels, Texas in a surprise move by CONNALLY. CONNALLY rejected their bid for early minimum wage legislation. CONNALLY said he would not meet with marchers in Austin on Labor Day and that he would not be in Austin at that time. CONNALLY said he would not greet the marchers even if he were to be in his office on Labor Day. He said he did not feel as Governor of Texas that he should lend the dignity and prestige of his office to dramatize any march. He told the marchers they did not need a march to get in to see him.

The Airtel continued reporting that at the Texas State Capitol, "Speeches were made by leaders of marchers and U.S. Senator RALPH YARBOROUGH and U.S. Representative HENRY B. GONZALEZ demanding $1.25 per hour minimum wage for farm laborers." And, the SAC, San Antonio redacted the name of one identified to be "CP leader in San Antonio, Texas, was observed in crowd at Austin on 9/5/66." The FBI agents and informants must have not known who César Chávez was or looked like, because his name is absent in the declassified files for these days.

Chávez appeared and spoke at the Labor Day rally on the capitol steps. Chávez had been with Walter Reuther of the UAW in Mexico City right after the DiGiorgio election. He made a stopover in Austin to walk in solidarity with his new UFWOC members and give them an encouraging talk, which he did.[25] Chávez's appearance at the Texas rally at the capitol not only uplifted the morale of the striking melon workers but also gave further impetus to the growing Chicano militancy among youth who saw César Chávez as one of their Four Horsemen of the Chicano Movement.[26]

Full Field Investigation of César Chávez

The White House, in a memorandum dated September 11, 1966, from Mildred Stegall to Cartha D. DeLoach, FBI, requested a full field investigation by the FBI on César Chávez. The form letter read: "The person named above is being considered for . . . [a] White House staff position." And two days later, Hoover sent an Airtel dated September 15, 1966, to SACs Washington Field-Enc. (4) and Los Angeles with "BUDED: 9/30/66." Hoover specifically asked Los Angeles to "obtain Chavez's complete background, including names of close relatives and set out appropriate leads. This should be done immediately in order that Bureau Files can be reviewed." The Director, FBI by Airtel dated September 16, 1966, adds two more SACs: Denver and San Francisco.

Back in San Diego, California

Although he was glad to not hear of any incidents or problems with police stemming from the Texas march now nearing the state capitol, Chávez had mounting problems with the local police. Basically, while posing as strikers or pickets, his union members would be subject to arrest and physical manhandling by the local police. When Chávez called the police for help and protection against grower violence and harassment, his calls were ignored. Tired of this constant police harassment and abuse, Chávez decided to go with several of the DiGiorgio workers who had not been paid and had been evicted for voting for the NFWA union in the election. They would go to the ranch housing where their belongings were and pick them up, and perhaps the overdue paycheck. The San Diego County Sheriff's Department, in conjunction with the private security guards for DiGiorgio, were ready for them. Chávez plus ten others were arrested and transported to San Diego for jailing. The six-page report filed by FBI field agent William S. Ovitt, dated September 28, 1966, on Césario Estrada Chávez is field office file #161-247. The report is straightforward: the eleven persons led by Chávez had trespassed onto private land without permission on June 29. The charge was trespassing. Court was set for July 7, 1966, but continued until August 3; all were found guilty and fined $500 plus a $26 penalty assessment. The report does not state that the eleven men were chained together while being transported from Borrego Springs to the county jail. Once arrested by the security guards, they were held in a locked, unventilated truck for five hours in the Coachella Valley sun and heat.

> At about ten that night sheriff's deputies arrived and arrested the trespassers, shackling Cesar, the two ordained ministers, and the workers with heavy chains. They were transported to a jail in San Diego where they were strip-searched and spent the night in jail.[27]

Expanding the UFW to Texas, the Midwest, and Florida

The documents released under the Chavez file for 1967 begin with an Airtel plus LHM from SAC, Chicago to the Director, FBI dated January 23, 1967. The message was informing the FBI HQ that a demonstration by the National Farm Workers Association had taken place at Zimmerman Liquor Store in Chicago mid-December 1966. On January 21 of 1967 the protest moved to Parkway Liquor Store. The NFWA was protesting the sale of wine distributed by Perelli Minetti Company of Delano, California. Leaflets passed out also called for the consumer not to purchase products from Schenley and DiGiorgio Companies, both of California. The SAC, Chicago alerted the U.S.

Secret Service and the Assistant U.S. Attorney plus the Coordinator (name redacted) of the 113th MI Group in Evanston, Illinois, the area military intelligence unit. The Midwest was coming alive for Chávez, as was the Rio Grande Valley of Texas.

On February 1, 1967, the Teletype was busy at FBI HQ printing out an urgent message from the SAC, San Antonio sent at 7:50 p.m. It read, "The following persons arrested by Starr County Sheriff's Office about two fifteen p.m. this date and charged with disturbing the peace after they entered the premises of La Casita Farms, Rio Grande City, Texas, to heckle non-union workers in fields: Father Sherill Smith, San Antonio, Texas, Catholic Priest; Father William Killian, San Antonio Catholic Priest; Father Harry W. Hayes, San Antonio Catholic Priest; Father D. J. Hefferman, San Antonio Catholic Priest; Charles Smith, Austin, Texas; Ismael Diaz, Rio Grande City, Texas; Gregoria Solis (female), Rio Grande City, Texas; Nenonar Garza (female), Rio Grande City, Texas; Anthony Orendain, aka Tony—an official of the National Farm Workers Association, Rio Grande City, Texas, and Delano, California; Benjamin Rodriguez, aka Benito Rodriguez, San Antonio, Texas. All above released on one hundred dollars personal recognizance bond shortly after arrested on February One, instant." Then at bottom the observation that "inasmuch as this appears to be part of a legitimate labor dispute involving a union, San Antonio is taking no action." The next day, SAC, San Antonio sent another URGENT teletype to correct the listing in his report of Charles Smith of Austin. "Was not among the ten persons arrested . . . and was not in the area to his knowledge." Curious wording, but not any more curious than adding the name of "Father Marvin Doerfler, San Antonio, Texas." I presume he was left off inadvertently to begin with and that he was also a Catholic priest.

While things were brewing in Texas, SAC, Los Angeles notified the Director, FBI via Airtel and LHM that the UFWOC was going to have a parade in Delano. He had alerted all the military intelligence units and others in the area. "Copies of this memorandum are being furnished to Region II, 115th MI, U.S. Army, Pasadena, California; OSI, Norton Air Force Base; Naval Investigative Service, San Diego; U.S. Secret Service, Los Angeles, and the U.S. Attorney, Los Angeles."

The parade had been given a permit by the city for March 25, 1967. The route was known. The approximate number of people parading was disclosed along with the times. But prior to the "march on March 25, 1967, there will be a luncheon, singing, and a theatre skit, and after the march a party is planned for the evening." What the Los Angeles FBI man found subversive, communistic, un-American, anarchist, and menacing about this event remains a mystery. Why the sharing of this parade information with the military intelligence units and Secret Service is equally mystifying. The City of Delano was not worried. They had seen Chávez march up and down the city and state time and again; it was always peaceful except for drive-by hecklers and their obscene gestures. Their main concern was police overtime pay straining their budget.

Back in Texas, Ernie Cortes, a student at the University of Texas-Austin, was leading the Valley Workers Assistance Committee out of Austin, so informed the SAC, San Antonio—the same person who viewed the matter as a legitimate labor dispute. This time in his URGENT teletype to the Director, FBI dated March 15, he added, "This is purely for information of the Bureau." And, he further explains that the Cortes group, some five hundred to one thousand people, will march from the church to the Texas state capitol grounds, where they will form to protest low wages. The farm worker wage for picking melons in South Texas at that time was 25 cents an hour. The FBI source stated that "legislative hearings on the minimum wage bill to be held at capitol tonight. Source state group intends peaceful demonstration."

From the content of a two-page letter without any heading dated March 21, 1967, from the Director, FBI to Fred M. Vinson, Jr., assistant attorney general, Hoover is responding to a prior request by the AG's office on UFWOC and La Casita Farms labor strike in the RGV. Hoover provides this information on the Filipino group, not Chávez's group: "Since October 1965, considerable information received by this Bureau has been furnished to the Records Administration Office of the Department relating both to Communist infiltration of the NFWA and various demonstrations by such organization in connection with efforts to organize farm workers in Texas and California." Hoover did state in this same letter that the NFWA and

NFWOC had merged in 1966 and become the United Farm Workers Organizing Committee (UFWOC).

The RGV melon strike of June 1966 was not initiated by the UFWOC. On the contrary, only once the fledging strike effort was in trouble and being victimized by the Texas Rangers, local law enforcement, and judiciary, did they reach out to the UFWOC. Chávez responded to the call for help and rescue from more disaster from the melon strike. And, Chávez referred to the ten arrested on February 1st. The second page of this letter contains a "NOTE" that contains heavily biased information against the UFWOC and in favor of La Casita Farms.

> Criminal Division advised of alleged violence as reported in newspapers concerning labor organizing activities of captioned Committee with regard to laborers of the victim corporation; requested advice of the situation generally and particular acts of violence coming to your attention; and indicated it would determine whether investigation was warranted under Anti-Racketeering (AR) Statute (18 USC 1951) which prohibits extortionate demands induced by violence.

Then, Hoover, in the next paragraph, admits that "labor organizational activities are not considered extortion as defined in AR Statue." He also admitted that

> investigation as to possible Communist infiltration of NFWA, independent labor union (now known as UFWOC), in the past did not indicate it was controlled by Communists, but that Communist Party members or sympathizers have furnished support in certain activities concerning grape growers in California.

However, Hoover, instead of closing the case on investigating the organizing effort, sent the same information to the SACs in Houston and San Antonio with specific instructions on the 23rd that "each office should insure that the Bureau is promptly advised of any incidents which arise in the future relating to organizational attempts or other activities of the captioned committee in the Rio Grande Valley." The SAC, San Antonio was prompt in responding to the Director, FBI by Airtel dated March 23, also with open source material from the extremely conservative *Valley Morning Star* published out of Harlingen, Texas, the last remaining white-majority city in the Rio Grande Valley at that time. He stated that the newspaper was reporting on car caravans coming from Houston and Austin, merging into one in Corpus Christi over the Easter holiday.

University Student Groups Join in Support of the Melon Strikers

The numerous chapters of the Mexican American Youth Organization (MAYO) across the state and other college-campus student groups such as Mexican American Student Organization (MASO) at the University of Texas-Austin solicited canned goods, clothes, and money for the strikers.[28] They were bringing "goods for farm workers and their families." The next Airtel with LHM the Director, FBI received was from SAC, Los Angeles, who also copied the military intelligence units in Los Angeles and San Diego plus the local U.S. attorney's office. The news was that the UFWOC "sponsored march at Delano on March 25, 1967." A redacted source stated it took an hour for the march, comprised of "strangers to Delano." The informant must have known everyone, including farm workers who resided in Delano, to make this statement. The same or another redacted source reported that "no problems were reported by his Delano Substation." This source must be a local police officer.

April 3, 1967, an Airtel with LHM was sent to the Director, FBI from SAC, San Antonio that his office was taking no further action "since strike activities described in instant LHM are part of a legitimate labor dispute." And, the LHM cited information taken from an open source, the *San Antonio Light*, that twenty-five cars made up the Easter caravan "carrying food, medicine, and clothing to striking farm workers in the Rio Grande City area." By April 12 the *Valley Evening Monitor* of McAllen, Texas, was reporting that the Mexican union Confederacion de Trabajadores Mexicanos (CTM) was picketing the border bridge on their side, preventing farm workers from crossing to break the melon strike in Starr County. Some refused to cross the picket line, but "approximately one hundred of these workers entered the United States after midnight this morning." The UFWOC were quoted in this article as having sent a telegram to President Johnson requesting that the Texas Rangers be investigated. "They said Rangers had shoved several union members and were acting as 'strike breakers.'"

César Chávez, meanwhile, kept traveling when he could to major cities promoting and supporting boycotters. On April 25, 1967, he was in Chicago, meeting with labor and church officials and urging they "send telegrams to Mr. JOHN TRIBUNO . . . New York, requesting him to cease purchasing vermouth from Perelli Minetti and urge Minetti to begin negotiations with NFWA," according to an LHM sent from SAC, Chicago to Director, FBI dated May 31st.

Another LHM from the SAC, San Antonio sent May 3 warned that on May 6-7, 1967, "a group of 50 demonstrators and strike supporters . . . from the Student Nonviolent Coordinating Committee and Students for a Democratic Society from upstate, probably Houston and Austin, Texas are being sought for the above event." The SAC is alerting the FBI HQ that early May "is the beginning of the melon harvesting season, and, according to source [NAME REDACTED] a strategic time to attempt a slowdown or stopping of the harvesting of this perishable crop, which is destined seasonally for the northern markets at a premium price." San Antonio FBI has more insider information: Eugene Nelson had moved to Pharr, Texas, to run a printing press "such as was done in a strike campaign held in the recent past among farm workers in Delano, California." Nelson was identified further in the LHM "as the author of a *Huelga* book of instructions, which he had issued during the activities in Delano, California." The book *Huelga* is not about instructions; rather it is a biography of the first one hundred days of that strike and the violence inflicted on striking workers and pickets. The replacement for Nelson was "James Drake, described as a 'missionary preacher.'" And the LHM further advised that "TONY ORENDAIN, another activist prominent in this Huelga, is a Mexican alien, who originated in the State of Michoacan." To the FBI, a Mexican is a Mexican is a Mexican alien forever, regardless of green card status, residency status, or citizenship by naturalization. Just four days later, on the 7th, the SAC, San Antonio reported to the Director, FBI that the striking workers were going to "prevent cantaloupe pickers from going onto farms by forming human chain across access roads. Also, they planned to prevent movement of melons to packing sheds in the same manner." But, "Since strike activities described are part of a legitimate labor dispute no further action being taken by San Antonio." Then why did the FBI continue monitoring, informing, analyzing, sending, responding, providing almost weekly activity being taken by farm workers in this legitimate labor dispute? Not only did the FBI continue its activity but it also escalated the level and scope of group activity among other intelligence agencies as revealed in its May 10th or so Airtel (section at top right masks date and other unknown information redacted) the Director received from SAC, San Antonio. The Orendain status "described as Mexican alien" was "disseminated locally to Immigration and Naturalization Service, Port Isabel, Texas and SAC, Houston," plus the second page of the document stated that "Copies of the LHM have also been furnished locally to the OSI, MIG, NISO, Secret Service, San Antonio and Secret Service, Austin, and Sheriff's Office in Rio Grande, City." The LHM was not disclosed.

On May 13, an unlucky day for Eugene Nelson, he was arrested according to the URGENT teletype sent to the Director, FBI from SAC, San Antonio, "after making threat against Texas Rangers by stating there would be some dead Rangers unless they lay off UFWOC pickets." The more telling story in the teletype of complicity between local judicial and county public officials and police is found in the steps taken by these entities following the arrest.

> Nelson immediately taken before Justice of the Peace who set bond at two thousand dollars. Bond signed by J.C. Guerra, Roma, Texas, who according to [NAME REDACTED] has only sixty-one acres of land valued at fifteen hundred dollars in his name, for this reason [NAME REDACTED] refused to accept bond until Nelson's attorney, James McKeithan of Mission, Texas, brought him a statement from the Texas [sic] Collector's Office indicating Guerra to own property of sufficient value to make his signature on bond acceptable. McKeithan refused to do this. Nelson was remanded to jail until acceptable surity [sic] obtained which has not been done to date."

There is no Texas Collector in Texas; there is a Tax Assessor and Collector who maintains property rolls and assessed values. More importantly, agricultural or unimproved land in South Texas during the late 1960s was not valued at $24.50 an acre.

Stern Hoover and More Arrests

Hoover notified SAC, San Antonio on May 16 that the Criminal Division of the Department "has previously expressed an interest in the activities of the United Farm Workers Organizing Committee . . . Bureau instructions regarding submissions of such LHMs is set forth in Bureau Airtel to Houston and San Antonio dated 3/22/67. You should see that such instructions are followed in the future." Stern Hoover was not pleased with whatever was reported in that LHM, but it was not disclosed or declassified in the Chavez file. That same day SAC, San Antonio sent an Airtel with LHM to Hoover with same information on Nelson's arrest and bond setting and the telegram sent to LBJ asking for investigation of the Texas Rangers for shoving pickets. This LHM, however, added new information taken from the *Valley Morning Star*: "Reverend ED KRUEGER, of Edinburg, Texas, and one DAVID LOPEZ, a member of the UFWOC, had filed a complaint . . . against Texas Ranger JACK VAN CLEVE which alleged Ranger shoved them during a demonstration at the International Bridge, Rio Grande City, the previous week." Nelson was also reported to have been released on bond posted by his attorney. And, "five melon growers of the Rio Grande City area had sent a telegram to Senator JOHN TOWER, Republican, Texas, charging the presence of pickets on the Mexican side of the Roma, Texas, International Bridge was 'an international conspiracy to block bridges and creat [sic] chaos." Another Airtel with LHM followed on the 19th citing information from the *San Antonio Express*, which said that "Henry Munoz, Jr., Director of the Equal Opportunity Department of the Texas AFL-CIO and member of the Texas Advisory Committee to the United States Commission on Civil Rights, had asked that that committee convene and investigate alleged violations of the civil rights of striking Starr County, Texas farm workers by Texas Rangers."

The LHM further informed that Gilbert Padilla, vice president, UFWOC, and twenty-two others, including the union's local president, Domingo Arredondo, had been arrested by Texas Rangers for "picketing within 50 feet of Trophy Farms and within 50 feet of each other." Padilla was considering filing "charges locally against the Rangers for 'pushing' pickets." The last substantive paragraph of the LHM quoted the *Valley Morning Star* of the 19th in which State Representative Lauro Cruz of Houston, Texas, was reported as having filed a House Resolution "asking Texas Governor John Connally to remove the Texas Rangers from the Rio Grande City area because of 'intimidation and harassment.'" In San Antonio, "Ernest Cortes, Jr. Boycott Coordinator of the UFWOC, had issued a statement protesting the arrest of the 22 pickets, saying the presence of the Texas Rangers in Rio Grande City is a 'crude attempt at union busting.'"

There was movement within the FBI to become more involved with this legitimate labor dispute as revealed in the Airtel dated May 27, 1967, from SAC, San Antonio to the Director asking FBI HQ and SAC, Los Angeles for information on "1. EUGENE NELSON, age 37, white male, UFWOC organizer. 2. WILLIAM CHANDLER, about 30, Los Angeles Police Department, No. LA 546-6456-C. 3. DOMINGO ARREDONDO, age 31, white male, President of UFWOC at Rio Grande City. 4. GILBERT PADILLA, white male, about 35, National Vice-President, UFWOC. 5. Any other members of the UFWOC in California presently known or believed to be in the Rio Grande City area." Perhaps the movement was in response to the Munoz request for the Texas Committee to the U.S. Commission on Civil Rights to hold hearings at Rio Grande City, Texas.[29]

The Subcommittee Hearing of the U.S. Commission on Civil Rights

The subcommittee met on May 26 and heard testimony from Gilberto Padilla to the effect that Nelson, Padilla, and Lopez were told by Texas Ranger Captain A. Y. Allee that they were under arrest as they were leaving a restaurant in Rio Grande City. Ranger Captain A. Y. Allee and Ranger Jack Van Cleve, rather than place those arrested in their car, instead got into their own car and drove away at a high rate of speed. Those arrested did not follow thinking the Rangers did not want them to follow. According to Lopez, one of those arrested, Ranger Van Cleve's action indicated he had been drinking intoxicating beverages and liquor could be smelled on his breath.

State Senator Joe Bernal took a tour of the strike zone in Rio Grande City during the days of the Civil Rights Commission hearings to learn firsthand about the labor dispute.[30] Just days prior to this, Roy Reuther of the United Auto Workers had made telephone calls to Governor John Connally and President Lyndon Johnson protesting the arrest of his employee Francisco "Pancho" Medrano by Texas Rangers for taking photographs of them committing violence. Medrano's bond was set at $500 for a misdemeanor "crime" that at most called for a maximum fine of $200. State Senator Bernal was confronted by Captain A. Y. Allee at the Starr County courthouse while he was trying to obtain information on the arrest of Dimas and Rodriguez. The meeting degenerated into a shouting match. "Allee told him, 'I never thought I'd live to see the day some senator would come down here' and do as Bernal had." Bernal was quoted as stating after that confrontation, "'I'm thoroughly convinced' that Allee is 'on the side of the growers.' Bernal did not think they should have come in at the request of the growers."[31]

Texas Ranger violence against the strikers reached epidemic proportions. Arrests were made daily and became commonplace. The brutality by the Rangers on the strikers was scandalous. The U.S. Commission on Civil Rights concluded this police abuse and violent practice was not uncommon:

> Widespread evidence compiled since the 1967 meeting of the Texas State Advisory Committee in Starr County reveals that this is neither an isolated nor unique instance of treatment Mexican Americans in the Southwest receive from law enforcement agencies. Many experiences were described to the Commission which exemplified what Mexican Americans allege to be common use of discriminatory, excessive police force against them.[32]

At the end of the month, the Missouri Pacific Railroad complained to the FBI or some unknown redacted source that mischief was afoot on the route north from Rio Grande City to Austin; the company claimed it was the

UFWOC: "the Missouri-Pacific Railroad Company has as yet sustained no material damage related to UFWOC activities." But what was the UFWOC being blamed for? To quote the report, "trains leaving Rio Grande City . . . had been stoned repeatedly by UFWOC pickets at most towns of any significant size between Rio Grande City and Taylor, Texas, some 300 miles away . . . Some locations included . . . Mission, McAllen, Edinburg, La Feria, Victoria, Falfurrias, Alice, San Antonio, and Austin, Texas. A switch engine running ahead of the main train . . . had located a few railroad spikes and tie plates on the railroad tracks . . . a rock on the track near McAllen, Texas, and two rocks at Donna, Texas." That is a lot of UFWOC pickets to have covered three hundred miles. More importantly, how could the Missouri-Pacific Railroad know it was UFWOC pickets and not just kids' mischief along the way?

The Airtel and LHM of May 31st are silent on eye witnesses or informants along the route. Another Airtel and LHM found its way to the Director, FBI the next day, June 1st, informing him that a UFWOC rally was being planned for the 3rd at a public park in Rio Grande City. The message also stated that twelve more members of the UFWOC had been arrested by the Texas Rangers for picketing at La Casita Farms, Rio Grande City, and "remanded to the Starr County Jail in lieu of $400 bond each." Two more, Mrs. William L. Chandler and Horacio Carrillo, were also arrested by a deputy sheriff, Roberto Peña, on orders from Captain A. L. Alyee [*sic*] of the Texas Rangers later that afternoon, but they languished in jail because "they had as yet not been afforded an appearance before a local magistrate and bond had as yet not been set." The SAC, San Antonio also reported that David Lopez was bringing attorneys to the Valley to "begin preparing a case through which they hope to bring civil actions alleging violations of the Civil Rights Act of 1870 against the Texas Rangers and other local law enforcement officials." They would be seeking a restraining order against further Ranger arrests. The following day, another Airtel and LHM went to FBI HQ from San Antonio, FBI to other SACs in Houston, El Paso, Dallas, Texas Department of Public Safety, San Antonio Police Department, and all the area military intelligence units plus the U.S. Secret Service, San Antonio and Austin. The LHM warned of another car caravan being organized to arrive for the Rio Grande City rally on the 3rd. This caravan was coming from Austin to San Antonio and then "arriving in Rio Grande City 11 a.m. and will be picketing for the remainder of the day." The SAC, San Antonio got his information from two sources, a leaflet announcing meetings for the rally obtained by the 112th Military Intelligence Group, Austin, Texas, and Erasmo Andrade, the state chairman of the Valley Workers Assistance Committee, San Antonio, Texas, who provided information on participants and the schedule of departure and arrival. The SAC contacted five area intelligence units and listed them by name (redacted) and time of call.

Rangers Hunt Down Benito and Magdaleno

June 2nd became a busy day for the FBI; it began with an Airtel and LHM from SAC, San Antonio to Hoover reporting on Texas Rangers severely injuring two UFWOC members. The LHM named Benito Rodriguez and Magdaleno Dimas as the victims of Ranger violence under the command of Captain A. L. ALyee [*sic*]. Captain Allee and his Rangers "appeared at UFWOC headquarters, Rio Grande City, armed with shotguns inquiring for . . . Magdaleno Dimas and Ben Rodriguez." Supposedly, William Chandler spoke to the Rangers but could not provide information on the whereabouts of the two men sought. "In Chandler's opinion, the Rangers were drinking. After the Rangers left . . . Chandler went to where Dimas, Rodriguez and other UFWOC members reside to warn them Rangers were looking for them. Rangers reportedly arrived at the house, broke down two doors, and arrested Dimas and Rodriguez. They showed no warrant. According to Kathy Baker, who also was staying at above residence, the Rangers beat Dimas and Rodriguez severely and used vulgar language. No charges were mentioned. Dimas and Rodriguez were taken to Starr County Jail, Rio Grande City." The first of three teletypes followed the LHM. The earliest sent "11:08 AM URGENT" to Hoover reported what David Lopez had complained to the local FBI, San Antonio about Ranger violence and named the victims; this message did change the disclaimer usually adhered to the end of all messages on this matter: "It is noted that this matter represents part of continuing labor dispute in Ro [*sic*] Grande Valley which has deep political implications . . .

between Governor John Connally and Senator Ralph Yarborough (D-Texas). In view of these political implications, it is not deemed advisable to conduct further investigation in this matter." Apparently, at that time FBI politics themselves trumped investigating civil rights violations. The next URGENT teletype, sent at 1:29 p.m., reminded the Director, FBI about the car caravan that arrived that morning and should be picketing all day before the rally on the 3rd at 7:30 p.m. The rally was billed as "Anti-Rangers Rally, according to [Erasmo] Andrade." The last urgent teletype sent to the Director, FBI at 5:39 p.m. stated, "June Two instant edition of *Valley Evening Monitor* . . . carries front page article captioned, 'Bernal says Connally will be asked to remove Texas Rangers.'" The article also stated that "Dimas suffered small cut near one ear and Rodriguez a small cut on one finger. Both were treated at a Rio Grande Hospital on orders of Justice of Peace Lopez." State Senator Joe Bernal was quoted extensively in the article, according to the teletype. Bernal had charged the Rangers with being "present at request of produce growers and not the people . . . making unjustified arrests . . . used violence . . . in arresting two union members." Bernal "said FBI had been asked to determine whether federal law has been violated." (Two redacted lines end page 2 with unreadable handwritten notes on side at bottom.) An accompanying note from General Investigative Division states the San Antonio office is handling the request for investigation made by Henry Munoz Jr.

The Beatings Were Brutal

The rally of the 3rd was comprised of local UFWOC organizers making speeches. "No significant events reported," stated the URGENT teletype of that day sent to Hoover from San Antonio, FBI at 12:20 p.m., but by 1:46 p.m. another URGENT teletype followed quoting open source material from the *San Antonio Express and News* that Dr. Ramiro Casso, who treated Magdaleno Dimas after the Ranger beating, stated that Dimas "'took the worst beating I have ever seen law enforcement officers administer' and that Dimas suffered brain concussion, a gash behind his ear, and 'tremendous swelling near the brain.'" According to the same newspaper, Allee was interviewed

over a Harlingen radio station and stated he and two other Rangers went
to find Dimas and Rodriguez to arrest them because "he feared violence if
they were left at large." During the arrest, the men had their hands under
the table where they sat when the Rangers busted into the house. Upon
orders to place their hands on top of the table, they didn't, and the beatings
began.[33] His boss at DPS in Austin, Homer Garrison, was quoted as saying,
"The charge of police brutality is the common defense and cry of a common
criminal and agitator. If the [*sic*] obey the law, no Texas Ranger ever has or
ever will molest them." The *Valley Morning Star*, the extreme-right newspaper in the Rio Grande Valley, reported that local citizens were signing
petitions addressed to Homer Garrison to keep the Rangers in the Valley.
And, the SAC added his personal opinion toward the end of the message:
"For info Bureau, Dr. Ramiro Casso, supra, is prominent in liberal political
circles in Rio Grande Valley." Apparently, the San Antonio, FBI also believes
medical diagnoses have liberal interpretations if they favor the victim and
blame law enforcement for the injuries. The two LHMs sent by Airtel that
accompanied the teletype did not contain much different information.
The Airtel and LHM of June 12 did report news to Hoover. It mentioned the
names of liberal state senators who supported the Rangers in opposition to
Bernal, and had figures on telegrams (100), letters (100), and names (1,800)
on petitions provided by DPS Director Garrison on the numbers for each
type of transmission, while only "ten letters critical of the Rangers." The
LHM also reported that Richard L. Dockery of Dallas, Texas, and with the
NAACP was investigating the charges levied against Rangers in the Valley
for his organization. The next day's Airtel from SAC, San Antonio to Hoover
reported on the civil litigation filed by the UFWOC and friends against
the Rangers and local law enforcement requesting they be enjoined from
making further arrests. The Airtel of the 14th from SAC, San Antonio to the
Director, FBI quoting open source material from the *San Antonio Light* of the
previous day, reported that indeed the Rangers were being sued in federal
court under the Civil Rights Act of 1966 by six of the victims of Ranger
abuse. The suit was against "Texas Ranger Capt. A. Y. Allee, Ranger Sgt. S.
H. Denson, Rangers Jack Van Cleve, T. H. Dawson, and Jerome Preiss, Starr
County Sheriff, Dr. Rene Solis, Deputies Raul Pena and Roberto Pena, Special

Deputy Jim Rochester, and Justice of the Peace B. S. Lopez." The article cited by the SAC mentioned that Rochester was "an employee of La Casita Farms," and his brother, Ray, was a "vice-president" for La Casita Farms "and general manager." Depositions in the case would begin in a few days, but not before "William Kircher, organization director of the AFL-CIO, is scheduled to meet with Gov. John Connally at 10 a.m. Wednesday in Austin."

The federal court case stemmed from arrests made from February 1, 1966, to June 1, 1967, and filed as a class action on behalf of many victims, including one, Francisco "Pancho" Medrano, whose name would become part of the style in the case, *Medrano v. Allee*.[34] The victims testified in federal court, and the judges hearing the case on appeal recited many of these incidents of Ranger and sheriff deputies' violence and abuse in their judgment.[35]

Governor Connally was being pressured at every turn by other politicians and national labor leaders. The SAC added more information about these meetings within quotation marks but did not cite the source, possibly the same article. Apparently "Union officers have made almost daily protests concerning the use of the Rangers and last Friday took their protest to the governor when he went to Laredo to speak at a banquet for a Mexican American organization." Of more importance was the last paragraph entry: "Cesar Chavez, national director of the union, ordered a halt to all pickets in Starr County shortly after his arrival at Rio Grande City last week. Chavez said the picketing would remain halted while the union attempts to file some legal actions." There is no document in the disclosed or declassified files on this visit to the RGV by Chávez. Levy, in *Cesar Chavez: Autobiography of La Causa*, does mention the Texas trip in passing and credits Chávez and Jerry Cohen, UFW attorney, in getting the Rangers out of the Valley:

> The first thing I did in 1967 when I came to the Union was go down to Texas with Cesar. The Texas Rangers had beaten the hell out of 140 strikers, and some of the men wanted to get the Rangers. They wanted to physically get them out of town. Cesar said, "You give me a chance." Now this was a classic situation. The Rangers were at the Rangold [*sic*] Hotel, and every day at about 4:00 they left the hotel and walked across the street to the Catfish Inn to drink beer. So, when the Rangers walked out of that hotel one

day, there were women, all related to our organizer Magdaleno Dimas—his grandmother, his mother, his sisters—dressed in black, praying for the Rangers' souls. And there were some people there to cover it from the press, of course. In twenty-four hours Governor John Connally had gotten the Rangers out of town.[36]

The *Valley Morning Star* of the 15th of June carried a front-page story that became the subject matter of the SAC, San Antonio Airtel to Hoover on the 16th. The SAC reported that according to this open source, the governor "had announced the previous day that Texas Ranger Captain A. Y. Allee had begun withdrawing Texas Rangers from Starr County since, in his judgment, things had quieted down enough to do this." And, the SAC also reported that Domingo Arredondo, one of the early victims of Ranger abuse and arrest, had sent "a telegram to U.S. Attorney General Ramsey Clark requesting Federal Marshalls [sic] be sent to the Rio Grande Valley to protect UFWOC members and their families ... from the Texas Rangers." Unreported by the SAC was the fact that the strike had been broken by scores of arrests, and the Ranger violence and the melon harvest were almost over; it would be quiet again until next harvest season in 1968.

The fact that the strike was in its last throes of life and the matter had moved into the slow wheels of litigation in federal court was lost on the faraway SAC, Los Angeles, who chimed in with an LHM, nine pages at least, to the Director, FBI on June 21, 1967, reviving the bogus "Communist infiltration" allegations against UFWOC due to its merger with NFWA back in 1966. The LHM listed by name and some description all the UFWOC personnel from California involved with the Texas strike, with special focus on Gilbert Padilla. "PADILLA spoke before the Los Angeles Socialist Workers Party (SWP) forum at 1702 East 4th Street on 6/3/66 on the topic, 'The Grape Strikers—How They are Building a Movement.'" The memorandum discloses that "Attendance at the meeting was disappointing, according to its sponsors. The SWP has been designated by the Attorney General of the United States pursuant to Executive Order 10450." This is followed by two entirely redacted paragraphs. Technically, the assertion by the SAC is correct; the SWP was listed on the Subversives List dating to AG Francis

Riddle and Hoover's tenure under FDR in 1941. However, the SAC is being disingenuous by stating this "fact" in 1967, knowing that SCOTUS in *Cole v. Young*, 351 US 536 (1956) found the term "national security" as justification for classifying hundreds of organizations in overly broad and vague terms, which was therefore unconstitutional.[37] The other proof offered by the SAC, Los Angeles of "Communist" presence was real in his mind because "SAM KUSHNER, Los Angeles Editor, 'People's World,' has been in the Rio Grande City area and has filed reports with the 'People's World' concerning the developments in that area." And, the SAC also sent the San Antonio Division "a xerox copy entitled, 'A Summary Outline of a Method of Organizing' by BOB SOLODOW, which is based in part on the teachings of CESAR CHAVEZ and FRED ROSS dated October 1966." This summary is on file with the Los Angeles FBI, according to this document. The remainder of the LHM sent by Los Angeles FBI to the San Antonio Division consists of several appendices on "communist infiltration" of the First Unitarian Church of Los Angeles; Los Angeles Committee for Defense of the Bill of Rights "formerly known as Los Angeles Committee for Protection of the Foreign Born"; W.E.B. Du Bois Clubs of America; and others not disclosed. The LHM ends with page 9, but it is clear that there is more material that should have been included.

It was not reported in records released or declassified whether Kircher of the AFL-CIO met with Governor John Connally or not, as scheduled, but the Airtel dated June 27, 1967, from the SAC, San Antonio to Hoover indicated in the LHM accompanying the report "that Gilbert Padilla . . . Pancho Medrano . . . and H.A. Moon of Dallas, also of the United Auto Workers, met with Texas Governor John Connally on the previous day at Austin, Texas, to discuss the Rio Grande Valley farm labor situation." His open source of information was the *San Antonio Light*. The governor is quoted as having stated to his visitors that "he was neutral in the dispute, as are the Texas Rangers assigned in the Rio Grande City area."

While the federal litigation was just beginning against the Rangers and local sheriff's department, a state district judge held a hearing and granted an injunction against all picketing at La Casita Farms effective June 28, 1967, according to the Airtel sent by SAC, San Antonio to FBI HQ on June 30th. The SAC, again citing an open source article from the *Valley*

Morning Star dated the 29th, reported that U.S. Senators Harrison Williams (R-New Jersey) and Ralph Yarborough, the Texas Democrat, had arrived at Harlingen, Texas, to hold the hearings on migratory labor.

U.S. Senate Subcommittee Hearings on Migratory Labor

A week later on July 6 the SAC, San Antonio sent Hoover an Airtel with LHM reporting on newspaper coverage in the *Valley Morning Star* of the migratory labor hearings. The newspaper concluded on the front page that the U.S. Senate hearing "showed open favor to unionizing farm labor." Moreover, in another related article of the same day, June 30, the newspaper ran a story indicating ratings by Americans for Democratic Action (ADA) and COPE, the AFL-CIO's political action committee, of Senators Ted Kennedy and Harrison Williams as voting correctly 100 percent and 95 percent, respectively, while a Republican member of the committee, Paul Fannin of Arizona, never voted right. The LHM concludes the report with news that Senator Harrison Williams stated that "he planned to turn the transcript of the hearings over to the Justice Department for study regarding alleged injustices to members of the United Farm Workers Organizing Committee."

The documents hide any role President Johnson may have had in the Rio Grande Valley strike. Perhaps nothing was hidden because Johnson did not care to wade into that labor strike. It was Governor John Connally on the frontline, not him. And, Governor Connally was not supportive of any dealings with Mexican Americans, including hosting the President's Cabinet hearings on Mexican Americans being proposed for the fall of 1968. In the memoirs of Lyndon B. Johnson, *The Vantage Point: Perspectives of the Presidency, 1963–1969,* there is no mention of any Mexican American leaders—not of Vicente Ximenes, his top aide, or Hector P. Garcia, his Texas operative, or Reynaldo Garza, the first federal judge, or Raymond Telles, the first ambassador—appointments made by Kennedy but recommended by Johnson.[38]

There is absolutely no mention of the slightest interest on the part of the White House in Mexican Americans found in any document until a letter dated July 7, 1967, from S. B. Donahoe to Mr. DeLoach with copies to

Rosen and Sullivan, higher-ups in the FBI hierarchy. Apparently, Marvin Watson, White House special assistant to the president, had Mildred Stegall call Hoover's FBI about the Rio Grande situation. It seems that Watson was "under the impression that the FBI has investigated and prepared a report on a series of incidents involving farm workers in Rio Grande City, Texas." Donahoe told her he "had no recollection of any overall investigation of this situation but that I would check, and we would send over a memorandum." Donahoe then wants "ACTION" and writes: "The General Investigative Division should prepare a concise, factual memorandum reviewing the background of this situation in Rio Grande City, indicating the extent and nature of our investigative activity in connection with the situation...This should be expedited." Rosen then sent a memorandum to DeLoach dated July 10, 1967, with a draft copy of the letter to Mrs. Mildred Stegall for approval. The official letter from the FBI "BY LIAISON" on July 11 was hand-delivered to Mrs. Stegall, and was accompanied by the promised report in memorandum form dated July 10. In the letter, however, the FBI person signing the letter (redacted) states, "While no active investigation has been requested by the Department of Justice in connection with the strike situation under the Anti-Racketeering Statute, the Department and other agencies have been kept apprised of information of interest to them on a current basis relative to developments obtained by this Bureau from sources and news media." Then, some revealing information follows: "This Bureau has conducted several civil rights investigations based on allegations of mistreatment as well as other deprivations of civil rights allegedly suffered by striking farm workers at the hands of law enforcement officers. The results of such investigations have been furnished to the Civil Rights Division of the Department of Justice. The Attorney General has not been provided a copy of this communication." No such investigations have ever been conducted by the FBI, much less reports of such disclosed in this file, released or declassified. The FBI always closed each communication from the field with the disclaimer that the situation was a "labor dispute"; later it added "with deep seated political implications" to the language. The official memorandum to Mrs. Stegall begins with background information taken from the Cesar Chavez file (#100-444762-72) and makes the assertion that "while the union was not Communist controlled, Communist Party members or sympathizers had furnished support to certain activities concerning the strike against grape growers in California." It continued with information on Eugene Nelson as the principal organizer in the RGV, assisted by an Austin-based resident, Charles McKinley Smith, and the long march from Rio Grande City to Austin, Texas, by "about one-hundred members of the National Farm Workers Association" that reached the capitol on Labor Day, September 6, 1966; the purpose was "to protest low wages paid to migrant farm workers." The prevailing wage was $0.50 an hour and no benefits of any kind. Nelson and a group of strikers, he wrote, "proceeded to the center of the International Bridge spanning the Rio Grande River between Roma, Texas and Ciudad Miguel Aleman, Mexico, where they stopped vehicles carrying farm laborers into the United States thus blocking traffic," for which they were arrested. More arrests are explained in the memorandum. Interestingly, the letter concludes with: "A number of civil rights inquiries have been conducted based on complaints of alleged mistreatment and denial of civil rights by law enforcement officials in connection with the strike situation in the Rio Grande City, Texas area. The results of these investigations are summarized hereunder." There were no summaries either attached to this letter or disclosed, released, or declassified (to my knowledge) corroborating that these investigations ever took place. The content of their findings and conclusions remains elusive.

Mrs. Stegall telephonically thanked someone at FBI HQ for the report the morning of September 12, and Donahoe quickly sent a memorandum to DeLoach. Curiously, the single item alleged of importance and interest to Marvin Watson, who was reviewing the report, was the mention of "Charles M. Smith" of Austin. Donahoe wrote, "Mrs. Stegall advised that Mr. Watson had requested that the Bureau furnish him additional data as to the background of Smith, his participation in subversive activities and the extent of his participation in the situation at Rio Grande City." It seems that Donahoe on his own initiative had already begun the check on Smith; he wrote at the bottom of the memorandum, "ACTION: The Domestic Intelligence Division is preparing appropriate data." Nothing more is contained in the released and declassified files concerning Smith or further White House interest in the matter. The shift of FBI focus on the UFWOC moves to other parts of the country. First, Chicago.

The SAC, Chicago notified Hoover via teletype on August 10, 1967, that six people were passing out leaflets in the vicinity of the Federal Building in downtown Chicago during the late afternoon. A copy of the wording of the leaflet was sent to Hoover. The leaflet contained information, according to the SAC, to the effect that the public should write to "Secretary of Labor Wirtz or Attorney General Clark protesting attempt by California growers to break farm workers union through use of Mexican nationals, aliens with work permits. Area remained peaceful, no incidents. USA, Military, Secret Service, advised. LHM follows." No such memorandum was released or declassified in the Chavez files. Then, SAC, Los Angeles chimed in on the same day as Chicago in his 3:35 p.m. URGENT teletype to Hoover. Earlier that morning the SAC reported "about one hundred fifty union members picketed front entrance of Federal Building, Bakersfield, Calif, carrying signs re current strike at FXXX [crossed out] Giumarra Farms, Inc., Edison, Calif." The rest of the message is entirely redacted as well as the next page, concluding with "picketing was orderly and no incidents. Local news coverage afforded picketing. Airtel LHM follows." The LHM is heavily redacted with only a partial sentence at its end which reads, "[REDACTED] Special Agent, 115th Military Intelligence Group, Bakersfield, is aware of this matter." The matter will remain a mystery. Another LHM dated August 11 followed. In this communication, the SAC, Los Angeles went into detail about the picketing at the Federal Building in Bakersfield. It began at approximately 9:20 a.m. and ended at 10:45 a.m. with Chávez leading the activity. The local police were alerted and arrived, "but there were no incidents in connection with the picketing." Apparently, as the SAC's LHM reported, "Approximately one week ago, UFWOC went on strike at Giumarra Farms, Inc. of Edison, California, and currently maintain picket lines at this location, although a recent local court injunction has limited the number of participants in the picket line at any given time." The next page of the LHM was entirely withheld. The third page is heavily redacted, mostly citing a "b (7) c" exemption, and closes as did the prior LHM: "[REDACTED] 115th Military Intelligence Group, Bakersfield, is aware of this matter." What possibly could be of military interest to this Intelligence Group is not evident to me. Unless the only purpose is to justify military involvement with civilian surveillance, there is no reason for this insertion.

Back in Rio Grande City, an Airtel arrived at FBI HQ dated August 15, 1967, from San Antonio, FBI with an LHM citing the *Valley Evening Monitor* of the previous day on the goings-on at the Political Association of Spanish Speaking Organizations (PASO) state convention held in Austin on August 13. PASO, it seems, passed a resolution opposing a fourth term for John Connally as governor and referring to the Texas Rangers as "strike breaking thugs." "The Rangers have shown they lack the necessary intelligence required to deal with human beings," it stated. If, as PASO's resolution asserts, Rangers lacked intelligence, the FBI's SAC in San Antonio was not far behind in lacking intelligence as to what is relevant and what is yellow journalism. The SAC reported in an Airtel and LHM dated August 29 that Magdaleno Dimas was arrested in Torreon, Coahuila, Mexico, for possession of marijuana along with another man, Oracio [*sic*] Carrillo of Corpus Christi, Texas. The *Valley Morning Star* carried the story on its front page. Gilbert Padilla is quoted as saying this was a personal problem and not a union matter, unless the arrest was based on a setup or drugs planted on the men.

The Labor Day approaching in 1968 would be the first anniversary of the UFWOC march to Austin from the RGV, and so reports the SAC, San Antonio in his Airtel and LHM on the 1st of September. Erasmo Andrade, state chairman of the Valley Farm Workers State Assistance Committee (VFWSAC), led the anniversary rally and symbolic march from New Braunfels to Austin. Only 150 persons attended the rally and twelve marched, the report stated, as did the accompanying 12:06 p.m. URGENT teletype to Hoover from San Antonio FBI. Quoting an unidentified source, probably newspaper, the SAC, San Antonio provided information indicating dissension in the ranks of the VFWSAC led by Andrade. The promised participation by organizations did not materialize, nor by scheduled speakers, prompting some to criticize these people for not showing up. Allegedly, Andrade, Rev. Novarro, and Rev. Sherill Smith made unfavorable remarks about those who did not attend. The LHM noted that New Braunfels Mayor Elliot Knox welcomed the group to the city and that other influential people were present: "Pete Tijerina,

Tom Cahill, Laverne Redwine, and Joe Guerra, Jr., vice-chairman of the Bexar County Republican Party." The day after Labor Day, September 5, the SAC, San Antonio sent another Airtel with LHM by registered mail. This report, which recounts the prior information about dissent and criticism, is amended to include another speaker, Reies Lopez Tijerina from New Mexico. The news came to his attention from the *Austin American* newspaper that Tijerina and his brother, Cristobal, had "stopped in Austin while on route home from Chicago where they were delegates to the Conference for New Politics." The numbers for the march were upped from fourteen to fifty arriving at Austin, "and that more than two hundred persons walked the last few blocks down Congress Avenue in downtown Austin to the Capital [*sic*] on Monday." This LHM was circulated to all area military intelligence units.

Dissension in the ranks of the UFWOC also apparently surfaced in connection with the prior notice of arrest for Magdaleno Dimas and Horacio Carrillo. The LHM accompanying the Airtel dated September 8, 1967, reported that the union had voted to expel the two from their membership. Moreover, the article from the *Valley Morning Star* providing the information stated that Dimas had pled guilty and cleared Carrillo of any involvement. Carrillo was being deported as an undesirable back to Mexico. The dissension continued, spreading to the Assistance Committee, the VFWSAC. In a new Airtel dated September 14, the SAC, San Antonio, reading from the *San Antonio Light*'s front page, quoted the material in his LHM. "The Valley Farm Workers State Assistance Committee ... has kicked President Erasmo Andrade, San Antonio, out of office, it was announced today ... because of the 'fiasco' Labor Day march and the invitation by Andrade to Reies Lopez Tijerina (RLT) of New Mexico to appear." Tijerina was known for his courthouse raid in Tierra Amarilla, Rio Arriba County, New Mexico, to arrest via citizen's power a district judge and district attorney for not protecting land-grant claimants in that area.[39] The FBI has an extensive file on RLT, which has been released to him with exemptions.[40]

The SAC, Los Angeles transferred the file on UFWOC #100-67440 to the new FBI office opened in Sacramento as reported on September 18, 1967, to the Director, FBI. The Sacramento file was under #100-197 while the Bureau file remained #100-444762.

In San Antonio, the FBI office received a telephone call from (redacted source) that the president would be coming to town to speak to a National Legislative Conference of state lawmakers the evening of September 29. "A confidential source who has furnished reliable information in the past, today, advised a group of Mexican-Americans who are interested in raising the standard of living of all Mexican-Americans including the farm workers in the Rio Grande Valley, plan to picket the conference at seven p.m. today." The presidential staff and Secret Service were alerted, as were the local police departments from Austin to San Antonio. Later that night in 8:48 p.m. URGENT teletype to Hoover (but attention DeLoach), the SAC, San Antonio informed on the demonstrators outside La Villita Assembly Hall in downtown San Antonio where the president was to speak. The Mexican American group were some "ten or fifteen . . . across the street . . . carrying such signs as 'Viva La Huelga Marcha,'" and the other group were "ten peace marchers." They were "carrying such signs as 'San Antonio Committee to Stop War in Vietnam.'" Apparently, the SAC, San Antonio knew his Communists in San Antonio because he identified them as being among the peace group. The names were redacted. Later still in a 9:44 p.m. URGENT teletype, the SAC to Director, FBI (but "Attention: Assistant to the Director De Loach") gave precise details as to the protestors at President Johnson's appearance in San Antonio: "ten persons in Mexican-American demonstration and fifteen persons in peace demonstration." When Johnson left the convention by car, the peace demonstrators shouted, "End the War." The Mexican American demonstrators shouted, "Box Thirteen," in reference to massive voter fraud in Duval County, Texas, during "President Johnson's early congressional election." The LHM that followed these teletypes indicated that the information he reported came not only from the local newspaper but also from an informant "SA-T-2 (9/29/67)" who provided information on the statewide peace group. An older informant "SA-T-4 (6/11/59)" provided more information, but it is entirely redacted without claiming an exemption from disclosure, noted usually on the right margin. Immediately above the informant-redacted information is this standalone entry: "ELIZBETH LYTLE," with no other words. More entries are made in similar fashion without redaction for *National Guardian*, *The Worker*, and SACWIV.

"SA-T-3 (9/29/67) can substantiate in part information furnished above by SA-T-2." In similar fashion as the criticism leveled at the no-shows at the farm-worker support group march and rally in Austin the previous Labor Day, the peace group also had its critics. The informant SA-T-5 (6/29/67) provided information on which persons were not part of the peace group but in close proximity of the demonstration. On page 6 and into the end on page 7 of this LHM is an entry with heavy redaction for most of the page, but apparently the source named the principal organizer and how she was "upset due to the fact that she had called many people to participate in the peace demonstration and these people indicated that they would. However, many of the people she called did not show up." The heavy redaction follows as if to imply that the actual names of the no-shows were provided to the informant by "she," the organizer. There are two additional pages, with the heading "APPENDIX," with information dating to the beginning of the year, January 26, 1967. It simply reports that a name change occurred then to San Antonio Committee to End the War in Vietnam. The prior name was not provided in this LHM page, but the fact that on May 29, 1966, at the convention of the Communist Party of Texas, John Stanford was elected chairman. He was also elected a member of the National Committee, CPUSA, on June 26, 1966.

The LBJ appearance in San Antonio had the local authorities and Secret Service present "throughout the demonstration and cognizant of activities." The SAC, San Antonio had made sure they were in the loop, with constant copies being sent to them and other military intelligence units, according to his Airtel dated October 2, 1967. This Airtel does contain revealing information about FBI communications with the White House. In this document, the names of the San Antonio informants, T-1, 2, 3, 4, 5, 6, and 7, were released to Jim Jones, presidential assistant, and Marie Sechmer, the president's secretary at the LBJ ranch. Airtel dated October 4, 1967, indicated that San Antonio FBI had photographed the demonstrators and sent twenty-five negatives to the FBI photo laboratory in D.C. and wanted six copies in print form sent back along with the negatives. The Director complied on October 11 and sent them back. The photos, the SAC noted, should be in the San Antonio local FBI file under #105-3237-1A3.

White House Vetted Chávez Again

Just after the Labor Day march and rally in Austin, and before LBJ made his way to La Villita in San Antonio to face a tiny number of demonstrators, he asked his White House staffer Mildred Stegall to obtain from the FBI a full field investigation on Chávez.[41] LBJ was considering him for a White House staff position. Hoover must have been livid. He begins the vetting process by Airtel dated September 15, 1966, to SACs in D.C. and Los Angeles; the next day in another Airtel he adds SACs in San Francisco and Denver. In this subsequent message, he provides information taken from FBI files by numbers and Airtels from these SACs that show "Communist Infiltration," "Communist Party, USA," "IS-C" and specifically instructs the DC Field Office to interview Congressman Harlan Hagen and his administrative assistant, George Baker. Hoover also wanted them to include in their reports "interviews with sources who have in the past furnished pertinent information concerning Chavez and contact security informants" (p.2). One can only imagine the mindset of the various SACs in the field about preparing a report on Chávez without including what the Director was providing them.

On September 17, 1966, SAC, Los Angeles to Director, FBI changes name of César Chávez to include Estrada as a middle name and provides a lengthy physical description of Chávez, which includes his arrest records. Chávez's wife is incorrectly identified as 'HELEN CHAVEZ nee SABELA," and the information on relatives including "cousin, MANUEL GONZALEZ CHAVEZ, FBI No. 1346428, who reportedly was released on parole from the penitentiary to work in the NFWA office" (p.3). The Director, FBI in Airtel to SACs in San Diego and Los Angeles dated September 19, 1966, sends copies of an "FBI arrest record # 428 846F which may pertain to captioned individual [Chávez]." This file number and another noted as "CII no. 2904329" were included in the September 17th Airtel from Los Angeles. SAC, Los Angeles responds to the Director, FBI on September 20, 1966, by teletype with repeat of all relatives' names and addresses, plus those of close associates, mostly ministers: Rev. Chris Hartmire, Rev. David Havens, Bishop Donohoe, Father McCullough, Father Keith Kenny, Dick Norberg, William Becker in the office of Governor Brown, and Bill Kircher of the AFL-CIO.

The FBI agents out of the Los Angeles office went to Delano to interview "personnel at National Farm Workers Association" on September 21, 1966, and by teletype to Director at 11:04 a.m. URGENT reported that Chávez himself had stated to them, "HE DID NOT KNOW OF ANY TENTATIVE AP-POINTMENT AND WOULD NOT ACCEPT ONE IF IT TOOK HIM AWAY FROM HIS PRESENT WORK AS HE IS DEDICATED TO WHAT HE IS DOING IN THE FIELD OF FARM LABOR ORGANIZATION. HE CONTINUED HE DID NOT INTEND TO LEAVE HIS WORK IN DELANO TO ACCEPT ANY APPOINTMENT OR ANY TYPE OF WORK OUTSIDE THE DELANO AREA." The next day Hoover wrote to Marvin Watson at the White House, who was special assistant to the president, and repeated the message: Chávez is not interested, nor will he accept such a job if it takes him out of Delano. But, he added, "In absence of advice to the contrary, investigation of Mr. Chavez is being continued. The Attorney General has not been provided a copy of this communication."

By September 26, 1966, the urgent request to vet Chávez was put "in abeyance pending further advice. Bureau requested to advise Milwaukee upon restitution of investigation."[42] On this same day, SAC, Chicago reported to SAC, Milwaukee that they interviewed Saul Alinsky of the Industrial Areas Foundation (IAF) while he attended a Johnson Foundation meeting about his former employee, Chávez, who worked for IAF from late 1954 to mid-1958. The FBI continued the investigation into Chávez by contacting Josephine Duveneck with the American Friends Service Committee, who had known Chávez since 1952, plus Ronald Haughton, who was appointed by Governor Brown to arbitrate Chávez's ballot issues for union representation.[43]

By the time the vetting process was winding down, given Chávez's refusal to accept any White House position, the California U.S. senators and several U.S. representatives received a "scathing telegram protesting the consideration of Chávez for Federal appointment from Kern County, Board of Supervisors, David Fairbairn." A copy of an article featuring this news from the *Washington Post* of September 26, 1966, was attached.[44] Mrs. Mildred Stegall from the White House stopped asking for an investigation on Chávez on September 27, 1966.

Hurricane Beulah Kills the Melon Strike

The SAC, San Antonio correctly assumed not much could happen in the RGV as a result of Hurricane Beulah and placed "this matter in a pending inactive status for three months." Apparently, his Airtel of November 29, 1967, reported to the Director "little agricultural activity in that region. Since almost all crops were destroyed by the storm, the seasonal influx of farm workers has not occurred and, therefore, no strike activity has been initiated at Rio Grande City." Then he adds a last, short paragraph: "The next scheduled agricultural season is the melon crop June 1968."

The last Airtel in these files dated December 22, 1967, has again amended the FBI disclaimer usually accompanying each message at bottom to read this time: "Inasmuch as this matter represents a continuing labor-political-religious dispute, it is being followed through established sources and news media."

When did the farm worker strike and/or march become a religious dispute? Which persons or groups made up the "religious"? Perhaps, the intelligent FBI agents upon seeing priests and nuns and other ministers picketing and marching along with the poverty-stricken farm workers thought it had become a religious issue as well: to be Christian is to be on the side of cash-poor working people. The LHM that followed informed the FBI HQ that the other victim of Texas Ranger Capt. A. Y. Allee's wrath and violence, Benito Rodriguez, had been arrested in the downtown streets of San Antonio on December 20. They confiscated four pounds of marijuana "which he allegedly brought illegally into the United States." And, it reminded the Director, FBI in closing that Magdaleno Dimas was convicted earlier in Mexico for possession of marijuana and expelled from the union; later his body was found in Mexico beaten to death. The crime remains unsolved to this day.

Back on the Picket Line and in Court

Chávez began to travel in the Southwest with a first stop in Denver on June 15, 1966. He participated with fellow Chicano leader Rudolph "Corky" Gonzales in picketing the local newspaper and promoting a petition to stop the war in Vietnam. Chávez was ambivalent about the war; he felt most union members supported the war effort. His position on the war put him in conflict with several of the union leaders and the staff of *El Malcriado*, which ultimately was irreparable.[45] Several months later, FBI agent Joseph C. Learned of the Denver office sent a lengthy report to Washington FBI dated September 28, 1966, on the activities of Chávez and Gonzales along with newspaper clippings reporting on the same. By that time Chávez was challenging the DiGiorgio Corporation in Borrego Springs, California.

The Texas Union Makes a Comeback in 1968

Events reported via the FBI files in late May 1968 took a different and more dangerous turn involving threats against Chávez and Dolores Huerta, together with reports of harm to union members. The FBI remained focused on happenings in the Rio Grande Valley of Texas during the early part of 1968. An FBI informant provided information to the San Antonio office on March 12, 1968, regarding the activities of "Reverend Edgar Allen Krueger, Kathy Baker, and Froben Lozada," who apparently had opened an office for the Texas Council of Churches in an old hotel in Donna, Texas. The activities reported by the San Antonio FBI office to undisclosed recipients the next day were that "they occasionally distribute free groceries to needy Mexican- American families and disseminate VISTA literature." The informant, however, reported on the recruitment of high school students and group discussions. "In the meetings, the group discusses general abuse and discrimination of the Mexican-American element by 'Anglo'-Americans and by the federal government." The informant was unable to provide more detailed information because "other local high school students whom he knows to be members will not discuss the organization in any way and

[REDACTED] has provided the above information confidentially and reluctantly." The redacted informant advised "that the organization is being divided into 'councils' of 16 members each."

Volunteers in Service to America (VISTA), a Domestic Peace Corps

On April 30, the San Antonio FBI office reported that the persons of interest identified in the earlier notice had moved their operation to San Juan, Texas. The FBI had recruited more informants, given the line space redacted in the report and plural reference to "Contacts with the above individuals developed the following information . . ." The reference to "VISTA" was clarified to mean "VISTA Minority Mobilization Project for Texas," but referred to as a "VISTA organization" rather than a federally funded national project with the "Southwest Regional Office of VISTA, Manager, Bill Hale, San Antonio, Texas." The report identified the RGV VISTA office in Donna as headed by "Reverend Krueger, a resident of Pharr, Texas, who received much help from Froben Lozada, a Donna, Texas, resident." The report continued with "The organization's avowed objective is to establish chapters similar to the Donna, Texas, chapter at Pharr, Rio Grande City, Bluetown, Gainesville, Santa Rosa, San Benito, Elsa, Santa Maria, Laredo, Santa Cruz, Laferia [sic] and Harlingen, Texas." Identified as the president of the Donna chapter was "Pablo Diaz, age 50"; "Brigida Castillo, female, 40 years of age" as the vice president; "Jose Escamilla" as the second vice president; and "Treasurer is Joe De la Rosa." These officers and others traveled to "Bartow, Tallahassee, Florida, and another unknown city in Broward County, Florida, to attend meetings." They returned "home" March 29, 1968. Supposedly, the travel and meetings in Florida were to learn about a teacher strike that occurred there and inform others of the farm worker strike in Rio Grande City. The informants also reported that "the speakers in Florida, identities unknown, allegedly stated they would come to San Antonio and Austin, Texas, next year to assist in teacher strikes there." Also of interest to the informants and FBI office reporting was "Susan Lau, an 'Anglo,' described as a white female American, age 20, reddish-blond long hair, 5'5" tall and always wearing a necklace of shells" and "very active in the local group as is (First Name Unknown)" (Five line spaces redacted almost entirely). Another Anglo female of interest mentioned by Lozada and Lau was "Cathy [*sic*] Baker" a "San Antonio girl who helps the group but neither [NAME REDACTED] nor [NAME REDACTED] has met her or seen her at a meeting." The report also indicates that "Members of the group, including Froben Lozada and Reverend Krueger, attended 'La Raza Unita' [*sic*] meeting in Laredo, Texas on March 24, 1968, to hear Senator Edward Kennedy speak."[46]

This FBI report closes with information that a photograph of a speaker during the showing of a film, *Anarchy, U.S.A.,* to a civics class at Donna High School was obtained and was apparently being forwarded to Washington FBI laboratory for identification; he was identified as "one of the Negro speakers his group heard during one of the above-described meetings in Florida." From this reference, it appears that one of the FBI informants was an infiltrator within the Donna group of officers or members to be able to physically identify the speaker at both locations. In a subsequent report dated May 15, 1968, the San Antonio FBI reports the specific address for the office as "103 West Fifth St." with telephone number "ST 7-5421." The FBI in this report changed the name of the VISTA "organization" to "Valley Community Service" and discusses dissension in the ranks of the project. Reportedly, one of the infiltrators/informants was "discontinuing his association with the Donna, Texas chapter of the Valley Community Service"; "Jose de la Rosa resigned his position as Treasurer"; and "Lozada stated he was leaving Texas because freedom of speech no longer exists in the state and intends to go to California where an individual can honestly express himself."

Names of other clergy from various denominations and locations are listed in the report, including two reverends who attended Martin Luther King's funeral in Atlanta, Georgia. The FBI clearly had an interest in Froben Lozada, because this report advised that he had "departed Donna, Texas, on May 6, 1968 on route to the San Francisco, California [LINES REDACTED]," and that the female informant/infiltrator reported "that the Valley Community Service was sending representatives to the Poor People's March on Washington, D.C., and has issued a call for volunteer vehicles and individuals. He emphasized to *her* [emphasis mine] that the struggle of the Negro is the struggle of the Mexican and predicted that both would eventually be victorious."

If Hoover and his top officials at the FBI did not already know about Rev. Krueger and his wife, Ninfa, from name checks of their affiliation with the VISTA Minority Mobilization Program or Texas Council of Churches, a newspaper article clipped by the San Antonio, FBI office was sent to him and to undisclosed recipients on May 29th. The terribly biased article, inappropriately headlined "For Enforcing Law in Valley Last Summer TCC May Drop Suit against Rangers," twisted the facts. The Texas Rangers unleashed gross violence against union members, supporters, and observers—perhaps even murdered Magdaleno Dimas, who was brutally beaten along with Benito Rodriguez. UAW organizer Francisco "Pancho Medrano," whose crime was to photograph Ranger violence, and Kathy Baker for being the domestic partner of Rodriguez, among others, filed suit against the Rangers for such brutality against them. Krueger and wife, while observing the picketing by the farm-worker union members, were also attacked by the Rangers. They sued. The article, however, states,

> The Texas Rangers were instrumental last summer in keeping law and order in the Valley, from Starr County on down, when demonstrators tried to stop the Missouri-Pacific trains hauling melons out of the area in which union and church outsiders from California, San Antonio and other points were trying to organize farm workers who didn't want to organize.[47]

Picketing Ramsey Clark, U.S. Attorney General

By late May 1968 Hoover learned that Frank Byer, representing Chávez, had announced they were going to picket the attorney general when he visited San Francisco to speak to the National Conference of Social Workers on the 29th. The information was shared: "Secret Service and appropriate intelligence agencies being advised." The purpose of the protest was over "a recent ruling regarding immigrant farm workers." Director Hoover promptly requested a name check on Frank Byer. "Based on information furnished by San Francisco, Los Angeles indices are negative on FRANK BYER." In plain language, no files on him were found by these two FBI officers other than the one now started by the FBI themselves, given the policy of checking into every name supplied to them. The only provocative item in this exchange of reports on the picketing of the U.S. attorney general and name check on Byers is the classification of subject matter to RACIAL MATTERS. This designation was utilized by Hoover for the surveillance of African Americans historically.[48]

The SAC, Chicago did find files on many organizations and forwarded this voluminous number of files, five each to the Bureau and SACs in Los Angeles, New York, San Francisco, four to Boston, and eight to Chicago. These files were identified by FBI file number and organization as Congress of Racial Equality, Students for a Democratic Society, American Friends Service Committee, Teamster Union, United Packing House Food and Allied Workers of America, plus César Chávez. The voluminous Chicago packet of files in addition to those listed above also contained three more, which were redacted.[49]

A subsequent May 30 teletype informed the Director that the picketing of the AG was peaceful other than "a power bullhorn interrupted speech with questions and recited pledge not to buy grapes. Majority of audience booed interruptions," and closed the report with the good news, or perhaps disappointing news, that "no incidents or arrests took place." And, by another Airtel message the next day, Hoover was informed that the AG was "met at SF International airport by SAC Charles W. Bates and delivered to Hilton Hotel San Francisco without incident. U.S. Attorney General proceeded back to Washington, D.C. after speech." This message is also coded (1-157-245) (Racial Matters, San Francisco Division) with copy to "Bishop," who was T. E. Bishop in charge of the FBI's Criminal Records Division. Bishop's primary job for Hoover, which continued into Patrick Gray's tenure as Director, was to investigate and gather information on members of Congress and political candidates to ascertain if they were friendly or hostile to the FBI.

Protests in Laredo, Texas

The League of United Latin American Citizens (LULAC) invited Governor John Connally to their state convention. Outside the convention hall were hundreds of anti-Connally protesters, over his treatment of farm workers and the situation in Starr County, Texas. Among those speaking to the pro-testers at their rally was César Chávez and Roy Reuther of the UAW.[50]

In preparation for the November presidential election, Johnson ap-pointed Vicente Ximenes to the Equal Employment Opportunity Commis-sion, with plans for him to head a Cabinet-level committee called Inter-Agency Committee on Mexican American Affairs from the White House. At this swearing-in ceremony on June 9, a nine-page press release was circu-lated that listed not only administration accomplishments but also future endeavors.[51] Among these was the equivalent of a White House conference long sought by Mexican Americans, but to be held in El Paso, October 26-28, 1967. Chávez, along with all the leaders of the emerging Chicano Movement, declined to attend and speak at this conference. Instead they organized with Ernesto Galarza to lead a rump conference termed La Raza Unida.[52]

The César Chávez and Robert Kennedy Connection

While César worked for the CSO in California during late November 1959, he met Robert Kennedy in Los Angeles for the first time and discussed voter registration among Mexican Americans in California. That was the work César had been doing for some years in the state.[53] Obviously, this was a move on the part of Robert to lay the ground for a presidential run by his brother John in 1960. The work in California regarding voter registration was made easier in that, unlike in Texas, registration was not subject to a poll tax. The poll tax was a means to disenfranchise the poor, who did not have $1.75 in extra pocket change to pay for the privilege of registering to vote. Moreover, California was a two-party state while Texas was a one-party dictatorship dominated by conservative Democrats since Reconstruction after the Civil War. And, Governor John Connally, a stalwart for Johnson, was presumed to be the leader of Johnson's presidential ambitions that year. Robert Kennedy asked César Chávez to pledge to John Kennedy for President. The Democratic National Convention was to be in Los Angeles that following year. Chávez agreed and worked within CSO to conduct the voter registration drives, and not with the official Kennedy campaign called Viva Kennedy! Kennedy barely carried Texas based on the Viva Kennedy! efforts led by Albert A. Peña Jr., Bexar County commissioner, and the Political Association of Spanish Speaking Organizations (PASO). And, Chávez failed to deliver California despite having registered about 140,000 Mexican American voters, 85 percent of whom voted for Kennedy.[54] Six years later, as U.S. senator, Robert Kennedy renewed his contact with Chávez at the hearings of the Senate Subcommittee on Migratory Labor and made a personal commitment to stand with farm workers from then on, including his presidential race in 1968. Kennedy joined the picket line at a DiGiorgio Fruit Corporation ranch after the hearings and vehemently defended Chávez as being a labor organizer not a Communist. Kennedy helped organize a fundraiser the following year in Marin County, California, to begin Chávez's farm worker clinic. Later, Robert or his wife Ethel would be at Chávez's side during his fasts to protest violence against farm workers.[55]

CHAPTER 4

The Arizona Battlefield, 1969–1972

GUSTAVO GUTIERREZ, CHÁVEZ'S man in Arizona, wrote a three-page letter to U.S. Attorney Richard K. Burke dated July 15, 1969, requesting an investigation into the actions and non-actions of the Maricopa County Sheriff's Department.[1] He was asking for help. He listed nine specific instances of misconduct that on their face also seem illegal. For example, the first item describes how "A Deputy Sheriff stood idly while a ranch foreman 'roughed up' a priest" (p.1). Items 4 and 5 address physical surveillance, warrantless stops, and seizures by the deputies (p.2). Items 2, 3, 6, 7, and 8 clearly describe actions by the deputies contrary to Arizona law about dismissing employees who signed a union card, picketed, and made conversation with nonunion workers. In item 8, a deputy made up his own law as to distance between pickets and forced them to stand 20 feet apart, plus rebuffed protests by the pickets, stating they were not a union, therefore had no rights. Item 9 detailed a dangerous practice of assault with a vehicle by the sheriff's deputies. Two deputies would drive their cars into each side of the picket line pushing the pickets into a tight group. In so doing, some pickets had been physically moved out of formation by the vehicles driven by deputies (p.2).

Gutierrez stated that these "incidents comprise only a partial listing of the abusive acts of the Sheriff's Department." He urges a prompt investigation into these illegal and dangerous practices because "the harvest will be completed within a few weeks." He provides his address and telephone number to Burke and assures him, "We will cooperate fully in any investigation" (p.3). The letter from Gutierrez has two more pages, numbered 6, 7, and 8, which are copies of articles from the *Arizona Republic* (May 11 and 12, 1969) and the *Phoenix Gazette* (April 6, 1969). The first from the *Arizona Republic* is an editorial against the strike and unionization of farm workers. It is doubtful that Gutierrez would send such a document as part of his letter. The other two articles are descriptive of activities by the pickets.

Burke's assistant U.S. attorney, Philip S. Malinsky, wrote to John P. Mull, the SAC in Phoenix, on July 18 asking him to interview Gutierrez and report back with specifics because "there may be a possible violation of 18 U.S.C. 242 or other federal law." This U.S. Code reference is for prosecution for deprivation of rights under color of law—such as the alleged actions by the sheriff's deputies. The SAC, Phoenix does not reply to Malinsky; instead he Airtels Hoover a week later on July 24 informing him of the letter and stating, "In the absence of a clear-cut violation of the civil rights statutes, as set forth in a three-page letter from GUSTAVO GUTIERREZ, no interview with the latter individual will be conducted pending Bureau instructions." The LHM accompanying the Airtel above contained copies of the letters sent between Gutierrez and Malinsky, plus "Pertinent newspaper clippings from the local press are also attached." The SAC then sent the articles of his choice and editorial on the matter at hand. The Assistant Attorney General of the Civil Rights Division of the DOJ received a memorandum with a copy of the SAC, Phoenix letter from Hoover dated July 29, 1969. Box B on the form was marked "xxx" and other illegible markings. This box is for informing the recipient that "The investigation is continuing, and you will be furnished copies of reports as they are received." At the bottom of the memorandum a note is entered informing the unnamed recipient at DOJ that "Pursuant to discussion between Mr. Charles W. Quaintance and SA [REDACTED] on 7-28-69, Gustavo Gutierrez, Arizona Representative, United Farm Workers Organizing Committee, will be interviewed for specific details." Hoover then notified by Airtel dated July 29, 1969, the SAC, Phoenix with this message: "In view of the allegations set forth in the letter from Gustavo Gutierrez . . . you should interview Gutierrez for specific details regarding any civil rights violations. Advise him that the interview is being conducted at the specific request of Assistant Attorney General Jerris Leonard of the Civil Rights Division." And, Hoover wanted a quick turnaround on this matter: "Handle immediately and suLHM within five days of receipt of this airtel." The SAC, Phoenix by Airtel dated August 1st notified the Director, FBI that Gutierrez was in California "and will not return until 8/4/69. He will be interviewed on that date."

On that same 1st of August, the SAC, San Diego informed the Director, FBI that "a branch office of the UFWOC was publicly opened in Office 8 of the El Rey Hotel in Calexico, California" in mid-July. The first page of this Airtel is completely redacted, as are four paragraphs of about four to five lines each. At bottom of page 2 of this document is a request made to the Sacramento FBI office for "pertinent background information regarding UFWOC, Cesar Chavez and Manuel Chavez, plus a photograph of Manuel Chavez, be expeditiously furnished for the use of San Diego." The Oklahoma FBI office was also asked to provide "registration data for Oklahoma plate XU 2099," and to search "indices for information regarding owner."

On August 5, the SAC, Phoenix reported to the Director, FBI with LHM with copy to the Phoenix U.S. Attorney about the interview with Gustavo Gutierrez conducted at his home in Tempe that same day. First, Gutierrez was made to sign a statement attached with two SAs as witnesses. Second, the LHM contains eight pages of notes regarding twenty-four incidents, each identified by a name at top implying that is the person with relevant knowledge of the facts as stated to the SAs conducting the interview with Gutierrez. The chain of information is troublesome for me as a lawyer regarding how the information was purportedly obtained by the FBI. The

SAC writes the report based on two SAs that interviewed Gutierrez, who provided information on what twenty-plus odd individuals (some are witnesses to more than one incident) told him at some point in time. Particularly troubling is the second paragraph of the SAC's Airtel that sets the context and characterizes the LHM regarding the interview as follows: "Mr. GUTIERREZ commented parenthetically that his organizing committee had the services of a legal committee of eight attorneys in the attached matter during the past ten days; that this 'legal committee' referred to the activities of the Maricopa County Sheriff's Office as subtle harassment, but not concretely within the meaning of the civil rights statutes." If this is correctly stated, why then would Gutierrez write the U.S. attorney if his own attorney committee opined it was "subtle harassment"?

Analyzing the twenty-four incidents cited, the names of victims and/or witnesses are provided to the FBI with specific alleged acts on the part of law enforcement officials acting under the color of law; dates and times are provided in some incidents, and names of those alleged to be the abusers are also provided. Reading about these incidents, it is obviously clear that these deputies are acting like the Texas Rangers did in breaking the melon strike by intimidation, arrests, assaults, bullying, vulgar language, and preventing the strikers from actual picketing and informing workers going into the fields about their strike. There is no further information provided in any disclosed FBI file as to the outcome of this investigation or the overall situation in Arizona.

SAC, Sacramento notified the Director, FBI; SAC, San Francisco; U.S. Attorney, Sacramento; and the U.S. Secret Service by Airtel with LHM on August 12 on a matter coded "Internal Security." "One copy has been designated for San Francisco because [NAME REDACTED] apparently is a student at the University of California, Berkeley, California." The national security matter was a protest by "sympathizers of United Farm Workers Organizing Committee" to be held two days later "outside the gate" of Mather Air Force Base near Sacramento, "and off the roadway so that there will be no traffic disruption and no possibility of any violation of statutes."

A Mass at Arlington National Cemetery

Another Airtel to the Director, FBI from his SAC downtown in Washington, DC, came in the next day with LHM with more "dangerous" information of national security interest, to be sure. The SACs in "Alexandria, Los Angeles, Sacramento, San Diego, San Francisco" plus the "AUSA, Secret Service, Military Intelligence agencies, MPD, WDC" received copies of the LHM from the Washington Field Office. The matter was that Chávez wanted to hold a two-hour commemoration at the Sylvan Theatre on September 7, 1969, then march across the Potomac to "hold a mass as close as possible to Senator Robert Kennedy's grave in Arlington National Cemetery, Arlington, Virginia." A spokesperson for Chávez, Mrs. Sylvia J. Laurenti had written to the National Capital Parks superintendent William R. Failor requesting a permit for the event. He in turn shared it with the FBI on August 11, prompting this Airtel and LHM to the Director and many others. "Mrs. Laurenti stated it is planned that Mrs. Ethel Kennedy would be the principal speaker 'with other nationally prominent people involved.'" On September 2, according to the LHM from Alexandria FBI, the Chávez group had sought the permit from the U.S. Army, "who had turned down the request." Supposedly to hold such an event at a gravesite, the applicant must include a "family member" as sponsor; "no indication on the application of any such sponsorship." Moreover, beginning September 2 and for three weeks thereafter, "the grave of JOHN F. KENNEDY would be blocked off to public access due to necessary construction and repairs at the site of his grave ... no one would be allowed within 30 feet of JOHN F. KENNEDY's grave." The Director, FBI notified via Airtel on the 14th of September all the SACs in the loop that the "Bureau's interest in this matter should be confined to determining if subversive organizations and individuals are attempting to subvert the legitimate purposes of this demonstration. In addition, the Bureau has the responsibility of disseminating any information developed regarding any potential violence which might evolve from this activity." The Chávez commemoration and Mass has now turned into a "demonstration" with "potential violence"; surely according to Hoover's mindset this qualified as subverting the "legitimate purposes of this demonstration." The SAC, Alexandria by Airtel with an LHM on September 2nd took the lead on the matter. He notified everyone in the prior loop and added to his list of LHM recipients: "116th MIG, OSI, and NISO" that his office "will afford appropriate coverage to the proposed ceremony at Arlington National Cemetery." With construction crews busy repairing the grave of RFK's brother John (their graves are adjacent to each other), the FBI offices engaged in a flurry of Airtels back and forth until September 15, 1969, when it was decided to close this matter since nothing the Director, FBI thought might happen had happened. For example, on the 3rd of September the SAC, San Francisco contacted four [NAMES REDACTED] of their sources and learned "they had not received any information concerning captioned matter," but assured the Director, FBI that "San Francisco will continue to remain alert for any information regarding captioned matter and will promptly notify the Bureau of pertinent developments." The SAC, Los Angeles on the 4th assures the Director, FBI that "Informants in the Los Angeles area were canvassed for any information concerning any delegation from Los Angeles area attending the captioned function, with negative results." And, as did San Francisco FBI, the Los Angeles SAC states, "The Los Angeles Office will continue to follow this matter and advise Bureau of any information indicating that a Los Angeles delegation will attend the Washington, D.C. program on 9/7/69." The Washington Field Office by teletype notified the Director, FBI and SAC, Alexandria that they learned from (redacted) that the commemoration plans had changed; now it was named the "Fourth Anniversary Pilgrimage" to Washington, D.C."; the new sponsors were "The United States Liturgical Conference" and the "Washington Lay Association," and the route was changed as well from the Mass at or near the Arlington National Cemetery to L'Enfant Plaza.

The eventful day arrived and the SAC, WFO notified the Director, FBI by teletype that "at two fifteen p.m. instant date a Special Agent of the FBI observed a group of approximately two to three hundred people assembled in the vicinity of the Sylvan Theatre, Washington Monument Grounds . . . At about three thirty p.m. instant date the group departed the above area and in an orderly fashion marched to the vicinity of L'Enfant Plaza, WDC where after several short prayers related to captioned matter the group dispersed by four forty five p.m. this date." And, the SAC of the Washington Field Office also assured the Director that Washington Field Office informants and sources, familiar with various phases of subversive and related activity in the WDC area, were contacted during September nineteen sixty nine were unable to furnish any information pertaining to the possible subverting of the legitimate purposes of this demonstration nor did they furnish any information relating to possible violence which might evolve from this affair."

The SAC, WFO provided the Director, FBI with the name of the SA performing the HUMINT and the names of his informants, as well as the names of the members of Congress who were "speaker[s] at this affair ... James G. O'Hara, Michigan and Don Edwards, California." To close this chapter of a threat to national security with a potential for violence by subversives that would subvert the legitimate purposes of this affair, the SAC, Alexandria sent an LHM dated September 15, 1969 to the Director, FBI. He writes, "In view of the events surrounding captioned activity having previously occurred and being held within the territory of Washington Field only, no further investigation being conducted in this matter by Alexandria." He copied all in the communications loop of his closing of the case. But not quite; the SAC, San Diego was late with his Airtel of the 15th to the Director, FBI in which he assured him, as all other SACs had done, that "Confidential sources, generally cognizant of Communist Party activities and racial matters at San Diego, California, advised during late August and early September, 1969, that no information has come to their attention regarding delegates from this area visiting Washington, D.C. to participate in a commemorative demonstration on 9/7/69 at the Sylvan Theatre or at the Arlington National Cemetery." I suppose this SAC did not read the last communication on this event informing all that the route had been changed to L'Enfant Plaza. The LA SAC, not to be outdone, sent yet another post-event LHM on the 22nd advising the Director, FBI that "Confidential sources and informants who are aware of Communist Party and racial activities in the Los Angeles, California area have advised that they know of no delegates from the Los Angeles area having visited captioned event in Washington, D.C." The Director must have been most pleased that his G-men were on this from the beginning and past the end; the Seat of Government was safe again. No Communists from the West Coast or subversives from across the land attended the event, and no Communists from the West Coast or subversives were reported after the fact as having been at the event. Chávez had to know how well he had played the FBI because he baited them with a repeat performance in late September 1969.

Chávez Goes for Seconds

The SAC, WFO again notifies via teletype dated September 25 the Director, FBI and SACs in San Diego and Los Angeles that Chávez is now going to hold a program at the Washington National Cathedral in the city the following Sunday, the 28th, at eight p.m. Then on Tuesday the 30th, Chávez is going to hold a 24-hour sleepover at the Church of the Reformation starting at 10 p.m. The SAC, WFO termed it a "Surprise-In" because those coming for the sleepover would be invited up at dawn to go to picket locations, which would be a surprise; hit-and-run pickets would have been a better term. This surprise picketing would be followed by a "big rally" at 212 E. Capitol Street in D.C. on October 1st. The SAC, WFO either had learned the Chávez tricks or had tired of Hoover's tautology on Chávez and "subversive Communists"; he notified the Director, FBI that "Washington Field Office will not cover, unless advised to the contrary by Bureau. RUC." The SAC, Los Angeles on September 26 sent an Airtel with LHM to the Director and three other SACs about news on Chávez. He is on the move, was the essential message. Apparently, the SAC, Los Angeles read the *Los Angeles Times* that very morning, which stated in its headline, "Chavez Begins 7-Week Tour of U.S." In the article, mention was made that he would go to forty cities; D.C. was not on the list. The SAC sent a copy of the article.

There is a huge gap in FBI documents released and declassified. The sequence of events in the transmission begins in early December 1969 and ends abruptly.

El Paso Visit

Whether Chávez, while on the forty-city national tour, stopped in El Paso or not cannot be determined from the declassified FBI records; but he and Helen did visit the city on December 2 according to the LHM sent by SAC, El Paso two days later to the Director, FBI. This LHM coded "Mexican American Militancy IS-Spanish American" was also sent to the local office of the Secret Service: "G-2 and 112th MI Group, Ft. Bliss, Texas, OSI, Biggs Field, Texas, and NISO, New Orleans, Louisiana"; all are military intelligence agencies. An FBI informant, "EP T-1," reported to his FBI handler that "about 500 people, most of whom were Mexican-Americans, gathered at Bowie High School on the south side of El Paso, Texas." The last page of these documents contains the caption "Mexican American Militancy." And, a character classification code provides names, perhaps of informants: "All sources (except any listed below) used in the referenced communication have furnished reliable information in the past." The names were not provided. The page is blank, without the usual black markings used for redaction of material in other documents and without any exemption claimed for denial of its release.[2]

Sometime after the meeting was underway, César Chávez "made an appearance and was granted permission to speak by Mayor de Wetter." The crowd went wild and "gave Chavez a tremendous ovation." Chávez "made no effort to propagandize his grape boycott." Helen, the informant must have told the FBI, reportedly said, "they could see the 'Chicano Movement' developing more and more wherever they went throughout the United States. Activist groups seem to be drawn to Cesar Chavez, have attempted to ride on his coattails, and then become more outspoken." The message from SAC, El Paso gets confusing in the remaining text because previously he wrote that the mayor of El Paso, Peter de Wetter, invited Chávez up to speak. Yet, he writes, "young Mexican-Americans connected with the Mexican-American Youth Association (MAYA) . . . took over the podium and called for Cesar Chavez to speak." And Chávez spoke, according to the LHM, about nonviolence and "that all that they had were their lives, and that there was no reason for violence taking place between people."

Chávez was jailed on December 4 in Monterey County on order of Superior Court Judge Gordon Campbell for refusing to obey Campbell's injunction against a boycott of Bud Antle Farm lettuce. The judge ordered Chávez to call off the national boycott of lettuce. The defiance of the court order cost Chávez twenty days in jail. The article containing this information was taken by the FBI from an open source, the *New York Times*, p.42. It also noted his jail release on December 23, 1970, "without bail pending the Supreme Court's hearing." While he was in jail, Chávez had important visitors. Among those visiting him were "Mrs. Ethel Kennedy, widow of Robert Kennedy," another open source document indicates, this one taken from the *San Francisco Chronicle* of December 8, 1970. This same article reports on two other significant developments in the lettuce boycott strategy. One, Harvard University was only going to serve Farm Workers Union lettuce; and two, union members erected a "shrine" to Chávez across the street from the Salinas, Monterey County jail where Chávez was kept and held all-night vigils. According to another open source document gathered by the FBI from the *San Francisco Examiner* of December 7, Mrs. Kennedy was escorted by Olympian decathlon star Rafer Johnson to the vigil and then into the Salinas jail.[3] She and Johnson were jeered at and "braved a barrage of catcalls and boos while in the jail facility." While she was at the vigil, anti-union grower protesters, numbering four hundred, sang songs such as "America, the Beautiful" and the most offensive Marine composition to persons of Mexican origin, "The Battle Hymn of the Republic."[4]

Back to Mexico

The shift occurs again in the declassified FBI documents on Chávez, internationally this time, to Mexico City. The SAC, Sacramento via memorandum dated October 15, 1971, to the Director, FBI enclosed seven copies of an LHM captioned "CESAR ESTRADA CHAVEZ" for dissemination purposes. A redacted source apparently provided information deemed important enough so "The Bureau is requested to forward seven copies of the LHM to Legat, Mexico City, for appropriate action." Additionally, at bottom of page is information of more entities being included in the loop to obtain the LHM on Chávez: "Copy to: CIA/State/RAO/Secret Service" (above CIA was written "CASTRO," and the "Secret Service" entry was also handwritten). Below that line, three other entities are typed but scratched out: NIS/OSI/USAINTC by routing slip for info." The forwarding of this information was done the next day by "THG/FJW."

The subject of concern was "regarding the conference scheduled by the General Union of Mexican Workers and Peasants (UGOCM) and the identities of the persons that might possibly be in attendance at that conference." The single-page document forwarded with the memorandum further clarified the FBI's concern. On at least three occasions, September 21 and 28, plus October 12, the FBI source (names and lines redacted) informed SAC, Sacramento that "Chavez or other members of United Farm Workers Organizing Committee (UFWOC)" were going to attend the UGOCM conference in either Mexicali or Mexico City. To be sure, "Dolores Huerta and Julio Hernandez, both recognized leaders of the UFWOC, have been designated to attend the conference along with other unspecified individuals. Also scheduled to be in attendance at the conference are a group of imported Cubans." Then, in an abrupt about-face, the SAC, Sacramento notified the Director, FBI on November 29, 1971, that his office was closing the investigation into this trip: "Inasmuch as source utilized was unable to develop further information regarding the identities of individuals connected with the United Farm Worker's Organizing Committee (UFWOC), that might be attending .. . this matter is considered closed by the Sacramento Division." Sacramento FBI in the LHM enclosed with the memorandum just quoted indicates the office tried the source three times—November 4, 1971; November 16, 1971; and November 22, 1971—regarding additional persons that were to travel to Mexico.

The Border Coverage Program (BOCOV): Another COINTELPRO

In 1970 Chávez had traveled to Mexico to visit a doctor, Julio Prado. Dr. Prado had become a person of interest to the FBI as early as the mid to late 1960s.

The FBI began implementing an illegal operation in Mexico sometime in the late 1950s named the Border Coverage Program, or BOCOV by its code name. William Sullivan was in charge of this program within the FBI.[5] Moving forward to 1972, the released FBI documents contain a four-page attachment dated June 20. These pages begin with quotes from open source material taken from the newspaper *Imperial Valley Press*, at El Centro, California. Of interest on the COINTELPRO labeled BOCOV are several paragraphs in this attachment, beginning with the first:

> As of November 30, 1970, Cesar Chavez continued to visit Julio Prado Valdez, a known member of the Mexican Communist Party (PCM). Chavez's interest in Prado reportedly was to have Prado run a health clinic in the Mexicali, Baja California, Mexico, area, for the United Farm Workers Organizing Committee (UFWOC) members. The health clinic would be subsidized by UFWOC funds as a supplement for the nominal fees charged to the chapter (p.1).

This information was supplied or supplemented by informants identified as "(SD T-1, November 30, 1970 SD T-2, November 30, 1970)." On the next page, bottom paragraph and continuing on the following page, is the money amount purported to be the subsidy to the Prado clinic.

> Cesar Chavez visited with Julio Prado Valdez in Mexicali, Baja California, Mexico, on October 3, 1971, at which time financial problems that Prado was having and the fact that he needed more money for the health clinic in Mexicali, were discussed. The UFWOC was paying 5,000 to 6,000 pesos (approximately $500.00) a month to Prado and was to send $200.00 to $300.00 more per month for the rent of the health clinic in Mexicali. (SD T-2, October 14, 1971). The medical clinic at Mexicali, Mexico, providing medical services to UFWOC members was closed due to a disagreement between Cesar Chavez and Julio Prado Valdez over the fact that Prado demanded more money for providing these services. (SD T-2, November 30, 1971). (pp.2–3)

Who Was Julio Prado?

SAC, San Diego proposed in late September 1968 to Hoover that a scurrilous flyer be distributed attacking Julio Prado. A copy was attached, and Hoover by return memo to both SAC, San Diego and W. C. Sullivan, dated October 25, 1968, approved the distribution of one thousand handbills and requested "Advise Bureau of success the informant realizes in distribution of the handbills and furnish positive results of this counterintelligence move in form suitable for dissemination." Prado's file number became 100-394842. The bilingual handbill, Spanish and English, contained this information:

> JULIO PRADO VALDEZ WHO IS JULIO PRADO VALDEZ? IS HE A DOCTOR? IS HE A FRIEND OF THE POOR? IS HE A COMMUNIST? DOES HE BELIEVE IN JUSTICE FOR ALL? NO! THE TRUTH IS JULIO PRADO VALDEZ IS RICH. HE IS A LANDLORD. HE HAS BUSINESSES. HE HAS A CLINIC. HE HAS NO INTEREST IN THE POOR. PRADO IS ONLY INTERESTED IN HIMSELF. NO ONE CAN BELIEVE WHAT PRADO SAYS. NO ONE LIKES THIS MAN BECAUSE HE IS A MILLIONAIRE AND SEEKS HIS WAY OF LIFE FROM A PARTY THAT DOES NOT EXIST. IT IS A FANTASY.
>
> Organized Committee of Baja California.

It is safe to surmise that the all-cap letters and malicious handbill from two years prior did not shut down Prado or his clinic in Mexicali. The FBI did claim credit in an internal memo from W. R. Wannall to W. C. Sullivan, dated January 29, 1969, for causing considerable dissent and concern as to the strength of Prado's leadership. The handbill's content did have a negative effect on his fundraising abilities. The handbill from 1968 did serve the purpose of using this COINTELPRO activity to link Chávez with Prado in 1970, if in fact Prado was a member of the Communist Party in Mexico.

The Plot to Kill Chávez: Cover-up or Bungled Investigation?

The *Washington Post* dated December 24, 1971, p.A2, posted a sensational story. The AP wire related the first details under the headline "Ex-Agent Sees Plot to Kill Cesar Chavez." The FBI clipped this article and placed it with the declassified documents for this year without explanation or any official document accompanying the open source newspaper article.

In a bizarre sequence of events detailed in the article, the FBI learned from other sources such as the *New York Times* that there had been a plot to kill Chávez in the works right under their jurisdictional noses in California.[6] The articles elaborated on a story that went like this: California state AFL-CIO leader John F. Henning called the state attorney general, Evelle J. Younger, to alert him of a plot to kill Chávez and ask him to investigate immediately. According to this article, Henning told Younger, "Cesar Chavez has been obliged to live with lights illuminating the area of his house at night and with police dogs guarding against anti-labor intruders." Hennings provided Younger with the name of the person who reported the death plot, Larry Shears. Allegedly, Shears was "a former undercover agent for the U.S. Treasury Department." Shears was interviewed on a Bakersfield television station and claimed that "he was paid $500 last Oct. 4 by the Internal Revenue Service's Alcohol, Tobacco, and Firearm Division to provide information about a plot to kill the 44-year-old farm labor organizer and to burn records in the union headquarters near Bakersfield." Shears, according to the article, "was promised $10,000 if he could substantiate his claim." A West Coast chief enforcement officer of the IRS, Mel Warner, confirmed the $500 payment to Shears, "but the government now considers the case closed because he failed to provide the evidence." The *New York Times* printed their story about this plot the beginning of the year on January 2, 1972. Earl Caldwell wrote, "The informer, Larry Shears, 32 years old, said that he had been offered $5,000 to participate in the plot and that he had witnessed what appeared to be the payment of $30,000 to carry out the assassination." The IRS in Washington, DC, was contacted about this assassination plot and confirmed they had investigated the matter. Donald W. Bacon, the former assistant commissioner for compliance at the IRS, recalled there had been an investigation. He said,

> At one time, there was a threat on Chavez's life. Sometime in early fall. There was an alleged plot. I authorized payment to an informant. I understood the information wasn't satisfactory and therefore he was not paid. The attempt was never made on his life. The investigation stopped.

Along with the newspaper clippings are two documents of great interest. One is titled "Public Voucher for Purchases and Services Other Than Personal," and the second is a copy of a check from the U.S. Government. The *New York Times* article described Shears's prior employment record and evidence mentioned above. Shears could support his contentions about the plot and the money. He had copies of the cancelled Treasury of the United States check no. 61,546,381 dated October 4, 1971, and made out to "Larry Shears c/o William J. Vizzard, a Spec Invest 650 Capitol Hall Rm 3508 Sacramento CA 95814," and a copy of the voucher dated September 27, 1971, indicating the services to be delivered on or about July 19, 1971.

> Informant will provide information and evidence necessary to identify Richard Petigo and those who are providing Petigo the funds to arrange the arson and murder of Caesar [*sic*] Chavez. CA E SI 71-552 (T-II). $500 [Signed] Mike Monzon Chief Special Investigator.

Shears had worked for the Kern County Sheriff's Department as an informer on drug deals. He did such good work that they referred him to the State Narcotics Bureau. While in this capacity, he learned of the plot to kill Chávez. Supposedly, he was recruited by a contact to burn an amusement slide, which he declined. He was then recruited to burn an office in Delano belonging to Chávez's union, steal some records from the office, then "make a 'hit' on Mr. Chavez"—that is, assassinate him. Shears claimed that at that point he sought out the Alcohol, Tobacco, and Firearms (ATF) Enforcement Division to report the assassination plot. He introduced the ATF agent assigned to the investigation, Lester Robinson, to the contact. The contact also provided Shears with detailed diagrams of Mr. Chávez's office, plus information on who the assassin would be. The "hit man" was already wanted for murder in both Kern and Ventura Counties and was arrested in connection with these other murders. The Chávez plot was put on hold. Shears claimed that the persons ordering the killing insisted that certain files be stolen before the assassination took place. His contact informed Shears that the guy would be there Friday to do the records. And, that Friday, a man showed up at the contact's house. Shears was waiting outside the house and witnessed the son of a farmer in the valley arrive about 4 p.m. with a brown paper bag that he assumed contained the $30,000. The contact came out, according to the *New York Times* article, and told Shears, "The money is here. The decision to go—we still don't have that decision."

The whole investigation into the plot to kill Chávez unraveled when even more bizarre developments occurred. The burning of the slide, which Shears declined to do, took place, and the police questioned the slide operator. In a dumb, irresponsible moment during the interrogation of the operator, the police mentioned Shears, the contact, and the plot against Chávez. The slide operator apparently relayed the information to the contact and the payoff man for the insurance proceeds from the burning of the slide, who immediately suspected Shears. Then, Treasury agents Bill Bertolani and William Vizzard decided to set up the contact for arrest, supposedly to keep him from Shears. They got another agent, Mr. Robinson, to purchase one thousand amphetamine pills from the contact. The Kern County Sheriff's Department assisted the Treasury agents in the arrest and confiscation of monies from the contact's home. They took $6,700 from the home, and from $20,000 to $22,000 was left there. Somehow, the Treasury agents and sheriff's deputies determined that money was not evidence. "The case is still pending, and the suspect is free on bail," the article concluded. Case closed. Other than holding these articles in their FBI files, the Bureau did little to investigate this assassination plot, did not interrogate the farmer's son bringing the money, and did not arrest anyone.

Early in 1972, the Washington FBI office met a delegation that wanted to register the murder plot against Chávez with them. UAW representatives

E. J. Moran, Stephen I. Schlossberg, and Paul Schrade, together with UFWOC attorney Jerry Cohen and the ATF informant, Larry S. Shears, made up the delegation. These persons, mainly Shears, repeated the story of the murder plot with names and amounts. The delegation expressed concern that the local authorities in California were too closely tied politically to the Delano farmers to conduct a thorough investigation of the alleged plot to kill Chávez. Cohen told the FBI that the ATF had closed their case and that the FBI had the evidence needed to continue with the case toward prosecution. Shears told the WFO, FBI he had numerous tape recordings of conversations between himself and others involved. And, he also sounded the alarm that he was fearful of being harmed. He recently had found five sticks of dynamite wired under the dashboard of his automobile. The delegation left their addresses with the FBI for further contact. Paul Schrade, who had been wounded in the head while in the company of Robert F. Kennedy when he was assassinated, echoed the fear and concern for Shears.

Jacques Levy provides more information obtained from Jerry Cohen, César Chávez, and, more importantly, the report filed by William Vizzard on the case.[7] Most of the critical information he and others found was presented to the FBI. Levy had tape recordings he made with Shears. Airtels flew back and forth from Sacramento FBI to the Director and back to Sacramento. The FBI wanted the Levy material, particularly since the FBI learned he was going to write a book about the plot. All in all, Levy had acquired twenty cassette tapes and 374 pages of written material on the plot. The FBI office in San Francisco sought out Levy in Santa Rosa, California, and Jerry Cohen in Delano; they obtained ten of the cassettes and 374 pages of written material on February 15, according to the report filed with enclosures and sent off to Washington, FBI on February 18, 1972. More tapes were to follow. Levy wanted the material back as soon as copied. And, the FBI did return the material after making copies for themselves and the U.S. Attorney General's Civil Rights Division Office. The Director, FBI by Airtel to the SAC, Sacramento wanted details regarding the material on pages 107 and 362 because it "indicates your office has had prior contacts with Larry Shears, the informant in this matter." The FBI agent is named (redacted) and Hoover wants complete details of Agent [REDACTED] contacts with Shears and any other information in your files regarding Shears. Insure prior contacts with Shears were properly handled. If not properly handled, obtain explanations and include recommendations for any administrative action.

The NOTE on page 2 of this report reviewed the events of the plot gleaned from the tapes and written material and concluded: "The transcription is a rambling, disjointed account of Shears' contacts with ATF and his associates . . . worthless as no mention or admission by these individuals were made." The last two sentences of the note indicate that the matter will be dropped and the FBI agent mentioned absolved of any wrongdoing.

Shears' allegations concerning the plot appear to be a complete fabrication and obviously, the result of refusal by ATF to pay him any additional money unless he could produce additional information of the plot against Chavez . . . in view of the unreliability and unpredictability of Shears, Sacramento being instructed to resolve the reference to Agent [REDACTED].

The FBI did not want to investigate the matter. They wanted someone else to solve the case. The material in the FBI files reads as if the Bureau wanted Shears to produce evidence of a "smoking gun," to use prosecutorial jargon, with names; otherwise they would not bother, except to clear the FBI agent of any wrongdoing in the handling of Shears.

Levy provided the remaining ten tapes with transcriptions to San Francisco, FBI, who in turn made copies for Sacramento, FBI and the Bureau in D.C. on February 29, 1972. Hoover appears concerned with the mention of contact with Shears by the FBI agent in the tapes. In his Airtel of March 13, 1972, he writes, "A review of the transcription, specifically that segment under caption, 'Tape 5' and 'Cassette 13' refers to contact with Agent [REDACTED]." He repeats the ominous admonitions about how the contact was handled by the agent and asks for recommendations if not handled properly. In closing he states, "If not already done, immediately respond to instructions set forth in reBuairtel." This reference is to his first expressed concern over this contact in mid-February. The NOTE from Airtel of the 28th is repeated in this communication, but for two new items. One is a reference to "a possible deserter-fugitive" Shears mentions to the FBI agent. The other is more damaging to Shears's credibility: "No one on any of the tapes furnishes any information of a positive fashion that would indicate a plot ever existed except in the mind of Shears."

Oddly, via Airtel of March 13, 1972, the SAC, Sacramento finally reporting on the agent's "handling" of Shears informs the Director, FBI that "On 6/21/71, SHEARS telephonically contacted the FBI Resident Agency, Bakersfield, California, and talked to SA [REDACTED]" asking for help since his cover had been blown and he feared for his life. The date of first contact is most significant: almost half a year before the first newspaper story came out and a couple of months before Vizzard of the ATF filed his report. The FBI knew as of that day about Shears, his role as informant for ATF, and the information he had on a plot to kill Chávez. The FBI knew about the plot and did nothing until pressured by the DOJ Criminal Division, who in turn was pressured by U.S. Senator Edward Kennedy, UAW officials, and the UFW people themselves—all of whom called or wrote letters asking for an investigation. This "looking the other way" posture and "hands off any investigation" despite information the FBI had from informants is like the role it played during the assassination of Malcolm X.[8]

Jacques Levy did get around to writing a book about the life of Chávez and not just this murder plot. He writes, "Much of the evidence is on tape and is reported in a secret U.S. Treasury Department report signed on September 23, 1971, by Treasury agent William J. Vizzard, head of the Bakersfield office of the Treasury Department's Alcohol, Tobacco and Firearms Division." Levy provides the critical names: the contact was Richard Pedigo and the assassin was Buddy Gene Prochnau.[9] The ATF raided Pedigo's home after his arrest for selling meth to Lester Robinson and found $6,830 (not $6,700 as reported in the newspapers) and $22,000 more in the refrigerator. The Vizzard report to the ATF is silent on the $22,000 found in Pedigo's refrigerator.[10] After Shears was interviewed on television in Bakersfield, "the cover-up starts," writes Levy. All major law enforcement and prosecutorial agencies from the State Attorney General, Kern County Sheriff's Department, and ATF involved in this investigation closed their cases primarily because they asserted Shears was not credible. Shears refused to take a polygraph test unless it was administered by an expert not associated with law enforcement. State AG Younger's office even went so far as to misstate facts and lie to the public, stating, "there never was a plot." According to Levy, the press statement read, "Lie detector tests have cleared two men Shears claimed were at the action end of the conspiracy" and that Shears had refused a polygraph.[11] Levy, in search of the truth, arranged to have Shears tested by a nationally recognized expert over a two-day period. "Shears is telling the truth on the key parts of his story," concluded the expert. U.S. Senator Edward Kennedy pushed the DOJ's Civil Rights Division to investigate. They offered Pedigo immunity to name the growers that provided the contract-to-kill money. Pedigo declined, and DOJ closed the case. Involved in the cover-up at DOJ was Robert Mardian, then an assistant AG heading Internal Security. Mardian's family claimed bankruptcy in Arizona after signing a contract with Chávez's union. Mardian also "was President Richard Nixon's political hatchet man in the Justice Department and is later convicted for conspiracy to obstruct justice in the cover-up of the Nixon Watergate scandal." Ultimately, Pedigo was sentenced to two to ten years each for his crimes of drug dealing and arson involving another Delano grower. Prochnau, the trigger man, received a life sentence for the Visalia murder.[12]

The End of Hoover's Machinations against Chávez et al.

Richard Hack termed Hoover the "Puppetmaster."[13] In his book, he recounts how Hoover maneuvered and conspired with Robert Mardian, not just to squelch the plot to kill Chávez but also, and more importantly for Hoover and Mardian, to get rid of William Sullivan, head of the Intelligence Division and fourth in command at the FBI. First, Hoover promoted Mark Felt, who later admitted his role as "Deep Throat" during the Watergate investigations, to deputy associate director, making him Sullivan's boss. Second, on August 31, 1971, Hoover summoned Sullivan, a thirty-year veteran of the FBI, into his office and proceeded to rant and rail against him for the next two and one-half hours. At the conclusion, Hoover ordered him to take a two-week vacation. Instead, Sullivan took one week. Upon his return, he found a new name plate on what used to be his office with the name "Alex Rosen," and the locks had been changed. He had been terminated.[14] Third, regardless of the fact that President Nixon had given Hoover use of Air Force One to return from his annual trip to Miami at the beginning of the new year in 1972, the Director heard Nixon wanted to fire him, after fifty-five years with DOJ. He made plans to hide and dispose of his secret and confidential files. But, his firing did not happen; his reign continued six more months. His last memorable deed was to fire off an angry letter to the CEO of Transworld Airlines (TWA) for compelling two FBI agents to leave the plane for not surrendering their guns. Hoover died May 2, 1972.[15] Chávez lived on to face more murder plots and violence, and to see Nixon become the first U.S. president to resign from office totally disgraced.

Chávez's Words on this Plot and Police Cover-up

César Chávez is quoted in the Levy book as follows:

> The Kern County district attorney and the sheriff's office are not our friends. So it is very easy for them to do nothing about the plot. They had hardly any pressure on them.
>
> The way Attorney General Younger responded, I'm pretty sure that he, too, was covering something up. At least he was very quick about saying there was no plot, and people believe it.
>
> On the federal level, I think the investigation was stopped by someone high up there, and the Civil Rights Division of the Justice Department just went through the motions.
>
> As for the existence of a plot, I think it shows that nonviolence is working. They wouldn't go as far as trying to kill me unless they were very worried about our success.[16]

CHAPTER 5

The Price of Leadership

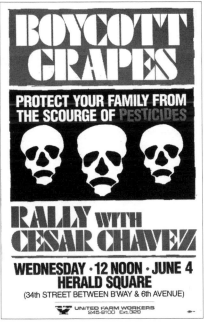

THE SAC SACRAMENTO INFORMED Washington FBI by URGENT two-page teletype on June 14, 1968, with follow-up in a two-page LHM later that day, of "possible threat against the President of the United States" and César Chávez. The Kern County District Attorney's Office in Bakersfield had received information from Jerry Cohen, the UFWOC attorney, of death threats made against Chávez and President Lyndon Baines Johnson "on or about June 9, 1968, during Kennedy Memorial March" (p.1 of teletype). Cohen supplied the name of the person who allegedly was "overheard to make a statement that Caesar [*sic*] Chavez was 'going down soon' and that Chavez and President Johnson 'are the only two left and they would be gotten'" (p.1 of LHM). This person was Juan Martinez. The names of witnesses with locations who heard the threat were "Porferio [*sic*] Borga Montion, who resides at the Pete Velasco Camp in Richgrove, California, and Al Vasquez, who can be contacted through UFWOC" (p.1 of LHM). The SAC also reported that "above information has been made available to the Kern County Sheriff's Office, Bakersfield, and the Delano Police Department" (p.1 of LHM). "Special Agent [NAME REDACTED], United States Secret Service, Sacramento, was notified of the above information by Special Agent [NAME REDACTED] at 11:43 A.M. on June 14, 1968" (p.2 of LHM). Curiously, nothing more is heard about any investigation by any of the four police entities— FBI, Secret Service, county sheriff, or city police—into this threat made by Juan Martinez, or at least interviewing the witnesses to corroborate Cohen's complaint to the FBI office in Bakersfield.

Another strange incident was reported to Hoover by the SAC, Sacramento on July 11, 1968. Chávez received a strange envelope postmarked late June at Gilroy, California, from a Tirso P. Mellosa, according to the SAC. The letter inside the envelope was handwritten in Spanish. Allegedly, the letter was translated into English by the editor of *El Malcriado*, the UFW newspaper, and a copy sent with the report to Hoover. The SAC transmission was coded "CESAR CHAVEZ-VICTIM EXTORTION"; marked "OBSCENE," given several words the letter contained; shared with San Francisco FBI office; and routed also to T. E. Bishop. An English translation by someone at the FBI (name redacted) dated July 18 has conflicting information in the heading. For example, the translation claims, "It is postmarked: San Jose, California, June 27, 1968, and Gilroy, California, June 27, 1968." The copy of the envelope is not clear or legible, but obviously a letter cannot be postmarked at two locations on the same day. It continues with, "The return address reads: Tirso P. Mellosa, or Malvosa, or Mellisa C: 29/1100, or 1168 San Jose, Cal." The letter in Spanish accompanying the report, however, is signed with the initials "T.P.M." without a name.

Hoover promptly sent the material to the Latent Fingerprint Section for analysis and responded to the SAC, Sacramento with the translation done by Fishlow of *El Malcriado*, which contains the menacing words "[We'll] Try. Grenades or mortars because the machine gun makes too much noise and you may run away frightened. To your better life." The report dated August

8 from the Latent Fingerprint Section makes mention of positive results, which are listed in a follow-up report dated August 13, 1968, from the San Francisco FBI office and filed under 9-2203 to correspond with Bureau file #9-48291, which is the number of the Latent Fingerprint Section. It reads, "one latent fingerprint of value developed on envelope and 7 latent fingerprints and one latent palm print developed on letter, AUSA, SF, advised he would authorize prosecution if Subject is located and admits writing and mailing the letter." All of these latent fingerprints were tied to FBI files under three names: Cesar Estrada Chavez, Cesar Humberto Chavez-Sanchez, and Cesar Elias Chavez-Baca. The FBI, as a result of this investigation, obtained the fingerprints of several UFWOC leaders, such as Tony Orendain and David Fishlow, who handled the letter, plus the postal clerks.

Chávez never saw the letter or received mention of it, according to the report dated August 7, 1968. On the contrary, some SA (name redacted) attempted to contact but did not reach Chávez on July 31, 1968; August 1, 1968; August 2, 1968, at Delano. Finally, it seems that on August 5, the SA reached Chávez, who "advised that he had not been previously advised regarding the threatening letter in this matter. He said he had not been in favor of making an issue over threats to his safety, but that he had been overruled by his attorneys in that they insisted that such threats be reported by an official of the union to the proper authorities." No such person under the name Tirso P. Mellosa was ever located by the FBI.

While the FBI was checking finger and palm prints on the Tirso P. Mellosa letter, the Sacramento FBI office reported to the Director, FBI by two-page teletype on August 14, 1968, that after an "accident and assault matter involving two male Mexicans investigated by SO [handwritten above this acronym is Sheriff's Office] and California Highway Patrol, Delano, Calif. Blame could not be placed and both parties were released" (p.1). The Airtel LHM, consisting of three pages, that followed this teletype clarified that the police entities "investigated a hit and run and assault matter" (p.1). The names of the parties investigated were redacted, but "both were released pending further investigation" (p.1). This incident, according to the chief of police (name redacted), Delano Police Department, was called to their attention by (name redacted) requesting police come to the "residence on the evening of August 13, 1968." Chávez was there waiting with "about 25 other persons, including [NAME REDACTED]" (p.1). According to this LHM, "Chavez berated the officers for lack of police protection and demanded some action concerning the [REDACTED] matter. The officers explained the accident matter was outside the jurisdiction of the DPD and left" (p.1).

Deciding jurisdiction requires a two-step analysis. First, jurisdiction is ascertained as to the nature of the alleged crime—in this case, a hit-and-run and an assault. Second, jurisdiction is ascertained as to the location of the crime. Did the offense occur in the city of Delano for the DPD or on a state highway? (to determine who was to have primary responsibility to investigate and prosecute). The reporting entity to the FBI was the Kern County Sheriff's Office in Bakersfield, California. But the exact location of the incident is redacted so jurisdiction is unknown except for the question of whether the hit-and-run and assault occurred in Delano or not, which is in Kern County. The Sheriff's Office did not investigate further; it referred the matter to the FBI. Hit-and-run is not a federal crime, unless the assault in some way involves a violation of civil rights. Regardless, Chávez did not buy into the runaround as to which police entity had jurisdiction. The LHM states that later that night

> UFWOC pickets appeared at the Delano Police Station at about 10:00 p.m., on August 13, 1968 remained until about 1:00 a.m., on August 14, 1968, protesting what they claimed to be lack of police protection for UFWOC members in Delano, California. The pickets returned on August 14, 1968, and as of 2:00 p.m., August 14, approximately 25 pickets including Chavez remained at the police station." (pp.1-2)

Chávez probably had been alerted by someone that a UFWOC member was one of the parties, but as the victim of the hit-and-run and assault. Hence, the picketing of the local police department overnight and into the next day. This is a serious commitment of resources and time by the UFWOC, and Chávez himself. The matter must have been of a serious nature to demand more police protection.

Unrelated but made part of this same LHM are a concluding set of paragraphs. The first states the chief of police for Delano also reported to the Sacramento FBI office that Chávez appeared on Los Angeles television that same August 13, 1968, evening to announce he was requesting that U.S. Attorney General Ramsey Clark furnish a sufficient number of U.S. marshals to police the proposed Labor Day UFWOC Parade at Delano, California. The chief of police stated that the City of Delano had denied the permit to parade because of safety concerns; the local police could not handle a parade crowd estimated to be upwards of 25,000 to 30,000 persons. The chief, according to the FBI report's last sentence of this paragraph, stated, "the above-mentioned picketing was planned in advance in view of Chavez's appearance on television in Los Angeles, California" (p.2).

The Continuing Threats in Delano, California

The FBI head of Domestic Intelligence Division, William C. Sullivan, also sent an initialed note dated August 15, 1968, presumably to Director Hoover alerting him to the Chávez request for U.S. marshals for the Labor Day Parade. The Airtels from SAC, Sacramento to the Director, FBI continued into August 16. Copies of this communication and the more descriptive LHM that followed that same day were furnished to various military intelligence agencies: Army, Navy, and Air Force, plus the Secret Service. In this LHM, Sacramento FBI was informed that the picketing of the 14th had continued into the night "with union members shouting, playing loud music and at times becoming quite belligerent" (p.1). The picket allegedly stopped mid-morning when "pickets left to attend a Congressional hearing being held at Delano High School regarding the living conditions of the farm workers. [NAME REDACTED] said the only violence occurred on the evening of August 14, 1968, when an elderly woman was struck by a rock which was thrown from the area of the picket line" (p.1).

The General Labor Sub-Committee of the House Education and Labor Committee, headed by Congressman John Dent (D-PA), held a one-day hearing at the high school in Delano that same day, August 15. The LHM also mentioned that the FBI's resident agent in Bakersfield was contacted by Assistant AG "Richard V. Boulger, Fresno, California," about a call made by Chávez to the DOJ in Washington, DC, "to the effect that one [NAME REDACTED] of the United Farm Workers Organizing Committee had been forced off the road in Delano by a car driven by one [NAME REDACTED] either during the evening of August 14, 1968, or morning of August 15, 1968" (p.1).

In another three-page LHM dated August 19, 1968, from SAC, Sacramento to Director, FBI, with copies going to the same military intelligence units mentioned previously and the Secret Service, a different incident of August 13th is mentioned involving a union picketer, Manuel Rivera, and another person, Ignacio Rubio. Rubio had "signed a complaint through the Kern County District Attorney's Office, at Bakersfield, California, on August 16, 1968, charging Rivera with battery." After a warrant for his arrest was issued by Judge McNally of the Delano Justice Court, "Rivera was apprehended at Delano by the Kern County Sheriff's Office, on the same date" (p.2). Picketing protesting this arrest ensued the afternoon of the 16th, the Sacramento FBI reports, and it adds fuel to the fire by passing on a rumor heard from a redacted source: "He said there is a vague rumor that Mr. Chavez has sent letters to militant groups throughout the United States, inviting them to join in the picketing at Delano" (p.2). The LHM reports that picketing continued with "25 to 30 pickets" on August 16; "an average of approximately 70 UFWOC pickets" on August 17; "no activity at the Police Station on August 18, 1968"; and "about eight UFWOC pickets . . . on August 19, 1968" (p.2). Curiously, the last page of this LHM has this statement in contradiction to what was previously written on page 2 about picketing on August 16:

[NAME REDACTED] advised on August 19, 1968, that [LINES REDACTED]. He advised that on the night of August 16, 1968, approximately 300 UFWOC pickets assembled in front of the Delano Police Department and became unnecessarily loud and unruly. UFWOC attorney Averbuck was called in to discuss the matter and was asked to cooperate; however, he was not very receptive to any suggestions on the part of the Delano Police Department. Immediately after Averbuck left the station, the pickets left the sidewalk and gathered at the door of the Police Station. Since they were interfering with the normal operations of the Police Department, they were ordered to leave, and only after all assembled forces were called in did the pickets leave without any further problems. [NAME REDACTED] stated that to date there have been no arrests in connection with this matter (p.3).

In Washington, the FBI Director, seeing an opportunity to charge the UFWOC—perhaps even Chávez himself—made a request of "Assistant Attorney General Criminal Division, Attn: Mr. J. K. Heilbron, Room 2110, Justice Building," on August 20, 1968. Hoover enclosed one copy of the August 14th teletype from Sacramento, which references the picketing at the Delano Police Department. Typed at bottom of this single page is: "This will confirm the conversation between [NAME REDACTED] and SA [NAME REDACTED] on 8/19/68. This matter was taken under advisement and an investigation was requested." The important words associated with this page are in the "Subject: United Farm Workers Organizing Committee, AFL-CIO, Delano, California, Information Concerning Antiriot Laws."

The DOJ does not investigate complaints; it prosecutes the investigations the FBI has completed. Hoover seems to be implying to DOJ that the Anti-Riot laws may have been violated, but declines to investigate unless requested. It reads to me as if DOJ's "Mr. J. K. Heilbron," who received the memorandum from Hoover, did not agree with the description of picketing being in violation of "Anti-Riot laws," despite the alleged loud and unruly behavior attributed by someone to the pickets, and declined an FBI investigation.

Nothing was released by the FBI on what was the outcome of the Labor Day Parade in Delano. The next FBI files in chronological order deal with a September 10th memorandum from the SAC, Sacramento to the Director, FBI reporting "no picketing or other unusual activity on the part of the above-captioned organization during the past week and none is anticipated in the near future. Consequently, this matter is being placed in a closed status." The FBI gave up monitoring Chávez for the time being. Instead, the FBI files indicated that the SAC, Sacramento submitted information on the finger and palm prints involved in the Tirso O. Mellosa threat. The records sent to the FBI, Laboratory were the "five fingerprint cards each containing finger and palm prints of DAVID MICHAEL FISHLOW; ANTONIO ORENDIAN, aka Tony Orendain; ROBERT S. SENINI; and WILLARD JOHN WIDMAN." The actual number of names listed was only four. By October 2, the FBI concluded that no viable prints other than the four identified persons were found and no leads were had on Tirso P. Mellosa in Gilroy or eight other areas in Kern County. Additionally, the FBI reported checking with six other agencies (names redacted) for information on the name of Mellosa, without success. While not explicitly stated in any record, the FBI closed the matter.

More Death Threats

Again, on October 3, 1968, a death threat reared its ugly head, this time via a telephone call. The Criminal Division of the DOJ received a telegram from a redacted source "alleging that the lives of Cesar Chavez and his assistant, Dolores Huerta, have been threatened by anonymous phone calls." Fred M. Vinson Jr., assistant attorney general, sent a one-page memorandum dated October 3, 1968, with the subject "Investigation of Phone Calls THREATEN-ING LIFE OF CESAR CHAVEZ," requesting the Director, FBI to "Please conduct a preliminary investigation into the nature and source of these anonymous phone calls . . . that constitute violations of 18 U.S. C. 875 (c)." In subsequent reports, the first from SAC, Sacramento to the Director, FBI, a one-page Air-tel dated October 14, 1968, relates an "investigation at San Jose, California, reveals Victim CESAR CHAVEZ, Director, UFWOC, 102 Albany, Delano, Calif., can reportedly be contacted at this location." The second transmission dated November 4, 1968, a four-page LHM from SAC, Sacramento to the Director, FBI, states "CESAR CHAVEZ . . . was interviewed at his residence, 1221 Kensington, Delano, and furnished the following information": Chávez reported two prior telephone threats about two years before made by "an unknown female who spoke English very rapidly with no detectable accent. Both telephone calls were apparently local calls and he believes they were made by the same individual" (p.3). The female voice accused the UFWOC members of being "Communists" and "we are going to get rid of all of you" (p.3). And, "During one conversation, the unknown female said, "What you

guys need is a good lesson abd [*sic*] We'll show you a little about violence"
(p.3). Chávez told the interviewer from the FBI that the UFWOC was getting
threatening calls "almost on a daily basis from unknown individuals." He
also referred the FBI interviewer to Dolores Huerta, who "may have received
some of these calls." And, Chávez gave her address as "the UFWOC office at
182 21st Street, Brooklyn, New York, telephone 499-6612" (p.3).

Hospital Threat

Critical to the issue of life-threatening calls was the Chávez revelation to an
FBI interviewer that his life was threatened while at O'Connor Hospital, San
Jose, California. SAC, San Francisco also reported in a five-page LHM to FBI
HQ on November 25, 1968, that while César Chávez had been hospitalized
the previous September 1968 at O'Connor Hospital, the doctor treating him
became concerned for his safety given a death threat that had been phoned
in to the operator handling reception. The information being reported by
SAC, San Francisco was taken from a Sacramento FD 302 dated October 3,
1968 (p.2). At the bottom of the LHM is the portion gleaned from the FD
302: "suspicious call was supposedly received by a hospital receptionist. Dr.
JEROME LACKNER, his attending physician, at that time, has the particulars
concerning this matter" (p.3, top right). The FBI interviewer asked Chávez
about a person named Charles N. Ella, but "he could not recall anyone by the
name" (p.4).

This LHM dated November 25, 1968, closes without a hint on who this
Charles N. Ella was, or why he was of interest to the FBI; instead, the report
provides a physical description of Chávez to include race, sex, date of birth,
place of birth, height, weight, color of hair, color of eyes, and marital status
(p.4, 11/4/68). We can only wonder if this FBI description would be useful to
anyone trying to identify César Chávez on the street or in a hospital bed.
No other information on the page with the substantive details of the calls
and caller is provided other than the narrative, and, at the bottom, that "On
10/30/68 at Delano, California File # SC 9-34 by SAs [NAMES REDACTED] CNS:
epg Date dictated 11/1/68" (p.3, 11/4/68, top right).

But this was not the first time Chávez had received threats. The doctor knew that, so he ordered that no information be given to inquiries about his room location or to visitors or contacts before consulting with him, according to the San Francisco FBI office to the U.S. Attorney's Office, also in San Francisco, in a five-page report dated January 28, 1969. Consequently, Chávez was moved intermittently from room to room and to different floors during his stay from September 8th to the 20th (p.2). What prompted the movement was an incident that occurred "several days after Chavez's admittance to the hospital." The facts detailed in this document are more descriptive than the earlier comments reported above: "[NAME REDACTED] received a telephone call from the Admissions Office of the hospital." The receptionist had taken the call "at approximately 2:00 a.m. one morning." The receptionist had just referred a call to the Admissions Office wherein an unidentified female had requested the room number for Chávez. The caller reportedly stated that she was calling for a doctor scheduled to treat Chávez in the morning and simply wanted the correct room number "so that the doctor would know which room to report. [NAME REDACTED] stated that an employee of the Admissions Office inadvertently furnished the room number to the caller at the time." The next four lines are entirely redacted. "[NAME REDACTED] stated that as a result of the police activity the press, who were cognizant of Chavez's hospitalization and were receiving daily releases concerning his condition, published articles reporting an alleged threat upon Chavez. The [REDACTED] was adamant that this information was incorrect" (p.2).

The closing sentence of this report is very carefully and clearly constructed: "at no time was any communication containing any threat upon Chavez received during his confinement" (p.3). The last page indicates that someone with the FBI investigated the incident and discussed it with "Assistant United States Attorney JERROLD M. LADAR, San Francisco." Mr. Ladar, however, ended the investigation by ordering that "no further effort be expended in this matter since all logical leads in effort to identify Unknown Subject have been exhausted" (p.4). The matter was followed up by the SAC, San Francisco in a report dated the 28th of January, 1969. This report, however, referenced a prior report dated November 25, 1968, which was not among the disclosed or declassified documents of the Chavez files analyzed in the previous chapter. A synopsis is contained in this document that repeats the information on these incidents. The interesting information is that the name of Tirso P. Mellosa and other variants of it are made part of the "Title of Case," and the "Character of Case" contains the word "Extortion." This was a different death threat made by letter, not telephone call.

The declassified Chavez file does not contain any other document until May 9, 1969, an URGENT teletype to the Director, FBI and SAC, Los Angeles from the SAC, San Diego. The urgency is to inform that Chávez is going to march again, this time from Indio, California, to Calexico. He would begin the next day and would stop overnight in various cities along the route. The "March will terminate in a rally afternoon May eighteen next at Calexico." It was rumored that Senator Edward Kennedy would participate in the rally.

Rabbit Trails

A letter sent to Hoover by an unknown sender (name redacted) dated May 14, 1969, is among the released documents in the declassified FBI file. The author of this letter wanted answers to several questions: "Was Chavez a Communist? Was the John Birch Society a good organization?" And, if Hoover wanted to speak with sender to "first call by telephone [REDACTED]; she could not reach anyone at Indio." Typically, the Director, FBI would have someone in his office respond to such letters, but in this case, he forwarded the letter to the SAC, Los Angeles for handling. Hoover's message indicates the sender to be a man and refers to "him" and "he"—so much for the redactions and concerns for protection of privacy. There are more redactions made to the body of Hoover's message to the SAC where the Director writes, "It appears that this individual is identical with the [LINES REDACTED]." The sender was not name-checked as others have been in the past when writing to the FBI. Usually, the FBI HQ person handling such a letter notes at the bottom that their files have been checked to see if this person is found in their records system (indicates if found or not found). Interestingly, however, is that once a person writes to the FBI, a file is created, so from that day forward a file will exist on the letter writer in the FBI records system.

The SAC, Los Angeles responded to the Director by LHM dated July 11, 1969, about this letter, claiming that no one answered his calls at the office in Indio. "The individual," the SAC assures Hoover, "was interviewed on June 27, 1969 by SA [REDACTED]." The LHM continues with the secondhand narrative of the interview as reported to him by the SA. It turns out that the individual did not have anything concrete to report other than opinions, concerns, and beliefs that "Cesar Chavez was a Nazi." And, he referred to similarities in statements attributed to Chávez in the press and "a book entitled 'Under Cover,' written by John Ray Carlson in 1943." This individual was reported to have said to the SA that "he felt Chavez wanted to overthrow the government through revolutionary means." The individual "was advised of the confidential nature of the information contained in Bureau files, and the Bureau was not in a position to offer any recommendation to him. He understood this fully and stated he merely wanted to bring Chavez to the attention of the FBI." The SAC closed his message to Hoover stating: "No further action with regard to [REDACTED] or information furnished by him is deemed necessary at this time." Despite this apparent closure to the matter, the SAC then inserted this last line in his message: "Information copies of this furnished to Sacramento as Chavez has his headquarters at Delano, California." It is utterly amazing to read, as in this exchange, how government resources are uselessly expended by the FBI while supposedly serving the public and protecting national security. What is the point of sending this query from a concerned person to the SAC, Sacramento?

First Real Look at Federal Violations

The U.S. Commission on Civil Rights in 1968 finally began to hold hearings across the nation to hear complaints from Mexican Americans regarding the lack of protection of their civil rights. The commission held several hearings in the Southwest, including San Antonio, Texas, and heard an earful at each location. They finally issued a comprehensive report and a *Summary*. The *Summary* booklet published by the U.S. Commission on Civil Rights contains the thirteen findings from the original report. These findings are on point with the above narrative of consistent, prolonged, and intentional harm directed at César Chávez and others in the UFW. Under "4. Inadequacy of Local Remedies for Police Malpractice" are found five items. Among them are that the only place to complain about local police behavior is with the local police; that there are noneffective police review boards, if they exist; infrequent civil litigation by victims against police with few successful local prosecutions; and when the FBI is contacted for relief, local police departments retaliate against the complainants. Under "5. Federal Remedies" are two clearly aimed at the FBI:

(a) Agents of the Federal Bureau of Investigation have often failed to interview important witnesses in cases of alleged violation of 18 U.S.C. 242 or interviewed such witnesses in a perfunctory and hostile manner.

(b) More aggressive efforts to implement 18 U.S.C. 242 by the Department of Justice are needed."[1]

At the time of these publications, the FBI had 772 top positions within the agency's field offices in the Southwest, but only three were Mexican Americans.[2]

Absent in the findings of this commission and the state advisory group is the fact that litigation is financially prohibitive for farm workers typically earning a wage of half a dollar an hour; it is protracted and time-consuming, and while the occasional court victory is vindication for victims, the remedy is too little too late. For example, the *Medrano* case took seven long years, from 1967 to May 20, 1974, for the Texas Rangers to be found at fault, prohibited from victimizing strikers and picketers, and removed from other labor disputes by order of the U.S. Supreme Court.

Protests of the 1970s

On February 16, 1970, Kansas City, Missouri, FBI reported that Chávez was due to appear in that city on the 12th of the month and did, according to an informant, "T-1." While there, Chávez, apparently with the T-1 informant in tow, met with folks, discussed strategy against Safeway, and set up a picket on the store at 3600 Broadway. Chávez continued to organize support for the boycott of Safeway stores in the city and spoke at various rallies, one of which was to an audience of approximately 1,500 people at Penn Valley Community College.

The protests organized and led by the UFW in cities across the agriculturally rich valleys of California and the country, such as Kansas City, Missouri, were peaceful, nonviolent events. If any violence occurred it was usually instigated by others, including the local police. On April 5, 1970, Chávez held a meeting and a barbecue at the city park in Coachella, California, for some five to six hundred persons, according to a two-page teletype sent by SAC, Los Angeles to the Director, FBI at 11:40 p.m. that night. This event was a prelude to the picketing of a grape grower in the Coachella Valley the next day. The teletype informed that "UFWOC meeting ended about six pm and dance sponsored by local Mexican Fraternal Organization began in same park which is located adjacent to Coachella Police Station." Within the hour, at approximately seven p.m., a group allegedly tried to take over the dance podium. The SAC, Los Angeles provided identification as "a group, exact number unknown, described only as 'Brown Berets,' who had come to Coachella from Los Angeles for UFWOC meeting" (p.1). When this group took over the podium and microphone, violence broke out.

> Coachella PD officers attempted to restore order at which time disturbance spread and moved from city park to adjacent police station where windows were broken with bottles and rocks and a black and white Coachella PD [scratched out and "police" handwritten] was overturned and burned. Tear gas used in attempt to disperse crowd. Unverified reports of shots being fired, and other cars parked on street being damaged and burned received. Mutual aid pact called into effect and officers from Riverside SO,

CHP [scratched out and "Sheriff's Office" and "California Highway Patrol" handwritten], Indio PD, and Palm Springs PD responded. Group attacking Coachella PD dispersed, however, other rock throwing incidents in other parts of city reported. Three or four arrests reportedly made, however identities of persons arrested as yet unavailable. No known injuries to officers or participants in disturbance reported. [NAME REDACTED] states order being restored and considers matter under control. USA, Region II [scratched out and "U.S. Attorney" and "Army" handwritten], and Secret Service being advised. LHM [scratched out and "LHM" handwritten] follows. (p.2)

No LHM on this matter was released until May 28, 1970. This one-page report from SAC, Los Angeles to the Director clarified that those involved with the Coachella disturbance could have been a Mexican college student group known as Mecha [sic], not Brown Berets. They also would hold a rally in support of Chávez in the Coachella Valley on June 6.

Scores of other SAC field reports on UFW and UFW boycott protests were submitted by teletype to the Director, FBI for the remainder of 1970. SAC, Chicago reported an April 16 protest at the Regional Food and Drug Administration offices and several grocery stores. SAC, Pittsburg reported a grape boycott demonstration in downtown's Market Square and marching over to the Federal Building on April 29, then to a supermarket located in the north side of town. May 1st was to be the site of another demonstration at Slaton House at the Village Green in Columbia, Maryland, according to the SAC, Baltimore, before they began the march toward Washington. DC. A May Day protest that was to take place at the University of Pittsburg was canceled by the grape boycott organizer Albert Rojas, from Pittsburg.

SAC, Washington reported on several protests in Maryland. On May 1st at Burtonsville, Maryland; on the 2nd in Jessup Blair Park in Silver Springs, Maryland, before entering D.C. to listen to Pete Seeger and Judy Collins. They had been invited to entertain the crowd, estimated to reach six thousand. And, the May 3rd protest march led by César Chávez was to occur at the U.S. Department of Agriculture (USDA) building, coming down Columbia Street. During these days, May 1st through 3rd, the SAC, Baltimore through daily teletypes kept Director Hoover informed of the crowd sizes involved in the protests and marches: 200 gathered at Slaton House; 1,500 were at Jessup Blair Park to hear Dr. Ralph Abernathy and David Sullivan; 500 protested at USDA; 180 left Columbia marching toward Burtonsville; and 600 more joined them marching toward D.C. The two-page LHM from SAC, Baltimore to the Director, FBI dated May 4, 1970, summarized the May Day protests and provided more specific information on numbers of protestors previously contained in the teletypes. For example, "a representative of the FBI observed about 200 people leave St. Stephen and the Incarnation Church toward North Agriculture Building . . . the above group merged with another five to six hundred demonstrators" (p.1). Besides Chávez as speaker, the roster of names submitted to Hoover contained: "Senator Fred. R. Harris (D) from Oklahoma, Representative Ogden R. Reid (R) of New York, Cynthia Wedel, head of the National Council of Churches, former Secretary of Labor Willard Wirtz, and representatives from the United Auto Workers, National Welfare Rights Organization, American Federation of Teachers, Consumers Federation of America, and the AFL-CIO" (p.2).

The FBI also began to monitor student activities at campuses in the Tampa Division. SAC, Tampa alerted the Director, FBI by Airtel dated July 17, 1970, that while there had been violence or unrest in the past two weeks within the Tampa Division, students at the University of Southern Florida had gathered twice, on July 9 and 16, to organize themselves into a Grape Boycott Committee in support of the UFWOC boycott of California grapes.

More Bombings in 1970—Hollister

An employee of the UFWOC in Hollister, California, called the RA in Salinas reporting a bomb explosion at their offices. The RA, Salinas notified the SAC, San Francisco, who in turn teletyped the Director, FBI at 12 noon on the 4th of November 1970. Reference in the two-page teletype is made to some officers who "were patrolling within two blocks of the building, which is located at seven two one and one-half San Benito St., when they heard the explosion. Officers responded to the scene and observed damage. Officers were at the explosion scene within a matter of seconds" (p.1). Apparently, the damage to the building did not exceed $500 and the building was unoccupied at the time. Moreover, the teletype states that "no threats or warnings received prior to explosion ... Streets were deserted ... No one observed near the scene ... No suspects developed to date" (p.2). The teletype mentions that explosive material found at the site was gathered, but the "Hollister PD has requested no investigation from Bureau. Facilities of FBI laboratory have been offered to the PD. Local offices of Secret Service and One One Five MIG have been advised" (p.2). This teletype does contain a revealing handwritten note as to the disposition of this case at the top of the first page just below the date and word TELETYPE: "Less. Atty. Ruff, Crim. Div. advised no investigation justified re E & ID or any other statute in absence of interstate commerce. 11/4/70, JRM" (p.1).

"E & ID" refers to Explosives and Incendiary Devices, which are a federal crime if used to destroy property or harm individuals. In this case, it was assumed dynamite—which is highly regulated with records of sales and purchases made by date, time, amounts, and purpose—was the explosive. The ATF investigates these crimes, but they were not included in the dissemination of this teletype or subsequent reports, if any. Additionally, grapes were being boycotted nationally by UFWOC and were in the stream of interstate commerce. How can the FBI person entering the handwritten note closing the investigation claim an absence of interstate commerce?

Other Bombings in 1973—Delano, Terra Bella, and Poplar

Henry E. Petersen of the DOJ sent the FBI Acting Director a memorandum dated January 31, 1973, repeating allegations made by César Chávez, and requesting a preliminary investigation into these incidents. The FBI response was to go to the Management and Labor Section of DOJ.[3] FBI Acting Director L. Patrick Gray sent an Airtel message to the SAC, Sacramento on February 1st enclosing the DOJ memorandum and asking for "Conduct investigation requested in enclosed memorandum and suRep on a prompt basis. Assign mature, experienced Agents and be most circumspect in any contact with Cesar Chavez."

Dynamite was used to blow up the UFWOC Delano office on January 22, 1973, according to Chávez. He also alleged that damage was done to other offices in Terra Bella and Poplar, and that union files had been taken. He had sent a telegram to the DOJ Assistant Attorney General Criminal Division reporting these incidents and alleging "that union members have been threatened with bodily harm." The Sacramento FBI office filed a six-page report on February 21, 1973. An additional twelve pages related to this report were deleted entirely. Oddly, two more pages of this report, numbered 19 and 20, informed Washington that the ATF "assumed jurisdiction in 1/17/73 dynamiting of the UFW Coop gasoline station, Delano (not UFW business office) and no suspects developed to date." In Poplar and Terra Bella, the Tulare County Sheriff's Department handled the investigation and found "broken windows and building not entered." The Sheriff's Office claimed that the Poplar UFWOC office had been "closed December 1972, and moved to Terra Bella." More importantly, the last sentence of the synopsis on the first page is most revealing: "USA, Sacramento, advised there are no apparent Federal violations, and recommended no further investigation." The report continues in cynical fashion, "[LINES REDACTED] all of the Kern County Sheriff's Office (KCSO), Bakersfield, California, all advised on February 9, 1973, that they have received no complaints from CESAR CHAVEZ or the UFW during the past six months." Yet in the next line, it reads, "[NAME RE-DACTED] stated that he turned the January 17, 1973, bombing matter of the UFW gasoline station over to Agents of the Alcohol, Tobacco and Firearms Department (ATFD) specifically to avoid any charges of bias by CHAVEZ." On the one hand, the Sheriff's Office claimed Chávez had not called in any complaints in six months, then states that last month, when he called in the dynamite bombing, they passed it on to ATF. Apparently the KCSO did some initial investigations into these complaints by Chávez because the FBI found "Records of the KCSO, as of February 9, 1973, reflected three reports … however, no suspects were developed by this agency." To demonstrate their bias toward Chávez, the KCSO [NAME REDACTED] provided the FBI with documentation that showed vandalism was done to growers in October 1972 and the past six months. Allegedly, vandals caused $53,700 of damage to 2,180 citrus trees near McFarland; $5,000 in damage to 3,200 grapevines in

Earlimart; $3,000 in damage to 75 peach trees in Hanford; $8,000 in damage to 6,000 new grapevines near Delano; and other instances in Fresno County. Vandalism had reached the point that "a $10,000.00 reward has been offered by farmers in Fresno County and an additional $10,000.00 by farmers in Kern County, California." The insinuation is obvious, if not the bias: Chávez must be behind this vandalism. But why would farm workers damage crops, their livelihood, and not do damage to buildings or offices or grower homes?

The ATF bomb squad found "that approximately one and one-half to two pounds of dynamite was detonated at the end of the garage area of the UFW gasoline station and, in his opinion, was placed where the explosion caused the least amount of possible damage to the facility. The result was an approximate two-foot diameter hole in the eighteen-inch wall of the service station, and damage to two old models 'junk' (inoperative) automobiles." The guard of the UFW gasoline station that night, the report reveals, came in late to work. No suspects were ever developed by any law enforcement or prosecutorial team for these incidents, nor the vandalism to growers' crops.

The report enclosed a clipping from the *Fresno Bee* in which Chávez is quoted repeating the same information about the bombing and break-ins at various offices. And, the report also contained two photographs and other reports sent January 29 and February 5. In the pages numbered 19-20, the FBI reports the Tulare County Sheriff's Office view of complaints filed by the UFW. In short, the sheriff disputed that the Terra Bella UFW office was broken into or damaged: "just several broken windows." The Poplar office "was abandoned by the UFW ... the structure was condemned." Their attitude toward the complaints is as follows: "[NAME REDACTED] advised that a typical attitude by the UFW representative upon responding to any complaint has been a total lack of cooperation, a refusal to furnish any statements, abusive language, censure of his department, and a curt referral to a UFW attorney." Moreover, the sheriff's source was of the opinion that "the many telegrams that UFW has sent to senators, congressmen, and the news media, have all been geared to get the maximum publicity to benefit the UFW movement."

Based on this information provided by the Sheriff's Office and an article in the *Bakersfield Californian* newspaper of February 14 citing damage estimated at $12,000 done to an office building in Richgrove, California, owned by White River Farms, the U.S. attorney made a determination regarding this current investigation. In straight three-way hearsay, the FBI quoted the Sheriff's Office quoting the U.S. attorney: "DWAYNE KEYES … advised that the variances between the allegations made by Chavez and the information developed by local and Federal law enforcement agencies and personnel casts doubts on the sincerity of the complaint by the UFW director." He further stated that the "CHAVEZ allegations are certainly vague and, in fact, for the most part, appear to be untrue." The blatant hearsay continues, "Mr. KEYES said that he does not feel that either the FBI or the U.S. Department of Justice should be used for political or publicity purposes by the UFW, and therefore, would not recommend contact with CHAVEZ or any other UFW official concerning this matter." An interesting investigative method is presented in the document—do not talk to the complaining party about their complaint; instead listen to hearsay. And, the investigation was closed by all federal and county law-enforcement officials.

The Black Bag Jobs Done on the UFW

Jerry Cohen called the DOJ Civil Rights Division sometime in late March about an extortion scheme developing against the UFWOC by Fred Schwartz. The DOJ person at the other end of the telephone call supposedly told Cohen to "tell Schwartz to contact FBI." The fuller story was detailed by teletype from Sacramento FBI to the Director, Los Angeles, and San Francisco FBI offices on April 1, 1971. Fred Schwartz was described as "white male, age 45 to 50, 6 ft. 2 ins.; 215 lbs., gray hair." Schwartz was to have met with Cohen on March 25 in Bakersfield, California. At that meeting, Schwartz asked for $35,000 for "certain documents … These documents offered by Schwartz supposedly relate to Calif. Growers who paid for break-ins of UFW offices and other organizations in 1960s." Cohen apparently rejected the offer, according to the FBI message, but met with Schwartz once again on March 31, at which time "the asking price was reduced to $25,000." The FBI observed this meeting, took photographs of Schwartz and Cohen, followed Schwartz driving "in 1974 Buick, Calif. License 814 JZH, and proceeded to Hilton Inn, Bakersfield. Car is registered to National Car Rental, care of [NAME REDACTED] San Luis Obispo. Hilton records reflect Ducote, [REDACTED] registered with same license number Mar. 30, 1974, and due to check out Apr. 1, 1974." In an attempt to ascertain if Schwartz and Ducote were the same person, Sacramento FBI contacted the California DMV for a copy of Ducote's photo, but as luck would have it, the Driver's License Photo Reproducing Section was under repair until April 2, 1974. They did, however, supply a first name: Jerry.

Addendum of FBI Files Recently Released

A lesson quickly learned in graduate school is to know when to stop researching; this work was to focus on the declassified and released files. But, under FOI/PA rules, if a person dies anyone can ask for release of those files, if any. A living person has to provide a notarized document expressly granting permission to access their files held by the FBI, if any, when someone else is making a FOI/PA request. In this case, Helen Fabela Chávez, Antonio Orendain, Gilbert Padilla, and Dolores Huerta were all alive when I began this work. None agreed to a notarized statement allowing me to file a FOIA request in their name. I could not locate Padilla. After Helen's death, I filed a FOIA request for her FBI files. I appealed the limited César Chavez files released under FOIA and asked for more documents held by the FBI from August 2, 1975, to April 30, 1993. On June 27, 2017, I received sixty-three more pages on César Chávez. A letter accompanying these new documents informed me that some records that might have been covered under my FOIA request had already been destroyed in November 1977.[4]

Antonio Orendain has also since died. I have requested his files. Files on Helen were denied under exemptions for national security. The only files received from the FBI were on Antonio Orendain. These pertain to his activities after he parted with Chávez; therefore, they are not included here. Padilla and Huerta are full of life and still active in civic affairs, especially Dolores. Those files must wait for public release.

FBI Hand-Washing of 9A-1191 C

SAC, Sacramento sent a three-page Airtel dated January 6, 1989, to the Director, FBI about the threatening phone calls received by César Chávez.[5] He provided a brief biography of Chávez in the first paragraphs and faulted Chávez in the second and third paragraphs for not being available to discuss the December calls "until after January 1, 1989" (p.1). On January 3, SAC, Sacramento wrote in his report that two agents (names redacted) met with Chávez at his office to get the details of the incidents (p.2). Chávez confirmed they originated within his own telephone system. Chávez told the FBI agents he suspected there was a spy within his organization for years, but had been unable to identify the person. The next line is a major concession by Chávez, if true. According to the FBI, "He explained that even when efforts are expended to conceal his whereabouts, itineraries, etc. he has been unsuccessful in maintaining privacy of his movements."

"The elements of the Federal Extortion Statute were tactfully explained to Mr. Chavez as well as the fact the FBI does not have investigative jurisdiction in this particular matter because of the intrastate aspect of the telephone calls" (p.3). Chávez then presented the FBI agents with a threatening letter dated January 3rd. They advised Chávez the letter would be sent to (name redacted) Attorney General's Office. The Airtel closes with "No further direct investigative efforts are being expended in captioned matter because of the lack of investigative jurisdiction, the threatening letter received at UFW headquarters." Then, why promise to send it up the FBI and attorney general chain of command and investigation if the decision made locally was to close the case? The Airtel references the case as closed with (C) made part of the file number.

Closed or Pending?

Once again, the FBI failed to find anyone at fault, despite an active suspect and identification of two latent fingerprints on the letters. They refused to investigate the telephone calls allegedly made from within the Chávez system of communication after he explained the ring codes, leading to the conclusion that they were inside calls. Is not a threat made over the telephone still a federal crime regardless of origin? Despite the fact that Chávez's UFW owned their own telephone system, it was still part of the satellite-controlled technology monitored by the National Security Agency (NSA) and subject to federal regulation and investigation. The FBI discontinued more investigations and closed more cases involving incidents against Chávez than it referred cases to any U.S. attorneys working for the U.S. attorney general in offices across the country for prosecution.

The Six-Year War with Teamsters

IN 1970, THE INTERNATIONAL Brotherhood of Teamsters union comprised of 2.3 million members made a move to usurp Chávez's newly organized farm workers in California. Their political friend from California, Richard Nixon, with the help of their generous financial contributions, was now president of the United States.[1] The growers, feeling the economic hit from Chávez's strikes, boycotts, and most recently, worker elections opting for the UFW, turned to the Teamsters and invited them to organize their workers in the fields. Unfortunately for César Chávez, the ex-Teamster boss Jimmy Hoffa was sent to prison in 1967 as Chávez was beginning to realize success from his organizing efforts. Hoffa had looked with favor on Chávez's gains and greatly admired his perseverance. His anointed successor, Frank Fitzsimmons, was too weak to oppose those within his membership that wanted to raid Chávez's contracts. They already had cannery workers and truckers in the fold; why not add the farm laborers? This battle continued for six long, bloody, violent years.[2] In 1974, George Meany of the AFL-CIO stepped up to the plate, sided with Chávez against the Teamsters, and provided funding to the UFW. The battle in the media was portrayed as a David vs. Goliath story, with much emphasis on Teamster violence against the farm workers. Once California's Agricultural Labor Relations Board (ALRB) was in place, the Teamsters began to lose worker elections, more often than not to the UFW. Chávez was able to defeat the Teamsters and win uncontested jurisdiction over most of the field-hand labor in the state—but not without great cost of lives, property, and financial resources.[3]

Teamster Violence

Chávez prepared and trained himself, staff, volunteers, and his membership on how to function as a union with hiring halls, ranch committees, governance rules, contract enforcement, and a myriad of administrative duties concomitant with large contracts. He and staff or UFW union members were prepared for the violence that ensued. However, neither he nor his people had trained for this eventuality; on the contrary, they were schooled in nonviolence and trained for that. The Teamsters by mid-July 1970 had signed sixty agreements with growers that included farm workers. Chávez turned to George Meany, his parent AFL-CIO president, for strong support against the Teamsters. Nothing was forthcoming from Meany. He turned to the Catholic bishops for help, and little changed. By August 20, 1970, it was clear that 170 growers were going to stick with the Teamster contracts. Chávez declared a general strike and ordered all lettuce to be boycotted. The next day, armed guards appeared at the farm roads and the violence began anew.[4] The Monterey County Court ordered restraining orders against the pickets at thirty-six grower locations.[5] Ronald Taylor writes,

> The UFWOC office in Watsonville was blown up; UFWOC counsel Jerry Cohen was jumped by a 300-pound, 6 foot-2 inches 'guard' who held him

in a bear grip while another guard beat him unconscious. Cohen was hospitalized for four days with a brain concussion and cuts and bruises.[6]

The Presidential Connections

On December 21, 1971, Jimmy Hoffa was released from prison after a plea for clemency by Nixon. A condition of his release was to stay out of Teamster union business. The federal parole board four months earlier had turned Hoffa down for the third time on his request for parole. What greased the wheels for the Nixon intervention was money, lots of money—over a million dollars in cash paid in various installments. The last payment of $500,000 in cash was delivered by Charles Colson, an ex-FBI agent, now part of the Nixon campaign staff.[7] Frank Fitzsimmons, as Teamster president, also asked all the Teamster vice presidents and organizers to each kick in $1,000 to Nixon's campaign. Frank himself sent in $4,000.[8]

In 1973, however, Hoffa, despite the restrictions of his parole, began making plans for a comeback by 1976. As he went across the country speaking to union groups, mainly Teamsters, Hoffa surprisingly began to speak of the necessity of cleaning out the Mafia from labor unions. He meant the Teamsters. Hoffa called on Harold Gibbons to aid him in the pursuit of the Teamster presidency. Meanwhile, Frank Fitzsimmons, the sitting president, became alarmed at the prospect of Hoffa becoming president. He called on Nixon to help him burn Gibbons and stop Hoffa. Gibbons was not only put in charge of shutting down Chávez in California by Fitzsimmons, but also was being subjected to an IRS audit ordered by the Nixon administration. Gibbons was doomed by both challenges. Moreover, others in the union made it clear to Gibbons that if he did not stop helping Hoffa, he would be out of the union feet first. This is when Hoffa disappeared feet first from society, and his body is yet to be found.[9]

Ronald Reagan Also Eats Grapes

Taking a page from Nixon's campaign book, Ronald Reagan also ate grapes in public and called the UFW names, such as "outside agitators," when he campaigned for the presidency. He called the UFW "immoral to boycott grapes."[10] From 1966, when he was governor of California, until 1974, when he left to pursue the White House, his team pursued a soft-power approach to court the Teamsters. The Teamsters in turn endorsed him for president. And, Reagan frequently visited his Hollywood chums, such as Frank Sinatra and his Rat Pack, during his eight years in Sacramento. Unbeknownst to Reagan, Hoover had an extensive file on Sinatra and his alleged links to organized-crime figures, probably including Ronald Reagan.[11] As president, Reagan is reported to have dismissed the allegations of corruption made by his close friend and appointee for U.S. attorney general, William French, and continued to consort with Sinatra while his casino license was pending, with, "Yeah, I know . . . we've heard these things about Frank for years, and we just hope none of them are true."[12] At the same time, Reagan's administration began to audit federal funds granted to Chávez and demanded return of $347,529; the IRS also wanted $390,000 in back Social Security and federal unemployment taxes not paid by the UFW.[13]

Hoover's Policy: Hands off the Mafia

Back in the 1930s, the top FBI man known to the public was Melvin Purvis, who almost singlehandedly brought down the most notorious criminals during the Depression years. He apprehended such Most Wanted criminals as John Dillinger, Pretty Boy Floyd, Baby Face Nelson, Machine Gun Kelly, and Volney Davis. Hoover resented the publicity Purvis always received, to the point that on April 4, 1935, in a Hoover memo to Tolson, he proposed a personnel shakeup involving fifteen agents, moving them from smaller assignments to larger cities—except one, Melvin Purvis; he was being reassigned from Chicago to Charlotte, North Carolina. Purvis resigned. Hoover and Tolson subsequently began the systematic removal of any mention of

Purvis from all FBI documents they could find. Hoover had been humiliated in a congressional hearing when he was pressed to answer how many arrests he personally had effected. None, was the answer.[14] These were the last years the FBI hunted down the top gangsters in the country.

In his tell-all book about his long tenure at the FBI, William Sullivan recounts the story about Hoover denying there was a Mafia in the United States. The story broke on November 14, 1957, that the New York State Police had interrupted a Mob meeting in a house in Apalachin, New York.[15] Hoover said, "They are just a bunch of hoodlums." Sullivan, however, explained further and in detail:

> Investigating the Mafia promised to be more difficult than rounding up juvenile auto thieves. Organized crime is far more complicated; the Mafia runs legitimate businesses as a front for their illegal operations. Mafioso are rich and can afford the best lawyers, while we have to use government lawyers, some of whom are excellent, some of whom aren't worth a damn. And, the Mafia is powerful, so powerful that entire police forces or even a mayor's office can be under Mafia control. That's why Hoover was afraid to let us tackle it. He was afraid we'd show up poorly.
>
> The Mafia has an ironclad rule—"Death to the informer!"—which makes investigating their activities even more difficult. Placing an informant in the Mafia is expensive and risky. We once found an informant in Detroit strangled and stuffed into the trunk of an automobile. Informing on the Mafia is more dangerous than informing on the Soviets—the Mafia is deadlier.[16]

Word in Washington and among politicians, according to Rhodri Jefferys-Jones, was that Hoover feared the consequences of hunting down those behind organized crime, the Mafia gangsters. He provides example after example of Hoover's neglect. Among the Hoover critics at the time was Robert Kennedy, whose focus early on was against President Eisenhower's DOJ lack of action against the racketeering activities of the Teamsters. As attorney general, he wanted Hoover to focus on organized crime and forget his paranoia over Communist subversion. LBJ and AG Ramsey Clark were both also critical of Hoover's soft-glove handling of the Mafia. Subsequent FBI top officials were critical of Hoover's hands-off policy even after his death, such as William H. Webster, FBI Director from 1978 to 1987.

Jack Conway, Ex-UAW Man, at the Center for Community Change

Back in Cincinnati, Chávez supporters and UFWOC staffers were printing and disseminating flyers protesting the arrest and jailing of Chávez in Salinas, California, for being in contempt of court. Judge Gordon Campbell of Monterey County on October 8 had ordered Chávez to stop the boycott of lettuce against the Bud Antle company. He ignored it. On November 17, 1970, he was ordered by Judge Campbell for the UFW to post a $2 million bond. Chávez ignored that also.[17] The FBI had copies of the flyers and copies of more open source material. Whitney Young Jr. wrote an opinion editorial for the *Cincinnati Post and Times Star* in strong support for the farm worker union and the boycott. Young's support in writing implicitly underscored the growing solidarity between Chávez and African American activists. In a subsequent open source clipping from the same newspaper, with date typed in stamped area of "12/16/70," is what appears to be an editorial. The heading reveals the thrust of the content, "Cesar Chavez Unjustly Jailed."

Just a few days before, on December 14, the FBI stamped "24" next to the *New York Times* on an open source article announcing a grant award from the Ford Foundation to the Center for Community Change based in Washington, DC, to help fund seven farm-workers service centers established by UFWOC. These service centers, it was reported, "advise 7,000 Mexican-American laborers monthly on such matters as welfare and social security benefits, the filing of tax returns and wage claims, and protection of civil rights." With this grant, the UFWOC was also going "to expand legal efforts to protect farm workers' health and safety."

The connection between Chávez, the Center for Community Change, and the Ford Foundation is illustrative of his growing reach into the offices of powerful change agents, the philanthropists of New York, because of his electoral work on behalf of the Kennedy brothers, John and Robert.[18] During the Chávez years of ascendency, the Ford Foundation was the world's largest grant-making institution; its budget exceeded that of many countries. Yet, philanthropy to Mexican Americans lagged behind all others in amount and number of grants, and still does. The Center for Community Change (CCC) headquartered in Washington, DC, was run by Jack Conway, senior advisor to the Reuther brothers of the UAW.

Scant Files from March 1970

The declassified files for 1970 are scant and contain huge gaps of time between documents provided. The year begins with a typical letter dated March 10, 1970, from an inquirer about César Chávez: "Has Chavez communist ties?" and a second question, "Is he really helping the workers?" Hoover responded a week later in typical fashion: "While I would like to be of assistance to you, information contained in the files of the FBI must be … confidential pursuant to regulations of the Department of Justice. I regret I cannot be of help to you in this instance." Signed with a signature stamp of his name at bottom.

Also at bottom of this letter below the stamped signature is a NOTE that indicates the person is a regular writer: "Bufiles reveal we have had prior cordial correspondence with [NAME REDACTED]." And perhaps the writer was female, because the Hoover letter begins with the salutation "My dear [NAME REDACTED]." The note continues with a review of the early special inquiry investigation of Chávez at White House request and the bureau coding of Chávez as a Security Matter Investigation. "He has been called a communist although this has not been corroborated. He repeatedly associated with 'left-wing' type individuals and allegedly distributes copies of 'People's World,' a west coast communist newspaper [illegible words] from his Delano office." Numbered sequentially are two sheets, an article from the *Daily World* with handwritten note "P.6." on the open source stamp list at bottom right of page, and a copy of a photograph of Chávez. The article, stamp dated at bottom left "56 NOV 16 1970," is favorable to Chávez and the grape strike and boycott. The story is critical of growers who are identified by name and business interest. For example, "J.G. Boswell and Co. alone received $4,091.81 in subsidies in 1967." The story also mentions another boycott: "For a while, there is a drive not to bank at Bank of America, the biggest bank in the world, which owns considerable land in the valley. And, Southern Pacific Railroad, people are told, has land amounting to 20,000,000 acres by virtue of early land grabs."

Bombing in Hollister

The declassified files jump to a teletype dated November 4, 1970, from San Francisco FBI office to the Director about "Explosion damage to United Farm Workers Organizing Committee (UFWOC) Office Bldg., Seven Two one and one-half San Benito St. Hollister, Calif., November Four, Seventy. Explosives and Incendiary Devices." The message reports the bombing being called in by a UFWOC employee to the "Agent at Salinas Resident Agency," stating it took place at 1:48 a.m. that day. In the third paragraph, a redacted source with the Hollister Police Department, it seems, also called in about the bombing and their investigation. A unit patrolling within two blocks heard the explosion and investigated: "officers were at the explosion scene within a matter of seconds. damage confined to front door and glass windows of building." The local police thought dynamite was used because they found "small shreds of white colored waxy type paper at crime scene." Apparently from the message, no FBI help was requested by Hollister police, but the San Francisco FBI office informed the Director that "Local offices of Secret Service and One Five MIG have been advised. LHM to follow." There was no LHM that followed in the declassified files.

According to a teletype dated November 28, 1970, the monitoring of Chávez picked up again when he appeared in Cincinnati, Ohio, to attend Mass and receive an award at St. Francis Church. Chávez was also going to speak to supporters "at Kroger Company building downtown." And, the message concluded with a redacted source, "Advised Chavez planned to fly to New York afterwards. Cincinnati closely following this matter." Whatever joy and good news Chávez was to bring back from this trip was short-lived.

Jail for Contempt of Court

With no money to spare, and hundreds being arrested daily, Chávez flew to New York's Riverside Church and Manhattan College to raise funds and rekindle the spark for the boycott of lettuce. He flew back in time to make his court appearance before Judge Gordon Campbell to answer why he did not post a $2 million bond to protect against Bud Antle's company losses due to the strike. Chávez had defied the judge by not posting the bond in a timely fashion. He stated to the press that they would continue the boycott. Judge Campbell ordered Chávez jailed until such time as he ended the boycott. By the third night in jail, Ethel Kennedy came into town. Rafer Johnson, the Olympian decathlon champion, did too. Then, Coretta Scott King came to visit César in jail. Hundreds of letters were delivered to the jail and UFW offices. On December 23, the California Supreme Court voted 6-1 to have Chávez released from jail by dissolving key parts of the injunction against the boycott.[19]

A diversion surfaced during this dramatic week that embarrassed many of the core UFW staff and the Chávez family. Richard, César's brother, had begun a sexual relationship with Dolores Huerta and she was now very pregnant and showing. Richard was still married to Sally, who had been a childhood friend of Helen Chávez since grade school. Not only that, but Richard and Sally had lost their eldest son in a car accident just a few years before.[20]

Eagle Eyes on Chávez in Cincinnati

At almost year's end, in a memorandum dated December 28, 1970, SAC, Cincinnati advised the Director, FBI that the Chavez file with the filing of this LHM "will be considered BUC." Case closed. The three-page LHM detailed the arrival of Chávez to the city and his itinerary down to the time he would receive an award, attend Mass at 6:30 a.m., eat breakfast, and fly out to New York. The Cincinnati office must have been very busy during Chávez's hectic schedule, interviewing informants and watching him as he deplaned at the airport and moved from activity to activity until he departed. SAC, Cincinnati also enclosed several clippings from the *Cincinnati Enquirer* and the *Cincinnati Post and Times Star* that covered Chávez's boycott activities against Kroger. Cincinnati is the headquarters for this national grocer and that was the target for Saturday morning, November 28. Chávez, according to the redacted source, and "about 125 individuals left the Sheraton-Gibson Hotel … and proceeded to march in an orderly fashion on the sidewalk to the Kroger Company building downtown. He stated this group stayed on the sidewalk, walked in a peaceful manner, and obeyed all traffic signals while en route to the Kroger Building. In conclusion, he advised that there were no incidents of violence as a result of Cesar Chavez being in Cincinnati Ohio."

War on the Department of Defense

Not one to be timid or cautious in pursuit of justice, Chávez filed suit against the Department of Defense for buying "scab lettuce." This was reported in the front-page article clipped by the local FBI field office from the *Sunday Star* in Washington, DC, dated January 17, 1971. The news was carried over UPI wire the previous day to thousands of outlets, such as the *Lodi News Sentinel* in Lodi, California. It was front-page news. The article listed Melvin Laird, defense secretary, and the commander of the Ft. Hamilton, Brooklyn, Army Base as defendants. Chávez and his legal team, headed by Jerry Cohen, got busy filing suits against the DOD and posting pickets at military installations. Richard Chávez led the picket committee and "estimated that his committee has picketed between 20 and 30 major military bases in the United States.

San Francisco FBI sent a teletype dated January 12, 1971, to the Director, FBI informing him of a demonstration at the U.S. Naval Station in Alameda, California. "Approximately eighty-five persons representing the United Farm Workers rallied at the Alameda Junior College … until twelve o'clock pm, this date, to protest against the purchase of nonunion lettuce by the United States Government. From there the group marched to the east gate of the United States Naval Air Station … where they passed literature …

until one fifteen pm, protesting the purchase of nonunion lettuce." The redacted source "advised that the group was predominated by Chicanos and contained a few blacks." Another redacted "source of unknown reliability advised" the Alexandria FBI, who sent a teletype with the information to the Director, FBI on January 25, 1971. The unreliable source passed on information that

> a group of approximately fifty persons of unknown affiliations would possibly attempt to infiltrate various government buildings in the Washington, D.C. area and disrupt lunch time crowds of people attempting to buy lettuce for their lunch. The purpose would be to draw attention to themselves by having themselves arrested and to suport [*sic*] the boycott by [end of page 1] Caesar [*sic*] Chavez against the purchase of non-union grown lettuce.

Supposedly, the informant was unsure of the exact buildings to be targeted, but mentioned "the Pentagon would be one target for the demonstrators." This rumor was made fact in a note sent by the Domestic Intelligence Division of the FBI to unnamed persons by affirming demonstrations to take place in various government buildings in the D.C. area. The rumor circulated widely: "Copy of attached sent Inter-Division Information Unit. Pertinent parts will be included in a summary to the White House, Vice President, Attorney General, Defense Intelligence Agency and Secret Service." Initials on the note are from various persons, but one set appears twice: "WCS," who was William Sullivan, number three man in the FBI in charge of domestic intelligence.

W. Mark Felt, "Deep Throat," Takes Over for Tolson

In July 1, 1971, Hoover bypassed William Sullivan, his friend, the way he had Melvin Purvis, and moved Mark Felt to the number two position within the FBI. Hoover's lifetime companion and partner, Clyde Tolson, had taken ill and missed too many days of work. Hoover needed a full-time number two man at his side. Mark Felt was the SAC in Kansas City for some time, and his main job was to investigate mobsters. He seldom could get anywhere with his investigations given the Mafia's ironclad rule—Talk and You Die! The police chief in Kansas City was Clarence Kelley, who like Felt would end up at the FBI. Kelley, when he could not solve gangland murders and crimes, would refer the matters to the FBI so they could share in the failure to prosecute. On the Mafioso Salvatore Palma case, Felt writes in his book that he and another "worked in Kansas City for more than five months, but we never built a case strong enough to present to a federal grand jury. We knew who the hit man was, but it was like investigating Watergate, nobody would talk."[21]

Soon, Felt's main job back in D.C. as the number two man in the FBI was to handle Nixon's White House and its continual and growing demands for political information. On Labor Day weekend, White House aides broke into the offices of Daniel Ellsberg's psychiatrist; Ellsberg, a military analyst for the RAND Corporation, had leaked the Pentagon Papers to the *New York Times*.[22] Nothing much changed after Hoover died in terms of illegal acts by the FBI. When Patrick Gray was FBI Director, he had instructed Felt in a written note about the bombings attributed to the Weather Underground in D.C. and the Pentagon: "Hunt to exhaustion—No holds barred." Felt "on at least five occasions . . . approved black-bag jobs."[23] W. Mark Felt would become the FBI official most instrumental in the investigation of the Watergate scandal, and his declarations led to the resignation of Richard Nixon as president. But he also was found guilty of federal crimes related to the black-bag jobs on the Weather Underground and was fined $5,000; however, he did not do prison time. He was pardoned by President Reagan in March 1981.[24]

Hard Research, More Data Uncovered

Meanwhile, Richard Chávez returned to Cincinnati and continued the protest against Kroger. The statistics obtained by the UFWOC on increased purchases of lettuce made by the Pentagon revealed a clear effort on the part of the Nixon administration via Defense Department officials, including former secretary of DOD Clark Clifford and Melvin Baird, to support Dow Chemical, the parent company of Bud Antle Farms, Inc., and help break the Chávez boycott.

This type of research on military purchases had proven invaluable during the grape strike and boycott. Utilizing the U.S. Department of Defense Fact Sheet (February 12, 1968) to do the math on the numbers of pounds and prices paid by DOD revealed purchases of grapes had tripled from 1965 at the beginning of the grape strike by the UFWOC. California grape growers contributed 90 percent of the national product in those years. And, South Vietnam became the world's twenty-fifth largest importer of U.S.-grown fresh grapes as a result. These facts, publicized by the UFWOC committees across the United States and internationally, made their case most convincing. It was not difficult to recruit boycotters of grapes or lettuce as opposed to openly protesting the war in Vietnam, which many did but others feared to do. Better safe not buying grapes or lettuce at Kroger and Safeway than risk being shot, as occurred at Kent State University, or beaten, as in the Los Angeles Moratorium of August 29, 1970. Housewives, students, and supporters of Chávez were moved by the article of January 27, 1971, in the *Cincinnati Post and Times Star* reporting on some of these statistics. Not only was the DOD buying scab lettuce in greater quantities, but they were also paying more of the taxpayers' money for the lettuce. The FBI article clipped from open source by Cincinnati FBI also included the news "that on Dec. 15 the Defense Subsistence Command bought 49,320 pounds of Antle lettuce at $5.54 a crate in Los Angeles, when the market quotation that day in the city for the highest quality wrapped lettuce was $3.50 a crate." The hike of $2.04 per crate showed DOD at its worst state of negligence in procurement and contracting. Consumers reading these types of news articles could associate the callous and hypocritical stance of the Johnson, then Nixon administrations' espousing a War on Poverty but keeping the poorest of the poor still poor by breaking their unionization movement at taxpayer expense.

Mr. Chávez Goes to Texas and Mexico

By Airtel dated February 1, 1971, the SAC, San Antonio informed the Director, FBI that Chávez was traveling to Austin, Texas, in support of the Economy Furniture Company striking workers. A redacted source gathered this information by attending a meeting of the Mexican American Youth Organization (MAYO) held at the University of Texas-Austin campus at which one of the Economy strikers announced Chávez would be speaking in their support at Austin's Montopolis Community Center on the 6th of the month. The SAC, San Antonio assured the Director, FBI that the information "is being furnished for information purposes as referenced communication 7/6/70 indicates that the Bureau does not desire an active investigation of CESAR CHAVEZ who will be the principle [sic] speaker at the above activity."

It is perplexing to analyze these documents when reading this type of disingenuous commentary stating on the one hand that the local agent knows not to investigate Chávez, yet reports that they not only are investigating MAYO and have an informer, but are also reporting on what they have learned about Chávez in the process. Equally perplexing in this Airtel is the coding for a convention referenced in July 1970 "captioned, 'Mexican American Texas State Convention . . . IS-SPANISH AMERICAN." Usually, the FBI reserved this coding for activity in New Mexico because those targeted refer to themselves as Spanish Americans or *Hispanos*.

Chávez arrived in Austin, made his presentation, and left town, according to the Airtel dated February 6, 1971, from San Antonio FBI to Director and marked 7:32 p.m. URGENT. In this message "a confidential source who has furnished reliable information in past" reported that "Chavez . . . spoke before fifteen hundred individuals . . . one of many speakers who appeared to urge support of the labor strike (Chicano Huelga) and boycott of the Economy Furniture Company (EFC) of Austin. Chavez gave a brief history of the successful organization of labor in Delano, California, and called for unity in the strike and boycott." The Washington FBI Office (WFO) back in D.C. was quieting the previous week's full alarm mode over "POSSIBLE DEMONSTRATIONS DURING THE WEEK OF 1/25/71"; it was relaying the information from

Assistant Chief (name redacted), Central Protection Force, General Services Administration. In short, the assistant chief had said "that no information had come to his attention, relating to any demonstrations in support of the CAESAR [*sic*] CHAVEZ boycott on lettuce having taken place in any government building in WDC, since he was contacted on 1/26/71." In hindsight, it would have been fitting justice if Chávez had in fact authorized this bit of misinformation to the FBI in a counterintelligence move of his own. But Chávez and his boycott committees were too busy with real work shutting down Safeway's nonunion lettuce-buying campaign.

Chávez headed to Las Vegas, Nevada. His trip to Sin City was reported by teletype dated March 3, 1971, from that FBI office to the Director and Sacramento FBI. Chávez in this Airtel was coded once again as "CESAR ESTRADA CHAVEZ: IS-SPANISH AMERICAN." The urgent message was citing an open source news item from February 27 in which the *Las Vegas Sun* reported Chávez was coming to join in protest of the state cuts to welfare organized by the National Welfare Rights Organization. Specifically, the Vegas office wanted Sacramento "to advise of any available information re proposed travel of Chávez to Las Vegas and plans to take part in demonstration." The intent of the request from my reading is clear: Vegas FBI wants to know if Sacramento FBI has intel on Chávez's travel plans and if they should infiltrate the demonstration. We are left in the dark because no follow-up document is among the declassified files.

The next declassified document in the Chavez file is dated June 11th. It is a letter requesting information on Chávez and Communism. The FBI Director regularly received these types of letters. He responded a week later with the usual formatted template denial letter to the inquirer from "Tipp City, Ohio 45371." Hoover used the self-addressed stamped envelope the person had sent with the letter. In the "NOTE" section at bottom, the letter writer's name was checked and "Bufiles reflect no record of correspondent" was written. And, as if to remind themselves periodically as to why the investigation of Chávez has continued for so long, it reads, "Chavez has been characterized as a controversial individual who had been openly called a communist, although our sources do not possess any corroborative information in this regard." Why, one must wonder, wouldn't the FBI just provide that information in their response to those inquiring if Chávez was a Communist, and be done with the question?

Again, in September 8, 1971, a clergyman from Cape Coral, Florida 33904, writes on the same subject to Hoover "pertaining to Mr. Ceaser Chevez [*sic*]." He asks directly, "Does he have communistic connections? Is he in any way out of step with the principles of our democracy or do you have any information which we need to know?" Hoover responds a week later with the standard denial letter, but in the note there is new language. It reads, "Has been characterized as a controversial individual and allegations made he is communist. Bureau sources have not corroborated this information; however, he has associated with 'left-wing' individuals. Chavez arrested on three occasions in past."

Efrain Fernandez and the Pharr, Texas, Police Riots

The FBI focus shifts a bit on Mexican Independence Day, September 16th, in a stamped "SECRET" communication to the Director, FBI from SAC, San Antonio.[25] The Secret message has the subject and referencing codes and classification of the matter redacted, but "All of these references originated with the San Antonio Office." But it particularly singled out a letter sent March 29, 1971, captioned "Disturbances, Pharr, Texas, Police Department, 2/6/71, IS-Spanish American," with an enclosure: SAfile 105-4658. The target of this separate investigation was Efrain Fernandez, with a request to further identify him and determine his contacts and activities. Efrain Fernandez was an active member of MAYO, originally from Kingsville, Texas. He had been a principal organizer in Kingsville and Robstown school protests and supportive of the farm worker march from the Rio Grande Valley (RGV) to Austin. After the family business in Kingsville, El Jardin restaurant, was boycotted by whites and ultimately burned to the ground mysteriously— without suspects, much less arrests for arson—he moved to the RGV.

Teamster Violence Intensified

During the protests at the White House on May 5, 1971, over the Vietnam War, President Nixon urged the beating of protestors, even murder! Summers, in his book, repeats quotes of a conspiratorial exchange between Nixon and Bob Haldeman, his chief of staff, regarding the use of Teamsters to hurt protestors:

> NIXON: Yeah … They've got guys who'll go in and knock their heads off.
> HALDEMAN: Sure. Murderers. Guys that really, you know, that's what they really do. Like the Steelworkers have and—except we can't deal with the Steelworkers at the moment.
> NIXON: No.
> HALDEMAN: We can deal with the Teamsters …
> NIXON: Yeah.[26]

No wonder the Teamsters had free rein to destroy the Chávez union from the White House down to the Department of Justice, to the FBI, to the Kern County Courthouse and other area judges; and to the Delano Police Department. This was not only the mentality of those in power but also their culture: not to let the workers partake in running the agricultural economy.

Bombings in the Delano Area

Dynamite was used to blow up the UFWOC Delano office on January 22, 1973, according to Chávez. He also alleged that damage was done to other offices in Terra Bella and Poplar and that union files were taken. He sent a telegram to the DOJ Assistant Attorney General Criminal Division reporting these incidents and "that union members have been threatened with bodily harm." Henry E. Petersen of the DOJ sent the Acting Director, FBI a memorandum dated January 31, 1973, repeating these allegations and requesting a preliminary investigation into these incidents. The response was to go to the Management and Labor Section of DOJ. The FBI Acting Director,

L. Patrick Gray, sent an Airtel message to the SAC, Sacramento on February 1st enclosing the DOJ memorandum and asking them to "Conduct investigation requested in enclosed memorandum and suRep on a prompt basis. Assign mature, experienced Agents and be most circumspect in any contact with Cesar Chavez."

Nothing happened for months, if we are to rely on the FBI documents that relate the entire history of events, until June 1973. A telegram campaign was started in support of Chávez and against the Teamster violence. The Bureau provided ten telegrams in the declassified files with sender names redacted. One telegram from (names redacted) on June 27 to Acting FBI Director William Ruckelshaus urged that "federal Marshalls assist Riverside County Sheriff's Dept. for maximum protection" of Coachella Valley Striking Farm Workers. At bottom of this telegram was a handwritten message: "No ack possible. No listing in telephone directory for above named individuals and organizations. No record identifiable in Bufiles." In someone else's handwriting below this entry is: "Crim Div advised he called AKSA Eric Nobels, Chief Crim Div, Los Angeles & informed him of name. Nobels reported Sheriff has matter under control & Nobel will contact FBI-LA if Bureau matter involved." My interpretation of these entries is that they were a request for the FBI to butt out of these local police matters.

U.S. Senator Floyd K. Haskell of Colorado wrote Clarence M. Kelley, the new FBI Director, on June 28, 1973. He expressed his concern over a photo in a newspaper: "picture in this morning's edition of the *Washington Post* indicates that violence is taking place in the Coachella Valley . . . am requesting that you exercise your appropriate jurisdiction in this matter in assuring that such civil rights are not infringed upon."

Ruckelshaus responded to the senator as he did all others: "Based upon the information you furnished and, in the absence of an indication that a Federal law within our jurisdiction has been violated, we have no authority to conduct an investigation."

The FBI handlers responding to similar correspondence for the Director added a NOTE at bottom: "We have had prior limited cordial correspondence with Senator Haskell." Hoover was known to keep scorecards on all members of Congress and the executive. As the power shifted to another director for the Bureau, it appeared the methods remained the same.

Unlike Hoover, who hid behind confidentiality of methods and privacy of individuals to deny any and all information, Ruckelshaus denied all requests for investigations in that language he used for Senator Haskell. The new Director wanted formal legal complaints referencing federal law conforming to Bureau jurisdiction from the public or other officials—otherwise, forget it. Consistent with prior Hoover practice, at bottom of his response, below his stamped name and signature, is a note that indicates the sender's name was checked in Bufiles, address in San Francisco telephone directory, and "Reply coordinated with the Accounting and Fraud and Criminal Sections of the General Investigative Division." The other note was more ominous. "Bufiles reveal that in February 1971, correspondent participated in an antiwar demonstration." Again, the reply was coordinated with the investigative division mentioned above. The other two replies also had a note: One, "Bufile disclose [NAME REDACTED] has been a participant in various civil rights and peace movements." The other noted: "Bufiles contain no record of correspondent." That is until July 3, 1973, when this communication began a file on that person. The FBI message remained clear: Don't write or communicate with the FBI or you may find yourself being investigated, not your complaint.

SACs at Seattle, Los Angeles, and Sacramento received a teletype from the Acting Director, FBI on July 2nd because "The following wire received at FBIHQ from [NAME REDACTED]," demanding investigation into Teamster violence against farm workers just like the FBI had investigated violence by whites against blacks; both are "part of the civil rights movement." A second wire from a (name redacted) was referenced, claiming Teamster violence against farm workers: "The farm workers are non-violent and refuse to retaliate against these violent attacks." Again, Ruckelshaus's hand is in the instructions to the SACs:

> Immediately interview above two correspondents in detail as to the specific nature of the violations alleged ... Make certain correspondent understands that matters involving disorder and personal safety are within

the jurisdiction of local authorities and, if indicated, appropriate local authorities should be advised.

Teamster violence had erupted in the fields, rural roads, and picket lines when UFW contracts with growers expired in April 15, 1973, and were not renewed. The growers entered into "sweetheart contracts," as they are known in organized labor circles, with the Teamsters. Chávez declared an all-out strike against all growers with Teamster deals the next day and set up picket lines. Sacramento FBI's teletype to the Director, FBI outlined a brief history of farm-labor organizing in California dating to 1963, when Chávez and the Filipino workers merged into one union under the AFL-CIO. It traced the organizing training Chávez obtained from the likes of graduates from the Saul Alinsky School of the Industrial Areas Foundation and their work with Community Service Organization. Between 1966 and 1967, the teletype explained, many growers signed contracts with the farm worker union that would expire in 1973. The Teamsters, the teletype also informed, were venturing into farm-related work unionization; they called it cyberization—combination of worker and machine—equipment operators, truck and tractor drivers, and produce-packing shed workers. In the early years of Chávez's unionization drive, the Teamsters were supportive through cash infusions for the struggling union for about three years. Competition for signing workers by both unions led to the early jurisdictional disputes. The Teamsters alleged that Chávez was unionizing produce-shed workers and truckers, while Chávez alleged that the Teamsters were signing up farm workers, not cybernetic workers. The growers, on the other hand, were critical of the UFW union-hall operations and accused Chávez of not sending enough labor when needed. The growers ultimately decided to sign with the Teamsters and not renew with Chávez; "this is the nature of the jurisdictional dispute in a nutshell." The teletype ended with summaries of local police, city, county, and state highway patrol complaints about Chávez. He does not provide them with information and numbers of picketers, so they can provide protection. He does not follow court-ordered injunctions. He has his members lie on the floor of the county jail. His members carry weapons and cause vandalism.

Jurisdictional Disputes Again

The Los Angeles FBI notified via a seven-page teletype the Acting Director, FBI, and three other FBI offices—Phoenix, Sacramento, and Seattle—of the dangerous situation between the UFW and Teamsters over the jurisdictional dispute on July 4, 1973. The fight in the fields ran all the way to the top of organized labor, with Frank Fitzsimmons, president of the Teamsters, on one side and George Meany, president of the AFL-CIO, on the other. Meany pledged $1.6 million for the UFW strike fund. The growers sought and obtained a court order from an Indio, California, superior judge that enjoined picketing by the UFW except under strict and limited conditions. The Farm Workers Union defied the order; mass arrests ensued. After some negotiation, the charges were dismissed, and new rules were put in place for picketing. "The pickets were instructed to picket within sixty feet of the property line and the Teamsters were to stay at the property line." The "Teamsters brought in approximately 350 members" to protect their union workers in the fields. The "UFW had in excess of one thousand pickets." The UFW complained that the Teamster members were nothing more than hired thugs from throughout California, especially San Francisco. "Fights and assaults between UFW members and Teamsters have occurred on the picket line and elsewhere and many arrests of Teamsters and UFW members have been made [REDACTED]."

The urgent teletype reported that "583 strike related incidents were reported [REDACTED] during 4-16-73, to 6-28-73, with 283 cases being reported by the UFW; 94 cases by the Teamsters; 174 cases by the growers; and 22 miscellaneous incidents." More importantly, the report provides a breakdown of arrests: "310 UFW members were booked … 42 Teamsters have been booked [REDACTED] during the same period." The report specified the charges by category and stated only "63 cases involved violations of court injunction." The remaining charges involved violence against persons primarily and some property damage. "Six arsons … three car fires … two Teamsters were arrested when they abducted an individual they apparently believed to be a UFW member and assaulted him with an ice pick." The Teamsters were "charged with kidnapping and assault with a deadly weapon." The report indicates that the worst is over in the Coachella Valley because the crop has been picked. Now, the report predicts, the battle will continue in the Arvin area of California and Maricopa County in Arizona.

The UFW also filed a huge lawsuit against growers in the Coachella Valley, seeking $32 million in punitive damages and $25,000 in actual damages as compensation. The suit alleged that the growers "maliciously and without justification entered into a conspiracy and a systematized campaign of terrorism, intimidation, threats, assaults, batteries and coercion to forcefully prevent the UFW from exercising their constitutional rights of free speech and expression."

The battle did move to Maricopa County, just northwest of Phoenix, Arizona. Phoenix FBI sent a teletype to Acting Director, FBI dated July 6, 1973, reporting that UFW contracts expired in Arizona on the same date as those in California; but the SAC adds, "No contract yet signed by growers with Teamster union or anyone else." The UFW's report adds, "presently picketing growers located in Maricopa County northwest of city of Phoenix with estimated 150 pickets. Principal growers involved are [LINES REDACTED]."

The report references a serious matter regarding a truck set on fire by pickets. "No arrests made. On July 3, 1973, complaint filed by growers in Superior Court, Maricopa County, Arizona 279173 against UFW for Temporary Restraining Order, Injunction, and damages regarding picketing of grape pickers. Temporary Restraining Order issued." The SAC reports that on July 5th, "approximately 25 UFW pickets arrested [NAME REDACTED] for violations of restraining order. No instances of violence occurred. Cesar Chavez, Head of UFW, arrived in Phoenix this date."

The Acting Director, FBI began a sleight-of-hand bureaucratic maneuver on how to handle the Arizona matter in his teletype to SACs in Los Angeles, Sacramento, Seattle, and Phoenix. He clearly did not want any investigation or report by them on any alleged violation of civil rights. He wants only "sufficient information for the department so that a judgement can be made by them as to the validity of certain civil rights violations alleged by recent correspondence with the FBI HQ." He continues with the new standing orders: "You are to specifically respond to bureau inquiry and conduct no further investigation." He wants any and all "leads outstanding to further follow the progress of the labor dispute . . . be immediately discontinued and not handled as part of this civil rights matter." Apparently, this new twist on FBI conduct was made directly to the SAC, Phoenix by telephone. The report reads, "This confirms BUTELCAL to Phoenix 7/6/73, in this regard." And, again to clarify the new FBI position in this matter, the teletype concludes with:

> Should some substantive violation or responsibility under Bureau jurisdiction become evident during the instant labor dispute, such violation or responsibility is to be handled separately under appropriate caption and not made a part of the civil rights inquiry presently being made.

In the NOTE entry that typically follows a communication sent by the FBI HQ are more revealing words about the Acting Director's intent to stifle and divert the field agents' work in Arizona, and his perception of who is involved. First, the note states, "In recent days, several communications have been received at FBIHQ asking for immediate FBI investigation into unspecified violations of civil rights of minority race members of United Farm Workers in Coachella Valley, California." The UFW members have now been perceived as "minority race members." I wonder if they mean the Filipinos, the immigrant Mexicans, or the Chicanos; who is in this new "minority race" category? Second, the note reviews their analysis of what to investigate and what to ignore:

> Our present interest in this matter is strictly limited to determining the validity of the alleged Civil Rights violations . . . Office involved have been responding to FBI HQ initiated inquiries but are expanding the matter beyond the area of immediate interest by advising that, "the matter (labor dispute) will be followed." Phoenix has carried the matter beyond the scope of Civil Rights interest by setting forth a lead for several offices to advise Phoenix regarding movement of the labor dispute into the Phoenix Division . . . This teletype is designed to get the captioned inquiry back on the intended Civil Rights track and to insure we do not become involved in an over-all investigation of the labor dispute under a Civil Rights caption.

The SAC, Los Angeles filed a 13-page Airtel on July 9 with the Acting Director, FBI covering much of the same history of the dispute in the beginning pages, but provides new information in the second half of the report. This SAC copied all previously admonished SACs in Sacramento, Seattle, and Phoenix, and the U.S. attorney in LA. The SAC, Los Angeles confirmed he understood the new rules of conduct: "The confrontation between the United Farm Workers and the Teamsters, as described in the LHM, is a union jurisdictional dispute and no further action is being taken by Los Angeles at this time, UACB." But, at bottom half of page 3, beginning with an entire paragraph redacted, the report states that UFW members in Brawley, California,

> had been taking license numbers of the Teamster workers in the field and thereafter published and circulated a list of these license numbers and their owners to their members, apparently in an attempt to intimidate the workers. Two cars reportedly owned by Teamster workers were burned during this period of time.

The implication is clear; the UFW is behind the burning of cars belonging to Teamsters.

Next, the Airtel report, with most of it redacted, contained a bit of insight as to how closely monitored the movement of UFW members and leader was at the time by FBI informants. "[LINES REDACTED] advised [RE-DACTED] that he had received information that there had been a meeting of officials of the UFW at the International Hotel located at the International Airport in Los Angeles on May 24, 1973, which included people such as [LINES REDACTED] . . . The Teamsters intimated that the UFW was bringing in 'hit men' in connection with their contact with [LINES REDACTED] (p.4). And penciled into the middle of the page between redactions is the underlined word "Nevada." A plain reading of this last section of a sentence implies the UFW okayed hiring hit men. It also could contain a typographical error with the word "contact," which does not make sense in the context of the sentence. If "contact" is changed to "contract," the meaning is clear. Furthermore, any amateur historian knows that Mafia and Teamster connections are found in Las Vegas, Nevada—not UFW unionization efforts, or even presence, at this time in history.

Pages 5 through 13 are full of anecdotal information on UFW wrongdoing against the Teamsters and growers. Rumors are reported by the SAC on the UFW "hit men" as actually being "heavies" from Las Vegas, members of the archrivals of the Teamsters, the Seafarers Union. On page 6, the SAC reports no less than three major confrontations between UFW pickets against Teamster guards and Teamster field workers. In one incident, UFW picket team captain Ray Huerta and six others were arrested. In another incident at an Indio, California, labor camp an unoccupied car was burned. During a rock-throwing scene described by UFW William Grami Sr., the director of the Western Conference of Teamsters Agricultural Organizing Committee, "had received a head injury and was bleeding profusely." In Mecca, California, 950 UFW picketers "moved into the small community . . . sealing off the town by blocking roads and harassing the grape workers in their vehicles and homes. Barbs shaped out of nails were scattered on the roadway, and the tires of the Sheriff's Office vehicles were flattened, according to." Another thirty to forty UFW picketers entered a field that same day. There were about ten Teamster guards and about fifty UFW picketers present. The lengthy report ends with the allegation that "three Teamsters had been badly beaten and they pointed out [LINES REDACTED]. According to [REDACTED] the Teamsters throughtout [*sic*] the strike have had orders not to resist arrest by law enforcement personnel and whenever a Teamster was arrested he immediately stopped fighting and passively submitted to the arrest."

An ugly scene occurred on June 23 (location is not provided other than it being an asparagus field) between UFW pickets and Teamster guards. The description begins on page 8 of the lengthy report. "One UFW line and one Teamster line bulged forward, contact was made, and a fight ensued. Someone in the other line of Teamsters yelled that a rock had been thrown and a fire cracker thereafter exploded after which the Teamsters moved out in unison toward the pickets. Numerous fights ensued with both sides using wooden clubs and irrigation pipe found at the scene, as weapons. Within one minute the Teamsters had swept the field clean of picketers. A short time later, about 100 Teamsters attacked approximately 50 UFW picketers in the field area." The incident was recorded on videotape. When the Kern County Sheriff's Office enforcements arrived, at least eleven arrests (six Teamsters and five UFW) were made. At bottom of the page, the UFW's sealing off Mecca and the Indio farm-labor camp were tactics that were "having a demoralizing effect on the workers as was the utilization of bull horns on the strike line by the UFW. Also 'camp visits' to workers homes and the farm labor camps were having an unsettling effect and making workers uneasy."

The Teamster hierarchy led by Jim Basly and fifty-two Southern California local union representatives met on June 23-24, 1973, and discussed strategy. They adopted a policy change to defeat the UFW, according to page 9 of this Airtel. In short, the strategy was to escalate the war with targeted sporadic violence on UFW leaders and picketers.

> The Teamsters, according to the plan, would attack the UFW pickets in bursts of violence to last 30 to 60 seconds. Principal objects of attack would be UFW leaders. During the afternoon and evening, floating squads of Teamsters would rove the Southern Valley areas performing "vineyard patrol, camp visits, and house visits" on both UFW and Teamster members.

These blitzkriegs would last until June 27, 1973, "when they expected that the UFW would fold under the pressure and leave the area. If the AFL-CIO called in 'heavies,' it was the Teamster plan to in turn call in sufficient additional manpower to sustain the activity." The Teamsters had "a total of 200 guards by June 25, 1973."

The orchestrated and planned violence continued at the crack of dawn, 5 a.m., Monday, June 25, as reported on page 10. Two car caravans, one UFW another Teamster, met on a roadway that was blocked by a Teamster vehicle. "Fights ensued, and a Teamster began smashing out the windows of a UFW car. Deputies [REDACTED] observed a Teamster kick one of the UFW members in the head. Two Teamsters were arrested, and the rest left the area."

Chávez showed up at one of the picket lines. "The Teamsters brought in about 100 men and surrounded the UFW [LINES REDACTED]." In an about face, however, the Teamsters quit the confrontation. "[REDACTED] a

Teamster Field Captain, told Lieutenant [REDACTED] that they had called off the attack because of the amount of manpower [REDACTED] had at the location and because of the cameras and news media at the scene."

Chávez apparently knew how to contain the Teamsters; as a nonviolent advocate, he put himself in harm's way for all the world to see. While calling the media to record the bloodbath was a most dangerous move, it was brilliantly timed. Cameras and photographers present during picketing had captured the Texas Rangers on film when they systematically took to beating union pickets during La Casita Farms strikes in the Rio Grande Valley. MAYO members placed themselves in harm's way in front of the Texas Rangers; but all had little Brownie cameras, and some had Polaroid cameras, to record any violence. Photographs of Texas Ranger violence introduced by attorneys for Francisco "Pancho" Medrano as evidence in a court case against them proved most damaging to the Rangers. Video recordings had been previously taken of Teamster violence without a deterrent effect, however. The same tactic of using cameras had exposed the violence in the South against civil rights protesters to the U.S. public via television and turned the tables of support in favor of the protesters and their cause.

The violence, however, continued into June 29. The UFW did not quit and neither did the Teamsters. Kern County sheriff's deputies in full riot gear began to station themselves between the two lines, pickets and Teamster guards. Occasionally "one or two Teamsters bolted through the lines and physically assaulted pickets." Finally, the Airtel quoting an article from the *Daily Enterprise* of July 5, 1973, page B-1, stated that William Grami, Western Conference of Teamsters director, had announced the day before that his union "will immediately withdraw all guards from agricultural areas being picketed by the UFW union." The 13-page Airtel closed with a final Grami quote: "We are leaving because we believe that local law enforcement agencies have realized the need for increasing their forces to the point where their protection appears adequate." And, the SAC adds, "No known incidents of police brutality have been reported or alleged in connection with the policing of this strike in the Coachella Valley by the RCSO, Indio Police Department or Coachella Police Department." The last page of the original message was entirely withheld under exemption FOIA

K2. The UFW had prevailed over the Teamsters and growers—a historic and unprecedented victory for now.

Pottinger Takes a Look

The correspondent rebuffed by the FBI due to insufficient details in his complaint on the 4th of July provided more details in a second complaint dated July 11. The complainant [NAME REDACTED] listed six specific instances of Teamster violence in the Coachella Valley. This time, the complaint had dates, names of victims, and brief descriptions of each assault. For example, in his first instance, he cites "a citrus rach [sic] foreman, mistaken by Teamster 'organizers' for a farmworker, was run off the road, pulled from his pickup, beaten, and stabbed. His attackers were apprehended in the act of dumping him into the Salton Sea by Riverside County Sheriffs." The second instance charges that "Teamsters or Teamster agents set fire in a midnight attack to the house trailer of Fancisco [sic] Campos, a migrant farmworker from Texas." Instance number six stated that on June 25, 1973, "Roving gangs of 50 or more Teamster agents attacked farmworkers as well as some United Church of Christ clergymen who witnessed the attacks." He repeats his request for an investigation into these attacks "in order to ensure that those persons who are violating the legal and constitutional rights of U.S. citizens are apprehended and stopped as soon as possible."

Finally, on July 11, 1973, the assistant attorney general, J. Stanley Pottinger, in charge of the Civil Rights Division, formally asked for an investigation by the FBI into Teamster violence against UFW pickets while the Kern County Sheriff's Office (KCSO) watched the attacks.[27] Pottinger supplied six names of victims with addresses; one was César's wife Helen. While the FBI's wheels of justice began to turn, to conduct the limited investigation requested, SAC, Sacramento informed the Director, FBI by teletype dated July 19, 1971, that four hundred UFW pickets had been arrested by the Kern County Sheriff's Office for violating a court order prohibiting such activity by the UFW.

Clarence M. Kelley, the permanent FBI Director, followed in the steps of his predecessors, Hoover, Gray, and Ruckelshaus, in the content of his responses to complaints received by his office. He denied jurisdiction unless a specific federal law had been violated. And, his office handlers of this type of material also followed protocol and added a NOTE to the bottom of his response with stamped name and signature. The NOTE to a July 20 and a July 30 response added the usual: "Bufiles disclose no record identifiable with [LINES REDACTED]" and "Reply coordinated with the Accounting and Fraud and Criminal Sections of the General Investigative Division."

Kelley received more complaints via telegrams and letters, and the SAC, Sacramento sent a teletype dated July 31, 1973, marked URGENT. The four-page teletype indicated more arrests were made by the KCSO, and redacted complainant stated, "some of her people were beaten this morning." The picketers had been at the Giumarra Ranch on Edison Road near Highway 58, east of Bakersfield, California. Another altercation occurred later in the evening with Teamsters attacking UFW pickets "at the Nalbandian Ranch on Panama Road near Vineland." The complainant further stated that "She advised the Kern County SO refused to accept complaints on the spot or to recognize citizen's arrest made by UFWU." The complainant alleged she was maced as she took photos of the violence. Jerry Cohen, the UFW lawyer, held a press conference in front of the KC jail entrance and stated, "this is shaping up to be another Selma, Alabama, and demanded private citizens go out to observe activities of Kern County SO to force them to do their job." Cohen claimed that "38 UFWU pickets have been arrested today of which 16 have been beaten."

The SAC continues in the URGENT teletype to inform Kelley that the "UFWU has been picketing at up to 15 different sites today at various locations in Kern County . . . the Sheriff's Office is strained to the limit and 50 California Highway Patrol officers have been requested through the Community Service Agency, Sacramento, California." In conclusion, the SAC claimed that

UFWU pickets attempted to provoke deputies into a shooting . . . pickets threw cherry bomb firecrackers into crowd simulating shooting . . . One picket attempted to steal gun from one deputy sheriff but was stopped by another deputy when he struck him across the arm with his nightstick, causing him to drop the gun in the road; however, the picket escaped into the crowd . . . windshields from two separate patrol cars have been broken out by pickets and tires slashed on at least one patrol car . . . deputy sheriffs were victims of rocks thrown by numerous persons on the picket line . . . tires were slashed on at least one patrol car during yesterday's activities.

More violence is reported from SAC, Sacramento on August 1st. The Sacramento FBI cannot locate for interviews, as required by FBI HQ, three of the persons listed as victims: Teresa Avila, Xavier Rivera, and Leonard Rodriguez. He does report that "25 USWU [*sic*] representatives who observed activities at the John Kovacevich Ranch on June 28, 1973 have provided signed statements, of the 25 statements three are victims." And, regarding the three missing witnesses, he closes with, "Active efforts are not being made to locate the victims by the FBI. However, they will be interviewed if they should appear at the Bakersfield RA." By five-page Nitel dated the 2nd but received on August 3rd, the SAC, Sacramento reports new arrests made, taxing the jail facilities in Kern and Fresno Counties: "143 new arrests made, all of whom refused or releases [*sic*] including . . . 20 nuns and six priests . . . 30 are still in custody from prior arrests, making a total of 443 in custody. Cesar Chavez made speech at Parlier, California . . . urging recall of Judge Blaine Pettit, who issued injunction limiting number of pickets, and Sheriff Melvin A. Willmirth, Fresno County Sheriff." The SAC continues on page 3 to list the accounting of loss of revenue for police actions by Kern, Tulare, and Fresno Counties. And, it reports gunshots and shootings of a picketer in Richgrove on the 1st at 3 p.m. The victim [NAME REDACTED] was shot "through rear window of vehicle and lodged in his upper right shoulder . . . witnesses stated approximately 12 shots were heard for duration of one to one and a half minutes . . . Freelance photographer, [NAME REDACTED] San Francisco, who was at scene reported one of bullets lodged in his car."

The next day the SAC, Sacramento sent another four-page Nitel to the FBI Director reporting "413 pickets remain in custody . . . Several nuns and priests remain in custody and have engaged in fasts while in custody . . . pickets pelted all cars with rocks in Arvin and Lamont . . . pickets assembled in streets of Delano blocking all streets leading from Delano in effort to prevent farm workers from going to fields. All other traffic was also stopped ... Force was necessary ... and approximately 40 pickets were arrested [REDACTED] rock throwing also took place in Delano. At least 17 windshields were reported broken [REDACTED]." An interesting stamp is at left bottom initialed by "WN" and dated "8/3/73" that reads: "Included in Summary to White House and Attorney General. Date____." Almost every other communication about this matter reviewed here has this stamp and is initialed by various persons depending on the date. Surely, this means the White House was apprised daily by the FBI about events in California involving the growers, law enforcement, UFW, and Teamsters. This stamp, however, is not found on all the documents; but the FBI does have control of what documents it has declassified, redacted, and released to the public and, more importantly, to the White House and AG.

More rock-throwing and arrests followed on the 2nd of August at the George Lucas Ranch and Roberts Farms; seven more picketers were arrested and jailed. The total in jail on August 6, according to the teletype from SAC, Sacramento to the Director, FBI, was 410, with the nuns and priests remaining in jail. They "have refused release unless everyone is released." In Kern County "four arrests made, two for disturbing the peace and two for rock throwing." Over in Tulare County "four strike related arrests effected before 2:00 pm. Congressman Edward Roybball [sic], Los Angeles, who appeared on scene, was quoted by UPI as stating he thought Tulare County SO was 'overreacting' to strike situation."

The Sacramento FBI submitted a lengthy report with enclosures, mainly photographs, on August 6, 1973, to Washington, FBI with copy to AUSA, Fresno. There were 137 pages withheld entirely and much redaction was made to individual pages; numbering of pages indicated also that many were missing altogether. The synopsis of the report indicates that twenty-eight Teamsters were arrested and jailed while four UFWU pickets were taken to the hospital. The first pages detail the difficulty had in arranging interviews with the six victims that made complaints; only Helen Chávez kept her afternoon appointment on July 26. Two more of the six victims, Frank Quintana and Lila Mancha, were interviewed on July 30.

Photographs were located that depicted the images of violence complained about by the UFW; copies were made and forwarded to Washington, DC. On a page numbered 53, several UFW persons called the KCSO for police protection only to be told "he does not have enough people to cover all of the picket lines," and that "he did not have enough men to furnish protection to everyone, and this terminated the conversation." The report concludes with information that Thomas T. Couris, the U.S. attorney for the Eastern District of California in Fresno, "does not desire further investigation at this point ... he does not feel this case has any prosecutive merit with respect to the Kern County Sheriff's Office."

Celebrities Pitch In

Joan Baez and Daniel Ellsberg joined the vigil being held while Chávez was in jail late afternoon August 7. She sang and he recited portions of the U.S. Constitution, according to the teletype of that evening sent to the Director, FBI by the SAC, Sacramento. The report also informed that Manuel L. Camarillo and Reynaldo G. Eridia were hit by "shotgun blast Sunday night" fired into their home near Sanger, California. "Camarillo told deputies he has been confronted on prior occasions by UFW pickets and was followed one time when he left work in fields." UFW pickets were "throwing rocks and assaulting workers ... About 23 arrests made with six deputies of Kern County SO injured, minor injuries." The UFW activity in Tulare County was described by the SAC, Sacramento as "hit-and-run" fashion, with "two homemade bombs ... thrown into field where there were workers." There were no injuries reported. The Kern County SO continued to have manpower shortage with so many incidents and arrests, plus "many units are disabled by barbs in roadway causing numerous tire failures." And, "objects confiscated this date from UFW pickets were one four-foot ax handle and one machete." The Director sent an Official Notification of Error to the SAC, Sacramento on August 9 admonishing the sender of the teletype to reference the matter as Administrative and "show at end what local dissemination is made; and, insure your office fulfilling responsibilities in this regard.

See MOI, S122B. Also, note correct spelling for Daniel Ellsburg" (scratched out, and penciled in is "Ellsberg").

The Director, FBI received another teletype from Sacramento FBI that same 9th of August informing him that Joan Baez and Daniel Ellsburg (*u* is crossed out and *e* written in on top of the *u*) were still entertaining those holding vigil at the Fresno Courthouse Park, across the street from the county jail. Inside the courthouse another drama was playing out. According to the report, UFW lawyers were seeking release from jail of all union members and other supporters arrested on their own recognizance (OR). The judge refused release without strict conditions of where, when, and how many picketers he would allow. Stalemate was the result; the jail remained full. The report informs the Director, FBI that Chávez will appear with guests "at Lamont Park at about 4:00 PM today and 2,000 expected to attend." The guests were Baez and Ellsberg.

UFW Counters Counterintelligence Moves

More arrests ensued in Kern, Tulare, and Fresno Counties for rock-throwing by UFW pickets; one caused a serious head injury to a female farm worker. The rock thrower allegedly had been arrested before: "This was his third strike related arrest in two weeks." A new tactic by the UFW was uncovered. Tulare County operated radio communication over two channels, and "Los Angeles County authorities indicating all available portable radios operating both on Tulare County Channel One and Two have been purchased from unidentified radio shop." And who made these purchases? The report states: "These units were reportedly purchased by 'farm worker types.'" If that was the case, the UFW was learning fast how to countermove against police communications by listening to them as they broadcast locations, destinations, and call codes.

The teletype of August 10 from SAC, Sacramento informed the Director, FBI that two UFW pickets were shot in Tulare County and a protest was organized by mid-afternoon in front of the Tulare County Sheriff's Office demanding arrest of the shooters. On the 13th the Airtel from SAC,

Sacramento informs the Director, FBI of a teletype complaint made against the Kern County Sheriff's Office for not arresting an overseer of Kovacevich Ranch near Lamont. The complaint identified the overseer as one throwing rocks at his own trucks. Upon refusal by a KCSO sergeant to arrest the violator, the complainants wanted to execute a citizen's arrest, but were not allowed by the same sheriff's officer. In a subsequent Airtel from the same source to the Director, FBI on August 8, a signed statement from two witnesses regarding Teamster violence was enclosed. The witnesses were two female hitchhikers crossing Bakersfield. They were picked up by three Teamsters who made such remarks as "they were going to 'knock some Wetbacks' heads in"; "going to make some other Wetbacks work in the fields in the sun so they would get strokes and die"; and that "they had been sent here." The report ends with the prediction "The Teamsters told [NAME REDACTED] and [NAME REDACTED] to watch the news the next day because there was going to be violence and heads busted open."

The shooter of the UFW picket was identified and arrested. The news was sent via teletype to the Director, FBI from Sacramento FBI on August 14. The report also contained updates on picketing in Fresno, Kern, and Tulare Counties together with estimates of costs to the law enforcement departments to police the Teamsters, growers, and UFW members: Tulare, $130,000; Kern, $200,000, and Fresno, $301,000. The shooter was (lines redacted) arraigned on assault with deadly weapon charge with bond set at an amazingly low figure of $5,000. The shooter posted the bail money and "has reportedly fled Tulare County to San Pedro, Calif." The more current news got to the Director, FBI the next day, 15th of August, when the SAC, Sacramento reported that the Superior Court reversed the ruling by the lower municipal court on not releasing those jailed on their own recognizance or "OR releases." The report stated, "Cesar Chavez appeared in Courthouse Park" to welcome the "359 UFW pickets released from Fresno County Jail Monday night." He urged the audience to "renew picketing and step up their boycott activities." Approximately one hundred more pickets remained in jail for reasons unstated in this communication. The other shooter of a UFW picket, a Teamster, was "still pending additional investigation." Toward the end of this teletype, the local FBI man in Sacramento provides an intelligence tip he obtained from (lines redacted): "info received that Chavez and UFW now without funds to pay for strike activities. [NAME REDACTED] also advised of receipt of info that AFL-CIO may drop Chavez and organization and conceivably may attempt to organize farm laborers on their own."

Another signed statement by a complainant was enclosed with the Airtel sent to the Director, FBI from SAC, Sacramento on August 14. The UFW legal team out of Lamont, California, furnished the SAC a copy executed by [NAME REDACTED] on August 2. She witnessed a sheriff's deputy order a field worker back into the field and not allow the worker to talk with a UFW picket. She interpreted this action as acting like a supervisor for the Mosesian Ranch and also refusing to allow communications between pickets and field workers. The report quoted the statement as "One of Mosesian's workers came out of the fields to talk to pickets, and deputy said 'Get back. Get back to work.' This worker went back."

On the 15th, J. Stanley Pottinger of DOJ's Civil Rights Division sent a ten-page memorandum to the FBI Director, of which eight pages were withheld entirely. The memo references the July 11, 1973, communication sent "to you." Pottinger relates that the Community Relations Service of the DOJ has provided him with twelve affidavits, which he attaches to the memo. He asks for "the following additional investigation": over five items. He wants to have "police reports or arrest records arising out of this incident"; to "identify the Sheriff's Deputies and Delano Patrol Officers present and interview them about the incident"; to interview the twelve victims about "what actions, if any, were taken by Kern County Sheriff's Deputies and Delano Private Patrol Officers before, during, and after the incident" and details of conversations the twelve may have had with police or deputies at the scene; to determine type of equipment Delano Private Patrol Officers are authorized to use, and what training they are required to receive before carrying such weapons; and specifically, to interview Marty Bozina about what he knew, when he knew it, and why he was talking with "law enforcement officials throughout the melee." Pottinger wanted to know if "Bozina had prior knowledge that teamsters were coming to the ranch and if so ascertain how he came to know this." The remaining pages of this memo were withheld, so nothing more can be inferred as to what more Pottinger was asking of the FBI concerning this incident.

The Police Killing of Nagi Moshin Daifullah

Pottinger would soon learn of another act of police brutality on a UFW picket, but first the Director, FBI learned of the killing of Nagi Moshin Daifullah by a KCSO deputy. The SAC, Sacramento version of events reported on August 15 that a barroom brawl occurred in the Smoke House Bar in Lamont, California. Three KCSO deputies responded to the call and attempted to control the crowd. According to SAC, Sacramento, Nagi threw a beer bottle and hit [NAMES REDACTED] and ran out of the bar with a deputy in pursuit. The deputy hit Nagi with his flashlight and he fell face first into the street from the curb. Nagi was taken to the hospital, where he died at 1 a.m., August 15. A blood test indicated Nagi was intoxicated with a 2.84 alcohol blood level. An autopsy revealed he died from a massive concussion of the skull. UFW attorney Jerry Cohen told KCSO he had witnesses who saw the deputy hit Nagi on the head, but would refer them to the DOJ rather than KCSO investigators.

The informant's intel on low financial resources on hand by the UFW came to light in a four-page teletype from Sacramento FBI to the Director, FBI the day after the notice of Nagi Daifullah's killing. The information obtained by the SAC, Sacramento was that Chávez had communicated with Fresno County picket captains, who were to inform picketers that "the UFW would no longer pay $75 a week in strike benefits it has been paying for several months." He would still pay pickets in Delano, where the picketing was now concentrated. The report also informed that most of Fresno County pickets in jail had been released OR and without conditions. At bottom of page 2, the report alluded to a new group joining in the strike, boycott, and picketing: Venceremos Organization from the San Francisco-Oakland Bay Area. Names connected with dates of birth were provided to the FBI HQ for "Richard Paul Curtis, DOB 11-17-36, Howard Bruce Franklin, DOB 2-28-34, and Wilbert Jackson, DOB 11-27-29." These birthdates indicate that the group of three were no college kids or hippie types. The oldest, Jackson, was forty-four years of age, and the other two, Curtis and Franklin, ages thirty-seven and thirty-five, respectively. And, they were coming "with weapons; purpose unknown."

More violence was reported between pickets and field hands in all counties with new arrests. None, however, were more alarming than the information on page 3 that Chávez's son Fernando was shot at but unharmed. Three bullets were lodged in a vehicle that shielded him from the six or seven fired in his direction. Fernando named his assailant, who had two prior assaults on UFW pickets committed on August 10. The assailant's name in the document is redacted, of course. Supposedly, the report indicates, Tulare County Sheriff's Office "expects their arrests shortly." In a new teletype on the 17th, another shooting is reported to have occurred on the afternoon of the day prior, the 16th. Allegedly "two Filipino individuals observed to drive by UFWU picket lines . . . they fired several shots into four or five UFWU vehicles . . . one 60-year-old UFW picket injured . . . UFWU pickets obtained license of passing vehicle, and Kern County SO now searching for vehicle." The last page, no. 3, of this report mentions that "[NAMES REDACTED] have now been arrested and charged with wounding of UFW pickets on 8-10-73." And, the report mentions that several state legislators have alleged "prejudice, breakdown of law and order, etc." by the Tulare County Sheriff. One of those was "state Assemblyman Richard Altore [*sic*], Los Angeles, who it was determined has never visited area, had received info pertaining to alleged conditions from Fernando Chavez, Jr. [*sic*], son of Cesar Chavez, who is in some manner associated with Alatore's [*sic*] office."

A four-page teletype dated August 17, 1973, from SAC, Sacramento to Director, FBI informed him of the turnout for Nagi Moshin Daifullah's memorial services in Delano: "Approximately 5,600 UFW members and sympathizers attended . . . and participated in related march . . . today." All picketing was suspended in the three-county area. The report also made mention of another UFW death, Juan Trujillo De La Cruz, who was shot the previous day, the 16th. "Kern County SO has arrested two male Filipinos [NAMES REDACTED] . . . both now [*sic*] union farm workers in Lamont . . . charged them with homicide." The final pages of the message report that Congressman Don Edwards (D-San Jose) telephoned the FBI's Senior Resident Agent (SRA) in Bakersfield about the "current civil rights investigation being conducted by FBI." But, "he was advised he was welcome to visit RA but SRA would not discuss case. On afternoon, 8-17-73, Congressman Edwards, his Administrative Assistant, and Jacques Levy appeared at Bakersfield RA." Apparently Congressman Edwards told the RA that the FBI was not doing enough to investigate civil rights violations. He was assured "sufficient manpower had been assigned at this time and SRA was not at liberty to discuss matter further." The congressman said, according to the report, that he "intended to take the manpower assignments up with 'Washington.'" The report then reviews who Levy is in relation to "Shears of Bakersfield, self-styled professional informant." At that time, Levy was by Chávez's side constantly while compiling material for the autobiography he would write about him.

The Los Angeles FBI office sent a "Message Relay" dated August 18, 1973, via teletype—a priority message classified under "Racial Matters Los Angeles" in handwriting, with copies sent to U.S. Secret Service; DOJ, Assistant AG Criminal Division, Internal Security Section, and General Crimes Section. The priority message was that Safeway stores would be picketed in Los Angeles by the UFW and "possibly the Western White House" (Nixon's house in San Clemente, California). The report indicated "over three hundred cars containing approximately one thousand persons heading south on U.S. 99 out of Kern County at about 8 or 9 a.m. today." Details of the picketing of stores were provided in the report, mostly for Los Angeles but making one reference that "half going by caravan to San Francisco and half to Los Angeles." Chávez held a press conference at one Safeway store and departed to "six different Safeway stores in the Los Angeles area." And, it concluded that "no information developed indicating that UFWU pickets would converge on Western White House." Either this piece of intel on the Western White House was totally off the mark, or Chávez was utilizing his own disinformation strategy to distract the federal police agencies. More importantly, who was the Secret Service protecting at the Western White House? Nixon was battling for his survival from impeachment brewing over Watergate in D.C.

The teletype of August 18 from SAC, Sacramento to the Director, FBI and SACs in Los Angeles and San Francisco confirmed that "45 cars with five to six pickets each, proceeded in car caravan from Parlier, Calif. to San Jose, Calif. for the purpose of picketing local Safeway stores." And, "Cesar Chavez called for 100 FBI agents to aid in investigation and protection of UFW pickets" and "the Delano Council of Growers also issued a call to the US Dept. of Justice for protection of their workers from the violent acts of UFW pickets." In closing, the scare of picketing at the Western White House was quieted: "There was an early rumor that the Kern County procession to Los Angeles might possibly picket at San Clemente. Further inquiry by Kern County SO revealed this to be strictly rumor and no basis in fact, however, Secret Service, Sacramento and Los Angeles advised locally."

In an exchange of messages on August 20 between SAC, Sacramento and Director, FBI over the twelve witnesses to interview regarding Teamster violence, confusion reigned high. On August 20 the Director ordered the cancellation of interviews with numbers 1, 3, 4, 5, 6, and 7. The NOTE appended to the report stated: "6 of these had previously been interviewed; therefore, Sacramento is being instructed not to conduct those again." Also, that day, SAC, Sacramento sendt to FBI HQ the affidavit of the two young women hitchhikers who heard the Teamsters boast of the violence they were going to direct on UFW members who they referred to as Wetbacks.

The next day, the Director, FBI informed the Assistant Attorney General via a memorandum, including a form with letters to be checked indicating what the matter was about. On this form, the letter "H" is checked, which reads: "This covers the receipt of a complaint and no further action will be taken by this Bureau unless the Department so directs." The matter was explained further in the typed NOTE referring to the "Nalbaudian incident" and "as being reported under a separate caption." There has been no prior reference to this "Nalbaudian incident"; perhaps it is just bad spelling of Nagi Daifullah's name, the recent victim of a KCSO deputy's police brutality. Sacramento FBI notified the Director, also on the 21st, that an agreement had been reached between UFW and the Fresno County district attorney on the jury trials set to begin in six weeks for those out on OR bond for picketing in violation of the court order. The agreement basically was that if any one of those arrested was not charged again for illegal picketing during the six months trials were postponed, the charges would be dismissed.

The remark Chávez made in Los Angeles about requesting one hundred FBI agents to protect UFW pickets drew bureaucratic blood from the SAC, Sacramento on August 21, 1973. By teletype the SAC informed the Director, FBI that both the U.S. Attorney's Office and U.S. Marshal's Office in Sacramento called for "an evaluation of current situation with UFW-Teamster dispute." Tersely, the message reported that "both were informed FBI does not engage in protective services and we were handling resulting civil rights complaints with available personnel." On a plain piece of paper with words "GENERAL INVESTIGATIVE DIVISION" at top, information is provided that an attorney representing growers had presented approximately one hundred affidavits to the Bakersfield RA alleging UFW violence against them. They wanted the FBI to investigate these civil rights complaints. In another teletype on the 21st from SAC, Sacramento to the Director, FBI, he makes mention of the similar affidavits from growers alleging civil rights violations by the UFW against them. Two pages of this document were withheld entirely. Enclosed with this communication was a nine-page newsletter titled "The Coachella Experience," prepared by six persons from Michigan who traveled to the grape strike zone in California to get the facts by personal investigation in the field. The newsletter sided with the UFW and against the Teamsters. The League of United Latin American Citizens of Northern California (LULAC) sent FBI Director Clarence Kelley a Mailgram requesting federal intervention to protect workers' civil rights. The names of LULAC officers sending the message were promptly checked in Bufiles and another FBI directory (not legible).

A teletype of August 22 from SAC, Sacramento to the Director, FBI reported that an officer of intelligence for the California State Department of Justice advised him why the Teamsters pulled out of organizing farm workers. Apparently, Teamsters assumed the Longshoremen's union would merge with them after their leader, Bridges, stepped down. Since Bridges was pro-UFW and the current dispute was antagonizing him and his membership, why continue the fight and risk losing the Longshoremen? Also, the report announced that the state was launching an investigation into the death of Nagi Daifullah at the request of the Kern County DA. Furthermore, the SAC was informing the Director that his daily reports would be discontinued given diminished activity between the Teamsters and UFW. But over in the melon fields between Firebaugh and Mendota, California, more violence had erupted between UFW picketers and farm workers, with many arrests. The SAC, Sacramento had to report all of this activity via Nitel on August 23. Again, on August 30, via another Nitel, he had to report more arrests—"60 adults and juveniles"—that included both UFW picketers and Teamster union workers at the Gallo Ranch near Livingston, California. This was the first report of violence in Merced County. Picketing the next day by UFW, the SAC, Sacramento reported, was "in orderly fashion and no incidents occurred." He also repeated that his daily reports would stop unless violence erupted again.

Over the Labor Day weekend, the SAC, Sacramento received information that Chávez was in Honolulu organizing a boycott of grapes in that state while another caravan of "approximately 125 vehicles with 400 to 500 UFWU members and sympathizers left Delano, California 8/31/73 in route to Phoenix, Arizona." From there his intel reported the pickets would spread out to other states to promote the grape boycott. The Sacramento FBI office sent a formal report to FBI HQ with a copy to the AUSA in Fresno regarding the training in weapons by the Delano Private Patrol. The SAC reported these police "armed with .38 caliber weapons carry no other equipment and receive no training." The report has 27 pages withheld entirely. The Director, FBI put on notice the SAC, Sacramento about the Kern County Sheriff's Office and UFW victims Frank Quintana et al.: "In your next report in this case, change title and include Deputies James Ernest Mathis and Gregory Sales as subjects, as well as Delano Private Patrolmen Donald Spence and Jerrel Lee Fortune."

As Teamster violence subsided and police activity returned to pre-strike levels, the Sacramento FBI office closed cases on all civil rights violations. In a September 15, 1973, communication to the Director, the SAC in Sacramento reports that two SAs [NAMES REDACTED] are returning to their respective offices in Los Angeles and San Francisco, and assures the Director they will continue to handle pending civil rights cases with available personnel. The

SAC does make room for one allowance: "If need develops for additional Spanish Speaking agents, the Bureau will be advised."

The previous day, September 14, Henry E. Petersen, assistant attorney general, Criminal Division of the DOJ, wrote a memorandum to the FBI Director. He was direct and specific about the records on three persons. He wanted the Bureau "to forward to the Criminal Division copies of all investigative reports pertaining to "Frank Quintana, et al, victims" and the violence at the Cavokovich [*sic*] Ranch; Lidia B. Manriques, victim, and the violence at the Giumarra Ranch; and Erlene Cuerto, victim, and the violence at the Nalbandian Ranch. No other files were declassified on these pending cases, much less the FBI response to this request.

From the East Coast the SAC, New York sent a memorandum to the Director, FBI on October 24, 1973, informing him that there is some connection between the Rapid City Welfare Rights Group, the American Indian Movement, and the UFW. Apparently, there were "fire bombings and damage to store windows . . . suffered by the A&P Tea Company as a result of the United Farm Workers Union (UFW) Union [*sic*] receiving nationwide popularity and support from local political members." The UFW presence in New York was referenced on the second page of this communication: "On 4/16/72, a dinner honoring Mrs. ROMANA BANVELOS [*sic*], Treasurer of the US, [was] held at the Waldorf Astoria Hotel. Fifty demonstrators from the UFW picketed the Park Avenue entrance of the hotel, protesting the hiring of illegal aliens at Mrs. VANELOS' [*sic*] tortilla factory in California." And the memorandum closed with yet another connection to UFW activity in New Orleans: "On 8/6/73 [REDACTED] a confidential source who is familiar with extremist activities in the New Orleans area, advised that on 6/19/73, an annual stockholder meeting of the A&P Tea Company was to be held at the Rivergate Hotel, New Orleans. In front of the Rivergate Hotel were demonstrators for the UFW, protesting A&P's continued policy of buying non-farm worker union lettuce." In the New York area, "the following sources, who are familiar with extremist activity . . . were contacted during the months of August, September 1973, for additional information they could provide concerning the UFW, with negative results: [NAMES REDACTED]. In view of the above, the NYO is no longer conducting investigation in this case." At least this FBI office soon realized there was nothing to investigate and closed the case. Regrettably, the SAC, New York not only did not spell the name of the U.S. Treasurer, Mrs. Romana Bañuelos, correctly, but also misspelled her name twice in his message.[28] We also learn that the FBI had sources that aided them in recognizing "extremist activities," and these included protesting at a hotel in New York and at a stockholder meeting in New Orleans, according to this message. On October 24, the SAC, Sacramento notified the Director, FBI that his office was moving on past the UFW and Teamster Union labor disputes: "This case is considered closed."

The last document declassified in the Chavez file for 1973 is a November 15th memorandum from C. L. McGowan of the DOJ on behalf of J. Stanley Pottinger to Mr. Gebhardt of the FBI about a meeting between Pottinger and Kelley. The eight-page memo thanks the FBI for outstanding work on the investigations requested. The pages contain much redacted material pertaining to other cases and not germane to the Chavez file except for mention made on page 6 under item 5, "United Farm Workers." The memo thanks the Director for temporarily assigning "two Spanish-speaking Agents to the Sacramento Office for the purpose of assisting in these investigations."

Despite all these investigations and reports, no federal grand juries were ever convened to hear testimony from the victims of physical harm caused by growers, Teamster violence, or state or local police brutality. Chávez continued his struggle without any local, state, or federal protection. Quite the contrary, he continued to face the real enemies daily, which were the growers and their hired security guards, local city police and county sheriff's departments, the state police, and both sides of the Department of Justice—the FBI, which is the investigative arm, and the Attorney General's Office, which is the prosecutorial arm of violations of federal laws.

CHAPTER 7

End of Hoover and Nixon

STOP THE GRAPES

March to Boston's Produce Center – Chelsea Market from Everett Station on **THURS. MAY 30, 7 AM** for info: 536-9465 or 288-0347

ON STRIKE
United Farmworkers AFL·CIO
boycott grapes·lettuce·gallo wine

IN THE EARLY 1970S, CHÁVEZ AND the UFW had to respond to new state initiatives that outlawed boycotts and strikes at harvest times and changed rules on how to (and who could) elect a union as the representative for workers. Chávez had to send his best people to Oregon in 1971, and Florida, Arizona, and California all in 1972 to fight these killer bills against farm workers. Chávez and his people learned that turning out the vote for a popular candidate like Kennedy was not the same as turning out legislators and voters to oppose a specific measure.

In Oregon, Governor Tom McCall was pressured by the UFW into vetoing the legislation. Chávez, with help from Fred Ross Jr. and the union's best lawyer, Jerry Cohen, was able to rally supporters involved with establishing the Colegio César Chávez in Mt. Angel, Oregon, as well as many others across the state. At a rally at the Salem capitol building, Chávez gathered five thousand persons to listen to his appeal for stopping the unfair legislation. Thousands more sent telegrams of support for Chávez and threats to boycott Oregon lumber products.[1]

Other Business as Usual

The UFW boycotters in Cincinnati, Ohio, were doing well picketing the Pogue's department stores, which sold California wine. The Cincinnati FBI sent word via Nitel a two-page teletype at 6:01 p.m. to the Director on February 18, 1972, that UFW people were planning to protest at Pogue's department stores in Cincinnati that day, and again on the 19th at all Pogue's stores unless they "ceased selling nonunion wine." The names of the sources of information given to the FBI Cincinnati are redacted on the second page. The 22nd of February, another Nitel two-page teletype was sent from Cincinnati FBI to the Director at 5:26 p.m. informing that forty-five protesters had been outside the Pogue's downtown store earlier that day, and that on the 19th a smaller number had been protesting at the Pogue's suburban store without incident. Again, on the second page of the Nitel the name of the information source is redacted.

The following month, a March 16, 1972, URGENT three-page teletype was sent from San Antonio FBI to the "Director ATTENTION: DOMESTIC INTELLIGENCE DIVISION" informing Washington that "COMMENCING AT APPROXIMATELY NOON TODAY MEMBERS OF UNITED FARM WORKERS ORGANIZING COMMITTEE WILL DEMONSTRATE IN FRONT OF REPUBLICAN PARTY OF BEXAR COUNTY HEADQUARTERS IN SAN ANTONIO, TEXAS." The demonstrators were protesting Nixon's appointment to the National Labor Relations Board of four "reactionary members" who recently ruled against the UFWOC. The FBI, San Antonio urgency is that it has been reported by their sources that at least two hundred will show up to demonstrate in that city and that such demonstrations will take place in at least twenty-eight other NLRB regions in the United States. They advise the Secret

Service and military authorities of this happening. Boston did have such a demonstration, according to Nitel two-page teletype from there to the Director on March 16, 1972, at 9:55 p.m. In Boston, the Republican State Committee headquarters was the site of the demonstration by twenty-five to fifty males and females "who conducted themselves in an orderly fashion." The police moved them from the front of the building to the back, and then back to the front in respect for a funeral service across the street. The protesters complied without incident. At end of page 2 it reads, "Special Agents [REDACTED] and [REDACTED] observed the demonstration." The next day, March 17, 1972, at 5:37 p.m., an "MSE PRIORITY" three-page teletype was sent to the President, Vice President, U.S. Secret Service (PID), and Acting Attorney General (BY MESSENGER) from the Director FBI titled "CONFIDENTIAL"; utilizing a reliable informant, it is advised that the VP will be picketed at the Americana Hotel at the "St. Patricks annual dinner this date at six pm." The Director identifies the UFW spokesman as "Moe Marano" and provides his address in Manhattan, New York, on page 2 of this teletype. Marano reportedly claimed fifty people would protest Agnew and the Republicans for their anti-farm-worker, pro-grower stance. On page 3, the Director specifies that Marano said the picketing would "take place on the west side of seventh street between fifty-second and fifty-third streets." The Director was only repeating the information he obtained in an "IMMEDIATE TELETYPE" from New York FBI that day at 2:30 p.m. In this communication, someone made a one-line scratch by the telephone number, 594 0694, for Moe Marano.

This next two-page teletype dated 12:45 a.m., March 18, 1972, from NEW YORK to "DIRECTOR ATTENTION DOMESTIC INTELLIGENCE DIVISION" would be hilarious if it were not so wasteful of taxpayer dollars, anti-democratic, and repressive of free speech in its content:

AT APPROXIMATELY SIX P.M. MARCH SEVENTEEN, SEVENTY TWO SPECIAL AGENTS OF THE FEDERAL BUREAU OF INVESTIGATION OBSERVED AP-PROXIMATELY SEVEN INDIVIDUALS FORMING A PICKET LINE ACROSS THE STREET FROM THE AMERICANA HOTEL, AT SIX TWENTY P.M. THESE INDIVIDUALS MOVED ACROSS THE STREET TO POLICE BARRICADES SET UP

NEAT [*sic*] THE AMERICANA. BY SIX TIHIRTY P.M. THIS GROUP MUMBERED [*sic*] APPROXIMATELY FIFTY INDIVIDUALS. A LARGE BANNER WAS CARRIED WHICH READ 'THE REPUBLICAN PARTY HATES THE UNITED FARM WORK-ERS.' OTHER SMALLER PLACARDS WERE CARRIED WHICH GENERALLY STATED THAT THE REPUBLICAN ADMINISTRATION IS DESTROYING THE UNITED FARM WORKERS (UFW) THROUGH THE REPUBLICAN DOMINATED NATIONAL LABOR RELATIONS BOARD.

And, in closing at last page, "IN VIEW OF NO INCIDENTS OR ARRESTS, NO LHM BEING SUBMITTED. E N D"

To the Sunshine State

In Florida, unusual situations existed for the UFW. An anti-union bill was defeated in 1971 but reintroduced in 1972. The UFW had won contracts from Coca-Cola's Minute Maid citrus workers and a dairy farm, H.P. Hood and Sons. The new Florida law banned union halls, restrained organizing, and limited the power of unions. Other unions in the state had not been active in opposing this law before, but now they wanted to fight. Chávez sent in his brightest protégé, Eliseo Medina, with no money and no staff. For fear of violence from the Ku Klux Klan in rural Florida and toward Tallahassee, the state capital, marches were put on the back burner. Oddly, Medina focused on a personal letter writing campaign, which ultimately netted them twenty thousand such letters within two months. He drove groups of farm workers to meet face to face with legislators, a first-time experience for both. This worked. Then, typhoid broke out at a labor camp due to con-taminated water, which the local health department had known about for two years. The scandal allowed Medina to bring in a congressional delega-tion to hold hearings on the matter. Several irregularities were discovered, and the state was made the culprit. Medina then found a grower holding twenty-nine farm workers under slave conditions, including armed guards preventing their escape; they had to pick the tomatoes. Most farm work-ers in the UFW were African Americans. Thousands of people sent protest telegrams to the legislators and governor. More farm worker teams visited the legislature. The bill was killed in committee 15 to 7.[2]

UFW Protests in Southern California

In coordination with national protests in key cities against the Republican Party and its officeholders, San Diego FBI reported that two hundred protestors in his city had met at New Town Park and marched from there to downtown to the Royal Inns at the wharf, the GOP headquarters for the National Convention, on March 16 in 1972.[3] Not to be outdone, the Los Angeles FBI office sent a four-page Nitel to the Director at 8:23 p.m., March 17, 1972, with two provocative subject heading titles: "PROGRESSIVE LABOR PARTY, IS-C, OO: NEW YORK" and "YOUNG SOCIALIST ALLIANCE, IS-C (TROTSKYIST). OO: NEW YORK." On page 2, the FBI man in Los Angeles reports that the flyer for a protest to be held by the UFW was printed by the Progressive Labor Party "ALTHOUGH PLP IS NOT NAMED AS SPONSOR OF DEMONSTRATION." The protest was to be against the APPEARANCE OF ROMANA BANUELOS, TREASURER OF THE UNITED STATES, AS A RESULT OF HER USE OF ALIEN LABORERS IN HER BUSINESS." Then the Nitel proceeds to give a brief history of the PLP and their adherence to the Chinese Communist Party line. On page 4, the final page, sources for this FBI information are apparently listed, but redacted. And, the dissemination of this communication was made to "Secret Service, Los Angeles, United States Attorney, Los Angeles, and One Hundred Fifteenth MIG, Pasadena."

On to Arizona and Gustavo Gutierrez

The Republican Women's Conference met in Phoenix during April 6-8, 1972, and were protested by members of the Tempe Peace Center, which was supporting the UFW. In Arizona, Gustavo Gutierrez had long asked Chávez to include his efforts at unionization of farm workers into his larger picture, and Chávez eventually did so. Gutierrez led the protests at the Phoenix location and at Sky Harbor Airport on the 6th to protest the arrival of the First Lady, Pat Nixon.[4] Gutierrez kept up the demonstrations during those days, and then moved to the capitol building on April 12 to protest the anti-farm-worker legislation being considered by that legislature.[5] The next month, May 12, 1972, the demonstrations in Phoenix were being led by César Chávez with four hundred others.[6]

Arizona Governor Jack Williams signed the anti-farm-worker bill within the same hour the legislature had passed it on the day Chávez was protesting outside the building. Chávez's advisors suggested they start a petition to recall the governor. And, they began the drive, which netted 168,000 signatures in four months, of which 100,000 were new voters. Personally, Chávez fell back to his regular public manifestation of sacrifice and suffering and undertook another fast until the governor was recalled. This time he was advised privately that the fast should not be done, *no se puede*. Dolores Huerta claimed credit for the slogan "Si Se Puede" to counter Chávez at that moment.[7] He gave up fasting for five days under doctor's orders before a huge crowd of four thousand farm workers. The recall did fail, and the law was not repealed, but the newly registered voters elected many Mexican American and Navajo public officials in the next elections, including a governor in 1974, Raul Castro.[8]

In Lincoln's Homeland and the Corn Belt

The Chicago FBI man sent URGENT word via teletype to the Director on April 11, 1972, that UFW demonstrators, according to his source (redacted), had begun a car caravan from Chicago to Springfield with plans to protest and possibly sit-in at the governor's office. The Chicago FBI estimated that twenty cars at best would make the journey, and there was no follow-up report on how many actually did. Perhaps the entire FBI bureaucracy was in a tizzy from the unbelievable news coming across all media.

Hoover Died, but the FBI Culture Remained

J. Edgar Hoover died on May 2, 1972, and was replaced by L. Patrick Gray III. He was pulled from the rank of assistant attorney general just hours after Hoover passed to become the Acting FBI Director. The FBI business continued without interruption. The Omaha FBI agent notified the Acting Director, FBI on October 12, 1972, that Chicano students at the University of Iowa and from Iowa City would hold a solidarity rally at the campus of the local university in favor of the UFW. It seemed that the UFW was protesting all over the country, and they were. The Acting Director of the FBI was perhaps behind the curve in his history of the UFW, because on June 20, 1972, San Diego FBI sent to the FBI, Washington a two-page LHM on the UFWOC, AFL-CIO with a history going back to 1970.

A Retouch of the Border Coverage Program (BOCOV)

On June 2, 1971, an LHM in the BOCOV files, a counterintelligence operation, reported on a visit by Chávez to Mexicali, Baja California. He went to see Julio Prado Valdez, a medical doctor, to entice him to run a health clinic for UFW members in that area. Apparently Chávez was convincing, and Valdez opened a clinic for UFW members. By October 1971, Chávez was subsidizing Valdez's clinic at $500 a month and was to raise that figure by $200 or $300 (p.2). Valdez, in prior years, had been an FBI target under the FBI's COIN-TELPRO BOCOV that sought to prevent Chicanos from collaborating and affiliating with Mexicans across the border.[9] BOCOV was one of many such COINTELPRO operations run by the FBI to destroy and disrupt organizations, activities, and persons the FBI targeted as needing to be neutralized.

Proposition 14 in 1974 was the Daughter of Proposition 22 of 1971

California's 1974 Proposition 14 had its birth with Proposition 22 in 1971. With 4,500 protestors at Sacramento, Chávez had been able to defeat

Proposition 22. This bill had the usual anti-farm-worker language prohibiting boycotts, strikes, and bargaining on work rules and conditions. California Secretary of State Jerry Brown agreed to sue the proponents of the measure for misleading those who signed the petition on what it was about. While Secretary Brown did not succeed, his publicity made it easier for UFW door-knockers to state their case for signing a new petition to put Proposition 14 on the ballot. The UFW had succeeded in defeating Proposition 22 in 1972 and began its own Proposition 14 for the 1976 elections. Brown, with UFW help, was elected governor in 1974 and promptly enacted in 1975 a UFW-tailored law, the Agricultural Labor Relations Act (ALRA), to protect farm workers. The growers, however, turned the law to their favor by challenging and litigating every aspect of the legislation. It exhausted the UFW legal department's resources, financial and human, and stressed Chávez immensely. Nevertheless, each battle was a clear victory for the ALRA, and the growers also tired of fighting Chávez. Jimmy Carter was the nominee of the Democrats in 1976, and the National Democratic Party sent word to Chávez to back off the petition drive lest he alienate support for the national ticket. He was informed that the growers would negotiate a deal to stop ALRA defunding efforts and court fights. Chávez ignored the advice. He proceeded to make three strategic errors. First, he raided the union coffers of huge sums of money that he gave to politicians for their support of Prop. 14. Speaker of the House Willie Brown alone received $700,000.[10] Second, being stubborn and headstrong, he called off the national boycott efforts, making it impossible to continue this national presence and effective pressure on gross sales of boycotted products. Chávez ordered the pickets to come home and work on the petition drive. They obeyed Chávez. With this decision, Chávez hurt *la causa* so badly, it would not recover. Those returning put their hearts and sweat into the campaign, which they eventually lost. As Randy Shaw writes, "This loss was a political disaster for the UFW, one entirely self-inflicted."[11] And, third, in the middle of the ALRA battle and devising Prop. 14, Chávez took off on what he called a 1,000-mile walk across the state, *la caminata*. This was not a march, not a speaking tour, not a caravan—nothing but a disappearing act. This walk, curiously, is not found reported, much less analyzed, elsewhere but in Garcia's work.[12] During all these battles in several states, Chávez had his own local problems stemming from the usual grower culprits, their security guards, and local police in the Delano area.

The Violence and Death Threats Renew against Chávez

In 1974 the Chávez people were still devastated from the voters passing Proposition 22, which opened new battlefronts over turf further south in the state against two crops, lettuce and asparagus, in Imperial County, California. The *San Diego Union* reported on the flare-up of violence between the sheriff's deputies and pickets, which prompted the SAC, San Diego to clip this open source article and notify Washington FBI on February 21, 1974, of its content. In summary form, the SAC, San Diego via teletype "Attn: Intelligence Division" reported that "16 persons were arrested . . . in connection with assaults on deputies." The Nitel provided three names of those arrested: "The names did not hit FBI gold, San Diego indices negative regarding Gilberto Rodriguez, Ignacio Guerrero, and Rosario Pelayo. San Diego conducting no investigation but will report pertinent developments to the Bureau." The account of the violence is not made clear in the report, other than "Sheriff's deputies clashed with approximately 400 UFW pickets six miles south of El Centro and two officers were hurt."

Reporting on another incident at another location, the same document reads that the UFW pickets gathered "around 2:00 am in Calexico at Farm Labor bus pickup points." The pickets urged those boarding not to break their strike and were "100 percent effective in keeping people off the buses." The remaining text—taken from the newspaper article, I assume—quotes Chávez and the planned activity by the UFW in other agricultural areas of California, including the Coachella Valley, to protest organizing by the Teamsters Union. The Chávez goal, according to the account, was to "bring about secret ballot elections by the workers to determine which union they prefer." The remaining two pages of this document were withheld entirely.

The "Correlation Summary" Document

An interesting 22-page document is found among the files dated in hand-writing "Feb. 13, 1975"; but actually it reads "Date Searched: 7/2/74" typed on the "Correlation Summary" report on "Subject: Cesar Estrada Chavez" and referencing files "Main File NO.: 105-157123 See Also: 9-48291, 44-51593, 139-2387, and 161-4719." First, the report contains no less than twenty-one variations of César Estrada Chávez's name, not the usual six-way search, and searched for two abbreviations, UFW and UFWOC, of the union name. It is interesting to note that their search did not include UFWU, the internal abbreviation used by local SACs in their messages. Second, the report has a heading and wording that is curious, "RELATIVE WHO HAS BUREAU MAIN FILE," and states, "The relationship, biographical data and activities of Cesar Estrada Chavez as founder and Director of the UFWOC were set forth in the serials of the main file on [NAMES REDACTED] as follows: [LINES REDACTED]." Only page numbers are left on the page, and of the five listed all but one are "(11)," and the odd one is just "(11.16)." The first record search mentioned is from June 3, 1965, yet the declassified file released to me under the Freedom of Information Act (FOIA) begins with a document dated October 8, 1965. This "letter dated 6/3/65 from the [REDACTED] which indicated that Cesar Chavez, MMA, 1221 Kensington Street, Delano, was under investigation by the [REDACTED] and requested to be advised of any reports or data known by the Justice Department which connected Chavez with Communistic or subversive groups. (No further information) Letter enclosed 100-7254-3996 ep.1 (23)." This tidbit of information indicates that the FBI motive for investigating Chávez was connecting him with Communism or subversion. Historically, the Communist Party USA was at its lowest membership and electoral efficacy in the mid-1960s, and Hoover knew that in 1965.

The summary has two references entirely redacted on page 3. It continues with references to every mention made in letters to the Director, FBI; newspaper articles; and FBI investigations of other groups such as SDS, of Chávez, the grape strike, UFW and UFWOC, and his connections with Saul Alinsky. All are from early 1966 to late 1966; then the focus shifts to a telegram. It reads in this pertinent section, "The Justice Department furnished copies of a telegram to Senator Ralph Yarborough dated 1/27/67 from Cesar Chavez of the UFWOC, Delano, Calif. in which Chávez alleged that false charges were lodged against Reverend James Drake and Gilbert Padilla in Rio Grande City, Texas, during a prayer vigil on 1/26/67. (No further information) Telegram enclosed 44-35329-6 p.1; ep.1 (2)." No indication is found here or in any other document that this telegram was furnished to the DOJ or surreptitiously obtained by the FBI. The FBI was known to employ such tactics during their investigations of persons. At least twenty other insertions referring to references that mention Chávez in this summary are redacted in this lengthy report. The first two redactions could indicate that FBI files on Chávez predate the June 1965 letter, because all entries are listed chronologically by date.

A Mention of Reies Lopez Tijerina

The FBI confirms the existence of yet another surveillance file on Reies Lopez Tijerina [FILE NUMBER REDACTED] with only the hint that his classification is "SI" for Security Index. The SA observed, and mechanically recorded, the rally speech by Tijerina on February 18, 1968, and in that speech, "Chavez was one of the individuals praised by Tijerina." Tijerina is known as one of the "Four Horsemen" of the Chicano Movement—a term used by Acuña in *Occupied America*, and Meier and Rivera in *The Chicanos*.

When Did the FBI File on Chávez Begin?

The "Correlation Summary" puts the beginning of FBI surveillance of Chávez earlier than even June 3, 1965 (p.5). "These references pertain to the UFWOC associations and activities of these individuals and Cesar Chavez, Director of the UFWOC, in California from 1962 to 2/26/68." According to this statement, there are FBI files dating to 1962 that mention Chávez in some fashion. Any name mentioned or stated in a letter to the FBI would be redacted for privacy concerns when released to the public, and if not, then a name search would be conducted by the FBI on that person, and a file created with that information. There is a reference in this document that "Dr. Martin Luther King, Jr., President, SCLC, would meet with Chavez on 3/16/68 in Delano, Calif. 157-8428-465 ep.5 (13)." This information, however, is not to be found in the FBI files on MLK Jr. (file number is 100-106670). The beginning file designation "157" means this document is classified under Civil Unrest. This meeting is not reported in any other of the FBI files on Chávez. Possibly the meeting never took place on that date, or later—because Dr. King was assassinated April 4, 1968. A more ominous entry is on page 6 at bottom with no redaction:

> In connection with the Assassination of Senator Robert Francis Kennedy (62-687), Caeser [*sic*] Chavez was interviewed by an SA at Indio, Calif. On 6/11/68 Chavez advised that he last saw and personally talked with Senator Kennedy in March 1968. Chavez stated that he did not see Kennedy on 6/4/68 as planned. He did not know Sirhan Sirhan [Robert Kennedy's assassin].[13]

Chávez also mentioned that he had never had an argument with Senator Kennedy or the Kennedy organization. Chávez added that he could furnish no information regarding the assassination. Bill Chandler, who was affiliated with Chávez in his labor movement, had commented to Chávez on June 10, 1968, that he knew Sirhan Sirhan, and Chandler had been at the Ambassador Hotel, Los Angeles, on June 5, 1968, where Kennedy was shot that same night (62-587-660 pp. 81, 82 [p.25]).

The information that Chávez and Chandler were interrogated about the RFK assassination is new but for this mention in the Correlation Summary. Furthermore, that Chávez would "throw Chandler under the bus" by stating that Chandler knew the assassin was a huge, ludicrous stretch if not an outright falsehood. Chandler may have been in the hotel that day and even a part of the entourage, as was Dolores Huerta, given all the electoral work done on Kennedy's behalf by the UFW; yet, there is no mention made of his presence in the literature about the assassination, much less that he knew Sirhan Sirhan as stated in the Correlation Summary.

In addition to Kennedy, five others were shot by Sirhan Sirhan and survived, including Paul Schrade, who Chávez did know and had worked with previously. The detour by Kennedy via the kitchen was a last-minute decision as he walked off the stage, not a publicized route of exit. The senator walked into Sirhan Sirhan's workplace, unfortunately. How Sirhan Sirhan would know the impromptu route will remain a mystery.

The complete redactions for half of page 7 are taken under exemption "b1," which is for national security matters. The remaining material, with many redacted lines, references some persons by name from Milwaukee, Wisconsin, in early 1969 who were to travel to California and meet with Chávez. The UFW publication *El Malcriado* is utilized as a reference in this summary, and there may be an FBI file on it despite the fact it is not a person, but could be the file for Luis Valdez, its founder—"100-453672-2." There are another one hundred files referenced, and pages that should be numbered 11, 12, and 13 are entirely missing from the summary. The summary referenced much other open source material to monitor the comings and goings of Chávez and his union leadership and his critics. For example, the *River City Review*'s article "Boycott Hamms!" in vol. 3, no. 4 referenced the call for the grape boycott to be extended in the case of Heublein Company to include their subsidiaries, Hamms Beer and Colonel Sanders' Kentucky Fried Chicken. The Brown Berets' *La Causa Brown Berets* newspaper was cited for its "We Declare a Nation" proclamation, which supposedly Chávez signed onto in support.[14] And, the *Arizona Republic* was also cited for carrying an article by Ralph de Toledano dated September 1, 1972, quoting some individual stating that Chávez should be killed.

Chávez supporter Richard B. Cook wanted "the FBI to question De Toledano and determine the identity of the person who made this threat against Chavez," as reported in his article.[15] By communication dated September 12, 1972, the Phoenix office was advised to "ensure that appropriate local authorities were aware of any threats to harm Chavez." This information, again, is more news, because the declassified FBI files obtained via FOIA and used in this book do not have any of these 1972 references, much less a new revelation that there may have been another assassination attempt or plot against Chávez in Arizona.

In September 1972, days before his landslide win of 60.7 percent of the popular vote over George McGovern, Nixon was in full control of his campaign, the FBI, the DOJ, and his entire executive branch. He would not have permitted his buddy Ralph de Toledano to be investigated or interrogated. Nixon's people and Toledano would have used journalistic privilege to protect their sources and withhold names. Hoover also would have helped stop any investigation into Toledano as well; he was one of his first biographers. When Toledano wrote for *Newsweek*, his beat was the FBI.[16] Nixon did have a coterie of Chicanos in his pocket, such as Dr. Henry Ramirez, who wrote an incredible entry about Nixon in his book:

> President Nixon had taken care of our issues and had made them systematically integral with the enforcement of the civil rights laws of 1964. Richard M. Nixon was the man who grew up with us Mexicans. He knew us, cared about us, and included us. Let history show that he was the only president who really and truly gave a damn for the Mexicans. He was nefariously lynched by Democratic hypocrites corrupted by power and by a cheering clique, the press, in August 1974. I belong to his official family. I resigned in August 1974.[17]

The *Los Angeles Times*, in an article cited as written by Frank Del Olmo, date not given, block date April 20, 1973, but under the heading "Illegal Grower Payoffs to Teamsters Charged," Chávez is mentioned as alleging he has proof of such a "conspiracy to destroy his UFW. Chávez called for a Congressional investigation of the allegations." Chávez would not have risked making such allegations to a reputable reporter like Del Olmo if he could not support with hard evidence the payoffs from growers to Teamsters. Yet, the FBI files are silent on this record of press statements by Chávez.

Beginning on page 20 and continuing to 22, which is the last page released or provided and may not be the end of the Summary, the narrative takes a new direction. The report includes: "The following references set out meetings and affairs of various organizations and groups which César Chávez, as Director of the UFWOC attended or planned to attend." The list of names, places, and dates contains an early October 28, 1967, event in El

Paso, Texas; another in Albuquerque with Tijerina's group Alianza Federal de Mercedes on the 22nd of October through the 24th, 1972; another with the American Indian Movement in Scottsbluff, Nebraska, on January 13, 1973; another in Honolulu, Hawaii, on September 4, 1973; and Dayton, Ohio, on April 8, 1974. The reference to this latter appearance by Chávez claims that "he spoke unless otherwise indicated." My interpretation of this statement is that the FBI may have recordings of Chávez's speeches that remain secret and unreleased. The FBI acknowledged it not only took photographs of Chávez and union members, but also instructed agents to tape-record interviews with UFW personnel, not to mention illegal wiretaps that may have also been done to Chávez as were done to other targets. These are not made available by the FBI.

On to Tomatoes

Near Stockton there are tomato growers, and Chávez set his sights on this target, according to an LHM dated July 26, 1974, coming from Sacramento FBI. During July 24-26, the San Joaquin County Sheriff's Office (SJCSO) arrested eleven pickets of the UFW. The SJCSO had met with growers and the DOJ's Community Relations Service over this escalating picketing and to listen to their contentions that their civil rights were being violated. The San Joaquin County Tomato Growers Association also complained on behalf of the public suffering from a reduced police force given their assignment to protect growers' interests against the picketing problems. Moreover, the LHM reported "four deputies sustained minor injuries on July 24, 1974; and, that more deputies had sustained minor injuries July 26, 1974." Apparently, the CRS representatives from the DOJ witnessed the "activities in the tomato fields during the early morning hours of July 26, 1974." The report ends without a conclusive declaration that the grower assertions were correct and corroborated by the CRS representative—unless that was not the case. This new front of picketing was also the subject matter for a Nitel teletype dated July 30th at 6:53 p.m. This communication, however, presented another version of civil rights violations; the SJCSO was identifying itself as a victim of civil rights. Both the Sheriff's Office and Assistant U.S. Attorney William B. Shubb had already conferred on the matter. The language of this communication is unique: "[NAME REDACTED] stated their position in this matter was that the civil rights of Sheriff's personnel and the Sheriff's Office (SO) was [sic] being violated due to the intimidation of Sheriff's personnel by the Mexican American tomato picker pickets requiring law enforcement assignment to the picket sites beyond normal strength and thereby are preventing other citizens of equal protection of law by virtue of the fact that they are not Mexican Americans." Later in the message, the sheriff is quoted from an open source article that appeared in the *Stockton Record*: "We are being compelled to be in attendance [at the tomato fields] in great numbers because of the conduct and misconduct of people at the scene. This denies the public's right to deputy protection. The public's right to be protected is in jeopardy." Shubb, the AUSA, admitted this was a novel theory and was not sure what relief the DOJ could provide: "This is kind of a unique thing and it has not been fully explored." The communication closed with this information: "Mr. Fred Grey, representative of the Community Relations Division, U.S. Department of Justice, San Francisco, California, has continued to be an observer to the picketing activity in the vicinity of Stockton, as of July 30, 1974." The Director, FBI was prompt in stopping any further investigation into this matter by his SAC, Sacramento. He told him so explicitly by Airtel dated July 31, 1974, which also noted that discussions were had with FBI attorney Frank Allen. Evidently, the Director, FBI was in need of advice and counsel from his own attorney on this matter. The LHM from SAC, Sacramento that followed an Airtel dated August 1st had more disturbing information. It reported that UFW pickets began a sit-in at a street intersection the previous day because they wanted the sheriff's deputies to arrest a man who drove his pickup into their picket line, injuring some of them. And, the San Jose County Sheriff's Office (SJCSO) personnel at the scene had refused. Manuel Chávez, cousin to César, accused the SJCSO of "being a racist police department, that they were on the grower's side, that they were going to hear from them, that they were going into the community to get them [SJCSO]," and stated that "f— the police, we are going to take them on."[18] The demonstrations by UFW pickets moved to "the county courthouse and it is anticipated that there will be some courtroom disruption when the Mexican-American defendants who have been arrested by the SJCSO are brought in for court appearance."

Nixon Resigns and Ford Takes Over

The focus for all U.S. citizens and the world, particularly the UFW, growers, and Teamsters on August 4, 1974, was not on themselves and their war with Chávez; it was on Nixon's downfall. Richard M. Nixon resigned the presidency on that day; Gerald Ford took over. Ford was the first unelected public official to ever assume the presidency of the United States.

Protests Continue Unabated

The demonstration at the Federal Courthouse in Sacramento on August 7 was reported via Nitel at 10:13 p.m. and stamped August 8, 1974. "Approximately 700 individuals associated with UFW appeared at U.S. Federal Building ... 400 individuals entered the building, congregating in hallways and lobby of building ... 300 remained outside peacefully picketing entire block." A U.S. marshal, Gerald McCarthy, "was able to determine demonstrators were in support of Calif. Assembly Bill AB 3370 guaranteeing free farm labor elections ... and protest Immigration and Naturalization Service (INS) against letting Mexican aliens into agricultural fields." Over in Arizona, the UFW was picketing the federal courthouse also, according to the Nitel of August 17, 1974, to the Director, FBI from SAC, Phoenix. The thirty-seven picketers, including six children, were in front of the courthouse on the 16th and "passed out leaflets demanding investigation of Immigration Services for allowing aliens into the United States to work." Although the demonstration was "covered by the Phoenix police," the SA notified both the "U.S. Secret Service and Assistant U.S. Attorney, Joel Sacks." The "Tomato Battles" between the UFW and growers began to take on the semblance of a war, with multiple fronts, because the pickets moved from county to county beginning at Stanislaus County. The SAC, Sacramento in a Nitel dated August 26 sent at 9:21 p.m. and stamped August 27, 1974, reported to the Director, FBI that the previous day,

> an estimated 200 persons attended a rally in Patterson, California held by UFW . . . an estimated 50 to 100 union members have been traveling in approximately 25 automobiles to various ranches where tomatoes are being harvested. Through the use of signs, banners, and voice the members have been urging that the workers leave the fields and support the UFW.

The few incidents reported were isolated and "rock or dirt clod throwing on the part of workers involved, but no major confrontations have occurred, and no arrests have been necessary. [LINES REDACTED]."

The Papal Visit

Back in Delano, César and Helen were packing to travel to Europe to ask for help from unions and consumers in boycotting lettuce, grapes, tomatoes, and other non-UFW union products being imported by European countries. His travel was sponsored by the World Council of Churches. The highlight for Helen and César was a possible meeting with Pope Paul VI in Vatican City arranged by Bishop Joseph Donnelly and Monsignor George Higgins. They left for Europe on September 16, symbolically Mexican Independence Day, accompanied by Jacques Levy and Richard Ybarra, son-in-law.[19] On September 24, 1974, after several most successful agreements had been reached with major European unions, Chávez was informed the meeting with the pope was to be in Rome at 10 a.m. the next day. Helen and César were in Stockholm. How to get to Rome by the next morning became the nightmare for all.

His group drove in a rush to catch a late-night flight out of Stockholm to London, and then hoped they could get seats on a Nigerian flight. There was one available flight, but no seats showing as being available. They gambled and made the flight to London, got seats on the Nigerian flight, and arrived at Rome. In less than twenty-four hours they had traveled 1,500 land miles across the Baltic Sea to Vatican City in Rome. The private audience with the pope became a reality. Chávez and his group had a private meeting with the pope on the 25th.

The same day Chávez and Helen were genuflecting before the pope and kissing his ring, the Yuma County sheriff in Phoenix was arresting demonstrators near Yuma. The SAC, Phoenix reported to the Director, FBI that "58 Mexican males belonging to United Farm Workers were arrested ... for unlawful assembly ... after Sheriff Bud Yancey ordered group of approximately 300 individuals to disperse as they were in violation of direct court order prohibiting more than 50 individuals to be assembled at one time at one locale." The arraignment took place on September 25, 1974, the day the SAC sent the teletype with the information. Each was released on $330 bond. The FBI files on Chávez contain no record of any previous "direct court order," hearings, much less injunctions, with conditions limiting picketing or prohibiting demonstrations by the UFW. Perhaps, Sheriff Yancey just made that up.

While Still in Vatican City

Chávez spoke to more than two hundred religious leaders gathered at the Vatican for the Pontifical Council for Justice and Peace. He was introduced to the audience by Archbishop Giovanni Benelli, one of the pope's closest aides. Benelli in his remarks rhetorically asked, "What is a Christian?," and proceeded to explain what it meant to be such, then said that César's "life is an illustration of this principle," according to Levy, who accompanied the Chávezes and took notes for his book.[20] From the United States, seventy bishops were meeting in Assisi, Italy; Chávez was informed that his meeting with and remarks made by the pope had been passed on to the gathering. On the return trip, the Chávez entourage made two important stops at Geneva and Brussels. Chávez met with Dr. Philip Potter, head of the World Council of Churches in Geneva, and in Brussels with leaders of the International Confederation of Free Trade Unions, the largest grouping of

European unions. After both meetings, Chávez received pledges of support to help his boycott and stop the Teamsters' challenge to his farm worker organizing. Upon return he learned that the Teamsters were sending their own representatives to Europe in an attempt to counter Chávez's internationalizing of *la causa*.[21]

The Push Back

Not all the press coverage from his European tour was favorable. Three critical articles by Victor Riesel on Chávez are in the FBI files.[22] The first is titled "World-Organizing Trip: Cesar Chavez' Supporters Invade Peaceful Conference of Christians and Jews Banquet" and condemns Chávez for picketing a hotel, entering the banquet, and disrupting the dinner. Little mention is made as to the purpose of the demonstration; the event was held to honor Robert R. Longacre, the president of the Great Atlantic and Pacific Tea Company Inc., the largest buyer of Teamster lettuce. Riesel accused Chávez of fomenting an intercontinental farm war. He questions why Chávez the Catholic is any different from the other Catholics in the mix. Most Italian grape growers were also Catholic. Frank Fitzsimmons, the Teamster boss, was Catholic. Why the favoritism toward Chávez? The next article in the FBI files is on Chávez and the pope, "Inside the Vatican: The Pope Receives Cesar Chavez Warmly." The articles were not favorable to Chávez or the UFW; in fact they were highly critical of what Riesel saw as a new dimension to labor organizing by the UFW, that of incorporating youth and clergy, a new socioreligious era being born.[23]

The Incessant Demonstrations

The federal courthouse demonstrations moved to St. Louis, Missouri, by October 8, 1974. SAC, St. Louis reports to the Director, FBI that the protest by UFW supporters was against John R. Rickhoff, a county circuit judge, for enjoining picketing at specified liquor stores for selling California wines made with nonunion grapes. St. Louis FBI closed its case almost within a week and notified the Director, FBI because no arrests were made, and no incidents of violence, injuries, or property damage resulted, according to the Airtel dated October 15. The LHM followed the Airtel on the same day with fuller description of this peaceful First Amendment exercise of the right to assembly and petition for grievances. There were two arrests made at a nearby Target store by University City police. This is the account per the LHM: "The arrests were made at the University City Police Station after the protest had ended. The group of protesters had marched to the police station to ask why they had been photographed while talking to customers in the Target Store. Police said members were photographed after they refused to identify themselves after attempts to question them at the store." Protesters filed suit subsequently against the University City Police Department and City in U.S. District Court and won, according to this document; no litigation timeline provided.

In Stanislaus County, California, the SAC, Sacramento in a memorandum to the Director, FBI dated October 24, 1974, states he is closing the investigation into the tomato wars: "The tomato harvest has been completed and [LINES REDACTED] ...No further investigation is being conducted within the Sacramento Division." But over in Dayton, Ohio, the picketing with arrests continued. In an Airtel dated November 8, 1974, sent from SAC, Cincinnati to the Director, FBI, he informs that "UFW pickets arrested by Montgomery County Sheriff's Office (MCSO), Dayton, Ohio, 11/2/74 for protesting sale of non-union grapes and lettuce and charged with disorderly conduct." The SAC followed up with an LHM that same day providing more details about these arrests. "It was reported that" the MCSO "had arrested 23 members of the United Farm Workers (UFW) union ... after they were stopped from picketing Fazio's Food Market ... where they were urging customers not to buy table grapes or head lettuce." The report indicates the picketing at this store had been going on for "the past six weeks." On this occasion, however, "a Deputy Sheriff was quoted as saying the pickets were 'clapping, chanting, and raving.'" The store spokesman "reportedly said that the pickets were disturbing the peace." From an open source, the *Dayton Daily News*, the SAC learned that those arrested "had entered pleas of not guilty and trial had been set." The SAC further reported that [LINES REDACTED] "he had sent a telegram to the Ohio State Attorney General seeking an investigation of 'reckless, high-handed, and illegal' behavior of the management of Fazio Stores and the Montgomery County Sheriff's Office in connection with the arrests."

The *Dayton Daily News* of November 6 provided more material for the SAC to inform the FBI HQ. David Koehler, the boycott director, had sent complaints to the FBI and DOJ, the newspaper stated. It was alleged that a drunken deputy "maliciously smashed the window of a UFW van, threatened people in a careless and dangerous manner with a gun and club." Other deputies allegedly pulled people out of cars and vans for arrest while they were trying to comply with the order to disperse or face arrest. The next day the Dayton RA received a call, the LHM stated; "he said all charges against the UFW pickets have been dropped by the prosecution at their court appearance . . . the UFW desired to withdraw any complaint made to the FBI and the United States Department of Justice." This version of events was corroborated for the SAC by another open source, the *Journal Herald* of November 8. A deal apparently had been worked out between the UFW pickets, MCSO, and Fazio's Store; picketing resumed. "About fifty UFW members and supporters immediately went back to the store . . . and set up a picket line for about an hour." The five-page LHM ends with the information that U.S. Attorney William W. Milligan was not pursuing any action.

Arizona Actions

SAC, Phoenix relayed to the Director, FBI by Airtel dated November 7, 1974, an eight-page LHM (heavily redacted) the same day reporting on events of the previous September. Apparently, immigrant lemon pickers working outside Yuma were confronted by 2,500 UFW members protesting their presence and illegal entry into the United States via Organ Pipe National Monument. The UFW protesters advised the park service there that they were going to patrol the park with five cars, each containing four UFW members. And when they encountered an "illegal alien" they would seek to convince him to return to Mexico (p.1). On September 16, there was a rock-throwing incident between the "illegal aliens" and the UFW patrols. The Yuma Sheriff's Office arrested twenty-five, including "illegal aliens" and UFW members. Subsequently, 250 UFW members protested across the street from the county jail (p.2). On September 25th, 58 UFW members were arrested by Yuma sheriff's deputies for unlawful assembly near Yuma, Arizona, under a court order prohibiting more than fifty individuals to be assembled at one time at one locale. Bonds were set at $330 each. Again, on October 7 the protestors were there, but no arrests were made because the ban was lifted by order of a superior court in Yuma allowing up to twenty-five pickets per field.

Earlier in the month, two cars and one bus belonging to Mexican workers were burned. UFWs member and César's cousin Manuel Chávez had set up the "Wet Line," as he called it, along the U.S.-Mexico border to apprehend and turn back illegal aliens (p.4). More violence was reported via phone call to U.S. Attorney William C. Smitherman, Tucson, Arizona, from FBI Special Agent (name redacted). The burning of a home was to happen in Somerton, Arizona, if its owner did not leave the citrus fields. And, out in the fields, lemon pickers were being threatened with harm if they did not leave the fields forthwith (p.5). On October 11 five vehicles belonging to immigrant farm workers were burned by unknown subjects in San Luis, Arizona. The remaining content is redacted (p.6). Finally, on October 16 the LHM had this notation in the report:

> A Xeroxed copy of a letter sent to President Ford from the Attorney General's Office of the State of Arizona written by N. Warner Lee requesting "to send investigators immediately to the Yuma, Arizona area" so the President could be prepared to discuss labor problems with Mexico's President Echevarria on October 21, 1974. (p.7)

The local FBI could not substantiate these allegations and so noted in the LHM (p.8).

The UFW Files Suit

Oddly, the Assistant Attorney General, Civil Rights Division, J. Stanley Pottinger, wrote a memorandum dated January 14, 1975, to the Director, FBI asking if any complaints had been received by them, and if any investigations into these were ongoing. He also asked for copies of any pleadings filed in the case alluded to in the newspaper articles attached to his memo. Four pages were deleted entirely on this communication. Hurriedly, the Director by Airtel notified SAC, Phoenix to begin a "limited investigation" of these legal papers, and report within fourteen days from January 16, 1975.

Chávez traveled to San Luis, Arizona, and addressed its members on January 31, telling them that a suit for $110,000 in damages was filed against a person or company whose name was redacted, according to the teletype from Phoenix FBI sent at 7:26 p.m. to the Director on February 3, 1975. Chávez also threatened a general strike if (redacted), and later at a news conference Chávez alluded to having evidence that (redacted). Chávez concluded the press conference by accusing the Yuma County court system as being "ruled by politics."

A two-page LHM from Phoenix FBI to Washington was heavily redacted, but made mention of an article that was not included. There were an additional two pages entirely withheld from this file under exemption "(b) (7) (C)." The referenced enclosure, "44-63337-3," perhaps was the newspaper article. It makes no sense to withhold an open source newspaper article, even if it contained names of FBI or sheriff's personnel; it is already in the public domain.

In March, the Phoenix FBI office sent copies to the Director, FBI of the Amended Complaint, Order of Court and Docket Sheet. On a single sheet dated March 27, 1975, from Phoenix FBI regarding Field Office file no. 44-802 accompanying these documents is found a one-line comment: "Attorney, Yuma, Arizona, declined to allow individuals to be interviewed. Court records reviewed." On another page dated March 24, 1975, is found the explanation that "attorney JAMES RUTKOWSKI representing the United Farm Workers (UFW), Yuma, Arizona, was contacted concerning making arrangements to interview [LINES REDACTED WITH PENCILED NOTATION

B7C AT MARGIN]. Rutkowski would not allow FBI interviews with his clients because the matter seemed to be "calmed down" and "an interview would only 'heat up the situation.'"

Procedurally, it seems that the UFW suit was a state court matter, and those parties had not been served. Perhaps it was a tactic by the Chávez legal team to see if the U.S. attorney would file a civil rights action, at which time they would withdraw their state claim.

Action Moves to Texas

J. Stanley Pottinger wrote to the Director, FBI on September 3, 1975, inquiring about a letter he was attaching to his memorandum concerning arrests of UFW pickets by the sheriff's departments of Reeves and Pecos Counties in Texas. Pottinger wanted listed items from the FBI: police reports, determination by the FBI on the status of the charges, interviews with several people (some names redacted), and specifically interviews with a law student who simply inquired about the charges and a surveyor who had stated the pickets were conducted on public property. The attached letter was dated July 25, 1975, from the UFW in San Juan, Texas, to Edward Levi, U.S. attorney general. It contained the allegations that thirty pickets on a public road were arrested in Reeves County on July 23 and that some of those jailed were children ages twelve to fifteen, who were locked up with adult inmates before they could be bailed out. Bail was denied some, and breakfast was denied to all the following day. The letter further made mention of fifteen more arrests taking place on July 25 in Pecos County. They asked for help from the AG. The signer's name was redacted under exemption (b)(7)(c). No response is found in subsequent documents.

Chávez Leads the Confrontation in Merced, California

The United Farm Workers Union had a rally and fiesta at the Merced County Fairgrounds on August 10, 1975, so reported the SAC, Sacramento to the

Director by Airtel dated August 11, 1975, and accompanying two-page LHM. The police had granted a permit to the UFW from 1 p.m. to 7 p.m. and listened to the Chávez speech. Chávez was the principal speaker at the event, which numbered approximately 1,200 persons. And, the informant or FBI agent wrote this about the talk: "Chavez spoke entirely in Spanish and the speech that he gave was reportedly basically the same one he had been giving during the course of a 1,000 mile walk through California."[24]

The music kept playing after the police sergeant made the call to shut it down at 7 p.m. The band refused to stop playing. The police sergeant declared the event illegal after the deadline and ordered the crowd to disperse. Chávez mounted the platform, took the microphone, and ordered the band to keep playing. He told the police sergeant it was a private party and that they had no right to stop the rally and fiesta. The police disconnected the electrical connections for the band and called for reinforcements. Some sixty to seventy UFW members left and set up pickets around the Merced police station. Within minutes, a brick was thrown through a window at the police station and a glass door was also broken.

For now, nothing more can be said on the outcome of this confrontation turning violent because there is only one page on this matter. Perhaps in the future more FBI files will be released.

The Final Unraveling of César Chávez

The promise of reforms under the ALRB was short-lived. The Teamsters did quit the fight, but the growers did not. In the legislature, they sought a reduction in funding for the ALRB, leading to case overload and little resolution of disputes. In the courts, they fought every decision rendered by the ALRB that was not favorable to them.[25] By 1978 César was tired of the court battles and disagreements with Jerry Cohen, his top lawyer. Cohen had refused to move the lawyers and legal department to the new compound in the Tehachapi Mountains, aka La Paz. Cohen had also asked for wage increases for his staff; César instead fired them all.[26]

Tired of the other never-ending battles, beatings, threats, murders, fundraising, worker issues, staff issues, the budget, volunteer recruitment, and contract enforcements, Chávez began to dream of getting away again from these daily hassles and conflicts. He had done that once before when he moved the office from Delano to the edge of town to Forty Acres to avoid the workers and their constant complaints and issues. Now, he was realizing his idea of a community for his *causa*, not his union, because no farm worker was to live at La Paz, only his family and some staff. La Paz was to be a mecca for the farm workers, who could come to relax, learn, and recharge. According to Caitlin Flanagan, an early volunteer recruited by her mother to work for the UFW, he had changed.

> He began to hold the actual farmworkers in contempt: "Every time we look at them," he said during a tape-recorded meeting at La Paz, "they want more money. Like pigs, you know. Here we're slaving, and we're starving and the goddam workers don't give a shit about anything."[27]

In 1955, he had envisioned communal farms for farm workers, but gave up on that temporarily. Now, in the spring of 1975, Chávez found a huge place, a former tuberculosis hospital and recovery center up in the mountains. His model was based on a vision similar to that of Charles Dederich, founder of Synanon, a drug rehabilitation program that evolved into a huge and much different business enterprise.[28]

Fallout from Playing The Game

The love affair Chávez developed with a group therapy exercise called "The Game" by its founder Charles Dederich began during the *caminata* of 1,000 miles in 1975. Members of Synanon played The Game in the evenings when not marching. Chávez observed the control of the leader by the release of tension and the formation of group solidarity among participants with this therapy. Chávez had known Dederich since the mid-1960s. He had a center in Santa Monica where the UFW sent members for free medical and dental care back then. Now in the 1970s, Dederich had a compound called Home

Place in the foothills of the Sierra Nevada Mountains near Badger, California, fifty-five miles east of Fresno. He built that empire by raising funds from donors, selling memorabilia, investing in real estate, collecting fees for services rendered by his volunteers to others, forming clubs to belong to Synanon, as he called his group—later a cult, and by 1975 a religion to avoid paying taxes. The membership in the club was paid monthly and he catered to the upper middle class in pursuit of what he called "looking for meaning in community." He had millions in assets by the late 1970s, according to Bardacke.[29]

Dederich invited Chávez to bring his staff and play The Game at Home Place, which he did. He rewarded Chávez for the visit with 22,000 pounds of food, children's clothing, building materials, and paper cups delivered in a 40-foot semi-truck to La Paz. The more Chávez played The Game or watched it played, the more he wanted to incorporate that practice into his model of community life at La Paz. And he did. Chávez mandated that on Sundays and Wednesdays the staff would play The Game. On Saturdays, the residents of La Paz would tend to the flower and vegetable gardens along with him and his family. Everyone should wear a UFW button daily and be fined $0.25 if not. He began to hold board and staff meetings when Marshall Ganz, Eliseo Medina, Gil Padilla, and Richard Chávez, his brother, were not present, so his motions could pass without debate.

His staff and volunteers began to quit. Rev. Jim Drake was among the first to quit over Chávez's reluctance to return to organizing a union. Leroy Chatfield left to help Jerry Brown win the governor's race in 1976. Chávez began to call his critics the "asshole conspirators." Next to go was Philip Vera Cruz, who had been with Chávez from the beginning just before Drake came on board, after a grueling and very personal attack on him. Chávez's wife, Helen, left him alone at La Paz for several months over allegations of infidelity and adultery in a letter she uncovered while working as a substitute in the main office in the spring of 1977. "Still, the letters kept coming. She also received several phone calls from women while her husband was traveling," wrote Matt Garcia.[30]

Falling Down on the Job?

Had the FBI been on the alert and on top of their surveillance game, they could have harassed Chávez over this alleged transgression to no end, as they did earlier in 1964 with MLK Jr. Back then, William Sullivan, the Assistant Director of the FBI, was put in charge by Hoover of blackmailing Dr. King over his sexual escapades when traveling around the country. They taped his conversations and lovemaking sounds with women and others in hotel rooms as he traveled about, until they hit their incriminating evidence. "Attorney General Robert F. Kennedy approved the above requests for technical surveillance on King at the SCLC office in New York City on October 10, 1963 and this was continued by AG Nicholas de B Katzenbach until June 21, 1966."[31] The tapes were played for President Johnson. A package containing transcripts and recordings with a letter drafted by Sullivan urging him to commit suicide before being internationally embarrassed by these revelations were mailed to King's office intended for Coretta King to open, which she did, but not until January of the following year, 1965.[32] Rev. King ignored the letter, and Mrs. King did not leave her husband's side. No damage to Dr. King resulted; LBJ ordered Hoover to patch things up with Dr. King.[33]

There is not one FBI document that makes any allusion to this adultery and infidelity on the part of Chávez. And, the FBI did have informants within the UFW, as the files indicate time and again, with clear references to sources as informants with names redacted. On the flip side of this argument is the fact that the FBI set up Dr. King and others with purloined letters, fake photos, tape recordings, even soiled lingerie under COINTELPRO operations. Maybe what happened to Chávez was the work of the FBI and that is why no documentary evidence to the contrary is in the declassified file.

The Unraveling Continues

Chávez arbitrarily moved Marshall Ganz to organizing, a department almost defunct since the Proposition battles in California. Chávez even signed up for a six-day class in Los Angeles on mind control. Upon return, he announced he now could cure ailments by laying hands (his) on people. The inner core, Huerta, Padilla, Ganz, Cohen, Medina, and Chávez's brother Richard, began to tell each other Chávez had gone crazy. Then Chávez insisted on not paying more money to staff; in fact, he wanted them to work for no salary. Medina took a leave of absence, as did Juan Govea and later Marshall Ganz. They never came back. When Jerry Cohen resigned as his lawyer, Chávez turned to the top assistant lawyer, Sandy Nathan, and asked him to stay on. Nathan refused and also left.[34] These were no ordinary staff persons; they were the keys to Chávez's many successes of years past.[35]

Nathan Heller succinctly puts the change in Chávez this way:

> Chavez became openly paranoid during the seventies. Increasingly seized by what Pawel calls a "basic mistrust of almost anyone with outside expertise," he began purging associates from the upper ranks of the union—quietly at first, and then in public confrontations. In 1977, taking a cue from Mao, he staged shouting matches at meetings to drive out colleagues. Sometimes he accused them of being spies for the Republicans or the Communists ("You're a fucking agent," he seethed at a confused plumber). The paranoia was not baseless—Chavez, like many figures on the left, was under F.B.I. investigation—but the reaction was extreme. When some he expelled tried to use the phone, La Paz security threatened to eject them forcibly.[36]

Randy Shaw has a more succinct listing of the causes for the unraveling of Chávez:

1. The defeat of Proposition 14 in 1976. Chavez spent millions of union funds and stopped organizing workers in this attempt. He never overcame this loss.
2. The fascination and dedication in 1977 to playing The Game and imitating Synanon's founder, Charles Dederich, in setting up a community based on cult. Chavez, despite internal opposition from Filipino members, accepted an invitation from dictator Ferdinand Marcos to visit the Philippines in August 1977. Philip Vera Cruz, an original founder, left the union. He was replaced on the board by Eliseo Medina.

3. Stopping the national boycott on May 5, 1978, and organizing new workers and removing Eliseo Medina from those responsibilities. Medina left the union August 1978. No farm worker sat on the National Board as of March 25, 1978.

4. Forcing the hand of his Legal Department to move to La Paz or be fired in June 1978. They resigned and left.

5. The Lettuce Strike of January 1, 1979, without Teamster competition since 1977 was an open door to organize 5,000 new workers from Salinas to Arizona. Chavez opposed the strike and sought to use a boycott strategy. Within six months, the strikers got contracts. The UFW hit its apogee in membership: 45,000 members. Marshall Ganz and Jessica Govea left the union. The emboldened strikers, led by Salinas leader Rosario Pelayo, sought seats on the executive board of the union in 1981; Pelayo had been a UFW volunteer since 1970 and president of her Ranch Committee since 1977. Chavez engineered the meeting to avoid a vote on the Pelayo slate; they walked out of the convention, never to return. Chavez fired nine of the paid worker representatives from the Salinas group. He later lost in court for wrongful terminations.

6. Chavez resumed total control over all aspects of the union, including bad management and poor service to workers on their contracts. By 1984 the UFW was down to fifteen contracts with grape growers when they used to have seventy. When he died in 1994, the UFW did not have a single grape contract. The following year, 1995, some 20,000 strawberry pickers voted in various elections for union representation; the UFW only won one contest for 750 workers. The federal government in 2001 reported the membership of the UFW at only 6,000 members.

7. Sixteen years of Republican rule in the state, from 1982 with the election of George Deukmejian to Pete Wilson's term ending in 1998, destroyed the ALRB and the Chavez political machine. It cost millions of dollars in campaign contributions from UFW coffers, and regained lost ground for growers.[37]

Missing from these three analyses by Heller, Pawel, and Shaw—as well as others who have authored critical works on Chávez—is the impact of the FBI surveillance on the man and the union. From day one, Chávez was under suspicion by many of being a Communist or being under the influence of Communists. Red-baiting was a most effective weapon against activists and dissenters during the 1950s through the Vietnam War years. The police assaults, coupled with judicial support and often misconduct directed at him, the UFW membership, and the scores of volunteers drained him daily of hope, money, and security. The murders of his members and extreme violence directed at strikers and pickets took a toll on Chávez, who resorted to marching and fasting to counter violence with nonviolence. Chávez knew, as did his family, staff, volunteers, and supporters everywhere, that he could be killed at any moment. The FBI also knew this for years and did nothing. How could Chávez ever feel secure at night, or by day as he moved about the fields, jails, courtrooms, campuses, picket lines, conferences, and the like? Is that why he kept moving his office from the center of Delano to the outskirts and finally to the mountains? Is that why he displayed paranoia time and again at meetings, dealings with staff, and processing of events?

Democratic and Republican presidents Kennedy, Johnson, Nixon, Ford, Carter, and Reagan were all aware of the troubles Chávez had with local police, state politicians, the courts, agricultural interests, and the Teamsters. The Teamsters did generously fund the presidential campaigns of several of them, and perhaps that had to do with their do-nothing attitude toward Chávez and his complaints to the executive branch. The FBI, plus the various U.S. attorney generals during these presidential administrations, never saw a prosecutorial opportunity to correct wrongs by state officials acting under the color of law, and repeated violations of state and federal laws by others.

Addendum of FBI Files Recently Released

I appealed for the limited Cesar Chavez file to be released and asked for more documents held by the FBI from August 2, 1975, to April 30, 1993. On June 27, 2017, I received sixty-three more pages on César Chávez. A letter accompanying these new documents informed me that in November 1977, records that related to my follow-up FOI/PA request on Chávez had already been destroyed.[38]

More Assassination Threats and Murder Plots

The recently released files begin with a three-page set of handwritten notes on letterhead titled Memorandum and dated December 21, 1988, from SA [REDACTED] to SAC, Sacramento (9A-new). The subject line contains an interesting entry: "UNSUB(s) Series of Threatening Calls to Cesar Chavez residence Keene [Kern Co.] California, 12/88 Extortion (OO:SC)." Apparently, these are notes from an agent in the field to his supervisor, the SAC in Sacramento, because OO means Office of Origin and SC is for Sacramento Field Office. The SA reported that

> on December 21, 1988 [NAME REDACTED] from the Attorney General's office at 15th and K Sts, Sacramento, tel # [REDACTED] advised that "his office has been responding to a series of 'veiled' threat calls, about 10 to 15 in total, received in early December 1988 by CESAR CHAVEZ, United Farm Workers leader at the CHAVEZ compound & residence located in Keene, Calif. [in the Tehachapi Pass area of Kern County]. (p.1)

The SA report states that

> the first call or two appear to be from an unknown white male voice, age 30s, who supposedly told victim CHAVEZ "we will get you and yours." Most of the other calls were hang-ups, nuisance-type calls, or no conversation. No calls have been received in the past 2-3 days. According to [NAME REDACTED], DOJ has already interviewed the CHAVEZ family and he [NAME REDACTED] will prepare a summary memorandum with all available details; and will drop this memorandum at the Sacramento office of the FBI on 12/22/88 (to the attention of SSA [NAME REDACTED]). In view of the above, it is recommended that the #3 desk await the delivery of Mr. [NAME

REDACTED] memo and then consider opening a 9A case for the Bakersfield RA. (pp.1-2)

This file was assigned number "SC 9A-1191-1A" indicating it is an Extortion file in the Sacramento FBI office (p.3).[39] Why it was classified Extortion and not Major Crime, Assassination, Conspiracy to Murder, or even a broad designation such as Civil Rights, is a curious question. There was no money requested by any of the voices during these calls.

State of California Department of Justice

The California Department of Justice also investigated these threatening phone calls by sending a special agent supervisor from the Bureau of Organized Crime and Criminal Intelligence. A three-page report with an additional two-page flyer—or what may have been one double-sided flyer copied onto two pages, Spanish and English—was filed by John B. Smoot, special agent in charge, in the Sacramento office on December 22, 1988. The flyer was found in MacFarland, California, and carries the logo imprint of the International Committee Against Racism (INCAR).[40] The woman leader of INCAR in the MacFarland area, according to Smoot, had long been an adversary of Chávez. The flyer said as much: "As usual, the Democrats have pulled out their clown Cesar Chavez ... The truth is one day this puppet of the bosses [Chávez] will be killed by workers who are tired of his garbage" (English side of flyer). The Spanish version reads differently: "La verdad es que un dia este alcuate de los patrones será linchado por los campesinos cansados de sus engaños traidores." The translation into English of this phrase would be very similar to the language used in the flyer, but for one word, *linchado*, which means lynched. And, in English she used "tired of his garbage" which is not the correct translation of "engaños traidores," which is closer to "traitorous cheating schemes."

Smoot, the SAC in Sacramento, reported much the same as the FBI special agent supervisor, except he added two noteworthy points. The second call on December 3 was thought "to be a male, possibly black. The voice might also have been disguised to sound black." And, that Chávez's home number was not listed except for an internal directory "for use by the many offices within the compound which includes his direct number" (p.1). Interestingly, SAC Smoot adds that "Both calls received were from within the compound or one of the three field offices." He was able to ascertain this from characteristics of the compound's telephone system that are "able to distinguish whether a call is originating within the compound and one of three outside offices located in Arvin, Delano and Coachella or an outside line." Smoot passed on his information to his superiors and the Sacramento FBI office (p.3). No mention is made in these documents that any investigation followed on their part to find which internal phone placed those calls. I assume this witch hunt was left up to Chávez to pursue and cause further division in the ranks with accusations of conspiracies and treason to the cause and leader.

The MacFarland flyer lists the INCAR telephone number and has several dates in August—13, 19, and 20—but no year. Both Smoot and the FBI assumed it meant 1988; but still, that flyer was from five months prior to these phone calls. The attachment of the flyer just seems a simple and local version of the former FBI's Operation Hoodwink, which tried to pit the CPUSA and the Mafia against each other with purloined letters, flyers, articles in the media, and letters to the editor.

More Inside Calls in 1989

Notes dated January 3, 1989, are from Field File #9A-1191-1A1 and written for an FD-340 form.[41] The code 1A1 refers to a file that may contain notes, photographs, surveillance logs, copies of publications, and signed statements. These handwritten notes indicate that Chávez was interviewed again about the phone call of December 3, 1988, by someone connected with the FBI; no names, offices, nothing to indicate who or from where are provided in these notes. In this report, Chávez is quoted as saying that the caller asked, "Is this César?" The voice was "cultured—no accent—very precise." When César allegedly said, "What?" the party hung up. What is surprising are the handwritten notes: "his call was to him thru at #104 (His office direct). They usually go thru #105 (Secretary)" (p.1). On the following page, the note writer indicates that a single ring from the phone indicates it originates from inside the compound or field offices; a double ring means outside. Chávez reportedly stated he "had no idea who caller was."

The next call, according to this report, was after 1 p.m., and "Live talker wanted to know if it was César—sounded like different voice. Said, 'We're going to kill you, you S.O.B.' That night dark sports car with Bas [unreadable] was near Cesar's place said they worked at CCI Tehahspi [*sic*, unreadable]" (p.2).

That same day, 3rd of January, but under a new file, 9A-1194-1A2, another FD-340 was prepared, eight pages, with a copy of a threatening letter that was directed at César Chávez. The original was sent to the FBI lab for analysis. The envelope containing the letter was one of Chávez's own self-addressed, stamped return envelopes used in fundraising appeals. The sender also used three non-postal-service stamps, distributed by the Humane Society, featuring a cat. Inside was a double-sided, long piece of paper or two pieces of paper, the "letter" with illegible words except for "Aryian brotherhood SSM" and notes from the FBI at bottom "Him 1/3/89 9A-new" and some unreadable initials ("RMH"?). The other piece of paper reads: "Fuck you Wetback Spick Mexican Whoop bastard I am going to kill you Mother Fucker" (pp.4–5). The last three pages are copies of the envelope sealing flap and the cat stamp (pp.6–7), and a copy of a page with title "Material Inside Q 2 (9A-1194) (P)" and what appears to be fibrous material (p.8).

Within two days, on January 8, 1989, SAC, Sacramento sent another three-page Airtel to the Director, FBI (Attention: Identification Division, Latent Fingerprint Section). The SAC entered "(9a-NEW) (P)" as the file number and scratched out "NEW" and penciled in "1194." This Airtel contains the "letter" with copy sent to Phoenix requesting the Fingerprint Section of the Identification Division to process the enclosure for any identifiable latent fingerprints. The Airtel provides useful information in that it identified the envelope.

This particular solicitation package, one of many on the mailing list, went to [NAME REDACTED] as evidenced on the UFW mailing label. Neither

Chavez nor [NAME REDACTED] know [NAME REDACTED] and have no reason to suspect him. It is pointed out that the writer of this particular
letter could possibly be a "nut" on the basis of the contents of the envelope
which consists of a soda can pull tab and straw in addition to the letter.
(p.3)

The letter produced and copied by the FBI referenced in their Airtels of
January 3 make no mention of a pull tab or straw. Someone (name redacted)
other than Chávez informed the FBI agents investigating this incident that
the letter had been handled by him or her, Chávez, and one of Chávez's sons.
This same person promised to, if latent print of value was found, "obtain
the identity of and other descriptive data regarding persons who handled
this letter for elimination purposes, if necessary." Phoenix FBI sent a copy
of their copy to Tucson FBI, with request they "display the letter for any
information of value or possible suspects." This Phoenix Airtel ends with
an ominous and uncalled-for conclusion in bold print and underscored:
"UNSUB CONSIDERED ARMED AND DANGEROUS" (p.3). If the person sending
the original letter is "Unsub" (unknown subject), then why is the person
considered armed and dangerous?

It turned out the letter was mailed from Tucson, from a rented post office box, and perhaps the FBI already knew that. The suspect was known to
be on the UFW mailing list. He sent donations periodically and he received
the monthly "Food and Justice Newsletter." The FBI agents from Phoenix
traveled to Tucson to interview this person about the letter. He explained
that it wasn't him who sent the letter, and it could have been anyone,
because he discarded right there while at the post office any unwanted material, such as a solicitation letter. He only kept it when he felt like making
a donation, which he did from time to time. The FBI agents learned from
the interview that the suspect was a graduate student, and checked him
out in city directories, U.S. postal service box rentals, and telephone service
records. They found nothing but a listing on him with the Arizona Department of Motor Vehicles with this information:

Disclosed a motorcycle instruction permit was issued on 10/28/88 to
[NAME AND BIRTHDATE REDACTED], 6', 130 lbs., brown hair and eyes, and

SSAN [REDACTED]. He was previously licensed in Colorado, with driver license [REDACTED] which expires in 1989.

An FD-302 was also sent with the Airtel above, containing the typed version of the interview with the suspect and a female student (possible roommate? girlfriend?); it did not explain how she fit into the scheme of the investigation. Too bad for her, because now the FBI does have a file on her. Further checking by the FBI found the suspect was enrolled in Optical Science Studies at the local university and had no criminal record. They also found he previously had been an undergraduate student at the Colorado School of Mines, Golden, Colorado, in 1981. No further information is disclosed as to why he continued to be a suspect.

The FBI laboratory in late February 1989 reported to SAC, Sacramento that they had found two latent fingerprints of value, and wrote: "the specimens are enclosed." They were not. They may have been, but not declassified and made part of the FBI Chavez file. The sender of this threatening letter will remain unknown, and possibly unprosecuted. Nine months later, August 17, 1989, the SAC, Sacramento by memorandum to the Director, FBI put in writing that

> Investigative efforts by Sacramento and Phoenix Divisions have failed to effect an identification or develop any suspects in captioned matter. Accordingly, this matter is being placed in a closed status.

Was All This Too Much for César Chávez to Take?

Is it possible that the totality of these circumstances made Chávez trust no one toward the end of his last decades of life? Is that why he turned against loyalists like Antonio Orendain, Gilbert Padilla, Jerry Cohen, Jim Drake, Eliseo Median, Marshall Ganz, Philip Vera Cruz, Jessica Govea, Rosario Pelayo, and hundreds more members and volunteers, suspecting them of disloyalty to him, his vision, his union? Is this why he turned to family as replacements for departed key staff members, keeping only the most loyal adherents by his side? Is this why he died in his sleep—just wanted to forever quit?

From Union Workers to Family Workers Post Chávez's Death

The persons most loyal and obedient to Chávez were his family members, nuclear and extended. As he removed the remaining non-family members from board positions, union departments and components, branch offices, and support service centers, he placed family members in those slots between the 1980s and the early 1990s. His children were grown, some married. Eliseo Medina was replaced with Arturo Rodriguez, a son-in-law, as heir apparent to Chávez to lead the union. Rodriguez still does so in 2018. Son Paul took control of the National Farm Workers Service Center, and then the Cesar Chavez Foundation. Son Anthony worked for Radio Campesina, and that was also taken over by Paul. More than a dozen family members work for some component of the union, service center, and foundation, plus the for-profit housing development projects; another dozen have quit working for Paul. The housing projects and retail strip-mall developments were built with nonunion labor. In March 2009, Anthony sued Paul over mismanagement of pension funds, $500,000. After the death of the UFW matriarch, Helen Chávez, on June 6, 2016, more family members moved out of La Paz and away from UFW activity. Others remain but do not speak to each other.[42]

CHAPTER 8

The Unraveling of Chávez

GUARANTEE FARM WORKERS THE RIGHT TO VOTE
YES ON 14

In 1972, Chávez was buoyed by the UFW win over Proposition 22, the Agricultural Labor Relations Act, which sought to end farm worker organizing in California. With the help of California's secretary of state, Jerry Brown, who probed and found massive fraud in the collection of signatures to place the initiative on the ballot, and that of the California AFL-CIO unions, who pushed voters to cast ballots against the measure, it went down to defeat.[1] Two years later, Chávez and his membership worked tirelessly for Jerry Brown's electoral victory to become governor of the state. As governor, he repaid the electoral favor by proposing to the legislature that they enact the UFW version of what the Agricultural Labor Relations Act (ALRA) should be the following year. Basically, this law created the process for fair elections on union representation and monitors to enforce compliance with other important terms, all favorable to farm workers. The growers rebounded from defeat of their proposition by challenging every election and ARLA procedure, thereby creating a shortfall in the ALRA's budget. There were so many elections held and contests over those election results, however, that the ALRA ran out of money too soon. The growers then stepped up the elections, knowing there was little to no state oversight due to budget shortfalls. At every turn, the legislators would either not schedule a vote in the legislative committee or vote down more supplemental appropriations for the ALRA. After a couple of supplemental appropriations were made, the legislature tired of this funding hemorrhage.

Chávez felt he knew best how to lead the UFW forward. Despite huge internal cracks as a result of resignations and purges in the organization's foundation, Chávez bravely conjured up a new strategy. He crafted a new Proposition 14 to prevent the legislature from interfering with funding for the ALRA. Chávez pledged that with this new initiative, "We are going to teach the growers a lesson they'll never forget once and for all."[2] He poured more money resources and volunteers into another ballot measure that greatly taxed the UFW treasury. The diverted staff and volunteers gathered over three-quarters of a million signatures of California voters, 850,000, in twenty-nine days.[3] Chávez redirected the union's money and assigned virtually every volunteer and sympathizer to the Prop. 14 battles. This steady shift from UFW resources dedicated to the organizing of farm workers went to handing out campaign contributions to politicians. Chávez gave Democratic Party Assembly Speaker Willie Brown alone more than $700,000 in political contributions.[4] This battle over Proposition 14 became the beginning of the end of it all. Chávez lost Proposition 14 resoundingly at the polls. From this day forward, Chávez began to unravel and the persona he used to be changed. He backed away from the most successful of his strategies: the consumer boycotts. His new focus was to keep winning elections in the fields under the ARLA without much help, if any, from state monitors. It was him and his farm workers against the growers all over again.

Looking backward from this defeat, we can trace the changes in Chávez —his character and worldview, the changes in his strategies and goals, and the organizational modifications away from that of a labor union to a family-owned corporation.

Jane Seymour Fonda and Purging the Communist Assholes

When Chávez was invited to attend the wedding of Jane Fonda to Tom Hayden, he could not believe his good fortune—another Hollywood celebrity to help with fundraising and publicity. Fonda and Hayden were married in 1973. Sure enough, she soon began to help the UFW with appearances and fundraising events with her name, and at times presence. She marched right next to Chávez on the *caminata* from Coachella to Calexico in 1975.[5] Pawel was able to pull that photo from the Chávez collection at the Walter P. Reuther Library at Wayne State University to use in her book.[6] The famous Hollywood movie star marched with him through the Coachella Valley to Salinas in 1979. It did not bother Chávez that Fonda had been dubbed "Hanoi Jane" by the national media since her 1972 tour in North Vietnam while the United States was at war with those Vietnamese. She was vilified as a traitor and a Communist sympathizer during those years for her trip and comments to the media opposing U.S. involvement in the war. Tom Hayden also had been to Hanoi earlier in 1965, and years later was part of the "Chicago Eight" and jailed for demonstrating in Chicago during the Democratic Party National Convention in 1968.[7] When Chávez heard that Tom Hayden, a former SDSer and author of the Port Huron Statement, had won his 1982 race for assemblyman in California (D-44), he was elated. He looked at this victory as another vote for the UFW.

By 1975, however, Chávez was seeing Communists under every California rock—even at La Paz. The law he wanted to protect union activity in the fields, ALRA, went into effect on August 28, 1975. "It's a union busting operation of the biggest goddam order. And the CIA is part of it . . . Communists will take over Mexico."[8] He believed in this conspiracy theory. Worse yet, Chávez was convinced that the immigrant issue was at the bottom of a deal between the Mexican government and the United States as a stand-in for agricultural interests.

In 1976 Chávez joined the chorus against Communists, Communist sympathizers, and leftists in general right after he lost the elections in California for president and U.S. senator, both Democrats, and Proposition 14. Chávez weighed in against the new recruits who had joined the UFW ranks as volunteers, alleging they were part of a plot that had killed Proposition 14. He fired the new editor of *El Malcriado*, Nick Jones, whom Chávez had hand-picked to try and revive it again for the third time. Jones had just been in charge of 329 boycotters in thirty-four cities before the reassignment as editor. Chávez had fired 92 of Jones's crew of volunteers and reassigned 57 others. Chávez forced 23 more to take an extended leave of absence. In effect, Chávez killed the boycott effort, and with that move, killed the national network organization. He instructed Marshall Ganz and Fred Ross Jr. to interrogate everyone who had worked on the campaign and root out all the "assholes," the word he used to encompass those he saw as spies, agitators, malcontents, and those with Communist leanings.[9]

> As far as Chavez was concerned, people who complained were questioning his judgment, and that alone was enough to warrant their dismissal. As Fred Hirsch had pointed out as early as 1968, Chavez viewed almost everyone as expendable. He prided himself on his unmatched work ethic and the union's ability to chew people up and spit them out. "I'm a son of a bitch to work with . . . and most of you could not work with me side by side. You could not keep up my pace. I work every day of the year. I just sleep and eat and work. I do nothing else.[10]

Chávez even fired the plumber, David McClure, who was working on badly needed construction projects at La Paz, accusing him of being a spy and an agent. The proof was that McClure was calling daily a person named Hayakawa, who was his consultant on heating issues. Chávez thought it was the new U.S. Senator Hiram Hayakawa.[11] Chávez refused to give McClure his truck and portable plumbing shop and tools when he was forcibly thrown out of La Paz. Liza Hirsch, the law student that Chávez had mentored, called Chávez trying to intervene and resolve the problem. Chávez fired her, threw her out of the union, and denounced her as a Communist.[12]

Getting Away

At Chávez's insistence, beginning in 1971, a deal was cut to buy a 280-acre facility previously used as a tuberculosis sanatorium. The place was high up in the Tehachapi Mountains near Keene, California, with the foothills ending near Bakersfield. La Nuestra Señora de la Paz became the main UFW community—a compound mostly for key Anglo staffers and the Chávez extended family.[13] Larry Itliong, among other core leaders, derisively called the place "Mecca," and the coterie of Anglos and Jews now living there "the Anglo Brain Trust." Chávez himself called his new home Mecca.[14] At Forty Acres, reduced to a field office, Itliong's office was two doors down from César's.

This radical departure from operations at Forty Acres was unknown to most members and supporters across the nation. At Forty Acres, members and even the public could drop in and visit, maybe even get to see César; not so at La Paz. Gates, security guards, unlisted phone numbers for the public, guard dogs, and detailed control of supplies, food, travel, and daily activity became the norm. Chávez wanted isolation from the daily turmoil of workers' problems so he could run the union his way. La Paz created a distance between Chávez and the union members. As Garcia observes, Chávez wanted to move toward more professionalism in his staff and for them to serve unpaid or for very little salary. He was moving away from the loyalty to an ethnic Mexican base of the movement to a volunteer army of the poor. "Now, the union has a Chicano thrust but that will change" into "an economic movement led by poor workers."[15] Once Chávez decided, it was his way through and through. Taylor quotes Jim Drake, longtime associate of Chávez, on his insight into the Chávez character and being.

> If there is a strike, Cesar *is* the picket line, he is there, with the people reacting. He is at his best when there is a lot of pressure, he is at his worst when there isn't much happening. When not much is happening, he goes off on tangents. At first, you know, I felt he was kind of godlike, that he didn't make mistakes, that he had some uncanny ability to see through everything. Now, I know he makes mistakes ... I don't think he is so much

the strategist as I think he embodies his strategy. You don't have to be right on target with your strategy, it's just that every strategy you decide on, you die with it, carry it to the ultimate. It isn't strategy that wins, it is commitment. Cesar can make a mistake in strategy and no one will know because he will adhere to it.[16]

Levy, the unofficial Chávez biographer, provides a glimpse of the life Chávez led while he retreated into the Tehachapi hills the summer of 1973. In summary, from Levy's notes:

June 19, 1973— Chavez recalled, "I got a very indignant call from Jack Henning, head of the California AFL-CIO. 'What's this I hear about you guys shot Grami?'"

June 20, 1973—Southern California Teamster Bill Grami was shot in the head at approximately 5 a.m. Tuesday, in the vicinity of a Coachella farm workers' labor camp.

June 21, 1973—Six Teamsters were arrested on charges of hurling rocks at a three-car caravan in which Cesar was riding from one picket line to another. No one was hurt. The men were released on a thousand dollars bail each.

June 22, 1973—Two Teamsters were arrested yesterday morning by Riverside County sheriff's deputies on charges of attempting to commit murder and kidnapping. Israel Guajardo, twenty-eight, was taken to Indio Community Hospital with ice-pick wounds to the back of his shoulder and neck.

June 23, 1973—Francisco Campos, his wife Patricia, and their two-and-a-half-year-old daughter, Elisa, all of Brownsville, Texas, nearly died early this morning when their small trailer was destroyed by flames in an open field. Campos joined the UFW in February. The fire destroyed everything they owned.

[June 24, 1973]—180 Teamsters charged into a UFW picket line with iron pipes, clubs, tire irons, and machetes. Deputies reported twenty-five to thirty persons injured, four requiring hospital treatments. Two UFW members were admitted with head wounds. The deputies made eleven arrests—six Teamsters and five UFW members.

Chavez recalled, "They drove up in trucks, got off, and beat the hell out of people with sticks and pipes and chains while deputies just watched. We had women, kids, and men, some older men ... Juan Hernandez, who was sixty, had his skull fractured and ribs cracked. Others were badly injured ... Although deputies arrested twenty-nine Teamsters, Leddy dropped charges on all but one, and he eventually got off, too. These were the same goons the Teamsters used in the Coachella Valley."

July 10, 1973—the nation's largest winery, Gallo Brothers, which had a contract with UFW for six years, signed a four-year Teamster contract. Gallo then tried to evict from its labor camps some seventy families who had been with the company up to fourteen years. The families, with four hundred children, were striking UFW members. But 288 arrests and imported strikebreakers helped break the strike.

Chavez recalled, "In four months, the courts in the four counties issued 58 injunctions, and there were 3,589 arrests. Fresno had the largest number, 1,993 people jailed, including 70 priests and nuns who came to Fresno to bear witness. We counted forty-four people that were beaten up by cops in the valley, where blood was drawn, and where workers were shot at from inside the vineyards ... We had nearly two dozen law students as volunteers who did a fantastic job ... At least one of them, Eduardo Rivera, was beaten by goons in Arvin on June 22. And often police refuse to distinguish between them and the pickets, arresting them illegally."[17]

The staffers between 1971 and 1976 who had been fired, resigned, quit, took leaves of absence, and otherwise left the union did not made public their discontent during those years. They suffered silently and kept the saintly, nonviolent image of César Chávez alive and well.

One can only wonder how Chávez suffered with the daily reports on violence that engulfed his members and volunteers. How could he sleep with the barrage of arrests, injuries, death threats, and court battles that were the daily diet of news from the field? Then, his most loyal people began to leave—some at his insistence, and others because of his eccentricities and paranoia. He made huge errors in organization by ending the boycott, depending on volunteers, and not evolving his staff into a union with departments to service contracts and worker members.

Three Years after 1976 Proposition 14's Defeat

Randy Shaw frames the demise of Chávez within years of Prop. 14's defeat. He writes:

> Whether a victory in the Prop 14 campaign in 1976 might have changed Chavez's post-election conduct cannot be known, but it is clear that within months of the staggering defeat he began viewing UFW staff and volunteers, rather than the growers who financed the No on 14 commercials, as the source of the union's problems. Chavez's introduction of the Game; the forced expulsion and voluntary departure of key organizers, volunteers, and legal staff; and Medina's exit left the UFW far weaker than it had been when the ALRA passed in 1975 ... Chavez also terminated the UFW's boycott apparatus on May 5 (Cinco de Mayo) in 1978. This decision was understandable in light of the union's need to focus attention on winning and servicing contracts in the fields, but it eliminated the volunteer positions that had been critical entry points for training so many young organizers.[18]

Matt Garcia saw an organizational defect as causing unnecessary problems for Chávez and suppressing dissent, but it was his own doing. Most unions have local union chapters at the company level. The UFW only had "ranch committees," which reported problems to the union headquarters. He gleaned this insight from an interview with Marshall Ganz:

> The loose governance structure of the union permitted such retreats from the nerve center of the union, but the lack of connection had its consequences. Chavez's harsh reaction at the Home Place meeting in February 1977 to Ganz's granting a two-week vacation to volunteers was just one example. According to Ganz, the executive board had talked about a more coherent structure leading up to the 1973 convention, but the confrontation with the Teamsters and the loss of virtually all the contracts that season created a "meeting of the government in exile" that put off such a discussion. In its absence, Chavez ruled by fiat over a vast, unwieldly

political terrain that produced more autonomy than obedience to the union leader. Rather than embrace the diversity of opinions and conditions extant among organizers, workers, and volunteers, Chavez tried to suppress expression. "Cesar was very, very suspicious," Ganz recalled. "He didn't want to have locals because locals develop their own politics."[19]

The Purges

The "Monday Night Massacre," as it became known, occurred April 4, 1977. It involved the "Veggie Kitchen" group, volunteers who were vegans and vegetarians, who preferred to prepare and eat their meals together and not with the entire gaggle of folks in the cafeteria, which was open all hours. At first Chávez was not concerned with the openness of the food hall, but eventually he grew suspicious of this group, so he ordered that the kitchen be open only for three meals at set hours and closed all other times. The Veggie Kitchen group protested, and Chávez called a meeting, which turned into The Game very quickly. The Veggie Kitchen group was the center of the attack. Some accusations were ridiculous and unfounded, like the one Chávez leveled at a young and new volunteer, David McClure. He had come to work on the forever failing heating system at La Paz. Chávez reported that one of his informants had heard McClure talking to Senator S. I. Hayakawa (R-California) about union business. McClure explained it was not the senator, but Hayakawa of the local Ayers & Hayakawa Energy Management Company. Regardless, Chávez ordered him to leave the building and premises of La Paz, regardless of how incorrect the Chávez in-house informant had been.

Guards and Chávez loyalists also literally forced many of the Veggie Kitchen group members to leave La Paz the night of that meeting, and others on subsequent nights. Within a month of that fateful meeting, thirty people had been purged, all Anglos except for one Mexican American. Chávez, while he had opposed Chicano nationalism in the past, now embraced his brand of a UFW cultural revolution and cult of personality. But Chávez defended his actions differently:

Chavez attempted to command loyalty by arguing that he had come under extreme pressure from subversive forces. "It has become fashionable to criticize me," he told them. He claimed that an "Anglo volunteer syndrome" permeated the union staff, conditioning them to judge any strong actions on his part as evidence that he had become a dictator.[20]

At a subsequent board meeting that went from June 30 to July 4, 1977, Chávez added these words:

> Chavez told them he would continue to purge suspicious characters from the union, concentrating on white volunteers because he knew "they got some more members," and because "getting a Chicano and a farm worker out is a different story." "We'll make some mistakes" he predicted, but assured the group that he would do it "with class" and avoid taking them "by storm" as they had done in April 1977. He would use special powers to run patterns in his mind to detect suspicious behavior and "find a nice way" to expel them. Either way, he told the board, "we gotta clean them" or else they would destroy the union.[21]

Gilbert Padilla

Padilla had been with Chávez since the CSO days of the mid-1950s through the founding of the NFWA and UFW until 1980. Padilla was secretary of the UFW and the main administrator for contracts. But Padilla had opposed Chávez's war against undocumented Mexican workers and did not enforce the rule of either being current in dues payments or not getting work from the union hall. Padilla knew how difficult it was for migrant workers from Texas and other places to send in monthly dues when not working in California; they could pay up when they made some money, was his view. He was sent to Texas to help with the La Casita Farms strike in 1967.

Chávez now grew to resent Padilla's recalcitrant ways. He assigned him away from California to lead the boycott in Washington, DC. Padilla and his wife, Ester, packed their bags and went. In June 1980, Chávez called him back to lead the contract negotiations with the Freedman Ranch in Coachella Valley—the largest single contract the UFW had at that time, the largest employer in the valley, and the first to sign a contract with the UFW in 1970.

Padilla entered the contract fray and found great discontent among the leaders of the Freedman Ranch committee, Armando Sanchez and Doug Adair. The Coachella UFW office was responsible for handling the paperwork for this ranch committee, but the volunteer staffers ignored them. The workers were expecting a $5 an hour wage, up from the $3.76 they obtained back in 1977. When Padilla reported these problems to Chávez, he shot back that the problem was that the ranch committee was agitating the workers, and he named Adair and two others, Rudy Reyes and Ahmed Shoibi, as the problem. Chávez exploded with rage: "The Commie, the Huk, and the PLO," he labeled the three, and blamed them for not reaching an agreement. An abortive strike was called by the angry workers in response to the contract expiring and only a two cents an hour raise. Padilla, with Marshall Ganz's help, persuaded the workers not to strike but to carry out a "pre-huelga," a slowdown and walkout before the workday. Freedman's manager upped his offer to $4.50 an hour for the first year of the new contract and $4.80 the following year. The medical plan contribution from Freedman went up by 75 percent and a hard worker under the bonus piece-rate incentive could earn up to $6 an hour. Meanwhile, Padilla and Chávez were at each other's throats, with Padilla defending the ranch committee and the workers' demands for $5 an hour. Chávez, opposing his recommendations, was chastising him for asking for a better car than the old Valiant he was assigned, which had a bad radiator, no air conditioning, and was basically falling apart. Chávez did not realize or care that the trip from La Paz to Coachella was four hours long in 100-degree plus weather.[22] The contract was signed by Chávez, who was present the last two days of the negotiations; but he skipped the celebration victory dance and barbecue with the workers and quickly returned to La Paz.

Within months, in October 1980, Padilla and Chávez were at odds again. This time it was over the expulsion of Maria Rifo, a Chávez loyalist dating to 1968, who was charged with counter-organizing at La Paz. Security literally deposited her outside the gates of La Paz. She called Padilla, who in turn called Chávez to complain bitterly about her treatment and challenged Chávez for facts on the alleged counter-organizing. Then, Padilla took on Dolores Huerta, who was accusing Fred Ross Jr. of being a traitor for working an alternative get-out-the-vote campaign. Huerta was conducting the UFW drive, which César had funded with nearly $300,000 in union funds to California politicians. Padilla and Huerta went at it at a meeting of the Credit Union chaired by Padilla. Huerta demanded Padilla resign from the union; Padilla walked out of the meeting, hearing a shower of curses from Huerta and others. Chávez took Padilla's call the next day and said, "Cesar, I am going to honor your wish and resign." With a curt "Okay" from Chávez, a twenty-five-year history of work together ended.

> When I left the union as the secretary-treasurer, there was more than $10 million in the RFK Medical Plan; $17 million in the Juan De La Cruz Pension Plan; and over $6 million in the MLK Service Center Fund.
>
> The union was my *whole life*—I gave it more priority than my family, often uprooting my children from their schools and friends to unknown destinations. I never thought of leaving the union, and I wanted to grow old working in the union on behalf of farmworkers.[23]

Two weeks later, Jerry Cohen resigned as head of the legal department over similar differences with Chávez.[24]

The Filipino Three

The Filipinos who Chávez joined in their grape strike, and who later helped him build what became the Chávez union, mostly left by late 1977; all three were directors of the UFW board. But the first one to go in 1971 was key; it was Larry Itliong, the first farm worker to organize and lead a strike against growers in the Stockton area, demanding higher wages in March 1965, according to *El Malcriado*.[25] There were other influential Filipinos that were behind Itliong: Pete Velasco, Philip Vera Cruz, Leo Lorenzo, and Al Masigat.[26] The wage increase to $1.40 an hour was based on the wage scale Secretary of Labor Willard Wirtz had specified should be paid to *braceros*. The Bracero Program had just ended, and Itliong knew the time was right to make the demand and strike if necessary, given the shortage of labor about to be faced by the growers. Moreover, cutting grapes required a skilled hand and eye, for these had to be cut at precisely the right time. Grapes stop maturing the moment they are cut.[27]

Larry Itliong: The Farm Worker Leader in 1959 and the Early 1960s

Itliong was fifteen years of age when he emigrated from the Philippines to California. He quickly gravitated to labor organizing as he faced the barbarous treatment of his Filipino brothers as laborers in fields, canneries, and fisheries. He worked with many organizing efforts up and down the Pacific coast from California to Alaska during the 1930s. In 1956, he formed the Filipino Farm Labor Union; three years later he was the recognized leader of the Filipino community in Stockton. He also rose to the position of vice-chairman of the Council of United Filipino Organizations of Northern and Central California.[28] Over the years, Itliong earned a reputation of being honest in his dealings with both growers and contractors. Mexican laborers resented but were captive to the labor contractors who negotiated wages and transportation to the fields for those who needed to work. Who didn't? The growers knew that the Filipino crews brought by Itliong into their fields would do a great job—better than those brought by the Mexican labor contractors. Itliong came up with the ingenious idea of charging $2 monthly dues to belong to his crews, as if he were the labor contractor, and met with great success. Itliong would negotiate with the grower on behalf of his crews.[29]

In August 23, 1965, Itliong requested by registered letter to Delano growers a meeting to discuss wages and working conditions. Only two growers responded. The Filipino workers led by Itliong voted to strike on September 7. Chávez and his group were caught unprepared for the strike. On September 16 the fledgling Chávez union voted to join the Filipinos' strike.[30] From then on, Filipinos and Mexicans became one union. Itliong became the number two man, assistant director, next to Chávez as director in the National Farm Workers Association, which became UFWOC. There were two other Filipinos in leadership roles on the executive board of UFWOC: Philip Vera Cruz and Andy Imutan, serving as vice presidents. Vera Cruz, like Itliong, had been active in Filipino labor circles since 1959; only Imutan was a recent immigrant.[31]

After the Teamsters were finally defeated in the fields by the 1970s, fissures within the UFW leadership developed, and strained relations between coleaders became the norm. Itliong was among the first to voice his dissatisfaction. As quoted in Ferris and Sandoval, Itliong, as he quit the UFW, said, "We in the top echelon of the organization make too many of the rules and we change the rules so quickly that the workers themselves don't understand what the hell is going on."[32]

Andy Imutan, an admirer of Ferdinand Marcos, also resigned from the UFW shortly after Itliong.[33] One of the main bones of contention between the old-school Filipino unionists and Chávez's *causa* union was the hiring hall. Many worker members began to see it as nothing more than a racket. If they paid their dues, they got to work—forget seniority, skill sets, and the so-called "ranch committees." The core staff surrounding Chávez was another crack in the foundation of solidarity. Itliong stated:

> I don't have any problem with Cesar; as far as I'm concerned, I have the greatest admiration for him. I am not quitting to make things harder for him . . . the thinking of these people [brain trust surrounding Chávez] does not relate to the thinking of the farm workers, and brother Chavez is . . . with them day in and day out. Instead of trying to understand the problems of farm workers he [Chávez] is swayed by the grandiose thinking of these people . . . who have created this monster organization on the behalf of the farm workers. I don't know how I would say it any other way.[34]

A third issue was wages for staff. The UFW had many, many unpaid volunteers who helped run the union. Itliong wanted the professional staff to run the union and be paid adequately. He had a family of seven to support on a salary of $500 to $550 a month. And only Anglos and Jews held key positions within the top hierarchy of the UFW; no Filipinos, no Mexicans, except Richard Chávez, César's brother, and new wife, Dolores Huerta. Itliong felt that when he complained of the mistreatment of Filipinos within the union, Chávez and the union leadership ignored him.[35]

Philip Vera Cruz Finally Resigns

When Chávez first mentioned an invitation from Ferdinand Marcos, the Philippines dictator, to tour the island nation, the executive board led by Vera Cruz and Chris Hartmire were opposed to accepting such an outrageous proposition. Chávez disagreed. He felt Filipinos would be appreciative that he toured their homeland. Vera Cruz clearly put it to Chávez: "It's a dictatorship. There are thousands of political prisoners, people are arrested without charges or benefit of trial."[36]

Catholic activists, UFW supporters and donors, not just Vera Cruz, insisted Chávez not go visit Fernando Marcos and help validate the oppression of Filipinos, including outlawing of labor unions and imposing martial law. Chávez, against their advice and opposition, accepted the invitation to visit the Philippines at the behest of dictator Fernando Marcos in August 1977. While on the nineteen-day trip, Chávez reportedly praised Marcos and accepted an honorary doctorate from Far Eastern University. Chávez, without consultation with the executive board, invited Marcos's labor minister, Blas Ople, to address the 1977 UFW convention. At that convention, Philip Vera Cruz, UFW board member and Filipino leader, was not allowed to speak in opposition to the remarks made by the labor minister.[37] His wife, Debbie Volmer, shouted at the labor minister as he was being introduced, "Abajo con martial law!" (Down with martial law) and was quickly escorted out of the convention hall. Vera Cruz resigned from the UFW at that moment. As he announced his resignation, he reminded the delegates and audience of the UFW's resolution approved the prior year denouncing the Marcos regime.[38]

Chávez had begun to suspect Vera Cruz of not just being in opposition to his trip to the Philippines but also as another traitor. He never forgot or forgave Itliong for not moving into La Paz with the others, choosing instead to continue to live in Delano. Chávez forced the executive board members to sign a pledge of silence to not criticize him or the union, and of loyalty to him. Vera Cruz refused to sign. Critical books began to be published in the 1970s with "truths" different from the Chávez UFW party line, as was the case with the departure of Vera Cruz and wife, Debbie Volmer. During one of the Synanon Game activities, this lengthy recording was made and quoted by Bardacke:

> The board is here to play the game, everybody is here except Pete and Philip. Pete agreed to play with the Executive Board only, which is a kind of change. Philip didn't because we got into a big fight with him at the board meeting for taking materials to write a book and refusing a legal commitment like all of us did that we will not take anything from the board to write a book. It came from when he told Kent [Winterrowd] about six or seven months ago that he was going to resign, and he was going to write a book blasting me and saying how corrupt the union was, and he was ready to do that. Anyway, we got into a big fight. He is married to Debbie Volmer, who is a fucking asshole, you know. She is part of the goddamned—we give her credit for all kinds of shit. Anyway, we gave it pretty hard, really hard, but he was well programmed. We really gave it to him. It was a game. Everybody, for more than three hours . . . Because of what happened with Philip, I have been having a running fight with the board, except Dolores. Everybody else has been kind of taking me on because, in their own way, like back-biting and going around my back and all those things that happen in a group because also, remember, we have been infiltrated by leftists and by Commies, and that's what they know. But, ah, how bad it was what Philip proposed, that we had to get to him.[39]

The Other UFW Wannabes

By 1975 it was clear and obvious to farm workers in Texas, Florida, Oregon, Wisconsin, Washington, and Ohio who had sought affiliation with Chávez and the UFW, now affiliated with the AFL-CIO, that no real assistance in their local efforts to unionize would be forthcoming from Delano. Affiliation meant placing themselves in a supporting role to Delano; their efforts must wait on Chávez. And, being people on the move in chase of harvest work, they could not wait. The situation of seasonal temporary field workers in the current economy is one of being "illegal people," according to David Bacon's analysis: "A globalized political and economic system creates illegality by displacing people and then denying them rights and equality as they do what they have to do to survive—move to find work."[40]

Cipriano Ferrel in Woodburn, Oregon

Cipriano Ferrel, a high school graduate from Delano, California, did volunteer work and was a paid staffer for the UFWOC before he migrated further north to Oregon in the mid-1970s. There, he joined efforts to create the Colegio César Chávez in Mt. Angel, Oregon, and to organize the *pineros*, pine-tree planters, in the Willamette Valley. Tree planting is lonely, cold, wet, and a backbreaking job. Planters are left along the mountainous areas of the Willamette Valley in Oregon, south of Portland and north of Eugene, with thousands of seedlings. Each seedling is planted in a tiny hole, then the next one, then the next one. It usually is rainy and very wet in the Willamette Valley because the clouds must discharge their water before crossing the mountain range. The wind stream coming from the Arctic regularly enters the United States at the Washington/Oregon land mass and forces the dumping of excessive rainfall. Sometimes weekly, often every two weeks, the contractor will pay a visit to resupply his workers with cold cuts, fresh water, more seedlings, and clothing. The planters have to pay for all those items and an occasional trip into the nearest town for toiletries, haircuts, liquor, and a decent meal.

The *pineros*, led by Cipriano Ferrel, formally organized themselves into the Pineros y Campesinos Unidos del Noroeste (Northwest Tree Planters and Farmworkers United) or PCUN in 1983. Chávez helped rescue the Colegio bearing his name from loan defaults, but not the upstart union. However, Colegio students did help the PCUN with support, publicity, and advocacy before Chávez. The PCUN managed without a Chávez affiliation to grow haphazardly until 1995, when Ferrel unexpectedly died. Ramon Ramirez, another transplanted Californian, took up the reins of the PCUN.[41]

Jesus Salas in Wautoma, Wisconsin

Manuel Salas from Crystal City, Texas, my hometown, was a labor contractor or *troquero* (literally means trucker, but in this context is the owner of the truck that recruits and transports workers to the fields).[42] The *troquero* is not held in high regard by workers because of corruption. Many *troqueros* would charge workers for the transportation and for water to drink. They would keep the Social Security deduction and not report it, and pick and choose who to give preference to for work. I grew up with the Salas children, Manuel Jr., Jesus, and Chacho, when they still lived or returned to live in Crystal City. A brother to Manuel Sr., Julian, was among my early supporters of the Raza Unida Party and an officeholder. Because of this personal connection, I can recall stories of organizing cucumber pickers by the Salas brothers—namely, Jesus—in Wautoma, Wisconsin.[43] The Salas family, like many others, settled out in the northern states after years of making the annual trek to and from Texas to the Midwest. There are sizable colonies of ex-Crystal City residents in Milwaukee and Racine, Wisconsin; Lansing, East Lansing, Kalamazoo, Pontiac, Grand Rapids, and Holland, Michigan; Moses Lake and Yakima Valley cities in Washington; Toledo, Ohio; Grand Forks and Fargo, North Dakota; and St. Paul and St. Cloud, Minnesota. Even the cities of Gilroy, Watsonville, and Hollister, California, and Pocatello, Twin Falls, and Moscow, Idaho, have settled-out migrants from Crystal City, Texas. Many other cities from South Texas also have their former residents in these northern communities.

The migrant workers move from state to state in search of crops to harvest. Cucumbers, for example, are a fast-growing, seasonal crop needing daily harvesting, sometimes twice a day, depending on the size of cucumber that is being harvested. It is a backbreaking job, dirty and itchy (cucumber plants have thorns), and paid by the bucket hauled to the weigh scale or *troquero* inspector. Manuel Salas Sr. tried for years to organize workers so he could negotiate better terms with the growers in the Wautoma area. Jesus Salas, the son, with help from his brothers, Manuel and Chacho, also tried to organize the workers, even calling a strike when the crop was most in need of harvesting. They got some concessions from some growers, but failed to draw the attention of César Chávez to help them in this unionization drive. Eventually, Baldemar Velasquez, another organizer of farm workers in the Ohio area, helped them, particularly when the strike was not just against the cucumber growers but the Vlasic pickle processor. The cucumber growers in Wisconsin began to copy the practices of those in Michigan and Ohio in the modified use of the sharecropper system. A picker would get half of the proceeds for his pick; they became independent contractors without need for *troqueros, contratistas*, or a union.

None of the farm workers in Wisconsin were able to interest Chávez in organizing them. I worked as a migrant in the Racine-Wind Lake area for a few years and recall the terrible problems we had with not only wages but also working conditions. The few workers able to cut a decent deal were those who broke with the *troquero* and established their own relationship with a specific grower to return to that farm year after year. I worked alongside the Simon Martinez family and our farmer was Howard Piper, at the outskirts of Racine, Wisconsin. The sod farm owner in Wind Lake has faded from my memory; there we just irrigated, cut, rolled, and loaded pieces of cut grass for replanting in suburban yards of the United States.

Baldemar Velasquez in Gilboa, Ohio

The only success story among the wannabes like Chávez is that of Baldemar Velasquez. He is from another settled-out family from Pharr, located in South Texas. At the age of four, Baldemar joined the family in field work in 1951. The family stayed in Gilboa, Ohio, that year and every year thereafter. The tug of home took him back to Pan American University in Edinburg, Texas, in 1965, now the University of Texas-Rio Grande Valley (UTRGV). But Texas-style racism was too much for Baldemar; he moved back to finish college at Bluffton College in Ohio. During an internship arranged by the Congress of Racial Equality (CORE), he lived with an African American family in Cleveland for a few weeks. He learned that inequality and oppression were not limited to Mexican farm workers. And he learned, during this time, of Jesus Salas and his work in Wisconsin's cucumber fields. He paid them a visit and stayed a few weeks. Another important facet of this visit was that cucumber pickers in Wisconsin more likely than not would move on to the next crop, which was tomatoes in Michigan and Ohio. If Salas and Velasquez could collaborate, they might be able to have a larger influence over both crops in other states.

Baldemar saw in Wautoma, Wisconsin, the same scenario as in Ohio and Texas of a disorganized group of workers who lacked so much that even the best of local leaders could not mount an effective resistance to grower power and systemic poverty. How can poverty-stricken workers go on strike when they need to eat the next day and the next? When he returned from those experiences and with a college degree, his father, his friends, and a small group of farm workers, at his insistence and passion, decided to form the Farm Labor Organizing Committee (FLOC) in 1967. The next year, emulating the Filipino tactic with the grape harvest, he contacted tomato growers in Lucas County, Ohio, and was rebuffed. He called a strike and quickly won. Tomatoes would rot on the vine if not picked in time. Thirty-three growers signed contracts with FLOC; Velasquez was on his way to building a union of farm workers modeled after the Chávez UFW. Like Chávez, he not only called strikes; he marched, held rallies, picketed, boycotted, recruited volunteers from campuses, invited clergy to be at his side, and he also fasted. His targets were the largest of the large companies depending on tomatoes: Campbell and Libby. In retaliation, the companies paid higher wages to their growers who did not pass on the increase to their workers, further aggravating the situation and increasing resentment.

Velasquez, like Chávez, also had severe problems with local police and grower violence. The growers hired goons with guns who pointed them at workers. Local police brought dogs to harass picketers and strikers, allegedly to keep them from trespassing on private property. The growers had picket lines sprayed with pesticides by "accident." One grower allowed a driver to run his pickup into a line of strikers, injuring many. A cross was burned at a FLOC strike headquarters. The owner of a migrant labor camp was also the director of the Findlay, Ohio, office for the Bureau of Employment Services. The public schools in some Ohio communities, as in Oregon, let out students so they could help growers by picking the crops. That did not last long, as children learned the ordeal of stoop labor in open fields without fresh water or sanitary facilities.[44] As Barger and Reza put it,

> Local Sheriff's deputies and police in particular harassed the strikers. Sometimes they showed up at picket lines with riot gear and attack dogs. They arrested strikers on a number of occasions for minor violations. In other circumstances, such charges would result in a ticket rather than being jailed.[45]

Chávez did support Velasquez in a very public way. In 1979, at FLOC's first constitutional convention, he was the keynote speaker and spoke to the need for worker solidarity and farm labor organizing. In 1982, Chávez again addressed the FLOC annual convention held in Defiance, Ohio, and praised their efforts. After that convention, Velasquez undertook a twenty-four-day fast to meditate on his life's work and the direction of FLOC.[46] Chávez continued to support Velasquez and FLOC in mobilizing external supporters who were also helping Chávez, but no affiliation with Chávez occurred. FLOC did become part of the AFL-CIO at that time. Velasquez had to fight alone, as Chávez was having to do in California and Arizona. Both were ignored in their complaints by the federal government. And, in many cases, the federal officials present and aware of violence, injustice, and arbitrary application of the law by local law enforcement looked the other way.

Velasquez expanded his organizing efforts into Texas and Florida, utilizing the boycott networks FLOC had established in those states. In 1986 and 1987, FLOC began obtaining significant three-year contracts with major companies: Campbell and the growers in Ohio, Vlasic in Michigan, Heinz in both Michigan and Ohio, and later Dean Foods of the Midwest. Among the gains in these contract negotiations was elimination of the sharecropping system and making pickers employees with benefits.[47] I suspect there is an FBI file on him and FLOC, but have not asked his permission to obtain it.[48]

Antonio "Tony" Orendain and the Texas Farm Workers Union (TFWU)

Tony Orendain was the only Mexican national to join and become an officer in the UFWOC from the beginning. He and Chávez did not get along due to Orendain's vocal opposition to white staff in high positions, excessive use of religious symbolism, and the inaccessibility of Chávez to workers. Orendain also always spoke in Spanish, making non-Spanish speakers rely on others to translate—in contrast to Chávez, who always spoke in English without Spanish translation except on rare occasions meeting with workers. Chávez kept Orendain at arm's length and finally exiled him to Texas in 1969.[49]

Antonio Orendain Is Sent to Rio Grande City, Texas

Some, like Eugene Nelson, saw a rift and break with Chávez coming early; he left the union before it became acrimonious. Antonio Orendain also saw this evolution developing, but stayed. As a cofounder with Chávez and others of the UFWOC, he sought to influence and shape a union for farm workers. He felt Chávez needed help on how to organize Mexican workers. Once he was sent to Texas in 1969, however, Orendain began to chart his own course based on the failed Texas melon strikes of 1966 and 1967. Miriam Pawel, in *The Crusades of Cesar Chavez*, quotes Orendain: "We decided the workers couldn't wait until Cesar Chavez was ready. The workers don't even know who Cesar is."[50] The fight between Chávez and Orendain, with workers caught in the middle, got ugly soon after he arrived in Texas. The building Orendain and the workers had constructed in Texas as the union office was taken over by Chávez, exerting proprietary rights since it was done during UFW tutelage. The attempts to raise funds by Orendain were stymied by Chávez's efforts to stop donations going to Texas, and they were branded as a maverick group. Chávez expanded his California Service Centers under the name of La Union del Pueblo Entero (LUPE) to San Juan, Texas, directly challenging Orendain's service work.

Orendain subsequently followed the crops out of the Rio Grande Valley and headed to Zavala County in time to hit the onion growers. Zavala County, home of the Chicano-controlled Raza Unida Party, protected the workers' right to strike and picket and march. I was the county judge at that time and Jose Serna the sheriff, and both of us as former farm workers were sympathetic to the cause. Their victory during the onion harvest season in Zavala County was temporary because Orendain decided to keep moving northwest to Pecos County in the Texas Panhandle—a more troublesome area for farm workers. The FBI picked up the trail there, not knowing Orendain was charting another independent union-organizing effort and no longer was part of Chávez's UFW. Regardless of whether the FBI knew or pretended not to know, the surveillance continued under the Chavez file code for Orendain as well.

Informant(s) Report on Orendain Meeting with Gus Hall

A meeting took place between Gus Hall, the U.S. Communist Party chair, and Antonio Orendain in San Antonio, Texas, in late March 1969. The FBI took great interest in this event and made sure informants got every word uttered between Hall and Orendain. Gus Hall had been in the crosshairs of the FBI for decades, just because he was a card-carrying member of the CPUSA. Among the first counterintelligence programs (COINTELPROs) authorized and instituted by the Director, FBI, was COINTELPRO-Communist Party on August 28, 1956. Actually, Hoover had been doing COINTELPRO-type disruptions and infiltrations of groups he considered radical since 1941.[51] The CPUSA was in decline in membership, dropping from half a million before World War II to "a paltry twenty-four thousand" in the late 1950s, and "by the early 1960s, its strength had dipped below ten thousand."[52] The CPUSA was heavily infiltrated by FBI informants and agents. According to William Turner, former FBI agent, citing another FBI agent, Jack Levine, and labor columnist Victor Riesel, the FBI had "an informant for every 5.7 Party members, which made the FBI, through its dues paying contingent the 'largest single financial contributor to the coffers of the Communist Party' —a minimum of $10-million in the past decade."[53]

Apparently Orendain was also of interest to the FBI, perhaps not as long but during 1950-1959 when his immigration status and apprehensions by INS became of interest. On March 22, 1969, an FD-306, a cover sheet for an informant report, was sent to SAC, San Antonio. The matter was first relayed by telephone (name redacted) and the conversation was reduced to a two-page transcript accompanying the FD-306. According to the informant (name redacted), Gus Hall and wife (name redacted) were feted by the San Antonio-based CPUSA National Committee member and southern organizer to a reception at their home (address redacted). Also present was Antonio Orendain, who "discussed the farm workers situation in the lower Rio Grande Valley." Allegedly, Orendain in the past had "made a statement that he would 'sleep with the devil' if it would help the farm workers union" (p.1). Orendain talked most of the time and went into a long history of grievances of the farm workers in the Rio Grande Valley and difficulties encountered by the union in organizing the farm workers. Hall told Orendain they "could count on him for anything in connection with his work adding that they would even buy equipment for him if he needed it" (p.2). Another FD-306 plus three-page report was sent on May 6, 1969 (name redacted) to SAC, San Antonio (name redacted) with copies to Los Angeles and New York FBI offices. The informant reported that the CPUSA 19th National Convention was held in New York from April 30 to May 4, 1969. During the proceedings,

> [Gus] Hall contacted [NAME REDACTED] and gave [NAME REDACTED] $1,000 in $50-bills, stating that this was the money he had talked to [NAME REDACTED] about for [NAME REDACTED] work in South Texas, obviously for [NAME REDACTED] involvement in the Huelga Movement in South Texas. (p.1)
>
> It is to be noted that upon returning to San Antonio, Texas, [NAME REDACTED] obtained 3 money orders for a total of $250. These 3 money orders were Handy Andy Money Order No. 3554185, 3554186, and 3554187. These were all purchased May 5, 1969, payable to Antonio Orendain, Farm Worker

Organization. It is to be noted that the first 2 money orders mentioned above were $100 each and the latter was $50. These money orders were mailed to Antonio Orendain in San Juan, Texas [ADDRESS REDACTED]. (p.2)

The report gave the name of the location of the Handy Andy store with its identifying number as HA-21-43583. The money orders were bought inside the store from San Antonio Savings and Loan Association (p.3).

More FD-306's

About two months later on May 14, 1969, SAC, San Antonio by two-page Airtel to SAC, Milwaukee, with distribution to FBI offices in Denver, Albuquerque, and Los Angeles, is alerting all that the National Presbyterian Convention is to be held in San Antonio with both Orendain and Chávez scheduled to speak. Orendain arrived early to speak one-on-one with delegates. Upon learning from Orendain that Chávez would not attend, the SAC, San Antonio concluded that the church meetings were legitimate, and of no interest to the Bureau. "This matter is being closed" (p.2). But the work of the informants continued unabated. Twice on May 13, and on May 15, May 17, May 19, and June 19–20 , FD-306's flowed back and forth from (redacted source) to the SAC, San Antonio about Antonio Orendain. The first three-page report of the 13th dealt with someone (name redacted) becoming a confidant of Orendain's who traveled with him to meet with (name redacted) of the Amalgamated Meat Cutters and Butchers Union (p.1). This unknown-to-Orendain FBI plant was reporting on his activities and plans while attending the National Presbyterian convention. He or she helped Orendain corner Presbyterian delegates to discuss their support for the grape boycott. Orendain had to leave for Rio Grande City on May 14, but would return the same day to San Antonio. This new "volunteer" was asked by Orendain to make contacts (p.2), which he or she did (p.3).

The second report on the 13th was prepared that evening after Orendain had returned to San Antonio. The subject was a meeting of Texas CPUSA members and national committee officers who had attended the

New York convention and brought back literature Gus Hall had promised someone (name redacted) (p.1). On the last page of the report, the insinuation is made that Orendain wanted to meet with Texas CPUSA members in San Antonio, and would this request be "all right"? (p.2). The report of the 15th inquired if Orendain had received the money sent by Hall (p.1). Orendain also wanted to know how Hall wanted this money to be used. "It is to be noted that [LINE REDACTED] sent money to Orendain in bits and pieces to help feed the Farm Workers in the Rio Grande Valley" (p.2). The CPUSA members on the 19th, according to the informant's report of that day, discussed how to help Orendain in "setting up a co-op for the Farm Workers in the Rio Grande Valley" (p.1). Then, they went to meet with Orendain at the "SNS Ice House" in San Antonio to discuss the co-op idea (p.2). They met again on the 20th at a Church's Fried Chicken location in San Antonio (p.1). A new member of the group was a representative from the W.E.B. Du Bois Clubs of America (DCA) who made the meeting on the 20th and again on the 21st.

The matter of helping form a co-op was becoming a difficult task for unknown reasons. The Texas CPUSA committee also was grappling with the Mexican American question, in part because there were many members in the CPUSA from Texas (p.3). Astonishingly, the report clearly stated that one of the Texas CPUSA committee members (name redacted) provided three names of persons who worked for the FBI (and one at the CIA) in the past who were among them in the Austin chapter (p.4). This past activity should not be held against them (name redacted) said (p.4). This report then turned to immorality on the part of others in the Austin group, which "approves of wife-trading and other immorality engaged in/by [NAME REDACTED]," and (name redacted) had also left "two rifles at her residence and she did not want them around her house" (p.5). These same CPUSA members from Austin were in attendance at the 181st General Assembly of the Presbyterian Church of the USA, and the Presbyterians "were so anxious to get them away from the assembly that they would even fly them to New York" (p.5). Someone went to retrieve the rifles and identified them by make and market value. The question then became "what should be done regarding the Austin situation" (p.6).

Other business was reported by the informant(s), with just one more issue raised by Orendain, which was of the "$250 of the $1,000 that Gus Hall stated should be used [REDACTED] for work among the Mexican-Americans . . . what strings Gus Hall had attached to the use of this money and [REDACTED] there were no strings attached" (p.8). They agreed to meet again to finish their business. The June report, 19th–20th, involved a telephone call from New Mexico intercepted by the informant. The call was from (name redacted) who needed $52 bus fare to get back to San Antonio because his wife was very ill. His brother was in jail for assaulting a federal officer. He promised to "send him the money to [REDACTED] Albuquerque, N. Mexico" (p.2). In between this item and the next, concerning another person in jail but in Austin, Texas, a mention was made that "Orendain would be in San Antonio this weekend and [REDACTED] and Orendain were going to get together" (p.3). On June 23, Orendain point-blank asked the CPUSA committee of San Antonio "if he could use the remaining $750 to help match a Ford Foundation promise to fund a service center in Rio Grande City" (p.1). The CPUSA informant reported that New York CP would send the money "as soon as he could as they did not see a reason why the money could not be used for that purpose" (p.2).

A New 105 File (Foreign Counterintelligence Matter) Is Opened

The FBI informants within the CPUSA continued to report any contact between that group and Antonio Orendain during the remainder of 1969 and into 1970. On August 19, 1970, some confusion arose among the FBI as to the identity of a new name, Antonio Bonataños from San Juan, Texas. SA Clay Zachry Jr. in the San Antonio's FBI office sent a memorandum to his SAC asking that a new 105 file be opened and assigned "to an agent in McAllen who covers San Juan." Zachry Jr. was reporting that at a meeting in Reynosa, Mexico, back in June 20, 1970, a person from San Juan, Texas, who had an early morning radio program offered to put any anti-U.S. commentary on the air. According to Zachry Jr. "the CCI is a Communist front organization for peasants (*campesinos*) in Mexico." He identified two names, redacted of course, who are the "leaders of the CCI located at *Rio Bravo, Tamps." Tamps.* is short for Tamaulipas, the Mexican state across the border from McAllen, Texas.

In another memorandum exchange between Zachry Jr. and the SAC, San Antonio dated October 9, 1970, several leads were reported as failing to identify Bonataños. They had checked the McAllen Credit Bureau, Hidalgo County Jail records, Radio Station KIRT, which had Spanish-language broadcasting programs, and Southwestern Bell Telephone records. They even considered that this Bonataños might be using a pseudonym. It took months before any clue as to the identity of Antonio was discovered, on November 11, 1970. The informant had given Zachry Jr. the wrong name. Radio Station KGBT in Harlingen had an early morning broadcast by the United Farm Workers at 6 a.m. each day. It was taped by Antonio Orendain. Moreover, in this dispatch, another memorandum from Zachry Jr. to SAC, San Antonio changed the name from Bonataños to Orendain, and subject matter headings to IS-Mexico and IS-Spanish American. It also reported that on June 20, 1970, both Orendain and César Chávez had met with Fausto Hernandez and another (name redacted) who were Communist leaders in Mexico. A burning question raised in the last sentence of this transmission was: "On[e] of the Director's original targets in the BOCOV Program was to detect what liaison existed between the PCM (Mexican Communist Party/ *Partido Comunista Mexicano*) and persons or organization in the United States." Undaunted by his own suggestion to change names, Special Agent Clay Zachry Jr. continued to search for Antonio Bonataños with the Immigration and Naturalization Service (INS). He found nothing on Bonataños, but did get information on Orendain, according to his memorandum dated January 29, 1971.

The INS Dirt on Orendain

Records from INS reviewed by Clay Zachry Jr. of the FBI office in San Antonio indicated that on May 20, 1967, an individual thought to be Antonio Orendain entered the United States at Brownsville, Texas, but did not present himself for inspection by a U.S. immigration officer. Zachry Jr. wrote in this memorandum dated March 4, 1971, "He was apprehended on 6/15/67. Form I-213 (Record of Illegal Alien Apprehended or Located) dated 6/15/67, contains the following: . . . wading across the river near port of entry . . . on 5/20/67, around 1300 . . . obtained a ride . . . to San Antonio . . . has no family and no equities in the United States" (p.1). The memorandum describes Orendain as "Male, Black hair, Brown eyes, 67" tall, 143 pounds, laborer," with "Cut scar near left eye; mole on right side of mouth . . . BP-Ranch check, 6/15/67, 1400 hours, 4-30 days illegally in United States, apprehended near Neche, North Dakota" (p.2).

The last page of this memorandum contains paradoxical information on whether these files are applicable to Antonio Orendain. Supposedly, Orendain was processed and fingerprinted at Grand Forks, North Dakota, and an FBI file number, while redacted, is on the page. Additionally, on January 25, 1971, at Hidalgo, Texas, a criminal investigator with the INS interviewed Orendain. The resident agent of the FBI in McAllen was sure this "INS file is the same as the ANTONIO ORENDAIN who is active in the UFW and is the driving force in attempting to organize the farm workers in the Rio Grande Valley." Yet, Pawel has Orendain in Hanford, California, organizing in the summer of 1962 with César Chávez the first statewide meeting of their union.[54] Bardacke has Orendain leading the *Viva* chants of *"Viva la Causa, Viva la Huelga, Viva César Chávez"* at the founding meeting of the NFWA, also in 1962.[55] Ronald Taylor writes that on September 30, 1962, "Antonio Orendain, a former illegal alien, former Bracero, and green-card immigrant, was elected secretary treasurer."[56] On April 17, 1971, a special agent (name redacted) in a memorandum to SAC, San Antonio reviewed the paper trail of the file opened by SA Clay Zachry Jr. and noted the problems in the data: "wrong name, wrong person identified, and wrong information in files." He probably was convinced that Zachry Jr. had been played by an informant. The memo concludes with these words: "A review of the file failed to reveal the subject is a member of any organization other than the United Farm Workers, therefore, it is recommended this case be closed at the present time."

Orendain Moves into the Panhandle of Texas

The FBI files pick up Tony Orendain in Texas mid-1975. An Airtel on June 14, 1975, from the SAC (name of place redacted) to the Director, FBI passed news from his "informants within United Farm Workers Organization of Hidalgo and Starr Counties indicating that all activities connected with UFWO strikes in Hidalgo and Starr Counties, Texas, ceased June 12, 1975." The bad news was that Orendain was taking the fight to Pecos and Presidio in West Texas and toward the Panhandle. The SAC, San Antonio reported by Nitel teletype on June 20 that Orendain was in the Pecos area but had returned to Edinburg in the RGV with "six of his closest associates in the UFW," where they were to be "feted."

The SAC, El Paso sent an urgent teletype to the Director, FBI and SAC, Dallas about civil unrest in Reeves County. On July 23, he reported that twenty-six UFW members, including eight juveniles, were arrested for criminal trespass by the sheriff's deputies. Orendain left before the arrests, and all those arrested had not made bond and remained in jail. At the hearing for the juveniles the next day, UFW organizer Paula Cruz was arrested for "disorderly conduct" and "creating a disturbance during juvenile hearing."

By letter dated July 25, 1975, from Antonio Orendain (with address listed as "United Farm Workers/AFL-CIO, P.O. Box 1493, San Juan, Texas 78589, (512) 787-5984") to Edward Levi, the U.S. attorney general, Orendain listed atrocities and abuses suffered by the melon pickers in Reeves and Pecos Counties, Texas, at the hands of local law enforcement—all supported with notarized affidavits from the victims. He asked for help in this manner: "National attention must be focused on the developments in Pecos and national pressure must be brought to bear on Sheriff A. B. Nail of Reeves County and Sheriff W. S. Ten Eyck of Pecos County that the law might be observed." Orendain graphically stated his personal fear for his life in a notarized statement accompanying the letter:

> On the way back to Pecos, I was stopped by a Highway Patrol Officer, Texas Department of Public Safety, who checked my van. Everything in the van and my driver's license was all right, with the exception of the left high

beam headlight which did not work. I was cited for the headlight at approximately 11:30 AM.

While the ticket was being written, a man, apparently a farmer, stopped and asked who spoke English. I said that I did. The farmer then said, "If you don't leave town, we'll kill you." I called this to the attention of the Highway Patrol Officer who told me that the County Sheriff handled problems of that nature, not the Highway Patrol. He also told me that the farmer had a right to freedom of speech. After being cited, I drove on back to our headquarters.

Some reporters told us that on their police monitors they had overheard several conversations between officers which in essence, indicated that the officers wanted to "get Orendain."[57]

LULAC's District Four of El Paso also demanded an investigation into the Pecos Sheriff's Office refusing to accept bonds on some arrestees and incarcerating juveniles together with adults, according to the Airtel of the 29th from SAC, El Paso to Director, FBI. The Airtel was accompanied by newspaper articles taken from the *El Paso Times* and *El Paso Herald-Post*, dated July 26, and a follow-up article from the former on the 27th. All three open-source clippings point out that upwards of forty-two persons were arrested over the course of two days in the two counties; however, only the Pecos sheriff refused to accept bonds for jail release. Such refusal once bond is set is a violation of state law. A subsequent Airtel from the SAC, El Paso to the Director, FBI on the 29th added to the civil rights violations by sheriff's deputies, including an allegation of physically pushing picketers and union sympathizers, and in one case confiscating a tape recorder from a member of an Austin-based film crew. The filmmakers were also arrested. This Airtel also had newspaper clippings attached from the *Odessa-American* in Reeves County dated July 25 and 26, which provided the SAC with his information.

The August 1st Airtel with LHM from the El Paso FBI office reported on a fact-finding committee of fifteen LULAC members traveling to the neighboring counties where the arrests were made. By teletype dated August 16, the SAC, El Paso notified the Director, FBI and the SAC, Dallas that he was closing the case because all picketing had ceased, and the union members and sympathizers had "departed for the Muleshoe, Texas area." He also notified the "U.S. Secret Service, El Paso and AUSA Wayne F. Speck, San Antonio, Texas" with this information. The Director, FBI was not pleased with the style of the Airtels. He wanted the message to state: "DEMONSTRATIONS AND VIOLENCE IN CONNECTION WITH FARM WORKERS ORGANIZATIONAL ACTIVITIES" and not use "POTENTIAL DEMONSTRATIONS." He was so upset with the wording that he returned the original teletype with the words crossed out in an August 18 message relay with copies to U.S. Secret Service, and three sections within the Assistant Attorney General's Office, the Criminal Division, the Internal Security Section, and the General Crimes Section. The Director, FBI had more corrections noted. He inserted the word "were" into the line referring to the Secret Service and AUSA to read, "were advised this date." And, he crossed out entirely the last two lines informing that the case was being closed. He either disagreed with the case being closed or simply did not want these words in this message. This error in format and style was brought up again by the SAC, El Paso to the Director, FBI in his September 29 Airtel indicating he was making the corrections pointed out to him. Moreover, this nine-page Airtel refers to a letter written on July 25, 1975, to the U.S. Attorney General by Antonio Orendain that was enclosed but not released to the public. The names with addresses of seventeen persons arrested are listed on seven pages with their local FBI file number. For example, the last entry on page 6 of the 9 has this information:

Arrest # 12308,

Name PAULA WADDLE CRUZ

Address 3711 Meredith, Austin, Texas

Age 27

Height 5'5"

Weight 115

Hair Brown

Eyes Brown

Date of Birth November 9, 1947

Place of Birth Dallas, Texas

Texas Driver's License 561 378 2

Offense Charged Disorderly Conduct

FBI # 177 381 P8

According to the narrative of the Airtel, Ms. Cruz was charged with disorderly conduct because during the juvenile proceedings "she allegedly created a disturbance." And, there is this wording about her, that she "is most identical to the law student arrested and whose interview is requested by the Department in the enclosed letter." There is no such letter disclosed. There are thirteen more names listed on pages 7 and 8. These "individuals were arrested by that department on 7/25/75, charged with Criminal Trespass, and released on $400.00 bond that same date in connection with UFW picketing activities."[58] It is unclear by the use of the words "that department" in which county these arrests actually took place, Reeves or Pecos. It is clear "that none of the individuals arrested were from Pecos County, Texas." And, "Docket # 4783 FRANCISCA CASTELA CALDERON" is listed twice among the thirteen names, the second being "Docket # 4798 FRANCISCA CALDERON (Second charge)."

A massive 39-page document was sent from the El Paso FBI office to the U.S. attorney in San Antonio, Texas, dated September 26, 1975, regarding their limited investigation into the arrests and allegations of official misconduct by sheriff's deputies in Reeves and Pecos Counties. This investigation was prompted by the Orendain letter—not attached, despite assertion that it was—and a request in letter form from the Assistant Attorney General of the United States, J. Stanley Pottinger.[59] The document continues to use the erroneous reference to "UFW" and "United Farm Workers" when clearly Antonio Orendain, under a new name, the Texas Farm Workers Union (TFWU), was leading these farm workers in the strikes and pickets from Hidalgo to Crystal City, to Pecos, to Odessa, to Presidio, to Muleshoe, Texas. The report made mention of the thirteen arrested by name once again, and adds on page 14, "none of the individuals listed are residents of the City of Fort Stockton. He also stated that no arrest reports were made in this matter." This is an amazing statement to attribute to any law enforcement agency that arrests individuals. Without an arrest report, there is no formal complaint as the basis for an arrest.

Nevertheless, the FBI in Austin was contacted, and a special agent attempted to interview Paula Waddle Cruz, without success. Her attorney advised her not to discuss any aspect of her arrest with the FBI while her cases were pending trial in both counties. There are five affidavits taken by the FBI special agents out of McAllen, Texas, conducting the interviews of persons previously arrested in this report, including one from Antonio Orendain and another from Jose Henry Salazar. These two persons are the only ones whose names are not redacted. All reports basically state the same facts that they were on a public road picketing and within minutes Reeves County sheriff's deputies arrested them. In Orendain's affidavit, he alleged a verbal death threat made by a local farmer who stopped as they were being detained by the state Highway Patrol at 11 a.m. in the morning. He was cited for a left front headlight that was malfunctioning at high beam. The arresting patrolman who heard the threat said that "The farmer had a right to freedom of speech" and declined to arrest him because "the County Sheriff handled problems of that nature, not the Highway Patrol." Five other affidavits were included in this report prepared by "JAMES HARRINGTON, Attorney, American Civil Liberties Union, representing the United Farm Workers (UFW), San Juan, Texas" and made on July 28, 1975. These affidavits were not tendered to the FBI until late September and October 10, 1975, according to the notations at bottom of these disclosed files. All the affidavits also make mention of maltreatment, verbal and physical abuse by the sheriff's deputies in both counties while being arrested, taken to jail, and jailed. They alleged they were not told they were trespassing on private property, told to leave, and warned of being arrested if not complying. They were arrested, and everyone, adults and juveniles, were jailed together in the same cells. Only hours later did the juveniles get removed to another cell. The Pecos sheriff allegedly informed another of the attorneys with the picketing group, Jim Douglas, that "his deputies had given no such warning." Furthermore, the sheriff allegedly added that no warning was given because "How can you warn a big group like that?"

On October 30 the San Antonio FBI office reported the difficulty of interviewing those arrested that lived in the RGV. Appointments repeatedly were made by special agents, the report states, but not kept by those being interviewed. None of the persons sought for interviews agreed to be interviewed or furnished a signed statement other than the ones previously mentioned as being tendered by James Harrington. There is one unsigned statement by someone (name redacted) who reportedly gave an oral version on October 24 of his account of events surrounding the arrests of July 23 in Pecos, Reeves County, Texas. In this oral version, the declarant is quoted as stating, "At about this time a Deputy Sheriff drove up and indicated that the road they were on was private property ... Another deputy came up and said that he would give them 10 seconds to leave inasmuch as the road was private property. He counted to ten and then arrested everybody." This version, containing a warning about trespassing and time to stop trespassing, contradicts all the other affidavits submitted by Mr. Harrington. From the narrative in the declarant's statement I infer he was not a picketer, not a worker who walked out of the field, and not an employee of the grower. But the attributed statement ends with, "He stated that he originally went to the fields to work, and when he joined the strike he did so believing that he would be on public land because the road appeared to be a public road. He stated that he does not personally have any knowledge regarding any efforts made by any member of the UFW organization to determine whether or not the road was public or private."

After this matter was orally shared with the AUSA in San Antonio, John M. Pinckney, by the El Paso FBI, the latter "stated that this did not appear to be a matter which would warrant prosecutive action or any additional investigation." Fortunately, "Mr. Pinckney requested that he be provided a copy of the investigative report prepared at San Antonio, Texas, for review by him and for completion of his files." To be sure, the taxpayers will know how things were done in Texas during the mid-1970s to save time and money. The FBI called the AUSA and told him the story. The AUSA found no violations of federal law and wanted the report so he could close his file. His mind was already made up from the FBI's oral version. No need to read affidavits signed and sworn to before a notary, or to call the respective sheriff's departments requesting arrest reports, much less check the underlying fact of whether the pickets were on a public road when arrested. The matter remains undisclosed as to its final outcome because there are no more records to analyze. I can only assume the case was closed with no relief afforded the complaining victims. The outcomes of trials in both counties were also not reported in these files.

Gustavo Gutierrez in Arizona

Another group of farm workers that sought Chávez out for help were those in Arizona led by Gustavo Gutierrez. In 1965, Fred Ross and César Chávez, while working with CSO, came to Arizona to conduct a training; Gustavo Gutierrez was one of those in attendance. The next year when Chávez marched to Sacramento, Gutierrez traveled to Delano to be part of the march and was able to make the last four days of the walk. He carried his own self-made sign, "Arizona Farmworkers Support California Farmworkers." In 1970, Gutierrez again traveled to Delano to witness the signing of the first grape contracts and stayed on to help with the lettuce strike in Salinas, California.[60] In 1972, Chávez underwent his fast in Phoenix, Arizona, at Gutierrez's home. There were occasions in the 1970s when Chávez came and supported Gutierrez's efforts at unionizing farm workers and intimated he would bring all groups under his UFW union. Chávez even sent his cousin Manuel to help Gutierrez and also sought ways to keep Mexican labor from crossing into the United States and causing the UFW problems in the fields in Arizona, California, and the Pacific Northwest. Gutierrez, without much help from Chávez, organized under the name Maricopa County Organizing Project (MCOP). When Gutierrez called a strike against onion growers, César Chávez called him to stop the strike. Manuel Chávez personally asked him to stop organizing and stop the strike. César even went as far as filing protests with state and federal agencies against MCOP's contracts with growers; he even urged a "no union" vote in an election involving MCOP. A grant that MCOP was awarded by the Catholic Church's Campaign for Human Development in the amount of $100,000 was withdrawn at Chávez's insistence, through the Phoenix bishop. Gutierrez quit his support for the UFW and Chávez and instead concentrated on exposing Manuel Chávez and his cruelty toward Mexican immigrants with his "wetline" operations along the border, especially in Mexicali.[61]

Joan Baez at Graceada Park

Late in February 28, 1975, a Nitel was sent by teletype to the Director, FBI from the SAC, Sacramento at 5:14 p.m. He reported that the two groups of protesters from the UFW had arrived in Modesto and would hold a rally at the National Guard Armory because Governor Jerry Brown Jr. had allowed it. From there the marchers would descend on the Gallo Winery the next day to present their petition demanding secret balloting in the election being held by Gallo on unionization. Another rally would follow at Graceada Park in Modesto. The SAC states, "Cesar Chavez, leader of UFWA, will join marchers in demonstration, and folk singer Joan Baez is expected to perform at rally at Graceada Park." The next evening at 8:34 p.m. the SAC sent another Nitel by teletype providing numbers in attendance at the rally: "Eight thousand persons estimated in attendance, many persons arriving early March 1, 1975, by chartered buses from various northern California areas." Victor Riesel was not far behind in reporting on Chávez's battle with Gallo. He circulated via his Field Newspaper Syndicate out of Chicago an article, "Drain the Vine," that was a five-page indictment of Chávez for taking on Gallo. He pointed out that Gallo had union contracts with others, including the Teamsters, and that George Meany of the AFL-CIO opposed the strike and boycott against Gallo; but Chávez did not take heed.

Chávez went on a business trip to New York that included a march entitled "Camino de Justicia." Chávez organized this demonstration to take place down New York's Fifth Avenue amidst the posh and plush boutique stores. Riesel called it the "Path to Justice" and suggested Chávez had another aim—to build a Chicano Movement as Rev. Martin Luther King, Jr. had attempted to do with black Americans. Chávez's goal, according to Riesel, was to take a combination of university students, Chicano youth, and clergy from all denominations, in addition to his farm workers, and weld them into a national coalition for the poor. Chávez's international support added to his growing clout among his union peers, including George Meany, who did not interfere with the march down Fifth Avenue on May 10.

On May 16, an Airtel with LHM from SAC, New Orleans arrived at FBI HQ. The message was that Chávez's group had picketed the federal courthouse the day before for thirty minutes. The odd thing about the LHM is that it mentioned eighteen picketers, divided between male and female and black and white. No Mexicans! And, no other farm workers or migrants seemed to be at the protest. It was a stretch to suggest that the placards he reported as reading, "Jobs Not War" and "Get Out of Cambodia" made this a UFW picketing protest.

Legats Are Curious Also

At the close of 1975 on December 18, the Legat, London (legal attaché) by Airtel with priority designation as "Confidential" wrote to the Director, FBI about the UFW and added on the subject line: "SM-C," which means Security Matter-Communist. The entire content is redacted, approximately twenty-two lines and possibly a block stamp at bottom right. And, during the first quarter of 1976, specifically March 19, the Legat, Bonn also wrote a memorandum to the Director, FBI with attention to the name check section. The subject was the UFW, and added on the subject line on this memo was "FPC," which stands for "fingerprint classification."[62]

The remaining few pages disclosed from the main FBI file on Chávez are dated from March 19, 1976, to June 14, 1978. A follow-up reference letter dated April 6, 1976, to the Bonn, Germany Legat from Director, FBI—perhaps a response to a request from Germany's FBI man—confirms who César Chávez and the UFW are. It also repeats the Communist line: "In response to an allegation that various officials of the National Farm Workers Association had subversive backgrounds, inquiries were made in 1965 which determined that while the union was not communist controlled, Communist Party members or sympathizers had furnished support to certain activities concerning a recent strike against grape growers in California." Then the *Mission Impossible*-type disclaimer: "The above information may be disseminated provided the FBI is not shown as the source." Old Hoover tricks of authorizing purloined and misleading information were hard to break in the post-Hoover FBI culture, apparently up to the years of the Carter administration in 1976. The misinformation was shared and disseminated to unknown agencies (names redacted) in a memorandum dated May 3, 1976, as indicated from the Bonn Legat to the Director, FBI.

I now fast-forward to June 14, 1978, for the last document released in the overall file, which was sent by the Director, FBI to multiple divisions and sections of the U.S. AG's office and the U.S. Secret Service. It was informing on civil unrest in Phoenix, Arizona. The civil unrest was a strike called by the UFW against Pete Pasquinelli and G&S Produce companies, based in Yuma, Arizona. The companies complained that they were victims of the civil unrest. Apparently, Chávez called for a strike against melon growers and subsequently was arrested. During the latter part of May 1978, a judge prohibited the UFW from picketing and ruled that Chávez had violated his anti-picket court order "not allowing pickets to interfere with farm workers of victims while working in fields."[63] A large paragraph of this teletype is entirely redacted on the second page, and a phrase is crossed out but legible at bottom: "no investigation being conducted by Phoenix Division, but will keep Bureau advised of pertinent developments."

Chávez learned a new legal maneuver early in his experience with anti-picketing orders issued by judges. Violate them by picketing despite the order and suffer arrest and jailing. Then, the UFW legal team would seek an injunction against enforcement of that order based on freedom of speech grounds. More often than not, Chávez obtained the injunction with the freedom of speech argument before appellate courts and had the original anti-picketing order set aside. The records released go no further in time, so the outcome of this arrest and jail time for Chávez are not furnished. We do know that Chávez continued his struggles to unionize in Arizona and California into the early 1990s.

End of Declassified File

There were no more declassified files disclosed by the FBI on César E. Chávez #100-444762 past this date in 1978.[64] No further documents are part of the declassified Chavez file, but one that is dated February 4, 1982, and incorporated in appendix 2 shows there are more Chávez unclassified files in existence and being denied FOIA release.[65] It is going to take litigation to attempt release of all documents on Chávez, his wife, and others belonging to the UFW beyond these dates. Chávez, however, continued his efforts for many more years well past 1978, until he died in 1993. It is remarkable that Césario Estrada Chávez was born in Yuma, Arizona, on March 31, 1927, and died in San Luis, near Yuma, on April 23, 1993. He had just celebrated his sixty-sixth birthday, an official holiday observed at La Paz, the month before. He was near Yuma, battling yet another court case, in which the growers claimed victimization by his boycott of their products, causing millions of dollars in lost profits.

What Could Have Been

One can only imagine what Chávez could have accomplished but for the problems he faced daily inside the union and outside La Paz. These FBI documents provide only a tiny glimpse of the FBI's role in destroying the man and the union by overt and covert actions. The FBI allowed local and state police and the growers to inflict injury and harm on thousands of UFW members, volunteers, and supporters, including the clergy. The many incidents reported went uninvestigated, or investigated by the FBI but not submitted for prosecution to the U.S. attorney general. Having gone through similar experiences during my own activism—in Texas, predominantly—I know what it feels like to live in fear, insecurity, paranoia, depression, and anxiety because there is no one to turn to for help or protection. The very officers whose duty is to protect you and yours are the main culprits and source of concern. The toll this takes on a person cannot be fathomed by anyone else.

After completing this manuscript, I pondered time and again what might have happened if Chávez had joined us in El Paso and helped in the building of the Raza Unida Party (RUP). Perhaps his presence and involvement could have prevented the rift between Rodolfo "Corky" Gonzalez and me. Could the four of us—Chávez, Gonzalez, Tijerina, and me—have built a national electoral base of power from the local level up to Congress and the

White House? Without him we already had a foothold and presence in seventeen states plus the District of Columbia at the time of the 1972 national RUP convention held in El Paso. The UFW Credit Union could easily have become a national bank for poor people across the country, which would have helped stop the spread of pawn shops, check-cashing operations, and loan companies charging exorbitant interest rates. The Colegio César Chávez could have become our first tier-one Chicano research university. What might have happened if he had affiliated FLOC and the other struggling unionizing efforts with the UFW? Migrant farm labor in California was organized by Chávez during the apogee of the UFW's contract signings by 1971. He was gaining ground in Arizona despite his anti-immigrant posture, policy, and the criminal activity of his cousin Manuel Chávez, with his "wetline" at the border. Chávez could have moved subsidiaries of his California operations into states with seasonal harvest of only one crop annually, such as cucumbers in Wisconsin, Ohio, Michigan; tomatoes in Ohio, Michigan, Florida; sugar beets in the Dakotas; cherries and apples in Michigan; and citrus in Florida and Texas. Truly, with eager, young, and competent leaders in those areas, like Baldemar Velasquez, Jesus Salas, Cipriano Ferrel, mentioned above, and others in the Yakima Valley of Washington, Florida, and the Red River Valley of the Dakotas, more could have been achieved. What might have happened if the boycott apparatus that reached globally before he shut it down without reason had continued, added to the FLOC boycotts, joined the women strikers against Farah and Levis, then expanded the boycott to other products and practices such as pollution, sand spoliation, use of airwaves, and obesity, for example? He was making great inroads with consumers with his educational campaign on pesticides and herbicides, and promoting organic food products. What might have happened if he had continued to embrace his *Chicanismo* and joined others like "Corky" Gonzales, who was mentoring and nurturing urban youth. Gonzales and Chávez were both against the Vietnam War and attracted thousands of youth to their causes. Instead, Chávez became Hoover-like and joined in the red-baiting chorus against those progressives, leftists, hippies, and militant Chicanos he once sought out for help and support. Reies Lopez Tijerina, in his quest for land recovery in the Southwest, could have added California,

Texas, Arizona, Colorado, Nevada, Oregon, Wyoming, and Utah, thereby buttressing Chávez's demands for those that worked the land. Tijerina faced the same problems as Chávez over the decades: Anglo trespassers, with help from the courts and police and military, took land not theirs and displaced the decedents and heirs of land grant claimants. These peoples continue to suffer and endure chronic unemployment in their homelands. With the return of some of these lands, mostly in federal and state control, Chicanos could have joined the farm-to-school fresh produce movement and gone from farm workers to farm owners supplying the nation's public schools with fresh and organic vegetables.

Chávez's UFW members are being displaced from the fields by machines, chemistry, and technology, not to mention U.S. government policy permitting agribusiness corporations to bring in thousands of H2-A and B visa holders to work in the United States. Chávez and most unions now realized their only future is in organizing immigrant labor coming into the U.S., legally or not. Could UFW members and Tijerina's members have been retrained to handle work in the national and state parks, fisheries, forests, mines, and the transportation of goods? How about moving into food processing and cooperative organic food production? Why not create a trucking, robotics, and drones division for new economic development ventures to move goods from farm to kitchen table? Why not use instructional television to retrain the unemployed in the new skill sets needed? Why did Chávez turn inward and away from the membership? Why did Chávez not seek collaboration with other Chicano leaders and erect a formidable united front of resistance and advocacy for social change?

We will never know. We do know it was possible, once. The coalescing of leaders did not occur, however, and Chicano leadership remained regional in the Southwest. We do know it can and will be made possible again by new, visionary, astute leadership with sound strategies. But, the twenty-first century will require new skill sets in leaders to control, harness, and utilize the technology of power.

Chávez and the FBI Surveillance

WHY IS THE CHÁVEZ FBI FILE DATing back some fifty-three years ago important in 2018 and beyond? The review of the documents yields several factual narratives. First, we learn of extensive, prolonged, purposeful government surveillance of a legitimate labor-organizing movement from its infancy to the creation of a formidable labor union that engaged in strikes, boycotts, pickets, marches, and demonstrations—all protected rights for unions.[1] During the fifty-three-year period, the surveillance described in the first two chapters was, most often, illegal and unconstitutional.

Second, we learn of cover-ups by local police (city, county, state) and federal agencies, including the FBI, which looked the other way at local and state police misconduct in all three states where the UFW tried to organize farm workers: California, Texas, and Arizona. After reviewing

■ 291

the FBI files cited here, there is a case to be made that the police agencies conspiratorially hid from scrutiny their violations of civil rights laws as they arrested, assaulted, jailed, mistreated in jail, and harassed striking UFW workers as they engaged in picketing, demonstrating, assembling, boycotting, and otherwise protested. The violence at the hands of the Texas Rangers, perhaps including the murder of Magdaleno Dimas, is the most revealing. The federal district case originated in 1968 during the thick of violent confrontations with the Texas Rangers in South Texas. The issues were not only the Ranger violence but also the right of farm workers to strike and picket. It took six years, until 1974, for the case to reach the U.S. Supreme Court, which ruled against the Texas Rangers and state courts; clearly this was delayed justice, which is no justice. The murders of farm workers in California and Florida also went unpunished or with a minor slap on the wrist. The federal government never brought a case during these years against anyone accused of violating farm worker rights. The bombings of UFW offices also went unprosecuted. On more than one occasion, local police cynically intimated it was the work of the UFW seeking to get publicity for their cause.

Third, we read in these FBI files of the complicity by local city, county, state police, and federal agencies with California growers and national agricultural interests to continue to deny farm workers a right to bargain for their labor, form a union to represent their interests, and go on strike without police repression.

Fourth, we learn of the maneuvers and manipulation of information by one federal agency toward another, sometimes even from a subordinate (Hoover) to his superiors (U.S. attorney general), including Presidents Johnson, Nixon, and Reagan. The documents also reveal instances of a president or intelligence chief not trusting his own subordinates and bypassing them to have his orders carried out, an often illegal activity. Jack Mitchell in *Executive Privilege* documents presidential misconduct from Washington to Reagan in 1989 in this regard. Not one president in the two hundred years of history depicted was free of corruption, *ultra vires* acts, and wrongdoing by them or their subordinates under their orders.[2]

Fifth, we read how these documents utilize code words, as Ian Haney in *Dog Whistle Politics* has revealed, to depict and characterize the persons and their organizations named as targets for surveillance as radicals, Communists, anarchists, subversives, protesters, minority racial groups, rabble-rousers, extremists, hate groups, troublemakers, security matters, racial matters, suspect, disloyal, and un-American, only because they exercised their First Amendment rights and freedoms.[3]

Sixth, the persons implementing the surveillance and committing the illegal acts, we can see in hindsight, were terribly flawed individuals in terms of ethics, morals, paranoia, and mental state, from presidents on down to Hoover and local police—wielding incredible power over others because of their position, whether elected or appointed. Does absolute power continue to corrupt absolutely as we witness the evolving Trump presidency?

Seventh, the documents held by government are not readily available, and are often costly to obtain even with the Freedom of Information Act (FOIA). The backlog of FOIA requests is legendary. There is no transparency in government agencies dealing with police, military, and intelligence matters. And, the FBI and other intelligence agencies go to great lengths to keep from disclosing information in their possession that is subject to FOIA and the Privacy Act. For example, the declassified files on Chávez end approximately in 1975, yet they included in these files a document dated in 1989 and copied in the appendices. On appeal, I received sixty-three more pages dealing primarily with hate mail Chávez received and more death threats via the postal service.

Eighth, we are a central part of the conspiracy to hide the truth. We, the public, have learned to ignore, tolerate, and deny this behavior from local police to presidents. We have traded privacy and civil liberties for security and safety. The pivot in values away from a prolonged external threat to our safety during the Cold War era to a post-9/11 focus on those among us has occurred at rapid speed. Similarly, the perceived and imagined enemy of today is not another nation or coalition of nations; instead it is groups termed terrorists, drug cartels, immigrants, and protestors in general. Admiral James Stavridis of the U.S. Southern Command (Latin America) states the new security-threat analysis best:

When it comes to security challenges, fortunately, we do not see any conventional military threats to the United States developing in the [Latin American] region, nor do we foresee any major military conflict between nations ... However, public security threats—such as crime, gangs, drug trafficking and use—pose the principal near term security challenges to the region ... Nearly 80 percent of the entire region lives on less than $10 per day. When you add the poverty figures—which represent millions of people trying to provide for their families—to the world's most unequal distribution of wealth and a high level of corruption, you have a strong catalyst for insecurity and instability.[4]

In general, the people, specifically the poor, are the new enemy and must be watched always. Those better off, by and large, are oblivious and apathetic and cynical about the world around them for two major reasons. On the one hand, they live in gated and privately secured communities, and work at their income-producing jobs a physical distance away from others not like them. The poor in their midst are service providers who disappear when the work day ends. And, on the other hand, those better off socialize and interact with one another in segregated enclaves, be it at the gym, church services, homeowner associations, private clubs, entertainment venues, sporting events (especially golf and tennis), and business ventures. The one large white group are homeowners; the other, larger nonwhite group are renters.

There is a general resignation and rampant pessimism about what individuals can do about the nefarious deeds of persons in elected and appointed public office—local, state, and national. That is, about what goes on in the international non-elected positions (e.g., UN, GATT, NAFTA, World Bank, WTO, and OAS, for example), the work of U.S. intelligence agencies, and the national media, which ignores the merit of ethno-racial social movements and actors, and reports mainly on whites, blacks, and Jews. LGBTQs are emerging as the new visible "minority group" as Latinos have become the largest minority group in the nation, with projections that one in three "Americans" will be Latino by 2050, and Asians not far behind as the second largest minority.

Ninth, we cannot begin to fathom what went on in César Chávez's mind, or in the minds of his family, his security personnel, his core staff, and the sponsors of events, twenty-four hours a day, seven days a week, about his safety given the murders committed on union people during these years. Chapters 5 and 6 discuss the death threats and real deaths of UFW members, particularly during the war with the Teamsters. There were countless serious physical assaults, bombings, death threats, and purported assassination attempts—none vigorously investigated at any level, much less prosecuted.

Tenth, who could Chávez turn to if his enemies used the government, federal to local, to wage war against him and the UFW?

Eleventh, we now have the best government money can buy using "legal" campaign donations. Money helps elect politicians to local governmental units of cities, school districts, community college districts, water districts, special districts, county governments, and the like, to state and federal offices. It takes inordinate amounts of money to win elections, and even more money to stay in office because each election cycle is more expensive than the last one. And, money donors want returns on their "investments" in the form of appointments, favorable legislation and regulations, and contracts. Government is very big business and expensive to influence. Chávez found that out when he also engaged in financing campaigns of select politicians such as Willie Brown, California's Speaker of the House. Over the course of two years, after 1982 when Jerry Brown no longer was governor, Chávez contributed $750,000 to various campaign committees leading to Willie Brown.[5] And, he punished other politicians who once were in his favor, such as Assemblyman Art Torres, by funding his opponents on three occasions.[6]

Twelfth, reflecting on the impact of the issues, actors (private and public), methods, actions, activities, technology, jurisprudence, economics, politics, and most importantly, the outcomes of this surveillance by the FBI on Chávez during 1965-1975 and into at least 1988, we can compare the totality of these events with actors and actions the public faces today. The methods and means of surveillance have improved and grown by quantum leaps. Intelligence agencies have proliferated. Military intelligence practices used against foreign governments in past wars are now part of the arsenal of weapons used post-9/11 for domestic intelligence activities. Yet, COINTELPRO operations were supposed to have ceased in 1971. People are the new enemy. Organized people are the greater enemy of the state.

Lastly, by 2018 what once was a dream to build a union of farm workers has become Chávez, Inc. He turned to selling the "brand" of his persona and his cause. "In 1990, Chavez spoke at sixty-four events, earning an average of $3,800 per appearance; planned on holding 240 fund-raisers, though they never achieved close to that number . . . The goal was to raise $1.2 million, plus $60,000 by selling items produced by ETG (El Taller Grafico Specialty Advertising Corporation)."[7]

The UFW's National Farm Workers Service Center component shifted to housing development, and by 1987 its real estate portfolio included 48 low-income apartments in Fresno and 81 in Parlier, according to Pawel.[8] And, at the time of her publication, the new UFW Service Center, with its subsidiary American Liberty Investments, had 70 single-family homes and 226 apartments on the drawing board.[9] To service the apartments, Ideal Minimart Corporation was formed by Chávez and Celestino Aguilar, his partner in the housing ventures of American Liberty Investments. Ideal operated two strip malls and a check-cashing store at that time. Richard Chávez formed Bonita Construction in 1987, and he had contracts for some of the construction work to build these buildings. None of the housing projects, however, employed union labor to construct the buildings.[10] In 1988, the total number of subsidiaries, nonprofit and commercial, tied to the UFW totaled eighteen. And, most of these entities are horizontally and vertically integrated into the UFW, which has about $2 million in assets itself. Some examples: the UFW Service Center bought $100,000 worth of stock in ETG and also paid the UFW Education and Legal Defense Fund to provide services at its field offices; UFW pays La Union del Pueblo Entero (LUPE), the legal name of the education and legal defense fund, to monitor the grievance boards required under contracts. Most entities pay the UFW for computer services and printing; the UFW credit union, operating as a bank, has over six thousand loans worth more than $7.7 million. The Martin Luther King, Jr. Trust Fund also invested in American Liberty Investments and became a private foundation with assets worth approximately $8 million in principal.[11]

The Power of Technology Has Become the Technology of Power

The ACLU has documented evidence, obtained via FOIA and Privacy Act requests, of the FBI's alleged community outreach program in Northern California. Under the guise of showing the good face of the FBI to the community at events to which they were invited, they used the opportunity to obtain information on the participants. For example, in 2008, a Pakistani community organization in San Francisco was targeted by the local FBI office to gather information on their activities and membership identities. In San Jose, the FBI in 2009 recorded information on the leaders, activities, and travel history of attendees at an Assyrian community organization's Career Day gathering. In 2009 at California State University-Chico, the FBI interviewed an unsuspecting student member of the Saudi Student Association during a meeting and forwarded the identity, social security number, telephone number, and address to the FBI office in Washington, DC.[12]

Faulty Facial Recognition Technology

The Full House Committee on Oversight and Government Reform on March 22, 2017, reviewed the FBI's law enforcement policies on facial recognition technology. It found that one in two Americans, more than 117,000,000 persons, primarily adults, are in an FBI facial recognition data base. These "facial recognition" photos come from passports, driver's licenses, visa applications, police arrests, student identification cards, military records, social media accounts, and surveillance photos taken for that purpose of protestors, picketers, sit-ins, and rallies without the person's consent. To date, eighteen states have a memorandum of understanding to share their facial recognition data with the FBI. The committee also found that the facial recognition technology is wrong at least 15 percent of the time. And, an additional 20 percent of the time it is wrong with dark-skinned persons such as Latinos, African Americans, Hindus, and Arabs. The FBI began using this faulty technology, Next Generation Identification, in 2010. What happens to the person wrongfully identified as an "enemy combatant" and sent to Guantanamo without trial? What happens to the person wrongfully identified as a criminal perpetrator and prosecuted based on facial recognition? There is no regulation over the use of this technology at this writing, nor is there a court case limiting its use and implementation. The technology is not under any control.[13]

Kakistocracy and Blackwater

Hoover and his G-men loyalists were bent on ferreting out any dissenter and group opposing the FBI's views during his fifty-five-year reign. They saw themselves as the "Seat of Government," as Hoover termed his office and agency, supplanting the White House in that role. Today, we face more threats to our constitutional rights and former semblance of a people's democracy, not a representative government. The United States of America of the 1790s has evolved from an aristocracy of the Founding Fathers to a plutocracy following passage of the Voting Rights Act of 1965 and the *Citizens United* ruling by SCOTUS in 2010. We are now into a kakistocracy. The kakistocracy is the billionaire class comprised of the richest men in the United States (there are few women), who are not the smartest in the world but are the busiest at privatizing all government services and programs.[14] We have the Koch brothers and Erik Prince, to name just three very wealthy individuals among the kakistocracy. The Koch brothers, Charles and David, matched the money spent by each of the national political parties in the 2016 election, about $889 billion.[15] In short, two men and the Republican Party spent $1.778 trillion to influence the 2016 presidential election—two Republican men spending nearly a billion dollars on electing the person they wanted. Erik Prince owns Blackwater, the private military force of mercenaries that is becoming the substitute for the official United States armed forces and internal police agencies.[16] Prince is the brother of Betsy

DeVos, secretary of education in the Trump administration, who in her own right is busy privatizing public education as we know it. Erik Prince is a huge defense department contractor that invoices for billions of taxpayer dollars to provide services to the Department of Defense. In turn, he also spends millions in campaign contributions to Republican candidates that support increased military and defense spending.

Erik Prince is "a radical right-wing Christian mega-millionaire who has served as a major bankroller not only of President Bush's campaigns but for the broader Christian-right agenda. Prince has never given a penny to a Democratic candidate."[17] Erik Prince, with help from President George W. Bush and Donald Rumsfeld, then secretary of defense, began building an empire with government contracts to militarize local police and corporatize military forces, with Blackwater being the major contractor.[18] Jeremy Scahill wrote:

> Today, Blackwater has more than 2,300 private soldiers deployed in nine countries, including inside the United States. It maintains a database of 21,000 former Special Forces troops, soldiers, and retired law enforcement agents . . . has a private fleet of more than twenty aircraft, including helicopter gunships, and a surveillance blimp division . . . its 7,000-acre headquarters in Moyock, North Carolina, is the world's largest military facility. It trains tens of thousands of federal and local law enforcement agents a year and troops from "friendly" foreign nations.[19]

George W. Bush staffed his Pentagon with top corporate officers from Enron, General Dynamics, Aerospace Corporation, and Northrup Grumman, for example. Donald Trump is doing the same thing as I write these last few pages: more corporate officers in the Pentagon and in the State Department. And, more retired generals in the White House.

Erik Prince is busy building facilities in Illinois (Blackwater North), in California (Blackwater West), and a jungle-training camp in the former U.S. Naval Base in Subic Bay, Philippines. This former naval station was the largest U.S. military base in Asia.[20] It is his private military fortress in the Pacific.

The Border Wall

The border wall proposed by the president will not only be costly but unnecessary for those who wish to come into the United States. The most preferred method of entry is with a visa that will expire and does; the holder simply stays in the U.S. To this day, the emphasis is on catching the border crossers, not the jumped-the-visa illegals. And, the visa jumpers provide names and addresses of their U.S. contacts to the State Department when filing. The least preferred method of entry is walking or wading into the United States, and the aim of the wall is to prevent such crossings. The wall, however, will only cover, if at all, 1,933 miles of U.S.-Mexico border. This limited perimeter is only 16 percent of the total border of the contiguous United States; Canada represents 33 percent. The shoreline or seacoast is another 5,000 miles of "border"—not counting Hawaii or Alaska.[21] To maintain vigilance along whatever length of wall is ultimately erected, as has been found out with the limited length of fence already in place—primarily in Cameron County, Texas—an extensive camera surveillance must be in operation. The cost of monitoring these cameras twenty-four/seven will exceed the wall expenditure, which is a one-time allocation. The response to a breach of the border wall will also be very costly and perpetuate the shoulder-to-shoulder militarization of the U.S.-Mexico border. Perhaps this is the next taxpayer-funded contract for Erik Prince in his quest to be the world's private security guard and mercenary army.

The New Voter Data Base and Microtargeting

The only differences between voter data from the 1960s, for example, and 2016 that are paramount are twofold. On the one hand, no one person or group was exempt from surveillance even in the 1960s. But in 2018, too many of us self-report our activities via social media, which in turn are handed over to the intelligence community by the very companies we pay to provide us with internet communication and storage. On the other hand, the awesome quantum leap in the power of technology has made possible a new field of study: the technology of power. "Dataveillance" is the term used by some, and metadata is another. These terms are often used in relation to the indiscriminate and illegal gathering of volumes of data, justified as a possible future need to maintain national security. The *Economist*, following the early reports by the *Guardian* and later the *Washington Post*, published a concise history of the National Security Agency and one of its surveillance programs, code-named PRISM. This surveillance consisted of gathering millions and millions of personal emails, telephone calls, photos, videos, file transfers, and their individual social-network data, for example.[22] Active partners in this government-sponsored surveillance were the giants in the field of information technology and computing, such as Dell, Apple, Microsoft, Google, and the like. These companies own our data based on the language of their service contracts. They, in turn, readily permit government access, free or for a price, to our personal data. This PRISM program collected during the early 2010s (and perhaps still does under some other name) millions of records on persons in the United States. These persons were not suspected of any crime or subversive activity, nor are they engaged in any anti-government protest or dissent; they just use social media like you and I do.

The Fight for Rights vs. the Technology of Power

In *U.S. v. Davis*, the U.S. Court of Appeals for the 11th Circuit for the first time ruled that law enforcement entities need to obtain a warrant to have cellphone companies provide them information on callers and those called. The U.S. Supreme Court, hearing cases from Massachusetts and the California case from the 11th Circuit, unanimously agreed on June 25, 2014.[23] Prior to that, in 2011 alone, the law enforcement agencies made 1.3 million requests of cellphone service providers for what is termed "tower dump" matter—who called, when, where, how long, and from what numbers.[24]

Racism and the Black/White Paradigm to Divide and Conquer

Millennials have gravitated en masse to social media, such as Facebook, yet the giant social network remains a bastion of male supremacy at 69 percent compared to 31 percent females around the globe. In the U.S. market, diversity fares worse: white 57 percent, Asian 34 percent, Hispanic 4 percent, black 2 percent, and two or more races 3 percent. The top senior-level echelons as well as the lower technical rungs of the employee structure remain predominantly occupied by white males, 74 percent and 53 percent respectively, according to *USA Today*.[25] The top white dominance, some speculate, is due to institutional racism that preserves those who have been in power in those positions with slow turnover. The bottom percentage of white males is more complicated to explain, but the industry does require entry-level employees to have technical certifications, and significant numbers of minorities have not obtained that type of training—for example, writers of code, or robotic operators and programmers. The fiction that the U.S. society is based on a white-black paradigm to the exclusion of all other peoples is perpetuated by this type of occupational stratification and segmentation. The fate of ethno-racial minorities for employment in the high-tech industry will continue in the hands of whites if these institutionalized racial policies affecting who is hired and in what roles continues.

The promotion of this black-white paradigm continues as well. The *Atlantic* magazine recently graced its cover with these words:

> 250 years of slavery. 90 years of Jim Crow. 60 years of separate but equal. 35 years of state-sanctioned redlining. Until we reckon with the compounding moral debts of our ancestors, America will never be whole. Such an argument is made in *The Case for Reparations* by Ta-Nehisi Coates.[26]

The *Smithsonian* magazine graced its September 2016 front cover during what is national Hispanic Heritage Month, September 15 to October 15, with a magnificent photo of the newly dedicated Museum of African American Culture in Washington, DC, along with a lengthy article on its creation and purpose. Not one word on the Hispanic presence in the United States is found in the entire issue. For that matter, not one word was uttered over national media about Natalie Romero, one of the 2017 victims run down in Charlottesville, North Carolina, a Chicana from Bellaire in Houston, Texas.

The FBI historically has been unconcerned, despite the potential for litigation for discrimination against Hispanics, about the lack of Latinas/os in the ranks of administrators, special agents, and field agents. The FBI has already been found to be discriminatory in hiring and promotion of Hispanics by a federal court. And, Latinos not only are the largest ethno-racial demographic group in the nation but also the fastest growing population compared to others. The future is a Latino USA. The quality of this future will also be contingent on the nature and extent of the FBI surveillance of Latinos/as they rise to high elective and appointed public offices, voice their dissent and opposition to White House policies, mobilize as voters, and become ubiquitous throughout the United States. Will the FBI once again seek to neutralize, destroy, and thwart their efforts to organize legitimate protest and social movements? Will the FBI and other intelligence agencies once again ignore the civil rights complaints emanating from this community as they did with César Chávez and the farm worker movement?

Application Addiction

Among the quantum leaps in technology is the new fad: "free" communication applications. Not only are they not "free," they are also dangerously invasive into personal affairs, values, likes, attitudes, behavior patterns, lifestyle, personal schedules, and user contacts. They do not cost money to install, but the price of installation is the forfeiture of privacy. The terms of service for applications, almost all of them, include language that waives the user's right to privacy and gives the provider full access to all user information as relayed by the times users visit their site and other sites. Rare is the person who has completely read the terms of the application's user agreement. In other words, once subscribed, the provider gets all data from a user's iPhone, laptop, tablet, and PC, plus that of others linked to their equipment, when they accepted installation of the "app."

Cookies and "As Is" Language

Cookies are implants on your computer hard drive that keep records on your activity on the computer. The consent to cookies is broad. This is a direct quote from my laptop:

> Our site uses cookies and other technologies so that we, and our partners, can remember you and understand how you use our site. Access our Cookie Consent Tool, as seen on every page, to see a complete list of these technologies and to tell us whether they can be used on your device. Further use of this site will be considered consent.

Better yet, let me quote the section of my agreement for use of an application in Section 4.3 of the terms of agreement. The title to this subsection is:

> NO REPRESENTATIONS AND WARRANTIES. Except as specifically set forth in section 4.1 or a schedule to the maximum extent permitted by law, each party hereby specifically disclaims any and all representations and warranties whatsoever, whether express, implied or statutory, in connection with the subject matter of this agreement, including regarding any of the license grants and the applicable licensed materials, including any and all representations and warranties regarding merchantability, fitness for a particular purpose or against infringement, without limiting the generality of the foregoing, each licensee acknowledges that the license grants and the applicable licensed materials are provided on an "as is" basis with all faults, and licensee assumes all risks in connection with its exercise of any rights under the license grants.

This is very broad, vague, unclear, and nonspecific as to what are the "license grants" and the "applicable licensed materials." As consumers, we don't read this small-font language; we just want to use the product.

Personality Profiles from Metadata

The internet is both a means to information and a targeted source for mining personal data. An application develops a database of the times a user visits a site, what they do when on the site, and how they use that site. Imagine this information as if it were a file with data on how many times a user clicks on the app, what times those are, how long they stay on, what they do when they are on, and the choices they make because of that click. The provider has a psychographic profile on them. Now imagine if someone pays for those data and for those of millions of users like them; they could target all of them with messages, links, ads, surveys, opinions, donation solicitations, and the like to help or hurt a political candidate.

Cambridge Analytica, a British company, did just that on 220 million Americans to build personality profiles, which they sold to the Trump campaign in 2016. Cambridge Analytica used applications for the data, but they also culled information from Facebook. Brad Parscale, a San Antonio, Texas, resident, was the digital director for Trump's campaigns from primary to general election. He spent approximately $70 million per month on Project Alamo, the name for the custom-designed program to mine voter data bought from Cambridge Analytica and Facebook, to influence voters. From Facebook, he bought $2 million in advertising and used Facebook's Custom Audiences from Customer Lists to match supporters with virtual doppelgangers. He then parsed these names by race, ethnicity, gender, location, and other attributes and identities. Another Facebook tool, Lookalike Audiences, pairs people with similar interests and qualities. The reliability of these matches to predict voter preference was enhanced with yet another Facebook tool, Brand Lift, that shows which person's likes, when targeted for advertisements, will increase sales of a product. A side benefit to this advanced microtargeting was fundraising. The Trump campaign, while identifying potential voters, also used the names for seeking donations. This program raised $250 million in donations.[27]

Don't Forget Our Cars

The installation of GPS devices on cars, especially rental cars, gets drivers road assistance when needed. It also allows tracking of every movement in that car. Sirius, the commercial-free music conglomerate station, also satellite-tracks the location of the car constantly to provide the service, and while doing so collects information on likes, dislikes, and favorite times the driver listens to certain programming. They get to know the driver, and the driver pays them to do so, just as the driver in past decades paid for membership in the American Automobile Association (AAA) for emergency road assistance such as tire repair, engine failure, or towing.

USA Today, in a special edition, "Transportation Today: Celebrating 50 Years of the USDOT," April 1, 2017, boasted of driverless cars in "smart cities," and even autonomous trucks driving themselves in our near future, based on artificial intelligence capabilities of computers and the new programs. Plans include sophisticated operating systems that will guide these vehicles to their destinations and avoid collisions while doing so. With passengers in the vehicle, the operating system controls everything, from locking doors preventing exit at will to instructions for locking on seat belts. The operating systems will "know" where the vehicle is, where it is going, who are the occupants, and the estimated time of arrival. Those who live in hot zones in the South know the ordeal of sitting and driving in a hot car where inside temperatures can reach 170 degrees Fahrenheit in minutes. What if the system malfunctions and does not stop the car when and where it should, prevents exit, saves fuel by shutting off the air conditioning system during hot weather? What guarantees will there be that no one but the owner of the vehicle can control the programming?

Then, there is ISAC. As a result of presidential directive PDD-63 in 1998, updated in 2003 by a Homeland Security Presidential Directive, HSPD-7, and more recently updated by PDD-21 in February 2013, cars will now have a built-in Auto ISAC to share information sent from a vehicle to a national vehicle center. A vehicle is the new snitch. It can and will record conversations inside and within a close range, take digital images of those inside the vehicle, analyze odors and smells inside and within a close range, and lock and shut off the engine if necessary to prevent combustion or unwanted acceleration. This Auto-IPAC is to be global information-sharing by the world's automakers and governments.

Consumers are to trust other governments, including the United States? Knowing the past history of the FBI and minorities, for example, and now the NSA in the use of metadata to track and profile huge segments of the U.S. population, futuristic vehicle owners are to feel protected in the privacy of their own vehicles?

The Big Trucks and Buses

Greyhound Bus Lines decades ago had an advertising jingle that said, "Leave the driving to us." Are passengers going to feel more comfortable leaving the driving to a computer program? Are passengers in cars going to feel more comfortable with a driverless semi-trailer coming at them at full speed or creeping up behind them as they both trek down the freeway? The tractor-trailer trucking industry is projected to reduce its 1.8 million drivers to a fully automated trailer-tractor fleet in a decade or two.[28] More importantly, for every robot in place, 5.6 workers will lose their job, according to a recent study by a pair of researchers, MIT's Daron Acemoglu and Boston University's Pascual Restrepo.[29]

The U.S. Intelligence Community Is Fundamentally Inept and Corrupt

Peter Lance, in *1000 Years for Revenge*, laid bare the culpability of the FBI in not preventing the attacks on the Twin Towers and averting the ensuing calamity that beset the nation. His investigative report reads like a novel, but concludes in no uncertain terms that "Each of the nation's spy agencies was responsible in part, but after an eighteen-month investigation, the evidence presented in this book shows that the FBI in particular had multiple opportunities to stop the devastation of 9/11 and simply failed to follow through."[30] Yet, President Bush and his administration, instead of admitting fault and cleaning house within the intelligence agencies, chose to ignore the recommendations by the various commissions charged with finding the weaknesses of the intelligence agencies. Instead they began looking for a scapegoat to blame outside the country; they found Saddam Hussein. Bush and his administrators formulated a plan for permanent war before embarking on retaliation based on lies. They packaged the message calling for an invasion of Iraq as the "War on Terror." The Homeland Security System was devised, and a color-coded terrorist threat scale formulated. They charted a path of fear with daily announcements of the color of the day for measuring the level of threat probability of another attack. Beginning in March 11, 2002, until April 27, 2011, nine years and nearly a month, the public was subjected to paranoia over the color of the day: red for severe risk of another attack, orange for high, yellow for significant, blue for general risk, and green for low. I do not recall a yellow, blue, or green day being announced; it was mostly orange. The follow-up to the color-induced paranoia scheme was tightened security and screenings at airports, courthouses, government buildings, major public events, and schools. The American public has now grown accustomed to this paranoia; it is the new normal.

Disrobing for Security

Reminiscent of Hoover's Security Index, a no-flight list of names was created post-9/11 that required personal screening and interrogation by airline personnel prior to boarding. The public has learned to expect long lines and waits to remove shoes, belts, jackets, personal effects, and to carry small amounts of liquids in carry-on bags. Later, invasive full-body x-ray machines were installed at major airports around the country. An air traveler can pay a fee for less scrutiny and no invasive personal searches with the Pre-Check program. This program provides a number to those who paid for the service when making a flight reservation. The boarding pass notes the holder is among the privileged who can pay for quick security clearance and faster screening. You enter a designated line, not the line for use by the general public. The Pre-Check program allows those designated to keep their coats, shoes, and belts on; not open attaché cases and remove laptops, other electronics, or purse/wallet; and skip the full-body x-ray. A ping at the screening portal entryway may subject the pre-checked person to a quick scan of their body with a hand-held metal scanner. Are we to believe that money can buy security?

Perpetual War

George W. Bush is long gone. Hussein is dead. The War on Terror, however, continues unabated. Jane Mayer in *The Dark Side* details the unbelievable level of FBI incompetence during these same years. She also provides an update to 2008, the eve of the Obama presidency, of how post-9/11 became an attack on American ideals and civil liberties.[31] Osama bin Laden was killed during the Obama administration.

The War on Terror has expanded beyond Afghanistan to become more U.S. wars in various places, as did the scope of U.S. involvement in other places in the Middle East and Africa.

The United States has been militarily involved in the Middle East—Pakistan, Afghanistan, and Iraq—and with other types of "assistance" in Syria, Libya, Egypt, Somalia, Philippines, Mali, Algeria, Sudan, and Niger by the end of 2017. The U.S. continues military involvement with "advisors" in Latin America as well. It is the world's largest supplier of military weapons across the globe, as history has revealed with the Iran-Contra scandal. Wars, for the United States, have become a constant. During post-9/11 and the Obama presidential administrations, the U.S. intelligence community grew to seventeen federal agencies with a combined annual budget estimated at $75 billion in 2013 and counting. There are 1,271 government organizations involved in gathering intelligence and 1,931 private contractors doing the same for these agencies.[32] The FBI's budget has grown to $6.04 billion to cover costs for 30,485 persons, of which 12,492 are special agents stationed in fifty-six field offices, sixty international offices, four hundred satellite offices, and the Washington, DC, headquarters.[33]

Information on the ineptness and corruption of the various U.S. intelligence agencies is readily available to anyone interested in reading such exceptional works as Jeffrey T. Richelson's *The U.S. Intelligence Community*; John Rizzo's *Company Man*, an exposé on the CIA; Bob Woodward's *The Secret Man*, about Mark Felt, one of the top FBI men who finally stepped forward with the truth about the Nixon presidency. Also Michael J. Cain's *The Tangled Web*, and Kevin Cullen and Shelley Murphy's *Whitey Bulger*, books about local police and FBI collaboration in crime with the Mafia in Chicago and Boston, respectively. After being outed as a CIA operative, Valerie Plame's *Fair Game* resulted in one conviction, Lewis Libby, and according to the Government Accounting Office the investigation cost $2.58 million. Libby was convicted and sentenced to 30 months' confinement plus fines and costs on March 6, 2007; but on July 2, after four months in prison, his sentence was commuted by President George W. Bush and he walked.

Presidential pardons have been used to protect wrongdoers time and again by both Democratic and Republican presidents. Some wrongdoers are never brought to light; they brag on their own without any fear of retaliation. For example, Jose A. Rodriguez, in *Hard Measures*, depicts his role as head of the CIA Clandestine Services and the implementing of the Enhanced Interrogation Program (EIT) operations on U.S. captives in Guantanamo Bay. The EITs are the methods President Bush authorized in 2002, which included the infamous "waterboarding." This method of pouring water into nostrils and mouth while a restrained person is in an inclined position is a tool to get suspects to confess. Other methods are to turn one group of suspects against another group, such as Communists against Mafia types.

Remember Hoodwink?

The collaboration between the FBI and the Mafia and the Teamsters had violent and deadly implications for farm workers during the UFW grape strikes. These details were revealed in various chapters in this book, mainly chapter 6. Other books, such as the first-person account by Hoffa's strong-arm man Joseph Franco on the deals cut with organized crime, the Mafia, the FBI, and President Nixon, are inculpating and incriminating.[34] Readers are encouraged to examine more closely the declassified FBI documents on Operation Hoodwink available on the FBI website for these relationships. While Hoodwink was aimed at pitting the Communist Party USA against the Mafia, the Communists did not fall for this divide-and-conquer strategy; the Teamsters did, however, as was the case in Boston and Philadelphia where the FBI handlers took on Mafia killers with offers of protection to eliminate other Mafiosi and Teamster bosses. Crime, organized or not, has continued, and so have the methods used by modern-day computer-savvy criminals.

Hacks and Hackers

Startling statistics were reported by a reputable consumer magazine: 29 percent of online consumers' home computers were infected with malicious software (termed "malware") in 2013. Malware can destroy files, erase content, and embed viruses that wreak havoc with the normal workings of the programs in the computer. Careless owners, 3.1 million people, had their cellphones stolen in 2013, and half that number in 2012. Most phones that are lost or stolen are because owners leave them unattended in public places. They forget them on business counters such as in grocery and department stores, gasoline pumps, bars, banks, and libraries. Another one in seven cellphone consumers were notified that their personal data had been breached in 2013—a 56 percent increase from 2012, and 62 percent of U.S. consumers took no measures to protect their privacy online, such as buying virus protection.

There were seven major security disasters reported in 2013-14. Target, the giant box retailer, admitted that during the 2013 Christmas buying spree, some 40 million credit-card users that made purchases had their card numbers stolen, and 70 million others had personal data taken by hackers. In April 2012, Web servers, two out of three of them, reported that a bug, Heartbleed, had taken passwords and other data that subscribers used online. Adobe Systems was hacked and payment information on 2.9 million customers was obtained; an estimated 38 million usernames and encrypted passwords were also taken. Tinder, a dating application, supposedly allowed app users to locate the other party to the nearest mile, but after they were breached, app users could trace the person to within 100 feet. Allegedly, the service corrected the problem on New Year's Day 2014. Advocate Health Care lost four of their unencrypted laptops to thieves at an office in Park Ridge, Illinois. Living Social, a deal-making site, lost 50 million usernames and encrypted passwords to hackers in 2013. Lastly, some Apple products, iPhone 4, iPad 2, iPod Touch (5th generation), were hackable by moderately sophisticated attackers. These hacker attacks yield passwords, emails, and financial information of hundreds of thousands of unsuspecting persons.[35]

Credit Scores

As if the average hard-working person does not have enough to worry about making ends meet, the latest midyear hack scandal of 2017 involves Equifax, one of three giants in the credit-history field of players. Equifax along with Experian and TransUnion hold in their databases almost all the residents in the world, over 400 million, who have ever made a transaction that was reported to the "Big Three" as a means of validating the customer's creditworthiness. Creditors pay the Big Three for this information. The Big Three score each and every one of us in their databases from 300 to 850, and lenders rely on those scores and credit history to decide how to process the transaction. Higher scores mean lower payments, lower interest rates, and better deals. Lower scores mean higher interest rates, perhaps denial. More importantly, the Big Three scores are now also used to determine a person's employability. Low score, no job. And, once negative information gets into a credit report of the Big Three, the person is the loser, unless he or she takes the time to challenge and correct the information. Most often the information is not corrected or erased; the customer's correspondence is just made part of the record. The score stands.[36]

According to the *New York Times*, Equifax was attacked by hackers, who made off with over 143 million records of credit histories that included name, address, credit-card account numbers, mortgage-loan account information, and Social Security numbers, among other important personal data. Equifax, in 2016, was contracted by the Social Security Administration to help them manage risk and mitigate fraud in the mySocialSecurity Web portal. They were paid $10 million to perform that contract service. And now someone else has all this information. If a person calls into Equifax or any of the other Big Three companies to freeze their account just to make sure no one steals their identity and data during this period of uncertainty, a hefty price must be paid to unfreeze the account later. In the meantime, what does a person do who is looking for a job, buying a house or automobile, opening a credit card account, or checking on their Social Security statement? Meanwhile, top executives at Equifax and at Social Security are not being held accountable for the breach or for the consequences expected from this huge hack of personal data.[37]

Panama Papers

The FBI and other intelligence agencies are investigating Russian and Chinese hacking of our internet network systems generally, as well as the systems used by organizations such as political campaigns. The leaked revelations from the scandal known as the Panama Papers indicates that the U.S. government also benefited from hacks done by others. The Panama Papers consisted of 11.5 million leaked documents on more than 214,488 offshore entities created by a Panamanian law firm, Mossack Fonseca.[38] The United States monitored communications of other world leaders, including allies, under PRISM conducted by the NSA. Among those hacked and eavesdropped on by illegal wiretapping by the U.S. government's PRISM program were the leaders of Germany, Canada, Costa Rica, Mexico, Argentina, Brazil, Venezuela, Peru, the European Union, France, Italy, Russia, Spain, United Kingdom, China, India, Israel, Pakistan, Syria, and Saudi Arabia, to name a few countries. The first leaked documents, 150, were published on April 3,

2016, and the International Consortium of Investigative Journalists posted full documents on its website. The information leaked revealed crime and corruption at the highest level of governments in over eighty countries. Google's Street View program also illegally collected emails, passwords, images, addresses, and other personal information from unencrypted computer networks, home and business. Google settled its lawsuit brought by thirty-eight state attorney generals in the United States for $7 million in March 2013.[39] Given this behavior, who would want to be an ally of the United States? And, why does the United States complain of foreigners hacking into U.S. accounts, public and private, when it has done, and probably is doing, the same thing to others?

Privatization of the Internet?

U.S dominance on the World Wide Web built in the last twenty-five years is being challenged by other countries. Arguably, some 3 billion persons subscribe to internet service, with hundreds of thousands of new accounts added daily in 2014. The internet is a behemoth business, $26 trillion in 2012, and a beehive of metadata information on any and all with little to no regulation. Traditional allies of the United States were alarmed to learn that their communications were monitored by the NSA. Data nationalism—a movement among nations seeking to keep information within their borders—is growing. Prior attempts to regulate and curb the power of the United States over the internet have failed. In 2012, eighty-nine member nations of the United Nations adopted a treaty to regulate the flow of internet data by an international body, the International Telecommunications Union (ITU). The United States and most European nations refused to sign on to this global treaty. Shortly after the ITU was formed, some African nations attempted to impose a "sending party pays" system to tax international data transmission, without success.

In the era of globalization and a shrinking world, some countries are reverting to regional accords to cope with international data transmission and hacking; they are proposing private pipelines between governments:

an underwater fiber-optic communications cable between them. Brazil and the European Union (EU) announced such a plan in 2014, as has Germany for just the EU countries, a regional internet walled off from the United States.[40] Globalization, it seems, has come full circle with regard to the World Wide Web and the development of a gated but global world of individual nations.

Cashless Society

The internet and globalization combined make for a marriage made in heaven for those who wish for complete control over people. Debit cards, credit cards, online banking all lead us toward a cashless society the world over. As we willingly surrender duties of check writing and cashing, making deposits at the bank, and balancing our bank statements, we need not worry about carrying cash. We just need the credit and debit cards to do transactions. It will be easier to get paid electronically. The companies we pay for the internet server system and software hold our money reserves. If they block access for whatever reason to a person's accounts, does that party have money? If users do not pay their fees for internet server, software, malware protection, etc., do these companies have access to their money from a user's account? More importantly, if they do not have electricity twenty-four/seven can they function? Better yet, do they exist?

Spy Chips

It is not just invasion by the local police and other law enforcement agencies that persons need to be concerned about regarding their privacy and theft of personal information. Major and dramatic advances by quantum leaps have occurred in technology across all business sectors that aid governments in continuing their quest for increased security. For example, small tracking devices known as RFID tags—radio frequency identification—are used in almost all warehouses to inventory, track, and find merchandise by way of a radio signal linked to a computer chip. Albrecht and McIntyre, in their book *Spychips*, explain the evolution of this tiny tracking device from a sizable and visible square chip to one as small as a grain of sand. They conclude from their research that RFIDs are going to be embedded in all products, documents (U.S. passports already are embedded), and soon perhaps within a person's body if industry and government have their way.[41] The military's historical reliance on "dog tags" that contain the soldier's information and are hung around their neck will soon give way to an embedded chip on their body.

LEDs as Cameras

Another product of concern for the future, among many, are the lights of the future, LEDs, light-emitting diodes. These lights are replacing the traditional bulbs and fluorescent tubes at a rapid pace across the globe. In Sunnyvale, California, deep in the heart of Silicon Valley and the birthplace of LEDs, most buildings, parking lots, streets, and homes have LEDs instead of bulbs or fluorescent tubes. It is not just light these diodes emit if they are enhanced with cameras and sensors, wired together and connected, and linked to a computer. Such a network can monitor every movement and relay the imagery to screen for analytics. Such cameras within these lights and other devices can capture a crystal-clear image of any item six inches in size at this point in time. Within a year or so, precision and clarity of imagery can be down to the size of a dime. Another example is voice recognition, not just to talk to the phone and have it convert the sound into text, but also for identification. When you reach a call center, at times you are informed the conversation will be recorded for security, and the recording then adds "for training purposes." These training purposes are to collect voice patterns, just like collecting fingerprints to have a mega-metadata base of voices—one of which is yours. At my former home institution, UT-Arlington, electrical engineers Smita Rao and J. C. Chiao have developed a tiny, tiny micro-windmill that can power batteries. It is 1.8 mm in size, or in terms we all understand, ten of these windmills can fit on a grain of rice.

This product could be the source of wind power to fuel a camera or drone or light or radio signal, and it is so minute it is undetectable.

Drones

A final example is "drones" or unmanned aircraft systems, vehicles used by both industry and the military since World War II by air, water, or land.[42] Robots that sweep, vacuum, and clean floors are readily available to consumers. These are all drones. This technology has progressed to the point now that drones are delivering merchandise to consumers, patrolling the border between countries, photographing and relaying imagery of pipelines in remote locations, killing targeted people with plenty of collateral damage, and monitoring troop movements and tropical storms. These drones can also be used as "Peeping Toms," to carry lethal weapons, and to capture and relay information. U.S. Senator Dianne Feinstein is reported to have discovered such a Peeping Tom disguised as a bird at her bedroom window one morning.[43] Seven states have statutes permitting use of drones for commercial purposes, while forty-three others considered such legislation during 2013.[44]

FBI Spy Planes

By April 2015, perhaps since 2003, the FBI began operating a fleet of spy planes over U.S. cities in eleven states and the District of Columbia. This operation is a huge leap into collecting metadata and placing all persons in a geographic area under surveillance for a particular or unknown reason. The FBI has utilized no less than thirteen fake companies registered to post office boxes in Bristow, Virginia, and another box shared with the Department of Justice to hide ownership of these spy planes. These 115 or more 182T Cessna Skylanes were used for video surveillance of people and cars below, and for "cell-site simulation" to intercept telephone, text, and email communication. Video footage assists in vehicle description and registration data, facial recognition of occupants, and even vehicle destinations. The cell-site simulation tricks a cellphone on the ground, regardless of being on or off, into sending its signal to the airplane instead of a cell tower. Such a practice reveals personal data and other subscriber information about the cellphone owner/user to the FBI airplanes.[45] The FBI has yet to explain, nor has it been asked to do so by Congress, why this spy plane operation is needed.

The new reality is how the U.S. government and businesses are devising ways to intrude into our lives with one purpose: complete social control. Old lessons learned but forgotten can serve us well. If all of us read books like this one to relearn what happened, how, and by whom to a man and a union, we are then better prepared and informed. Chávez, with a lifetime goal for justice in the fields for farm workers, was not, and he paid the ultimate price. He died leaving unfinished business, for others to pick up and carry on.

Methodology and Research Note

We Fought For It.

Demand The Union Label.
United Farm Workers of America, AFL-CIO

FOR THE BENEFIT OF FUTURE RE-
searchers, the entire Chávez collection of the declassified FBI file I obtained consists of 2,085 pages.[1] These
declassified FBI files are presented
as seven parts but further broken
down into seventeen packets. These
seventeen packets each consist of
approximately 111 pages on the low
end and 147 pages at the high end. The face or cover sheet of each of the seven
parts of the seventeen packets reads, for example, "Part # 2 of 7" or "Part # 5
of 7." Other packets of the seventeen that do not have first-page covers just
begin with a document or a simple inscription, for example, "Subject: Cesar
Chavez & United Farm Workers et al File: #100-444762 Section: 4."

Pagination Problems

To make matters worse for researchers, each of the seven parts has an entry at bottom of the webpage corresponding to that set of documents that reads, for example, on part 2 of 7: "Pages Available This Part 338." This pagination scheme serves no purpose but to cause confusion. The electronic page of the webpage has an additional entry at bottom of the electronic page for each packet, for example "Page 1 of 114," and that numbering system disappears when the actual page is printed. Additionally, the page numbers inside each part of the seventeen packets do not correspond to any page therein. Instead, there are penciled numbers at bottom right on each page in every part and packet without regard to any consistency or chronology.

I did not use any of the FBI page numbers supplied to reference documents used in this manuscript. Instead I listed the documents as endnotes for each chapter narrative with enough description for the reader to crosscheck the document with the electronic version on the webpage or a downloaded hardcopy that has been reorganized by dates.

Lastly, the actual documents in each declassified part or packet are not in chronological order by date. In any given packet you will find a document dated March 3, 1967, for example, followed by another dated November 17, 1971. The first page of packet 6 consisting of 114 pages, for example begins with "page two" of an undated and missing subject title document with penciled page number of 230. The last two-page document in packet 6 is dated January 12, 1971, with penciled page numbers 342 and 343. Where are the missing pages? Did the FBI miscount the pages? In the last packet, #17, the content is to consist of 101 pages, yet the penciled-in numbers on documents start with 102 and end the last page with 201. Where did the other two pages go? Did the FBI miscount these pages as well? This packet begins with these 99 pages of documents dated from January 18, 1973, to August 30, 1973—a brief seven-month period. Is this last document the FBI's way of letting us know that the surveillance of Chávez and the UFW ended then? I do not believe this and filed an appeal in early 2017 based on a new FOIA request for documents held after this date to the day after his death.

Where to Find Organized FBI File on Chávez

The staff of the Julian Samora Research Institute (JSRI) at Michigan State University and I had to rearrange the pages of the seventeen packets into chronological order by month and day for each year of the surveillance, nearly ten years. The rearranged file is on deposit under my name with the Julian Samora Research Institute at the Michigan State University Library, East Lansing, Michigan. Additionally, other related FBI files used in this manuscript will also be archived there. A declassified file, not rearranged, is on deposit under my name with the Nettie Benson Latin American Collection at the University of Texas-Austin. Anyone can download these pages from the FBI website The Vault, under Cesar Chavez, file #100-444762. I could not make sense of the files as released without downloading them; reorganizing them by date, month, and year; and proceeding to analyze their content. There is no substitute for holding in my hands a paper copy of an original FBI document while my eyes travel the page looking for clues as to the who, why, how, when, and what happened during the surveillance.

As previously stated, these "official" declassified files on Chávez posted on the FBI website are what the agency wishes to disclose. It is probably not the entire file on him or the UFW. The awkward separation of the released file into packets; double pagination, penciled or posted, on the webpage frame; and the total disregard for chronology by date of the documents in each packet all serve to raise this doubt.

The FBI Numbering System for Files

Douglas M. Charles, in his work on the FBI files on gays, states that by 1947 there were 94 categories for FBI file numbers. That is to say 94 different subject headings for the categorization of files.[2] The Chavez file number is 100-444762-000. The 100 is the main file or case file number for a domestic security investigation. The 444762 number refers to the specific file number assigned to Chávez. These numbers are assigned in sequence of cases opened. In this case, the Chávez file was the 440,762nd security investigation opened by the FBI. If there are additional numbers after the second set of numbers, such as 100-444762-110, this third set is for serializing or tracing the order of the document, as in this case, the 110th document received on this matter. Not all documents are serialized or marked in order of preparation; some have a checkmark after the assigned file number, or the letters UR for unrecorded. Another problem with file numbers is that there could be more than one file number if a person was investigated by different field offices for different reasons. Each FBI field office has its own number, and the file would start with that geographic code for that office followed by the numbers for that specific file. The Los Angeles FBI office is coded as LA, for example. SA is either San Antonio or for Special Agent, SC is for Sacramento or Special Clerk, SD is for San Diego, SF is for San Francisco, and SOG is for Seat of Government, Hoover's favorite term for his office.

Appendix 2 provides copies of FBI documents to show how they look, file and subject name, who sent and received each file, who else signed off on each file, what handwritten notes may be found, what other agencies also received copies of each file, and what exemptions are claimed for the redactions on a page.

In Appendix 3, I provide a listing of all presidents, U.S. attorney generals, and FBI directors in the event any readers want to place in historical context which national public officials were in charge of the FBI at any given time. More Chavez files are to be found in these presidential archives. I visited the Johnson, Nixon, Ford, and Reagan presidential archives in search of documents related to César E. Chávez and the UFW, and found photographs and additional documents, mostly correspondence and memoranda on Chávez. The Cesar Chavez Foundation, Los Angeles, California, has photographs, posters, and other information and memorabilia for sale. The Wayne State University's Walter Reuther Labor Archives in Detroit, Michigan, has the FBI file, more documents, and the posters used herein as chapter covers.

After the deaths of Helen Chávez, Richard Chávez, Manuel Chávez, Antonio Orendain, and Larry Itliong, all active with the UFW and Chávez, I filed FOI/PA requests for their files and am waiting. Other FBI files on Saul Alinsky, Stanley Korshak, Charles Tolson, Richard Nixon, for example, are also available. The easiest route is the FBI website to find declassified files by name, and then the online FOIA request. In the case of those not listed but deceased, then an obituary or proof of death must accompany your FOIA request for files on that person. I was unable to convince Dolores Huerta to authorize me access to her FBI files and could not find Gilbert Padilla.

Explanation of Exemptions

SUBSECTIONS OF TITLE 5, UNITED STATES CODE, SECTION 552

(b)(1) (A) specifically authorized under criteria established by an Executive order to be kept secret in the interest of national defense or foreign policy and (B) are in fact properly classified to such Executive order;

(b)(2) related solely to the internal personnel rules and practices of an agency;

(b)(3) specifically exempted from disclosure by statute (other than section 552b of this title), provided that such statute (A) requires that the matters be withheld from the public in such a manner as to leave no discretion on issue, or (B) establishes particular criteria for withholding or refers to particular types of matters to be withheld;

(b)(4) trade secrets and commercial or financial information obtained from a person and privileged or confidential;

(b)(5) inter-agency or intra-agency memorandums or letters which would not be available by law to a party other than an agency in litigation with the agency;

(b)(6)   personnel and medical files and similar files the disclosure of which would constitute a clearly unwarranted invasion of personal privacy;

(b)(7)   records or information compiled for law enforcement purposes, but only to the extent that the production of such law enforcement records or information (A) could reasonably be expected to interfere with enforcement proceedings, (B) would deprive a person of a right to a fair trial or an impartial adjudication, (C) could reasonably be expected to constitute an unwarranted invasion of personal privacy, (D) could reasonably be expected to disclose the identity of confidential source, including a State, local, or foreign agency or authority or any private institution which furnished information on a confidential basis, and, in the case of record or information compiled by a criminal law enforcement authority in the course of a criminal investigation, or by an agency conducting a lawful national security intelligence investigation, information furnished by a confidential source, (E) would disclose techniques and procedures for law enforcement investigations or prosecutions, or would disclose guidelines for law enforcement investigations or prosecutions if such disclosure could reasonably be expected to risk circumvention of the law, or (F) could reasonably be expected to endanger the life or physical safety of any individual;

(b)(8)   contained in or related to examination, operating, or condition reports prepared by, on behalf of, or for the use of an agency responsible for the regulation or supervision of financial institutions; or

(b)(9)   geological and geophysical information and data, including maps, concerning wells.

SUBSECTIONS OF TITLE 5, UNITED STATES CODE, SECTION 552a

(d)(5)   information compiled in reasonable anticipation of a civil action proceeding;

(j)(2) material reporting investigative efforts pertaining to the enforcement of criminal law including efforts to prevent, control, or reduce crime or apprehend criminals;

(k)(1) information which is currently and properly classified pursuant to an Executive order in the interest of the national defense or foreign policy, for example, information involving intelligence sources or methods;

(k)(2) investigatory material compiled for law enforcement purposes, other than criminal, which did not result in loss of a right, benefit or privilege under Federal programs, or which would identify a source who furnished information pursuant to a promise that his/her identity would be held in confidence;

(k)(3) material maintained in connection with providing protective services to the President of the United States or any other individual pursuant to the authority of Title 18, United States Code, Section 3056;

(k)(4) required by statute to be maintained and used solely as statistical records;

(k)(5) investigatory material compiled solely for the purpose of determining suitability, eligibility, or qualifications for Federal civilian employment or for access to classified information, the disclosure of which would reveal the identity of the person who furnished information pursuant to a promise that his/her identity would be held in confidence;

(k)(6) testing or examination material used to determine individual qualifications for appointment or promotion in Federal Government service the release of which would compromise the testing or examination process;

(k)(7) material used to determine potential for promotion in the armed services, the disclosure of which would reveal the identity of the person who furnished the material pursuant to a promise that his/her identity would be held in confidence.

FBI/DOJ

N. T.

36 (Rev. 5-22-78)

FBI

TRANSMIT VIA: PRECEDENCE: CLASSIFICATION:

☐ Teletype   ☐ Immediate   ☐ TOP SECRET

☐ Facsimile   ☐ Priority   ☐ SECRET

☒ Airtel   ☐ Routine   ☐ CONFIDENTIAL

☐ UNCLAS E F T O

☐ UNCLAS

Date ___2/4/82___

TO: DIRECTOR, FBI

FROM: SAC, WFO (58-1908) (P) (C-7)

███████████ NATIONAL
FARMWORKERS SERVICE CENTER
(NFWSC) / UNITED FARMWORKERS
UNION, LA PAZ, KEENE,
CALIFORNIA
POSSIBLE COI
(OO:WFO)

      Re letter from K. William O'Connor, Inspector
General, Community Services Administration, to WFO dated
9/2/81.

      Enclosed for Bureau are the original and three
copies of an LHM regarding captioned matter. One copy of
the LHM is being disseminated to Assistant United States
Attorney Timothy J. Reardon, Fraud Section, United States
Courthouse, Washington, D. C.

N 15—10898—1

②- Bureau (Enc. 4)
2-WFO   7 FEB 8 1932
████ kio
(4)

1-CRIM
1-CIVIL
1-CSA
2/9/82

Approved _____ Transmitted _____ _____ Per _____
                             (Number)   (Time)

254

(R U.S. Department of Justice

Federal Bureau Federal —

Bureau of Investigation

Washington, D.C. 20535

November 8, 2016

MR. JOSE ANGEL GUTIERREZ
1020 WILD OLIVE CT
BROWNSVILLE, TX 78520

FOIPA Request No.: 1360817-000
Subject: CHAVEZ, HELEN FABELO

Dear Mr. Gutierrez:

This acknowledges receipt of your Freedom of Information request to the FBI. The FOIPA number listed above has been assigned to your request.

You have requested records concerning one or more third party individuals. The FBI recognizes an important privacy interest in the requested information. You may receive greater access to these records if they exist by providing one of the following: (1) an authorization and consent from the individual(s) (i.e., express authorization and consent of the third party); (2) proof of death (i.e., proof that your subject is deceased); or (3) a justification that the public interest in disclosure outweighs personal privacy (i.e., a clear demonstration that the public interest in disclosure outweighs personal privacy interests). In the absence of such information, the FBI can neither confirm nor deny the existence of any records responsive to your request, which, if they were to exist, would be exempt from disclosure pursuant to FOIA Exemptions (b)(6) and

5 U.S.C. 552   and b

Express authorization and consent. If you seek disclosure of any existing records on this basis, enclosed is a Certification of Identity form. You may make additional copies of this form if you are requesting information on more than one individual. The of your request should complete this form and then sign it. Alternatively, the subject may prepare a document containing the required descriptive data and have it notarized. The original certification of identity or notarized authorization with the descriptive information must contain a legible, original signature before FBI can conduct an accurate search of our records.

Prpof of death. If you seek disclosure of any existing records on this basis, proof of death can be a copy of a death certificate, Social Security Death Index, obituary, or another recognized reference source. Death is presumed if the birth date of the subject is more than 100 years ago.

Public Interest Disclosure. If you seek disclosure of any existing records on this basis, you must demonstrate that the public interest in disclosure outweighs personal privacy interests. In this regard, you must show that the public interest sought is a significant one, and that the requested information is likely to advance that interest.

Fax your request to the Work Process unit at (540) 868-4997, or mail to 170 Marcel Drive, Winchester, VA 22602. If we do not receive a response from you within 30 days from the date of this letter, your request will be closed. You must include the FOIPA request number with any communication regarding this matter.

For your information, Congress excluded three discrete categories of law enforcement and national security records from the requirements of the FOIA. See 5 U.S.C. S 552(c). Assuch, this response is limited to those records, if any exist, that are subject to the FOIA. This is a standard notification that is given to all our requesters and should not be taken as an indication that excluded records do, or do not, exist.

You may file an appeal by writing to the Director, Office of Information Policy (OIP), United States Department of Justice, Suite 11050, 1425 New York Avenue, NW, Washington, D.C. 20530-0001 , or you may submit an appeal through OIP's FOIAonline portal by creating an account on the following web site:

https://foiaonline.regulations.gov/foia/action/public/home. Your appeal must be postmarked or electronically transmitted within ninety (90) days from the date of this letter in order to be considered timely. If you submit your appeal by mail, both the letter and the envelope should be clearly marked "Freedom of Information Act Appeal." Please cite the FOIPA Request Number assigned to your request so that it may be easily identified.

You may seek dispute resolution services by contacting the Office of Government Information Services (OGIS) at 877-684-6448, or by emailing ogis@nara.gov. Alternatively, you may contact the FBI's FOIA Public Liaison by emailing foipaquestions@ic.fbi.gov. If you submit your dispute resolution correspondence by email, the subject heading should dearly state "Dispute Resolution Services." Please also cite the FOIPA Request Number assigned to your request so that it may be easily identified.

For questions on how to reasonably describe your request, please email us at foipaquestions@ic.fbi.gov. You may also visit www.fbi.gov and select "Services," "Records Management," and "Freedom of Information/Privacy Act" for additional guidance.

Enclosed for your information is a copy of the FBI Fact Sheet and a copy of the Explanation of Exemptions.

Sincerely,

David M. Hardy
Section Chief,
Record/Information
Dissemination Section
Records Management Division

Enclosure(s)

ev.

Notes

Preface

1. Richard Gid Powers, *G-Men: The FBI in American Popular Culture* (Carbondale: Southern Illinois University Press, 1983), 127. Powers was the first to explode the myth of the FBI as the top crime fighters who always got their man. See also Matthew Cecil, *Branding Hoover's FBI: How the Boss's PR Men Sold the Bureau to America* (Lawrence: University Press of Kansas, 2016), for a most comprehensive study of the packaging and marketing of Hoover and the FBI over the years.

2. Rhodri Jeffreys-Jones, *The FBI: A History* (New Haven: Yale University Press, 2007), 81-82, which describes these antics.

3. A couple of recent histories of the agency are Athan Theoharis (who has long been writing about the FBI), *The FBI and American Democracy: A Brief Critical History* (Lawrence: University Press of Kansas, 2004); and Jeffreys-Jones, *The FBI*, which traces its growth up to 2001.

4. See David J. Rothkopf, *National Insecurity: American Leadership in an Age of Fear* (New York: Public Affairs, 2014), 307-38, for a discussion of how greatly the abuse and illegal deeds by presidents and directors of intelligence agencies have increased as an official response to the specter of "terrorism."

5. After Hoover's death, the term of office for the FBI director was set at ten years

by Congress in 1973, "unless special exceptions are sought by the President and Congress." Robert S. Mueller, appointed on September 4, 2001, served twelve years, as requested by President B. Obama on May 12, 2011; Congress extended his term two more years. He served until September 4, 2013.

6. See Betty Medsger, *The Burglary: The Discovery of J. Edgar Hoover's Secret FBI* (New York: Vintage Books, 2014), for the story of the brave activists who stole FBI files and made them public via major daily newspapers.

7. Jeffreys-Jones, *The FBI*, 123–24.

8. William C. Sullivan, with Bill Brown, *The Bureau: My Thirty Years in Hoover's FBI* (New York: W.W. Norton & Co., 1979), 128.

9. I thank Ernesto Vigil, author of *The Crusade for Justice: Chicano Militancy and the Government's War on Dissent* (Madison: University of Wisconsin Press, 1999), for giving me a copy of documents he obtained from sources that reveal and confirm a massive national surveillance project by the FBI aimed at persons of Mexican ancestry titled Mexican American Militancy (MAM). It is very probable that MAM is yet another COINTELPRO.

10. See Nelson Blackstock, *COINTELPRO: The FBI's Secret War on Political Freedom* (New York: Pathfinder Press, 1988), 9. See also *The COINTELPRO Papers: Documents from the FBI's Secret Wars against Dissent in the United States*, by Ward Churchill and Jim Vander Wall (Boston: South End Press); both 1st and 2nd editions have in the fourth chapter an analysis of the Puerto Rican COINTELPRO. Theoharis, *The FBI and American Democracy*, 120–22, lists the COINTELPRO operations by year of inception but ignores and leaves out the Puerto Rican one, as does Rhodri Jeffreys-Jones. According to both Athan Theoharis and Rhodri Jeffreys-Jones, the subsequent COINTELPRO aimed at the Socialist Workers Party was instituted in October 1961; the White Hate program was begun on September 2, 1964; the Black Nationalist Hate program was begun in August 1967; and the last one, allegedly, on the New Left was started in October 1968. The Black Nationalist Hate COINTELPRO launched another secret program titled Racial Matters. This code name was to seek out and evaluate Communist influence in racial matters (Theoharis, *The FBI and American Democracy*, 123). James Kirkpatrick Davis, *Spying on America: The FBI's Domestic Counterintelligence Program* (Westport, CT: Praeger, 1992) omits any mention of a Puerto Rican COINTELPRO. Churchill and Vander Wall make a case in their book that a COINTELPRO-AIM also was instituted in the 1970s in response to growing Native American militancy. Lastly, I had released to me FBI documents titled Border Coverage Program or BOCOV. The content of the BOCOV documents clearly indicate the aim was to prevent collaboration,

communication, and contact between Chicano groups in the Southwest borderlands with Mexicans on the other side of the border. I believe BOCOV was another COINTELPRO derived from the 1956 one aimed at disruption and destruction of Communists and their sympathizers. According to Ernie Vigil, who obtained FBI documents titled "Mexican American Militancy," he suspects this was the Chicano COINTELPRO; all the tactical elements are described in the content of such documents. According to Jeffreys-Jones, during the Nixon years, Hoover and the Internal Revenue Service collaborated to harass the target with audits.

11. See "Documents Show FBI Harassed Puerto Rican Separatist Parties," *New York Times*, November 22, 1977, 26. See also William Lichtenstein and David Wimhurst, "Red Alert in Puerto Rico," *The Nation*, June 3, 1979, 780-81.

12. See Ignacio Garcia, ed., "Chicanos and Mexicanos under Surveillance, 1940-1980," Renato Rosaldo Lecture Series Monograph (Tucson: Mexican American Studies and Research Center, University of Arizona, 1986).

13. See Churchill and Vander Wall, *COINTELPRO Papers*, 2nd ed., 107-12.

14. See Churchill and Vander Wall, *COINTELPRO Papers*, 2nd ed., 108, for copy of the FBI memorandum from G. C. Moore to W. C. Sullivan, dated February 29, 1968, that refers to the first letter, dated August 25, 1967 (p.109), that instituted the first COINTELPRO against black nationalists. See also the Airtel from the Director, FBI (100-448006-17) to SAC, Albany dated March 4, 1968 (pp.108-11), which lists the field offices that received the memo expanding the number from twenty-three to forty-one, the first set of instructions on implementation, the goals, and the targets. This first year resulted in the recruitment of over four thousand informants from the black communities that used to be called TOPLEV, for Top Level Black Community Leadership Program, to a new name, Ghetto Informant Program, aka Ghetto Listening Post, at bottom of page 110, not narrative in the Airtel.

15. I began requesting files on Chavez and the United Farm Workers in the early 1980s. Files obtained are no exact match to those posted on the Web by the FBI under his name; many documents are the same. An interesting stamp on those early 1980s documents reads "DECLASSIFIED 1980," yet it was not until the mid-1990s that the file documents the FBI wanted to release were made public on their website.

16. Richard Steven Street, "The FBI's Secret File on Cesar Chavez," *Southern California Quarterly* 78, no. 4 (Winter 1996): 347-84.

17. Ibid., 348-49.

18. "The Rise and Fall of the United Farm Workers," in *Labor Notes*, May 12, 2010, a review of Miriam Pawel's *The Union of Their Dreams*. See www.labornotes.org/blogs/2010/05/rise-and-fall-united-farm-workers.

19. See, for example, the work of Ernesto Vigil on the Crusade for Justice, and earlier Mauricio Mazon monograph on the zoot-suiters and military and police riots of the 1940s in Southern California.

20. See https://vault.fbi.gov and utilize the A-Z index link to find Cesar Chavez. The file is organized into seventeen packets of varying page lengths and is not chronological. More importantly, the pagination scheme is varied. The packets are numbered electronically on the cover page when you click on any packet, and numbered in pencil on the actual pages, plus the cover page to each packet has yet another number of pages. None of the pages match the actual pieces of paper downloaded and printed out. For this research, I have printed all pages from all packets and reorganized them chronologically by date, and will reference the date of the document rather than a page, with one exception. When a document is two or more pages in length, I will use the date plus the page number it should be if I were to number the pages of that document. And when a document contains addendums such as a newspaper clipping or other non-FBI generated document, I will describe it as best I can and note it is an attachment to the original document. The complete FBI file used for this manuscript will be placed on archival deposit at the Nattie Lee Benson Library of the University of Texas in Austin under my name.

21. A quick online search under his name will provide information on him, his family, and the union he founded, as well as links to other Chavez entities now in existence, such as his foundation and national monument. In the bibliography of this work are found the major publications utilized to prepare a lengthy timeline of his life, events, activities, and activities of others, namely, the FBI and other oppositional actors.

22. For a basic introduction to the history of Mexican people in the United States, I relied on two sources above all: The early work of Wayne Moquin and Charles Van Doren in their 1971 book, *A Documentary History of the Mexican Americans* (New York: Praeger), particularly parts 4 and 5 on the periods of 1911 to 1939 and 1940 to 1970, respectively. This book contains readings by prominent scholars and journalists of the era. And Rodolfo Acuña's first edition of *Occupied America: The Chicano Struggle toward Liberation* (Canfield Press, 1972), in which he describes with excellent reference material the history of labor organizing by Mexicans and Chicanos in the United States from the late 1880s to Cesar E. Chavez's early efforts. *Occupied America* is now

in its 8th edition, 2014. The story of the Filipino farm workers that immensely helped make Chavez and the farm worker union a success is not ignored any more than the invaluable early and sustained contribution by Dolores Huerta as Chavez's coleader. This work is focused on Chavez and his FBI file. For a personal history of one of the early Filipino leaders that joined Chavez in making a union, see Craig Scharlin and Lilia V. Villanueva's 2000 book, *Philip Vera Cruz: A Personal History of Filipino Immigrants and the Farmworkers Movement* (Seattle: University of Washington Press). Dick Meister and Anne Loftis have a more comprehensive work on the making of a farm worker union in the United States, beginning with Filipino labor since the Anglo colonization of the Philippines and their migration to Hawaii, then the Pacific Northwest, to the Chavez story in *A Long Time Coming* (New York: Macmillan, 1977). There is no major work on Dolores Huerta, only scattered articles in popular magazines and frequent mention in the Chavez literature.

23. I spent parts of the summers of 2016 and 2017 at the Julian Samora Research Institute at Michigan State University, writing letters of inquiry and draft proposals to foundations and funders with some stated interest in the subject. Not one letter or draft from the summer of 2016 was accepted for further review. The summer 2017 letters are awaiting response.

24. See Kenneth O'Reilly's two books on this subject: *Racial Matters: The FBI's Secret Files on Black America, 1960–1972* (New York: Free Press, 1989), and *Black Americans: The FBI Files* (New York: Carroll & Graf, 1994), edited by David Gallen, which includes files on Marcus Garvey from the 1920s and Paul Robeson from the 1930s, among others more contemporary.

25. See Jan Jarboe Russell, *The Train to Crystal City: FDR's Secret Prisoner Exchange Program and America's Only Family Internment Camp during World War II* (New York: Scribner, 2015), on the lives of such detainees in an internment camp from 1942 to 1948. Crystal City, Texas, is my hometown, and that detention camp when closed became the segregated middle school for Mexican-ancestry students like me.

26. During this case history, the Office of Naval Intelligence withheld a report finding no evidence that Japanese Americans were spies or sending intelligence to Japanese submarines. It took thirty years for this information to be disclosed and for Fred Koramatsu's conviction to be voided. See Lawrence B. Lindsey, *Conspiracies of the Ruling Class: How to Break Their Grip Forever* (New York: Simon and Schuster, 2016), 83.

27. This legislation dating to 1996 was basically the only law on the books for investigators and prosecutors to respond to the Oklahoma City Federal

Courthouse (1995) and World Trade Center (1993) bombings that allowed for suspension of habeas corpus while conducting investigations—that is, holding suspects indefinitely for interrogation without legal interference by defense attorneys, posting bail, and presentation of evidence, even circumstantial. It also was used to hold suspected "terrorists," mainly persons of Arab descent or profile.

28. Davis, *Spying on America*, 171-72, 175, states that FBI director Clarence Kelly on February 2, 1975, informed the attorney general of the United States, Edward Levy, that he had discovered five more COINTELPROs in operation not previously disclosed, and released 52,000 pages on twelve COINTELPROs on November 21, 1977.

29. The first direct legislative response to the 9/11 attack was the Patriot Act, pushed by President George W. Bush in October 2001 and later expanded by President Obama in May 2011 and renamed the USA Freedom Act in June 2015. The Entry-Exit Registration System was first implemented by President Bush in 2002, specifically targeting those profiled and suspected of being Muslim. President Obama suspended implementation of this law on December 22, 2016. Oddly, shortly after the U.S. created the Border Patrol and the Immigration and Naturalization Service, Congress passed the Alien Registration Act of 1920, which requires to this day the annual registration of all persons who hold a valid Resident Alien card.

30. See Jack Gillum, Eileen Sullivan, and Eric Tucker, "FBI is Operating Fleet of Spy Planes over U.S.," *Fort Worth Star-Telegram*, June 3, 2015, 1A, 19A. The article also mentions that a 2010 federal budget document revealed an allocation for 115 airplanes.

31. Betty Medsger, *The Burglary: The Discovery of J. Edgar Hoover's Secret FBI* (New York: Alfred A. Knopf, 2014) is a detailed account of that break-in and removal of FBI files, which revealed that partisan political ends had been the main business of the FBI, not crime-fighting. For the story on Ellsberg, see *The Pentagon Papers* by George C. Herring (New York: McGraw-Hill, 1993); and Ellsberg's audiobook, *Secrets: A Memoir of Vietnam and the Pentagon Papers* (HighBridge, 2004).

32. He claims to have coined the word. See rogerclarke.com.

33. On Snowden from the taking of NSA files to obtaining exile in Moscow, see Luke Harding, *The Snowden Files: The Inside Story of the World's Most Wanted Man* (New York: Vintage Books, 2014). Chelsea Elizabeth Manning is serving a 35 year sentence for violating the Espionage Act by copying and releasing

what became known as the Iraq War Logs, just over 400,000 documents from the U.S. State Department, military reports, and information on detainees at Guantanamo. She will be eligible for parole in 2020.

34. Millions of FBI records have been destroyed. The FBI requested the National Archives and Records Service (NARS) to destroy records from 1910 to 1938. NARS did not consult Congress or the president, or examine the records to ascertain whether they contained information of historical or legal research value, or any other value, and destroyed the records. Again in 1945 and 1946 the FBI requested NARS to authorize destruction of FBI field office records and was approved without any inspection of these documents. In May 1975 the FBI requested authorization to destroy more field office records, index cards, and materials on closed cases. The three types of "closed cases" are those where investigation led to no prosecution; investigations where the perpetrators could not be found; and investigations where the charge was unfounded, "not within the jurisdiction of the FBI," or preliminary inquiries. This latter category is crucial in the Chavez investigation because field office files on preliminary inquiries were the only files kept, not duplicated in the D.C. office of the FBI, and a preliminary inquiry was typically a domestic-security intelligence file. These files are lost forever and the extent of FBI field-office work on preliminary inquiries will never be known. See Ann Mari Buitrago and Leon Andrew Immerman, *Are You Now or Have You Ever Been in the FBI Files? How to Secure and Interpret Your FBI Files* (New York: Grove Press, 1981), 35–43, for a history of this destruction of records and a federal case that enjoined the FBI from further destruction up to 1981, when this book was published.

35. John Burma, *Spanish-Speaking Groups in the United States* (Durham, NC: Duke University Press, 1954), gleaned from chapters 3 and 4.

36. Steve Rosswurm, *The FBI and the Catholic Church, 1935–1962* (Amherst: University of Massachusetts Press, 2009). The cover of this book features a photograph of Hoover receiving an honorary doctorate degree from the University of Notre Dame in 1942, to be found in the National Archives, photo no. 65-H-671-1.

37. Sam Kushner, *Long Road to Delano* (New York: International Publishers, 1975), 6–22.

38. See part 3, chapters 8 through 11 specifically, of Roger Burbach and Patricia Flynn, *Agribusiness in the Americas* (New York: Monthly Review Press, 1980), 140–219, for an exhaustive examination of the operations of this megacorporation in the U.S., Mexico, Pacific, and Guatemala. The appendix in this book, "Multinational Investments in Latin America," 253–82, lists the top sixty U.S.

corporations doing business in Latin America up to the 1980s.

39. Italians, fundamentally practicing Catholics, began arriving in California in the 1880s. They began as laborers for other European winemakers in California and quickly moved into becoming wine producers on the rich grape-producing lands taken from the Spanish and Mexicans just two decades earlier. See Simone Cinotto's *Soft Soil, Black Grapes: The Birth of Italian Winemaking in California* (New York: NYU Press 2012), for the history of three renowned Italian winemaking families in California: Gallo, Rossi, and Guasti. The oldest winery in the Americas, U.S. included, dates to 1597 and is still known as Casa Madero in Mexico. Franciscan missionaries introduced grapes in Spanish California beginning in 1650, and Junipero Serra established the first vineyard and winery in what is now San Diego, California, in 1769 until Charles II prohibited the making of wine in Mexico, except for religious purposes, to prevent competition with Spanish and other European wines. With independence in the 1820s, Mexican winemaking resumed; 90 percent of Mexican wine is still produced in the Baja California region across the border from San Diego, California.

40. See Steven W. Bender, *One Night in America: Robert Kennedy, Cesar Chavez, and the Dream of Dignity* (Boulder, CO: Paradigm Publishers, 2008) for a lengthy examination of Latino vote turnout in various elections, but with focus on the role Chavez played in California's electoral politics.

41. See Tom Chaffin, *Fatal Glory: Narciso Lopez and the First Clandestine U.S. War against Cuba* (Charlottesville: University Press of Virginia, 1996).

42. Joan M. Jensen, *Army Surveillance in America, 1775–1980* (New Haven, CT: Yale University Press, 1991), 49–108.

43. See www.strategypage.com/militaryforums/478-1312.aspx#startofcommands/. See also Juan Gonzalez, *Harvest of Empire: A History of Latinos in America* (New York: Penguin, 2000).

44. See a personal account by Clifford Alan Perkins of his experiences as the founding director of the Border Patrol based in Arizona and Texas, in *Border Patrol with the U.S. Immigration Service on the Mexican Boundary, 1910–1954* (El Paso: Texas Western Press, 1978).

45. Timothy J. Dunn, *The Militarization of the U.S.-Mexico Border, 1978–1992: Low-Intensity Conflict Doctrine Comes Home* (Austin: University of Texas Press, 1996); Joseph Nevins, *Operation Gatekeeper: The Rise of the "Illegal Alien" and the Making of the U.S.-Mexico Boundary* (New York: Routledge, 2002). And for the border wall, see Reece Jones, *Border Walls: Security and the War on Terror in the United*

States, India, and Israel (London: Zed Books, 2012).

46. Robert J. Rosenbaum, *Mexicano Resistance in the Southwest: The Sacred Right of Self-Preservation* (Austin: University of Texas Press, 1981), 4.

47. Ibid., xi.

48. "Mexican" as a racial or ethnic descriptor was born along with the independence from Spain of that territory in 1820. The new country opted for Mexico as their name and subsequently their nationality. The term *meshicano*, however, was in use by the reigning tribal clan at the time of the Spanish conquest of the same territory in the 1520s. They called themselves *meshicanos* (meh-shee-can-ohs) while the Spanish called them a similar name, *mejicanos*, inserting a "j" and later an "x" for the "shee" sound. The British and other Europeans called this tribal clan Aztecs. The language of the Aztecs, *meshicanos, mejicanos*, Mexicans was Nahuatl. Similarly, the language of the British was English, but rebels in the American colonies, while they continued with English, chose American, not British American, as their nationality. The question of race classification also has long roots, but for purposes here we will limit the explanatory narrative to classification schemes employed in the United States up to the twentieth century. The British colonists in the United States of America referred to themselves as Anglo-Saxons, claimed a white racial classification, and were Protestants until the 1680s when new Europeans also immigrated to the United States. In 1790 the Continental Congress of the United States of America passed its first racist law to circumscribe citizenship in the new country. The 1790 Naturalization Law recognized as citizens only those "free, white males" over the age of twenty-six years and with property. These first U.S. citizens did not perceive the Spanish or the Mexicans as a racial category; rather they saw these peoples as mixed bloods, hybrid races, and Catholics. The Spanish in the Iberian Peninsula, while they may have had Norman, Gallic, and Roman conquerors at one time, also had Islamic African Moors as conquerors from 711 to the early 1490s. Modern-day Spain was born with the expulsion and genocide directed by the Catholic kings against Jews and Islamists. The hybrid race of Spaniards conquered and intermarried with indigenous tribes of Mexico and bred modern-day Mexicans. The Anglos held to both a racial and ethnic classification as White Anglo-Saxon Protestants (WASPs) until the late 1970s. In May 1977 the Office of Management and Budget issued Directive 15, which institutionalized the four racial categories of people in the United States as white, black, Asian Pacific Islander, and Native American; and one ethnic group, Hispanics. All hyphenated "Anglos," e.g., Polish Americans, Italian Americans, German Americans, Jewish

Americans, Greek Americans, along with all other European-based immigrant groups, became white, a broad, expansive racial umbrella. All progeny from the Spanish hybrids became Hispanics without any other national origin. When speaking Spanish, however, these Hispanics will resort to a nationality identifier to distinguish themselves from their designated broad, expansive ethnic umbrella. Moreover, the Hispanic ethnicity promotes division among the mass when as individuals they must choose a racial classification, e.g., white Hispanic (Costa Rica), Asian Hispanic (Filipino), Native American Hispanic (Chiricahua Apache), or Afro-Hispanic (Puerto Rican). For a typical biased account of immigrant groups in the U.S., see Carl Wittke, *We Who Built America*, 2nd ed. (Cleveland, OH: Case Reserve University, 1964). Among the last books utilizing a white ethnic framework opposing assimilation, see Michael Novak, *The Rise of the Unmeltable Ethnics* (New York: Macmillan, 1972), and opposing multiculturalism and diversity see Arthur M. Schlesinger Jr., *The Disuniting of America: Reflections on a Multicultural Society* (New York: W.W. Norton, 1991). I will use "Mexican" to refer to those from Mexico, and "Chicano" for U.S.-born Mexicans, and white and black for those racial categories employed in the U.S. since 1977.

49. See chapter 2, "American Intervention," in Joseph Smith, *The Spanish-American War: Conflict in the Caribbean and the Pacific, 1895–1902* (New York: Longman, 1994), 28–47, 28 nn. 1 and 28.

50. Arnoldo De León, *They Called Them Greasers: Anglo Attitudes toward Mexicans in Texas, 1821–1900* (Austin: University of Texas Press, 1983); and chapter 11, "Anglo-Saxons and Mexicans" in Reginald Horsman's *Race and Manifest Destiny: The Origins of American Racial Anglo-Saxonism* (Cambridge, MA: Harvard University Press, 1981).

51. See Guadalupe San Miguel, *Let All of Them Take Heed: Mexican Americans and the Campaign for Educational Equity in Texas, 1910–1981* (College Station: Texas A&M University Press, 2000).

52. Perez v. Sharp, 32 Cal. 2d 711, 198 P.2d 17 (Cal. 1948). Texas, among other states in the Southwest, never had miscegenation laws on the books.

53. Hernandez v. Texas, 347 US 475 (1954). See Michael A. Olivas, ed. *"Colored Men" and Hombres Aqui: Hernandez v. Texas and the Emergence of Mexican American Lawyering* (Houston: Arte Publico Press, 2008); and Ignacio M. Garcia, *White but Not Equal: Mexican Americans, Jury Discrimination, and the Supreme Court* (Tucson: University of Arizona Press, 2008), for fuller analyses of these cases and historical facts.

54. For David Cole's analysis of the recently passed House bill the USA Freedom Act, and its elements for increased utility of metadata, see *New York Review*, June 18, 2014, 16-17.

55. For a political history of this political party of the 1970s, see Armando Navarro's *La Raza Unida Party: A Chicano Challenge to the U.S. Two-Party Dictatorship* (Philadelphia: Temple University Press, 2000). See also the 2013 six-hour PBS documentary on Latino civil rights struggles, particularly the segment "Prejudice and Pride" for specific information on these four leaders, www.pbs.org/latino-americans; and the companion book by Ray Suarez, *Latino Americans: The 500-Year Legacy That Shaped a Nation* (New York: Celebra/Penguin Books, 2013).

56. See Representative Patsy T. Mink's article "The Cannikin Papers: A Case Study in Freedom of Information," in *Secrecy and Foreign Policy*, ed. Thomas M. Franck and Edward Weisband (New York: Oxford University Press, 1974), 114-31. The case style is *Mink et al. v. Environmental Protection Agency et al.*, 464 F.2d. 742 (D.C. Cir. 1971), 410 U.S. 73 (1973). While the case was ultimately lost, the president replaced the 1953 Executive Order (EO) on classification of documents with a new EO 11652 permitting a portion-by-portion classification of documents rather than denial in their entirety; and subsequent amendments to FOIA, such as including the Privacy Act, have made the process somewhat more transparent and accessible. Backlog of requests and time to response are as big an issue as denial. The destruction of records in 1977 also has closed the door to many documents from the past.

57. Requests to the Texas attorney general John Hill and later via Paul Rich, who was a deputy attorney general for Jim Mattox during his tenure, produced no results and denials that such files existed on Ramsey Muniz, the RUP, the Mexican American Youth Organization (MAYO), and me. Yet, Robert M. Utley, *Lone Star Lawmen: The Second Century of the Texas Rangers* (New York: Berkley Books, 2008), found access to records detailing the surveillance. See chapter titled "Latino Uprising" for the extent of surveillance on MAYO, the farm workers, and me by the DPS and Texas Rangers, with references to documents and sources now on deposit at the Texas State Archives. Texas Ranger H. Joaquin Jackson, now deceased, provided me a folder of documents on MAYO he had in his possession during a personal visit. See his and David Marion Wilkinson's book on his activities in Zavala County, Texas, during the 1969 school walkout and early years of the RUP electoral challenge to the local power structure: *One Ranger: A Memoir* (Austin: University of Texas Press, 2005), chapter 5, "The Reconquest of Aztlan: An Angel on My Ass, 1972."

58. For a personal account of a journalist's travails with FOIA requests, see William Vollmann, "Life as a Terrorist," *Harper's*, September 2013, 39–47.

59. I never was able to get reciprocity on documents obtained from Dolores Huerta, coleader of the UFW with Cesar E. Chavez, or Rodolfo "Corky" Gonzales and his heirs. I did collaborate with Ernesto B. Vigil and Richard Gonzales, former brother-in-law to Corky, and exchanged documents. See Vigil's *The Crusade for Justice: Chicano Militancy and the Government's War on Dissent* (Madison: University of Wisconsin Press, 1999). Reies Lopez Tijerina authorized me to obtain his FBI, New Mexico State Police, and U.S. Bureau of Prisons records, which I have, and I plan to follow up this work with a manuscript on him and these files.

60. Garcia, "Chicanos and Mexicanos under Surveillance, 1940–1980."

61. Mauricio Mazon, *The Zoot-Suit Riots: The Psychology of Symbolic Annihilation* (Austin: University of Texas Press, 1984). Another book by Mark A. Weitz, *The Sleepy Lagoon Murder Case: Race Discrimination and Mexican-American Rights* (Lawrence: University Press of Kansas, 2010), on the controversial 1942 case *People v. Zammora* [*sic*], 66 Cal. App. 2d 1966 (1944), completely ignored the FBI file on the Zoot Suit Riots, relying instead on court procedure and appellate process.

62. See *Perez v. Federal Bureau of Investigation*, 714 F. Supp. 1414 (W.D. Texas 1989). Lucius Bunton was the presiding judge.

63. See, for example, news articles such as that of J. Michael Kennedy and William Overend, "FBI Discriminated against Latino Agents, Judge Rules," *Los Angeles Times*, October 1, 1988; UPI article "Hispanic FBI Agents Describe Bias," *Deseret News*, August 19, 1988, and Brainmass, "Discrimination, Hispanic FBI agents, Rule: 5.1.4. Title VII," http://brainmass.com/law/business-law/91540. The 2012 statistic on Hispanic agents is found at http://www.politico.com/story/2015/02/fbi-black-hiring-115185.

64. Sari Horwitz, "As U.S. Pushes Police to Diversify, FBI Struggles to Get Minorities in the Door," *Washington Post*, March 12, 2015.

65. David Correia, *Properties of Violence: Law and Land Grant Struggle in Northern New Mexico* (Athens: University of Georgia Press, 2013), 128–31, 140–45, 150.

66. Under FOI/PA rules, anyone with proof of death can request the FBI file on any deceased person. These Chavez cohorts are still alive at this writing, but Antonio Orendain and the Filipino coleaders are not. The live ones have not given me notarized permission to request their FBI files. Orendain has passed and I have requested his file, but as of June 6, 2017, the FBI has refused

to expedite release of any document to me and will place the request in the normal queue. See letter with that date from David M. Hardy to me on FOIPA request no. 1375477-000.

Onomasticon

1. See other government sources, such as U.S., Congress, Senate, Select Committee to Study Government Operations with Respect to Intelligence Activities ("Church Committee"), *Final Report*, book 1, 1976, pp. 617-29; contains an extensive list of terms and acronyms, but books 2-6 of the Church Committee reports also have other terms and acronyms. The U.S. General Accounting Office, Comptroller General, published six reports during 1976 and 1979 that also have a glossary: *FBI Domestic Intelligence Operations—Their Purpose and Scope: Issues That Need to be Resolved*, 1976; *FBI Domestic Intelligence Operations: An Uncertain Future*, 1977; *FBI Taking Action to Comply Fully with the Privacy Act*, 1977; *Impact of the Freedom of Information and Privacy Acts on Law Enforcement Agencies*, 1978; *Timeliness and Completeness of FBI Responses to Requests under Freedom of Information and Privacy Acts Have Improved*, 1978; and *An Informed Public Assures That Federal Agencies Will Better Comply with Freedom of Information/Privacy Laws*, 1979. For books during this era that also have terms, acronyms, titles, names, and the like, e.g., glossary, see also Sanford J. Unger, *FBI* (New York: Little, Brown and Co., 1976); Tyrus G. Fain, ed., *The Intelligence Community: History, Organization, and Issues* (New York: R.R. Bowker Company, 1977), 967-79; and Ann Mari Buitrago and Leon Andrew Immerman, *Are You Now or Have You Ever Been in the FBI Files? How to Secure and Interpret Your Files* (New York: Grove Press, 1981), 160-215.

2. U.S. Department of Justice, FBI, FBI Records Management Division, *The Central Records System*, Washington, DC, 1978; and see also the *Federal Register*, vol. 44 (1979): 58981-86. Any changes in the classification system are reported annually by the DOJ/FBI in the *Federal Register*.

3. See Buitrago and Immerman, *Are You Now or Have You Ever Been*, 177-79, glossary, for listing as of publication date on form numbers.

4. Ibid., appendices D and E for addresses of 59 field offices in 50 states and Puerto Rico and Washington, DC, with phone numbers in use at that time; 12 Liaison Offices (Legats); map of Field Offices; and 477 Resident Agencies in the 50 states, Puerto Rico, Virgin Islands, and Guam. Each Resident Agency reports to its parent field office in that state or territory and not to FBI HQ in D.C.; pp. 97-98 for D, and pp. 100-101 for E.

Chapter 1. The Target and the Architects of Oppression

1. See Rodolfo Acuña, *Occupied America: The Chicano Struggle toward Liberation* (New York: Harper and Row, 1972). This book has become the classic history text in Chicano studies courses and details with ample references and citations this degradation by violence from a governing class of people against a governed and powerless minority. It is now in its 8th edition under a new title: *Occupied America: A History of Chicanos.*

2. See table 7.2 in Thomas D. Hall, *Social Change in the Southwest, 1350–1880* (Lawrence: University of Kansas Press, 1989), 46; and Oscar J. Martinez, "On the Size of the Chicano Population: New Estimates, 1850–1900," *Aztlan* 6 (Spring 1975): 50–56.

3. Dick Meister and Anne Loftis, *A Long Time Coming: The Struggle to Unionize America's Farm Workers* (New York: Macmillan, 1977), 5.

4. See recent scholarship on this horrible practice in the Southwest, comparable to what blacks faced in the South as well, by William D. Carrigan, *The Making of a Lynching Culture: Violence and Vigilantism in Central Texas, 1836–1916* (Chicago: University of Illinois Press, 2006); William D. Carrigan and Clive Webb, *Forgotten Dead: Mob Violence against Mexicans in the United States, 1848–1928* (New York: Oxford University Press, 2013); and Richard Delgado, "The Law of the Noose: A History of Latino Lynching," *Harvard Civil Rights–Civil Liberties Law Review* 44 (2009): 291–312.

5. Elton Miles, *More Tales of the Big Bend* (College Station: Texas A&M University Press, 1988), 158–65. See also Kirby Warnock's self-made and distributed documentary *Border Bandits,* which depicts the violence against Mexicans in South Texas.

6. While there is ample biographical information on Chavez, the most helpful and complete are two works: Jacques E. Levy, *Cesar Chavez: Autobiography of La Causa* (Minneapolis: University of Minnesota Press, 2007), and Susan Ferris and Ricardo Sandoval, *The Fight in the Fields: Cesar Chavez and the Farmworkers Movement,* ed. Diana Hembree (Harcourt Brace & Co., 1997). For this incident, see Levy, *Cesar Chavez,* 7.

7. See Levy, *Cesar Chavez,* 8–9; and Ferris and Sandoval, *The Fight in the Fields,* 11–27.

8. Jean Maddern Pitrone, *Chavez, Man of the Migrants: A Plea for Social Justice* (New York: Alba House, 1972), 18.

9. John H. Burma, *Spanish Speaking Groups in the United States* (Durham, NC: Duke University Press, 1954), 72–81.

10. The use of the short-handled hoe requires the worker to be bent over for

hours on end, if not the entire day, while spacing or weeding crops to prevent possible harm to other plants—backbreaking work. This practice, as opposed to using a long-handled hoe for the same work, is to prevent the accidental cutting of good plants due to the inaccuracy inherent in a longer implement. *El cortito* was outlawed in California and subsequently in many states because of the injuries to the spine and pelvis. See Douglas L. Murray, "The Abolition of El Cortito, the Short-Handled Hoe: A Case Study in Social Conflict and State Policy in California Agriculture," *Social Problems* 30, no. 1 (1982): 26-39.

11. Ronald B. Taylor, *Chavez and the Farm Workers* (Boston: Beacon Press, 1975), 43-44.

12. Meister and Loftis, *A Long Time Coming*, 27-39.

13. See Devra Anne Weber's article "The Organizing of Mexicano Agricultural Workers: Imperial Valley and Los Angeles, 1928-34: An Oral History Approach," *Aztlan-Chicano Journal of the Social Sciences and the Arts* 3, no. 2 (1973): 307-50, for more information on agricultural-labor organizing and unionization in that area of Southern and Central California.

14. Meister and Loftis, *A Long Time Coming*, 71-86, for an account of Ernesto Galarza's efforts. See Galarza's own books on the subject of *braceros* and farm workers in California: *Merchants of Labor: The Mexican Bracero Story* (Charlotte, NC: McNally and Loftin, 1964); and *Spiders in the House and Workers in the Field* (Notre Dame, IN: University of Notre Dame Press, 1970). For a new look at *braceros* in a globalized world, see Deborah Cohen, *Braceros: Migrant Citizens and Transnational Subjects in the Postwar United States and Mexico* (Chapel Hill: University of North Carolina Press, 2011).

15. Levy, *Cesar Chavez*, 84-85.

16. Ibid.; and Ferris and Sandoval, *The Fight in the Fields*, 33. This incident is included in the 2014 PBS documentary *Latino Americans*.

17. For a female view of being a migrant farm worker, see Fran Leeper Buss, ed., *Forged under the Sun/Forjada bajo el sol: The Life of Maria Elena Lucas* (Ann Arbor: University of Michigan Press, 1993).

18. Peter Matthiessen used that name as part of the title to his book on Cesar Chavez, among the first publications to focus on Chavez and his organizing of farm workers. See *Sal Si Puedes: Cesar Chavez and the New American Revolution* (New York: Dell Publishing Co., 1969).

19. Basically, 10 percent of a worker's wage was withheld by the U.S. government between 1942 and 1949, and not paid out until litigation commenced in the last two decades. In states with an income tax during these years, they also

deducted these dollars and have not paid out. States have not been sued, yet. See "Braceros: History and Compensation," *Rural Migration News* 12, no. 2 (April 2005); and for a general review of treatment of labor, including *braceros*, see Philip Martin, *Promises Unfulfilled: Unions, Immigration, and Farm Workers* (Ithaca, NY: Cornell University Press, 2003).

20. See Julian Samora, *Los Mojados: The Wetback Story* (Notre Dame, IN: University of Notre Dame Press, 1971); and a subsequent work by Juan Ramon Garcia, *Operation Wetback: The Mass Deportation of Mexican Undocumented Workers in 1954* (Westport, CT: Greenwood Press, 1980).

21. Frank Bardacke, *Trampling Out the Vintage: Cesar Chavez and the Two Souls of the United Farm Workers*, chap. 24, "The Wet Line" (New York: Verso, 2012), 488–506.

22. Levy, *Cesar Chavez*, 25–27.

23. Bardacke, *Trampling Out the Vintage*, 57–66.

24. Marco G. Prouty, *Cesar Chavez, the Catholic Bishops, and the Farm Workers' Struggle for Social Justice* (Tucson: University of Arizona Press, 2006), 12–13.

25. See Industrial Areas Foundation's report *IAF: 50 Years Organizing for Change* (Franklin Square, NY: IAF, 1990) for that history of the Community Service Organization and the other organizations that developed later into the 1990s.

26. Prouty, *Cesar Chavez*, 26.

27. Craig Scharlin and Lilia V. Villanueva, *Philip Vera Cruz: A Personal History of Filipino Immigrants and the Farmworkers Movement*, 3rd ed. (Seattle: University of Washington Press, 2000), 33–34, 48.

28. Bardacke, *Trampling Out the Vintage*, 8.

29. See Glenn Anthony May, *Sonny Montes and Mexican American Activism in Oregon* (Corvallis: Oregon State University Press, 2011) for the story of the Colegio Cesar Chavez in Oregon and the role Chavez played in keeping this institution operating and from defaulting.

30. Miriam Pawel, *The Crusades of Cesar Chavez: A Biography* (New York: Bloomsbury, 2014), 380–82.

31. Some records on the organizing and founding of the Texas Farm Workers Union by Orendain after he resigned from Chavez's UFW are found at the Nettie Lee Benson Latin American Collection, University of Texas, Austin, under the name TFW Union Collection, 1977–1980.

32. Scharlin and Villanueva, *Philip Vera Cruz*, 124–37.

33. Ibid., chap. 8, "Some Were More Equal Than Others," for a review of the program's implementation at La Paz (156–91). See also Bardacke, *Trampling*

Out the Vintage, chap. 26, "The Game," for a deeper history of relations between Chavez and Chuck Dederich, Synanon's founder and leader "dating to mid-sixties" (542). Dederich would send a car for Chavez to travel to his center in Badger, some hundred miles from La Paz (542). As a result of this experience, Chavez modeled his community at La Paz after Synanon's hierarchical and authoritarian structure (547).

34. Matt Garcia has a short commentary on the impact of the boycotts, based on a *Los Angeles Times* article, *From the Jaws of Victory: The Triumph and Tragedy of Cesar Chavez and the Farm Worker Movement* (Berkeley: University of California Press, 2012), 283-84.

35. Pawel in *Crusades* details this course of action (448-54). See the various departments of the foundation and its leadership at www.chavezfoundation. org.

36. Simone Cinotto, *Soft Soil, Black Grapes: The Birth of Italian Winemaking in California* (New York: NYU Press, 2012), 178-81.

37. 816 P.2d 919 (Ariz. App. 1991).

38. *Rural Migration News* 2, no. 2 (April 1996).

39. Anthony Summers in *Official and Confidential: The Secret Life of J. Edgar Hoover* (New York: G.P. Putnam's Sons, 1993), 421.

40. Athan Theoharis in *From the Secret Files of J. Edgar Hoover* (Chicago: Ivan R. Dee, 1992) produces documents that reveal Hoover maintained perhaps as many as six secret files, many destroyed, in his office, the FBI basement, Clyde Tolson's office, Louis Nichols's office, Helen Gandy's office, and a floating file of "Do Not File" files between him and Gandy, sometimes Tolson. Theoharis discusses five of these file categories on pp. 3-11. Anthony Summers in *Official and Confidential* claims Hoover had no files at all in his office (425).

41. See Summers, *Official and Confidential,* 12, 254-55.

42. Richard Hack, *Puppetmaster: The Secret Life of J. Edgar Hoover* (Beverly Hills, CA: New Millennium Press, 2004), 272-75.

43. Curt Gentry, *J. Edgar Hoover: The Man and the Secrets* (New York: W.W. Norton & Co., 1991), 159, 179-80, 192, 240, and 531.

44. Theoharis, *From the Secret Files of J. Edgar Hoover,* 330-31, 346-56.

45. Richard Gid Powers, *Secrecy and Power: The Life of J. Edgar Hoover* (New York: Free Press, 1987), 169.

46. See the first introductory pages without numbers in Darwin Porter, *J. Edgar Hoover and Clyde Tolson: Investigating the Sexual Secrets of America's Most Famous*

Men and Women (New York: Blood Moon Productions, Ltd., 2012).

47. Marc Aronson, *Master of Deceit: J. Edgar Hoover and America in the Age of Lies* (Somerville, MA: Candlewick Press, 2012), 37–47.

48. Ibid., 419. Mark Felt and John O'Connor, *A G-Man's Life: The FBI, Being "Deep Throat," and the Struggle for Honor in Washington* (New York: PublicAffairs, 2006), 150.

49. The FBI file on Clyde Anderson Tolson is no. 67-9524; there are eleven parts to the declassified file, available at the https://vault.fbi.gov website. For more on the Hoover-Tolson relationship, see Powers, *Secrecy and Power*, 169–73. Tolson was one of Hoover's first hires, dating to 1923. Tolson was recommended to Hoover by the Republican National Committee member Dr. E. B. Clements from Missouri. In a Clements letter to Hoover after the Tolson nomination was accepted is prophetic language: "Think he will make you a good man." Tolson accepted appointment as special agent on March 16, 1928, and was appointed on April 2 that year. At the time, Tolson was a single man, age twenty-seven, from Iowa, but had been in Washington, DC, the previous nine years. He passed the bar exam in the District of Columbia and was admitted into the practice of law the second week in March 1928. Tolson continued with Hoover for decades and became the number two man within the bureaucracy, Assistant Director of the FBI, in fewer than 28 months of first hire. He had a stroke in 1964 and retired at Hoover's request upon reaching age seventy, but was rehired under a special program until 1974. He died April 14, 1975.

50. Hack, *Puppetmaster*, 19–58. Summers, in *Official and Confidential*, 424, interviewed neighbors who insist they saw at dawn men removing a big quilt with some heavy object they assumed was a body. He suggests Hoover may have been poisoned and discusses several attempted break-ins at the Hoover residence, 414–16.

51. Hack, *Puppetmaster*, 5 and 329–31.

52. John Ehrlichman, *Witness to Power: The Nixon Years* (New York: Simon & Schuster, 1982), 167–68.

53. David K. Johnson totally refutes these allegations made by Summers in his work *The Lavender Scare: The Cold War Persecution of Gays and Lesbians in the Federal Government* (Chicago: University of Chicago Press, 2004), 11–12. More pointedly, Douglas M. Charles in his book *Hoover's War on Gays: Exposing the FBI's "Sex Deviates" Program* (Lawrence: University Press of Kansas, 2015), 3, simply poses the question in the opening chapter, "Does It Matter?"

54. Summers, *Official and Confidential*, 9–34. See Ann Mari Buitrago and Leon

Andrew Immerman, *Are You Now or Have You Ever Been in the FBI Files? How to Secure and Interpret Your FBI Files* (New York: Grove Press, 1981), 195, for explanation of "O&C" or "Official and Confidential." According to these authors, the words or letters are not a national security classification authorized by executive order. These were other files kept by Hoover in his or Ms. Gandy's office or the basement of the DOJ building. These O&C files and the "Personal and Confidential" files contained incriminating information on many prominent and influential persons, public figures, and private citizens. Kenneth Ackerman, in *Young J. Edgar: Hoover and the Red Scare, 1919–1920* (Washington, DC: Viral History Press, 2011), 407, adds that this other set of separate files were kept by Hoover in his desk and marked "Personal and Confidential."

55. Hack, *Puppetmaster*, 33.

56. Gentry, *J. Edgar Hoover*, 64-65.

57. Ibid.

58. Hack, *Puppetmaster*, 34-42.

59. See Stanley Cohen, *A. Mitchell Palmer: Politician* (New York: Columbia University Press, 1963), 217-18.

60. See Barbara Tuchman, *The Zimmermann Telegram* (London: Constable and Co., 1959) for a history of this teletype message. In short, the telegrams from the German foreign secretary to their ambassador in Washington, DC, contained war plans and specific instructions to relay to his counterpart from Mexico: Germany offered to return the Southwest to Mexico if they joined forces. According to Tuchman at p. 7, the coded words in exchange for Mexico's assistance with the German war effort were "To regain by conquest her lost territory in Texas, Arizona, and New Mexico."

61. Ackerman, *Young J. Edgar*, 49, 65, 217, 321.

62. Gentry, *J. Edgar Hoover*, 265n.

63. Immigration to the U.S. from Europe was running at 87 percent of all immigrants prior to World War I and 64 percent for the five years after the war, according to Roger Daniels, *Guarding the Golden Door: America's Immigration Policy and Immigrants since 1882* (New York: Hill and Wang Publishers, 2004), 50. More importantly, a racial quota was made into policy with passage of the Immigration Act of 1924. Vincent N. Perrillo's 8th edition of *Strangers to These Shores* (Boston: Pearson Education, 2006), an introductory college text for race and ethnic relations courses, has on the front inside cover a printed chart that indicates that immigrants during 1900 to 1910 numbered 8.8 million, and 5.7

million by 1920. These 14.5 million newcomers were the object of the "Palmer Raids" and became Hoover's assigned targets for identification, surveillance, and apprehension as potential subversives and radicals.

64. Ackerman, *Young J. Edgar*, 6-7.

65. Gentry, *J. Edgar Hoover*, 101, 6-7, and Hack, *Puppetmaster*, 407, for more names.

66. Frank Donner, *The Age of Surveillance*, 49.

67. For history of the U.S. Communist Party, see early work of Theodore Draper, *The Roots of American Communism* (Piscataway, NJ: Transaction Publishers, 2003); and Philip J. Jaffe, *Rise and Fall of American Communism*. In summary of federal court cases, prosecution of Communists was made possible by the Smith Act of 1940 and strengthened in 1954 with passage of the Communist Control Act (see 50 US Code 841), but SCOTUS intervened in a series of cases that in essence stopped the juridical hunt for Communists and those that espouse communistic goals. The first SCOTUS case is *Dennis v. United States*, 341 US 494 (1951), which upheld convictions of U.S. Communists for "advocating the violent overthrow of the U.S. government." Then came SCOTUS case *Yates v. United States*, 354 US 298 (1951), which weakened *Dennis* in holding that "concrete steps toward" the advocacy of overthrow was necessary and central to any prosecution. The Smith and Communist Control Acts were virtually unenforceable thereafter. The last SCOTUS case with that type of effect was *Communist Party v. Catherwood*, 367 US 389 (1961), which prohibited a state from denying federal benefits to a member of the Communist Party USA. In the electoral arena, the CPUSA never posed a serious challenge in any presidential election. The CPUSA had the lowest national turnout of 1,077 votes for its presidential ticket in 1968 and the highest turnout of 0.26 percent in the 1932 presidential election. One can only imagine the early glimpse of "congressional gridlock and polarization" if the U.S. electorate had ever placed a Communist to head the executive branch, federal or state. The historic claims made by many influential persons that Communism is a threat to U.S. national security is not supported by reality and is more a fiction utilized for political purposes and red-baiting.

68. Draper, *Roots of American Communism*, 50-51.

69. Ibid., 53-55.

70. Joseph A. Stout Jr., *Spies, Politics, and Power: El Departamento Confidencial en Mexico, 1922-1946* (Fort Worth, TX: TCU Press, 2012), 10.

71. See Arnold J. Meltsner's edited volume *Politics and the Oval Office* (San Francisco: Institute for Contemporary Studies, 1981), 3-9, for a collection

of readings on this dynamic and tension between presidents and staff, among others, and in particular the opening memo by the editor directed to President Reagan on how to lead.

72. Barry Rubin, *Secrets of State: The State Department and the Struggle over U.S. Foreign Policy* (New York: Oxford University Press, 1985).

73. David Priess, *The President's Book of Secrets: The Untold Story of Intelligence Briefings to America's Presidents from Kennedy to Obama* (New York: Public Affairs, 2016), surveys this phenomenon through various presidencies.

74. Ibid., 55.

75. See posting by Josh Dawsey and Nancy Cook, "Trump Assembles a Shadow Cabinet," *Politico*, January 24, 2017.

76. For a review of actual documents filed by Service, see the edited volume by Joseph W. Esherick, *Lost Chance in China: The World War II Dispatches of John S. Service* (New York: Random House, 1974). SCOTUS case is *Service v. Dulles*, 354 US 363 (1957).

77. James Cross Giblin, *The Rise and Fall of Senator Joe McCarthy* (Boston: Clarion Books, 2009); see pp. 164–65 for that anecdote.

78. See John Barron, *Operation Solo* (Washington, DC: Regnery Publishing, 2014), and Daniel Leab, *I Was a Communist for the FBI* (University Park: Penn State University Press, 2000) for biographies of the most famous of U.S. spies on the Communist Party in the Soviet Union and the United States. Moishe Chilovsky, aka Morris Childs, born in Kiev, Ukraine, on June 10, 1902, was first recruited to spy for the Soviets in the U.S. in 1929; he turned double agent in 1952 and became "Solo" until 1982 when he retired. His identity and existence were kept secret by Hoover from the CIA, but more importantly from the president and secretary of state until 1975. The Leab book is on Matt Cvetic, also a U.S. spy on the CPUSA and Russia since 1943, but not as successful as Childs.

79. See Robert Welch, *The Blue Book of the John Birch Society*, first self-published in 1959. According to this source written by the founder, the John Birch Society was organized on December 9, 1958, in Indianapolis by Welch and at least ten others. A partial list of those in attendance is found in Milton A. Waldor, *The John Birch Society: Peddlers of Fear* (Newark, NJ: Lynnross Publishing, 1966), 16. The list includes Fred C. Koch, president of the Rock Island Oil and Refining Company of Wichita, father of the current right-wing political funders and philanthropists Charles and David Koch, and William J. Grede, president of Grede Foundries, Inc. of Milwaukee and past president of the National

Association of Manufacturers. All were white men of means and influence. See also Benjamin R. Epstein and Arnold Forster, *Report on the John Birch Society, 1966* (New York: Random House, 1966) for a critical analysis of the organization written from the perspective of a targeted group by the anti-Semitic "Birchers."

80. See Summers, *Official and Confidential*, 11-12; Gentry, *J. Edgar Hoover*, 691, 699-703; and Hack, *Puppetmaster*, 394.

81. Ronald Kessler, *The Secrets of the FBI* (New York: Broadway Paperbacks, 2012), chap. 4, "Secret Files," 37-45.

82. He is currently the senior advisor to the Open Society Foundations with his office in Washington, DC. See https://www.opensocietyfoundations.org for information on staff.

83. Morton H. Halperin, Jerry J. Berman, Robert L. Borosage, and Christine M. Marwick, *The Lawless State: The Crimes of the U.S. Intelligence Agencies* (New York: Penguin Books, 1976), 64.

84. Porter, *J. Edgar Hoover*, 225.

85. See Morton H. Halperin et al., *The Lawless State*, which surveys four of the nineteen intelligence agencies in operation within the U.S.: FBI, IRS, NSA, and CIA. In the introduction (1-12), they provide the code names for the domestic intelligence programs in place by agency.

86. Porter, *J. Edgar Hoover*, 227-30.

87. Ibid., 247.

88. Nixon's FBI file no. is 67-102459 and is available at the Vault website, https://vault.fbi.gov.

89. Porter, *J. Edgar Hoover*, 511.

90. See his book by that title, David K. Johnson, *The Lavender Scare: The Cold War Persecution of Gays and Lesbians in the Federal Government* (Chicago: University of Chicago Press, 2004).

91. Charles, *Hoover's War on Gays*, 32. A companion file, 105-12198, was opened for Sex Perverts in Government Service in 1942. Later, one, termed Obscene File, for pornography.

92. Porter, *J. Edgar Hoover*, 230 on monitoring "young men on their way to the top," and 511-13 on Bebe and the Florida White House. *Bebe* is Spanish for baby.

93. See chap. 10, "Hoover" (156-68), for these specific incidents and attributed quotes. Ehrlichman also confirms that Gray was too late in recovering the secret files Hoover maintained; see 167-68.

94. Ehrlichman, *Witness to Power*, 156–68.

95. He and Haldeman were fired, indicted, convicted, and served prison time for their crimes related to the Watergate cover-up. Ehrlichman was responsible for creating the Plumbers unit in 1971 that carried out the black-bag jobs and bugging of the Democratic National Committee. President Ford only pardoned Nixon, an unprecedented move since Nixon was not yet indicted for any crimes. Ehrlichman died on February 14, 1999; Haldeman passed earlier on November 12, 1993; and John Mitchell died even earlier on November 9, 1988. The Ehrlichman papers are part of the Nixon Presidential Library and Museum, but held in custody by the National Archives and Records Administration.

96. After a year in office, Nixon escalated the war in Vietnam by expanding the fronts to include bombings of Cambodia without congressional approval; massive antiwar demonstrations took place across the country, and students were killed by U.S. National Guardsmen at Kent State University in May 1970. Nixon became the target for severe criticism by the media and the general public. He called the heads of the intelligence community to meet and discuss how to curb domestic unrest and radicalism among the youth and minorities. He made Hoover the head of the committee and presented his Huston Plan. Hoover refused to adopt the plan unless he was ordered by AG John Mitchell, who refused to make the order. Nixon turned the plan over to the NSA for implementation, which continued until 1973. See www.globalsecurity.org/intell/ops/huston-plan/htm/.

97. See Summers, *Official and Confidential*, 59, and Gentry, *J. Edgar Hoover*, 280, for information on blacks in the FBI that Hoover inherited when he became Director in 1935. Among them was James Crawford, his driver, and Sam Noisette. "Mr. Sam" was the "major-domo of Hoover's office" whose job duties entailed getting the Director a fresh towel when he emerged from the bathroom, swatting flies, ushering persons into the office, and helping him into his coat. Hoover also dismissed the handful of white women in the FBI at that time. It wasn't until 1972, when L. Patrick Gray became Director, that the first women, both white, were hired by the FBI and made special agents.

98. December 14, 1970, 16.

99. "Hispanic Agents, in Testimony, Call F.B.I. Biased," *New York Times*, August 17, 1988, as reported by the Associated Press the previous day. From that testimony in the case, several evidentiary facts were reported, such as in 1916 Manuel Sorola was hired to work in the El Paso Bureau of Investigation office and made special agent in 1922. In 1938, he disappointed Hoover on some

assignment and was demoted and placed on limited duty until retirement. Julius Lopez, son of immigrant Spaniards who settled in Biloxi, Mississippi, was the first special agent in charge (SAC) of an office in Puerto Rico in 1943. The places of assignment, the Southwest and Puerto Rico, for Spanish-speaking FBI agents were known as the "Taco Circuit." Assignment to Puerto Rico was the destination for one third of the Spanish-surnamed FBI agents, as opposed to only 2.4 percent of non-Hispanic agents. El Paso was termed the "dumping ground" for FBI agents assigned to that post. Perez, the lead plaintiff in the class-action case, was first hired as a mail clerk and messenger in the D.C. FBI office in 1960 and made special agent in 1979. The FBI spent $200,000 on a commissioned study to refute the charges of discrimination. The EEOC investigated and found no discrimination. The court, however, was moved by the statistical evidence of one Hispanic as special agent in charge of an FBI office out of 58; six Hispanics as special agents of 440; ten Hispanic agents out of 7,000; and the testimony of forty-four Hispanic agents on the racial slurs and name calling commonplace in the work environment, such as "spic," "greaser," "taco belly," and "Pancho" from white agents, usually Mormons at the Los Angeles office. See http://www.equip.org/PDF/DM510.pdf. The FBI website has a link to history and background on each division, such as Puerto Rico or El Paso, which provides information on Hispanic agents.

100. See John Service's own *The Amerasia Papers: Some Problems in the History of US-China Relations* (Berkeley, CA: Center for Chinese Studies, 1971).

101. See the trilogy beginning with *The Years of Lyndon Johnson: The Path to Power* (1982); *The Years of Lyndon Johnson: Means of Ascent* (1990); and *The Years of Lyndon Johnson: Master of the Senate* (2002) for a detailed examination of how Johnson rose from obscurity as a school teacher in a segregated school for Mexican American kids in South Texas to the Senate majority leader on the verge of becoming the vice-presidential nominee. All three books were published by Alfred A. Knopf.

102. Robert Dallek, *Lone Star Rising*, vol. 1, *Lyndon Johnson and His Times, 1908–1960* (1991), and *Flawed Giant: Lyndon Johnson and His Times, 1961–1973* (1998), both published by Oxford University Press.

Chapter 2. Hoover's "Commonist" of 1965

1. All FBI documents cited hereafter are from the declassified file on Cesar Chavez entitled Cesar Chavez & United Farm Workers Et al. File: 100-444762 and found at https://vault.fbi.gov. The first file cited here is the first document in this extensive file from part 1 of 17, section 1, penciled page 3, and the

narrative begins on penciled page 4 of the document. The actual report has no page number on the first page and page "-2-" typed at bottom of the actual memorandum with pencil page number 5. For precise identification of each document cited and referenced as an endnote hereafter, I will cite the type of file, the persons exchanging the communication, the date of the document, other persons receiving the document copies if necessary to place the content in context, and other agencies cross-fertilized with the document.

The reader is forewarned that to find the documents cited here, the declassified file must be downloaded and reorganized chronologically by date to follow my references. The FBI purposely has no order by date, no order by typed page, and no order on pages cited on the webpage of The Vault for the entire set of declassified documents. A complete set of the declassified file organized by date is on deposit at the University of Texas-Austin Nettie Lee Benson Latin American Collection, Main Library, under my archival deposit name, and another set is found at the Michigan State University Library under my archival deposit name.

2. Roberta Strauss Feuerlicht, *America's Reign of Terror* (New York: Random House, 1971), 85.

3. Ibid., 90.

4. Ibid., 93.

5. Frank Donner, *Protectors of Privilege: Red Squads and Police Repression in Urban America* (Berkeley: University of California Press, 1990) is a thorough review of anti-labor, anti-immigrant, and anti-Communist practices in the U.S., particularly his chap. 2, "The Growth of the Red Squads from the Thirties to the Sixties," the period of Hoover's ascendency to FBI Director and the birth of his style of repression culminating in COINTELPRO (44-64); and chap. 3, "The Surge of the Sixties" (65-89).

6. The document that provided Hoover the cover he needed was Executive Order 8840, issued by President Roosevelt on July 30, 1941, creating within the White House another Office of Coordinator of Inter-American Affairs. This new office gave Hoover the rationale to conduct surveillance in Latin America.

7. Richard Gid Powers, *Secrecy and Power: The Life of J. Edgar Hoover* (New York: Free Press, 1987), 229-30.

8. "Deke" DeLoach was the deputy associate director of the FBI under Clyde Tolson, who was the associate director under Hoover, numbers three, two, and one, respectively. According to Bruce Weber, writing on the occasion of DeLoach's death, he claimed that DeLoach as Hoover's liaison to LBJ was

asked to conduct political intelligence investigations for the president and have FBI agents as part of his security detail. See "Cartha D. DeLoach, No. 3 in the FBI, Is Dead at 92," *New York Times*, March 18, 2013.

9. The FBI also has a file on Larry Dulay Itliong No. 1328894-0, who is mentioned in this first LHM in the Chavez file. However, in a three-page LHM dated "6/18/69 FROM: S. B. DONAHOE TO: MR. DE LOACH on the "Subject: [FIRST LINE REDACTED]" then second line "LARRY ITALONG [*sic*] SECURITY MATTER," which is in response to a telephone query by U.S. Senator George Murphy (R-California) to S. B. Donahoe about "Larry Italong (precise spelling unknown to the Senator), whom he described as a Filipino, is operating as a front for Chavez and is reported to have a background as a communist sympathizer."

10. Marshall Ganz, *Why David Sometimes Wins* (New York: Oxford University Press, 2009), 60-82, discusses the role AWOC played in curbing recruitment and use of *bracero* labor during these years. Specifically, on page 64 is a biographical sketch of Larry Itliong and his role in the AWOC.

11. The FBI uses various exemptions authorized within the FOIA. See Ann Mari Buitrago and Leon Andrew Immerman, *Are You Now or Have You Ever Been in the FBI Files? How to Secure and Interpret Your FBI Files* (New York: Grove Press, 1981), chap. 2, "The FBI and the Freedom of Information and Privacy Acts," for an examination of these two acts, particularly pages 49-78 for an explanation of the exemptions in the FOIA such as (b)(7) and the Privacy Act's two major categories listed as (J) (1)(2) and (K) (1)(7).

12. Harlen Hagen, a Democrat, represented the 14th district from 1953 to 1963, when redistricting changed the boundaries into the 18th district, and lost to Republican Bob Mathias. Hagan was born and raised in Hansford, which is 17 miles from Corcoran, California, the site of the largest and bloodiest strike led by the Cannery and Agricultural Workers Industrial Union representing thousands of Mexican cotton pickers during September to October 1933.

13. William C. Sullivan, with Bill Brown, *The Bureau: My Thirty Years in Hoover's FBI* (New York: W.W. Norton & Co., 1979), 87-88.

14. Jacques E. Levy, *Cesar Chavez: Autobiography of La Causa* (Minneapolis: University of Minnesota Press, 2007), 104-8.

15. Airtel from Director, FBI to SAC, Los Angeles dated October 11, 1965, three pages.

16. These dates are taken from content of the memorandum dated October 8, 1965, and purported to be the first file in the entire declassified FBI file. Obviously, these dates stated in this memorandum contradict the first records

of surveillance of Chavez.

17. Airtel dated September 15, 1966, from Director, FBI to SAC Washington Field Office and Los Angeles.

18. Ignacio M. Garcia, *Viva Kennedy: Mexican Americans in Search of Camelot* (College Station: Texas A&M University Press, 2000), 175.

19. Julie Leininger Pycior, *LBJ and Mexican Americans: The Paradox of Power* (Austin: University of Texas Press, 1997), 154. Pycior, in an email to me dated January 27, 2014, in my possession, writes on this question, "My impression from the WH files, and from my interview with Joseph Califano (the chief domestic advisor at that time), was that the Johnson Administration dismissed Chavez (and Galarza, Corona, Gallegos, Samora, Bernal et al.) out of hand as Bobby Kennedy supporters, which of course was the kiss of death with LBJ. Just shows you how wrong-headed the FBI could be." She technically is correct if we are researching events and documents from 1968, but this memo is dated 1961. Kennedy was president and his brother the attorney general; it is possible Chavez was considered or even applied in 1961. See also Alex Poinsett, *Walking with Presidents: Louis Martin and the Rise of Black Political Power* (Lanham, MD: Rowman & Littlefield, 1997) for a history of Martin's work with several presidents. Martin was an Afro-Latino, son of a Cuban father and African American mother.

20. Pycior, *LBJ and Mexican Americans*, 154–55.

21. Joseph Califano at that time was the special assistant to the president. He was the top aide for domestic affairs. In 1977, he was appointed secretary of Health, Education, and Welfare by President Jimmy Carter until August 1979.

22. Letter from David S. North to Mr. Califano dated December 23, 1966.

23. Madeline Neighly and Maurice Emsellem, "WANTED: Accurate FBI Background Checks for Employment," National Employment Law Project, New York, July 2013. See www.nelp.org. The project found that in 2012 the FBI processed 17 million such background checks for employment; this is six times the number from 2002. According to the report, 50 percent of the FBI reports on background for employment fail to be completed and are therefore inaccurate. The most neglected item is final disposition of the case involving the person being checked; approximately 1.8 million workers are affected by this neglect (1). The FBI had in 2012 criminal history records on more than 75 million persons in the U.S. States keep the records, forward them to the FBI, and therein is the problem. The majority of the U.S. population lives in states where more than 30 percent of the records do not contain final disposition

of a case (2). A map on page 12 of the report shows Texas, California, and Arizona as states with 50-69 percent of arrests in a database containing final disposition, but in New Mexico, Michigan, Tennessee, South Carolina, New Hampshire, Alaska, Maine, South Dakota, Louisiana, and Delaware this final disposition data is not provided. These states represent 12.1 percent of the U.S. population. In Colorado, New York, Oklahoma, Montana, Mississippi, and Alabama 0-49 percent contain final disposition, and these states represent 13.7 percent of the U.S. population. Background checks were first authorized in 1954 for federal employment during the Cold War by EO 10450. In 2004 the background checks were expanded to cover millions more in the private sector, and were employed by federal contractors by Homeland Security Presidential Directive 12 (p. 6) 2 in 2004 (HSPD-12).

In 2006 the U.S. AG found 50 percent of the FBI records did not contain the final disposition of a case or arrest. One in four U.S. adults has an arrest or conviction record. African Americans are 28 percent of those arrested despite being only 14 percent of the U.S. population. Hispanics are 16 percent of the U.S. population. African Americans have more incomplete records. The NELP report is silent on this point regarding Hispanics. Estimates are that 600,000 persons are negatively affected by these faulty records and unemployable by those who rely on background checks (3). When it comes to buying guns, an incomplete record is no impediment; it can be cleared up within three days by the FBI to comply with the Brady Handgun Violence Prevention Act ("Brady Act"). Why not clean all records up? the NELP asks (4).

24. Memorandum from M. A. Jones to Mr. DeLoach, dated October 15, 1965, two pages. This memorandum was sent to all the top-level associate and assistant directors of the FBI; hereafter this would be the practice to keep all top FBI officials in the loop with copies.

25. See Airtel from SAC, Los Angeles to Director, FBI, dated October 20, 1965, two pages, and the full 13-page letterhead memorandum (LHM) of the same day, which utilizes the entire code "Internal Security-C." The Airtel has two redacted sections eliminating names of sources and/or informants. The page listing those who received this packet of documents is missing except for San Francisco, Los Angeles, Cong. Harlen Hagan, and OEO.

26. Frank Bardacke, *Trampling Out the Vintage: Cesar Chavez and the Two Souls of the United Farm Workers* (New York: Verso, 2012), 128-33, for a short story on the beginnings of *El Malcriado* and the real worker behind the newspaper, Bill Esher, who was married to Wendy Goepel. It was Goepel who recruited Esher to work on the newspaper in Delano.

27. Steven W. Bender, *One Night in America: Robert Kennedy, Cesar Chavez, and the Dream of Dignity* (Boulder, CO: Paradigm Publishers, 2008), 20-22. Bender makes the argument in these pages that Robert Kennedy's visit to Delano and his support for Chavez began to turn the tide against the Communist charge.

28. Http://latinopia.com/ for his interview and comments on this first visit to the picket line.

29. Several other sources, such as George Mariscal's *Brown-Eyed Children of the Sun* (Albuquerque: University of New Mexico Press, 2005), 138; Richard Griswold del Castillo and Arnoldo de Leon's *North to Aztlan*, 2nd ed. (Wiley, 2012), 162; Frank Bardacke's *Trampling Out the Vintage*, 488-89; and Pakal Hatuey's *End 1492* blog (http://end1492.blogspot.com) contain references to this racist language condoned by the UFW. Both del Castillo and de Leon and Hatuey's work reference Chavez's cousin Manuel being in charge of a union program, "Wetline," implemented near the Yuma, Arizona, border with Mexico to prevent Mexican workers from crossing into the U.S. See http://thinkmexican.tumblr.com/post/80947508130/c.

30. See, for example, these issues of *El Malcriado*: June 7, 1967, 6; and June 15, 1968, 16. A collection of *El Malcriado* newspapers are found at J. Paul Leonard Library, San Francisco State University.

31. The FBI has a manual, *FBI Domestic Investigations and Operations Guide* (DIOG), posted on its website, http://vault.fbi.gov. The U.S. Attorney General also has a manual for the FBI to use with confidential human sources, *The Attorney General's Guidelines regarding the Use of FBI Confidential Human Sources*, from 2006, which I examined. For more recent analysis of the policy and practice, see Trevor Aaronson, "The Informants," *Mother Jones*, September/October 2011 issue.

32. From FBI, Los Angeles to Director, FBI and unnamed other persons, ten pages with two appendices on the Du Bois Clubs.

33. Drake worked for the California Migrant Ministry beginning in 1962 and was assigned to work with Chavez and the NFWA for three months, but stayed on until 1978. While with Chavez, he became his administrative assistant and director of boycotts. After Chavez he continued his work in labor organizing in Mississippi, South Texas, and other locations until he died in September 2001. His papers, under the name "Reverend James Drake Collection Papers, 1961-1977," are archived at Wayne State University, Detroit, Michigan.

34. Steve Allen was a radio and television personality with several successful prime time shows. In 1966 he wrote a book about agricultural labor and the

plight of farm workers. See *The Earth Is Our Table* (Garden City, NY: Doubleday Books).

35. Merle Miller, *Lyndon: An Oral Biography* (New York: G.P. Putnam's Sons), 468–69.

36. Ibid., 468.

37. Ibid., 467.

38. Western Union telegram from SUSP CUPE LONG PD DELANO Calif 23 1141A PST to J. Edgar Hoover asking him to confirm if the three mentioned in narrative were Communists: Wendy Goepel for going to the 1958 Youth Conference in Helsinki, Valdez for going to Cuba, and "Modesto Dulay Itliong alias Larry Duley [Larry Itliong]" for taking part in "the Huk Uprising in the Filipine islands."

39. Letter from Hoover to redacted name in Delano, California, dated February 25, 1966.

40. Airtel from SAC, Los Angeles (62-0) to Director, FBI, dated March 3, 1966, two pages. Noted at bottom of first page is designation of "COMINFIL" of National Farm Workers Association. The classification of NFWA has moved from infiltration to IS-C to now a full-fledged COINTELPRO-COMINFIL for Communist Party.

41. That is the wording in the second paragraph after redacting the source of the information in the LHM sent from FBI, Los Angeles to the Director, dated March 9, 1966, three pages.

42. Teletype from Los Angeles (100-67449) to San Francisco (100-55900) and Director (100-444762). Dated 450PM PST URGENT 3-14-66 PLS, one page.

43. My FOIA request to the Secret Service on Chavez and the United Farm Workers Union yielded limited results. The first record obtained from this agency is not dated to coincide with this forwarded FBI communication; it begins with the date February 24, 1970, and reports on a United Farm Workers demonstration that occurred at the White House. This document reveals that about fifteen participants were involved in the demonstration and two were arrested. Names of agents, field offices, participants, etc., cross-referenced are redacted along with the file number for this record. Secret Service documents are more sterile and redacted than FBI records.

44. Airtel from SAC, Los Angeles (100-67449) to Director, FBI (100-444762) subject: COMINFIL NATIONAL FARM WORKERS ASSOCIATION, DELANO, CALIFORNIA, IS-C, dated March 14, 1966, two pages, with accompanying LHM titled "Proposed March Sponsored by Congress of Racial Equality, Delano

to Sacramento, California, March 18, 1966 to April 10, 1966 Information
Concerning," six pages with two pages of appendix on Du Bois Club that have
no relation to or bearing on the Peregrinacion March except to inflame and
associate by reference a group of interest to the Director, FBI from a previous
decade.

45. Bender, *One Night in America*, 22.

46. Ibid., 11-26. Recent documentaries that feature this verbal confrontation
    include *Latino Americans* (PBS, 2014) and the 2015 *Willie Velasquez: Su Voz es Su
    Voto*.

47. Bender, *One Night in America*, 22-24. For a complete statement on the plight of
    farm workers entered into the Congressional Record 114, no. 169, October 11,
    1968, by Senator Harrison Williams, see Peter Matthiessen, *Sal Si Puedes: Cesar
    Chavez and the New American Revolution* (New York: Dell Publishing Co., 1969),
    363-72.

48. Levy, *Cesar Chavez*, 208.

49. Teletype posted URGENT at 4:50 PM PST dated March 14, 1966, and again at
    10:28 PM PST to FBI WASH DC reporting on a protest march set to begin 9
    a.m. March 17. After the march began, FBI, Los Angeles informed Washington
    FBI in a two-page LHM that no permit had been sought or obtained and the
    route had been changed at the last minute and that was what the police
    confrontation was about.

50. See Richard W. Etulain, ed., *Cesar Chavez: A Brief Biography with Documents*
    (Boston: Bedford/St. Martin's Press, 2002), 56, for this source, and the next page
    for a photograph of his office with such images.

51. Luis D. Leon, *The Political Spirituality of Cesar Chavez: Crossing Religious Borders*
    (Los Angeles: University of California Press, 2015), 21-22.

52. Frederick John Dalton, *The Moral Vision of Cesar Chavez* (Ossining, NY: Orbis
    Books, 2003), 85-87.

53. See Timothy Matovina, *Guadalupe and Her Faithful: Latino Catholics in San
    Antonio, from Colonial Origins to the Present* (Baltimore: Johns Hopkins
    University Press, 2005); and Roberto Trevino, *The Church in the Barrio: Mexican
    American Ethno-Catholicism in Houston* (Chapel Hill: University of North
    Carolina Press, 2006). While these two works are Texas-based case studies, the
    Mexican American Catholic community across the United States is universal
    in their belief system and practices.

54. Dated April 4, 1966, quoting the news item in the newspaper of April 3, 1966, 27.

In the LHM in the last paragraph, the report maker adds that some redacted source informs the office that "the above march was an annual 'sidewalk parade' of Spanish speaking Americans who marched between churches in connection with Holy Week."

55. Airtel from SAC, Los Angeles to Director, FBI, dated April 5, 1966, three pages, and LHM from same source to Director same day, two pages.

56. Airtel (REGISTERED) from SAC, Los Angeles to Director, FBI dated April 8, 1966, and inserted below subject line is "OO: Los Angeles" and turf protection language at bottom.

57. LHM from Los Angeles, California, to Washington, dated April 8, 1966, two pages.

58. Levy, *Cesar Chavez*, 211-12. In the PBS documentary *Latino Americans*, a segment that focuses on the Chicano Movement leaders contains several minutes on Cesar Chavez with mention that his sore feet were from walking in new boots, not old shoes.

59. Ganz, *Why David Sometimes Wins*, 4.

60. Levy, *Cesar Chavez*, 215-18. In Richard J. Jensen and John C. Hammerback, eds., *The Words of Cesar Chavez* (College Station: Texas A&M University Press, 2002), 29. Chavez is quoted as claiming it was April 6 in Stockton when he got called by the Schenley representative.

61. FBI file on Korshak dates to 1963 and is numbered 92-5053 in Washington FBI files, File no. 92-742 in Los Angeles, File no. 92-789 in Chicago FBI files. FBI main file nos. are 159-2194 and 183-3658. See subsequent newspaper articles on Sidney Korshak's activities in *(Chicago) Sunday Today*, September 10, 1972, and *New York Times*, June 30, 1976. Korshak's involvement with the Teamsters in an FBI targeted COINTELPRO program from 1966 termed HOODWINK is the subject of FBI File #100-446533.

62. Jensen and Hammerback, eds., *The Words of Cesar Chavez*, 29.

63. Schenley Industries, Inc., Rockefeller Center, 1290 Ave. of the Americas, New York, N.Y. 10019, dated April 11, 1966, to Honorable J. Edgar Hoover and underscored in caption: PERSONAL AND CONFIDENTIAL from redacted source with handwritten note at bottom from the Director: "Let me have summary on Union & Korshak.

64. Memorandum is dated April 14, 1966, and is titled "Synopsis," five pages, and covers known information in FBI files about Chavez and his leadership cadre. Nothing was included on Korshak.

65. Levy, *Cesar Chavez*, chap. 11, "Schenley Signs a Contract," 215-18.

66. Ibid., 221-27.

67. Ibid., 223.

68. The recruitment may have continued, but in late 1996 revelations emerged that the CIA was funding the U.S. National Student Association. Evan Thomas in 1996 published his book *The Very Best Men: Four Who Dared: The Early Years of the CIA* (New York: Simon and Schuster) with that information on pp. 329-30. Vice President Hubert Humphrey speaking at Stanford University disclosed as much in his remarks in February 1967. Phil Agee Jr., not a CIA favorite, also chimed in the fall of 1991 in *Campus Watch*, "The National Student Association Scandal," 12-13. Recently in the June 20, 2013, edition of the *New Yorker*, Hendrik Hertzberg, "Unwinding 'Unwitting'" revisits the CIA connection to the National Student Association while reviewing CIA Director James Clapper's testimony before a congressional watchdog committee on warrantless spying on Americans.

Chapter 3. The UFW Eagle Comes to the Lone Star State, 1966–1968

1. See Eugene C. Barker's two books, *The Life of Stephen F. Austin, Founder of Texas, 1793-1836: A Chapter in the Westward Movement of the Anglo-American People* (Nashville, TN: Cokesbury Press, 1926), and *Mexico and Texas, 1821-1835* (Dallas: P. L. Turner Co., 1928) for these historical developments, migrations, and rebellion.

2. There are countless history books that cover this period of time and events. See Weston Joseph McConnell, *Social Cleavages in Texas: A Study of the Proposed Division of the State* (New York: AMS Press, 1969), 30-33. A unique proposal by the Texans was to divide the land into five slave states; being rejected, they settled for one accepted into the union by Joint Resolution of United States Congress, March 1, 1945. See also *Congressional Globe*, 28th Congress, 2nd Session, 171.

3. Charles W. Goldfinch and José T. Canales, *Juan N. Cortina: Two Interpretations* (New York: Arno Press, 1974).

4. John R. Chavez, *The Lost Land: The Chicano Image of the Southwest* (Albuquerque: University of New Mexico Press, 1984), 4-5. For an oral-history memoir of a family who lost their land grant in New Mexico, see Mike Scarborough, *Trespassers on Our Own Land* (Indianapolis, IN: Dog Ear Publishing, 2011).

5. Julie Leininger Pycior, *LBJ and Mexican Americans: The Paradox of Power* (Austin: University of Texas Press, 1997). See chap. 5 for LBJ's first steps leading

to the presidency (87-108), and chaps. 8 and 9 (163-214), which reveal the close connection of the president with local South Texas politics and with the governor during the farm worker strikes in Texas and California, both attributed to Chavez.

6. Sheila Allee, *Texas Mutiny: Bullets, Ballots, and Boss Rule* (Victoria, TX: Redbud Publishing Co., 2003). Also see McConnell, *Social Cleavages in Texas*; the original work in 1925 was published by Columbia University Press. Chapters in part 2 deal with the historical development of the various proposals for a Texas as state or states, while the chapters in part 3 deal with issues of slavery, the German population, Mexican illiteracy, and geographic distribution of these populations. Texas became a state in 1845, and the first U.S. Census enumeration occurred in 1850. At that time, Texas was 30.2 percent black slave population, or 182,556 according to McConnell (167). According to the Texas Comptroller of Public Accounts, *The Changing Face of Texas*, August 1992, table 1, "Texas Long-Term Demographic Trends, 1850-2026" (10), the "black population in 1850 was 58,558 or 28%." Population numbers for persons of Mexican origin or ancestry were not provided in either source. Perhaps this category of persons in the state were not counted at all. McConnell does provide geographic distribution of Mexican people: "Prior to 1900, Mexicans residing in Texas were confined mainly to a narrow strip of territory lying east of the Rio Grande and to a few cities not far distant from the border, but their movement toward the interior by way of San Antonio is very perceptible in recent years" (177).

7. Deborah Cohen, *Braceros: Migrant Citizens and Transnational Subjects in the Postwar United States and Mexico* (Chapel Hill: University of North Carolina Press, 2011), 202-5.

8. For a Ranger perspective on the history of his agency, see H. Joaquin Jackson and David Marion Wilkinson, *One Ranger: A Memoir* (Austin: University of Texas Press, 2005), 37-42. Jackson also has a quick observation on the forced retirement of Captain Alfred Y. Allee of Company D and reflections on his own retirement that are indicative of the Ranger mentality and character (243-50).

9. Miguel Antonio Levario, *Militarizing the Border: When Mexicans Became the Enemy* (College Station: Texas A&M University Press, 2012), 19. See Timothy J. Dunn, *The Militarization of the U.S.-Mexico Border, 1978-1992* (Austin: Center for Mexican American Studies, University of Texas at Austin, 1996).

10. See Kirby Warnock, *Border Bandits*, for a critical documentary on the myth and legend of the Texas Rangers at www.borderbanditsmovie.com. For an informative book about the political work on behalf of the powerful growers

by the Texas Rangers, see Robert M. Utley, *Lone Star Lawmen: The Second Century of the Texas Rangers* (New York: Berkley Books, 2007), 238-47.

11. See John Shockley, *Chicano Revolt in a Texas Town* (Notre Dame, IN: University of Notre Dame Press, 1974) for a prime example of containing the growing Chicano vote in my hometown, Crystal City, Texas.

12. See Utley, *Lone Star Lawmen*, 238-47, for an apologist treatment of the Texas Rangers in the La Casita Farms strike of 1966-67.

13. Erasmo Gamboa and Kevin Leonhard, *Mexican Labor and World War II: Braceros in the Pacific Northwest, 1942-1947* (Seattle: University of Washington Press, 2000), 111-19. The more important early works on this program are Ernesto Galarza, *Spiders in the House and Workers in the Field* (Notre Dame, IN: University of Notre Dame Press, 1970) from the U.S. Chicano perspective; and Manuel Gamio, *The Mexican Immigrant: His Life Story* (Chicago: University of Chicago Press, 1931). Incredibly, the Gamio book was not translated or published in Mexico until 1969. See also Jerry Garcia and Gilberto Garcia, eds., *Memory, Community, and Activism: Mexican Migration and Labor in the Pacific Northwest* (East Lansing: Julian Samora Research Institute, Michigan State University Press, 2005).

14. Dennis Nodin Valdes, *Al Norte: Agricultural Workers in the Great Lakes Region, 1917-1970* (Austin: University of Texas Press, 1991).

15. *El Malcriado*, March 17, 1966, 11-14.

16. Marshall Ganz, *Why David Sometimes Wins: Leadership, Organization, and Strategy in the California Farm Worker Movement* (New York: Oxford University Press, 2009), 106.

17. Lisa Garcia Bedolla, *Latino Politics*, 2nd ed. (Malden, MA: Polity Press, 2014), 79-82, 259 n. 35.

18. See Eugene Nelson's book on the grape strike in Delano, *Huelga: The First Hundred Days of the Great Delano Grape Strike* (Delano, CA: Farm Worker Press, 1966). He was Chavez's secretary beginning in August 1965, and his primary job was to translate written documents from articles in *El Malcriado* to flyers, letters, memorandums, reports, and the like from Spanish to English and English to Spanish. Nelson was the son of a grape and orange grower in Modesto, California, until a bank foreclosure ended the family enterprise. Like Chavez's experience, the Nelson family became destitute. Unlike Chavez he did not stay working in the fields or join the military; instead he attended Handy Writers' Colony in Illinois for two years. Then, he joined Chavez as a volunteer, then became picket captain, then Texas director of the boycott,

then strike leader in the RGV. He has published other works and is best known for his 1972 novel, *Bracero* (Culver City, CA: Peace Press Publishing).

19. Photos of the marchers are found at the University of Texas-San Antonio Hemisphere Campus, Special Collections, San Antonio.

20. A 34-page photo journal titled *Sons of Zapata* contains many images of farm workers involved in the strike from 1966 to 1967 and was published by the UFWOC-AFL-CIO out of Rio Grande City, Texas, in 1967. A copy is at the University of California San Diego libraries.

21. Airtel from SAC, San Antonio (62-New) dated June 28, 1966; one page makes reference to an earlier LHM from San Antonio dated June 7 and 22, 1966, regarding bomb threats at the Starr County Courthouse. No such documents are included in the declassified Chavez file. This earlier LHM was widely disseminated to Houston, Los Angeles, El Paso, Brownsville, Secret Service-Austin, Austin Police Department, Travis County Sheriff's Office, 112th INTC, OSI, 10th District, and ONI.

    The LHM from FBI, San Antonio to Washington dated June 28, 1966, utilizing an open source, the *Valley Morning Star*, reporting on a proposed march from Rio Grande City to Austin, Texas, the capital, to arrive during Labor Day into the capitol building.

22. See Nelson, *Huelga*, for a dramatic insider report on what it was like to be nonviolent in the face of threats, cars and trucks running into you, insensitive police officers, being shot and beaten, being sprayed with pesticides, and not being immobilized with fear. Nelson was a local who befriended the farm worker cause and stayed loyal for years. Chavez sent him to Texas to help Antonio "Tony" Orendain organize the South Texas farm-worker factions and build a movement to expand the UFW influence and reach.

23. Miriam Pawel, *The Crusades of Cesar Chavez: A Biography* (New York: Bloomsbury, 2014), 545; she indexed all the references to Antonio Orendain, most of which are conflicts between Tony and Cesar that led to his being sent into forced exile in Texas.

24. July 15, 1966, teletype, 8:05 p.m. CST URGENT with "AM COPY TO HOUSTON."

25. Ganz, *Why David Sometimes Wins*, 106.

26. Matt Meier and Feliciano Rivera, *The Chicanos: A History of Mexican Americans* (New York: Hill and Wang, 1972), 128. The other three "Horsemen" mentioned are Reies Lopez Tijerina, Rodolfo "Corky" Gonzalez, and José Angel Gutiérrez, this author.

27. Frederick John Dalton, *The Moral Vision of Cesar Chavez* (Ossining, NY: Orbis Books, 2003), 55-56; Matt Garcia, *From the Jaws of Victory: The Triumph and Tragedy of Cesar Chavez and the Farm Worker Movement* (Berkeley: University of California Press, 2012), 50-52.

28. Mark R. Warren in *Dry Bones Rattling: Community Building to Revitalize American Democracy* (Princeton, NJ: Princeton University Press, 2001) presents the history of the various groups formed under the aegis of the Industrial Areas Foundation and the work done by Ernie Cortes. This history is post Cortes's involvement with MASO, MAYO, and the Texas Institute for Educational Development (TIED), all affiliated with MAYO. Cortes led the collection and delivery to Starr County while at UT-Austin.

29. The U.S. Commission on Civil Rights investigated in 1967 and 1968 the complaints filed by Mexican Americans across the country and issued their findings in *Mexican Americans and the Administration of Justice in the Southwest* (Washington, DC: U.S. Government Printing Office, 1970), and also a *Summary* (U.S. Government Printing Office, Clearinghouse Publication No. 26, 1970). The Texas State Advisory Committee to the U.S. Commission on Civil Rights and the commission itself held hearings in Starr County in 1967, and in 1968 in San Antonio, Texas.

30. Senator Bernal, together with Julian Samora and Albert A. Peña Jr., wrote a critical monograph on the Texas Rangers, *Gunpowder Justice: A Reassessment of the Texas Rangers* (Notre Dame, IN: University of Notre Dame Press, 1979). The information on Senator Bernal's visit to the Rio Grande Valley is found on 147-53, with details of the Medrano case on 154-56.

31. Bernal et al., *Gunpowder Justice*, 149, citing the *Texas Observer*, June 9, 1967, 23.

32. U.S. Commission on Civil Rights, *Summary*, 3.

33. Utley in *Lone Star Lawmen*, 240-42, gives a radically different version of events involving the arrests of Magdaleno Dimas and Rev. and Mrs. Ed Krueger, but states some incriminating facts about the arrests and search warrants necessary to enter a premise.

34. See my oral-history interview with Medrano at http://library.uta.edu/ tejanovoices, 1997, and another with John Castillo in 1996. The Houston PASO chapter was most active in providing support to the strikers and finding lawyers for the countless cases filed against them. See also Utley's favorable rendition of these Ranger arrests and the Medrano case, *Lone Star Lawmen*, 238-47.

35. The first case filed was styled *Francisco Medrano et al. v. A. Y. Allee et al.*, 347 F.

Supp. 605 (1972), and on appeal the title is reversed to *Allee v. Medrano*, 416 US
801 (1974). The U.S. Supreme Court case was decided on May 20, 1974.

36. See Levy, *Cesar Chavez*, 451, for Levy's account of the visit and Chavez's feat as
related to him by Jerry Cohen, who apparently accompanied him to Texas.

37. In other, later cases in 1974 and 1983, federal courts continued to uphold the
SWP as a legitimate political organization. In *Socialist Workers Party v. US
Attorney General*, 642 F. Supp. 1357 (1986) the court found for the SWP against
the FBI for maintaining surveillance over the organization and membership
for over thirty years, and awarded them nearly a quarter of a million dollars
in damages and ordered the release of 1 million or so pages of FBI documents
on the SWP. From October 12, 1961, to approximately June 20, 1973, initially
under U.S. AG Robert Kennedy, the FBI began a COINTELPRO on the SWP. See
chap. 3, "COINTELPRO-SWP," in Ward Churchill and Jim Vander Wall, *The
COINTELPRO Papers: Documents from the FBI's Secret Wars against Dissent in the
United States* (Boston: South End Press, 1990), 49–62, for details of this program.

38. Lyndon B. Johnson, *The Vantage Point: Perspectives of the Presidency, 1963–1969*
(New York: Holt, Rinehart and Winston, 1971).

39. See a journalistic view of RLT's movement by Richard Gardner, *Grito! Reies
Tijerina and the New Mexico Land Grant War of 1967* (Indianapolis, IN: Bobbs-
Merrill Co., 1970); and Patricia Bell Blawis for a sympathetic view of the land
recovery movement and leader in *Tijerina and the Land Grants: Mexican Americans
in Struggle for Their Heritage* (New York: International Publishers, 1971). In 2000
I translated and edited into English his autobiography published in Mexico
in Spanish, *Mi lucha por la tierra*, under the title *They Called Me "King Tiger": My
Struggle for the Land and Our Rights* (Houston: Arte Publico Press).

40. The files are archived under his personal papers at the Zimmerman Library,
University of New Mexico, Albuquerque, New Mexico.

41. Memorandum from The White House to Mr. Cartha D. DeLoach, FBI dated
September 13, 1966.

42. Teletype from Chicago to Director and Milwaukee dated September 26, 1966,
one page.

43. Airtel from SAC, Los Angeles to SAC, San Francisco dated September 26, 1966,
one page.

44. Memorandum from W. V. Cleveland to Mr. Gale, dated September 26, 1966, two
pages. Additionally, several FBI offices—Phoenix, Chicago, Denver, and Las
Vegas—sent in their reports on the investigation; all were short and brief with
no findings.

45. Frank Bardacke, *Trampling Out the Vintage: Cesar Chavez and the Two Souls of the United Farm Workers* (New York: Verso, 2012), 273–76. The last issue of *El Malcriado* was dated August 16, 1967.

46. No major politician of any political party was ever invited to speak at La Raza Unida Summits held during 1968, much less official party conferences held after it was formed in Texas in 1970 and nationally in 1972. See the *Brownsville Herald*, March 25, 1968, 6, for a news account of that meeting and the *Corpus Christi Caller Times*, April 7, 1968, 20, for coverage of two summits. The Raza Unida summits were one-day issues conferences held by the Mexican American Youth Organization (MAYO) in various cities of Texas; precursor to the formation of La Raza Unida Party.

47. *Valley Morning Star*, May 25, 1968, 1.

48. See Kenneth O'Reilley, *"Racial Matters": The FBI's Secret File on Black America, 1960–1972* (New York: Free Press, 1989), and the companion work by him as editor and Clayborne Carson with Spike Lee, *Malcolm X: The FBI File* (New York: Carroll and Graf, 1991); and Michael Friedly and David Gallen, eds., *Martin Luther King, Jr.: The FBI File* (New York: Carroll and Graf, 1993).

49. Airtel handwritten date of May 26, 1966, from SAC, Chicago to Director, FBI and those other SACs listed.

50. Pycior, *LBJ and Mexican Americans*, 199.

51. Ibid., 200.

52. Ibid., 203–14.

53. Oral history interview with Chavez, January 28, 1970, 3, Walter P. Reuther Library, Wayne State University, Detroit, Michigan.

54. Steven W. Bender, *One Night in America: Robert Kennedy, Cesar Chavez, and the Dream of Dignity* (Boulder, CO: Paradigm Publishers, 2008), 2–7.

55. Ibid., chap. 2, "Viva la Huelga!," 8–26.

Chapter 4. The Arizona Battlefield, 1969–1972

1. The Gutierrez letter begins with its first page marked at bottom "3" by the FBI and penciled in "303" at bottom right. Gutierrez himself noted his pagination sequence at top right. I will cite by Gutierrez's pagination.

2. For the 2015 policies and practices of handling informants, see the FBI's manual *Confidential Human Source Policy Guide* (CHSPG), September 21, 2015. See also Trevor Aaronson, "How the FBI Recruits and Handles Its Army of Informants," *The Intercept*, January 2, 2017. The FBI also has the Domestic

Intelligence and Operations Guide (DIOG) and the CHSPG must not contradict the DIOG. During the 1950s era of Operation Wetback, U.S. border officials would hold border-crossing cards upon entry from Mexican workers with threats of no return unless they spied and reported on activities by persons and groups of interest to them. The practice was continued by the FBI on members of the Mafia. See Trevor Aaronson, "The FBI's Secret Rules: When the FBI took on the Mafia in the 1980s," *The Intercept*, January 31, 2017, 1. Apparently, FBI agents were never short of leverage to use to recruit informants. If a low-level Mafia soldier was popped for stealing a car, the FBI line was simple: Hey, would you rather work for us or go to prison?" Potential Muslims are offered a variation after 9/11: "Hey would you rather work for us or be deported?" (2). The FBI and other intelligence agencies can get immigrant S visas for assets and informants. Yassine Ouassif, crossing from Canada into New York in November 2005, had his green card taken by U.S. border officials, was on a bus to San Francisco with instructions to see FBI agent once he arrived for a visa or be deported (3). FBI regularly coordinates with U.S. Customs and Border Protection (CBP) for these purposes and they also use Deferred Action Program, not DACA for students, but immigrants who cannot travel to a foreign country and return to the United States. Significant Benefit Parole Program is another. Bring in inadmissible or deportable informants if they can and will assist in investigations and prosecutions despite the fact that coercion can produce bad intelligence (5).

3. This clipping in the area of the stamped source information under "Character" has the typed notation "IS-C," indicating that Chavez is still being coded under Internal Security-Communist despite all the information obtained in the past half-decade by the FBI.

4. This song contains the stanza "From the Halls of Montezuma to the shores of Tripoli …" which is a reference to the U.S. invasion of Mexico and taking of Mexico City in 1846.

5. Anthony Summers, *Official and Confidential: The Secret Life of J. Edgar Hoover* (New York: G.P. Putnam's Sons, 1993), 167.

6. No date on *NYT* clipping, just byline by Earl Caldwell, "Informer Says He Was Part of Coast Plot to Kill Cesar Chavez," and stamped bottom right by the FBI as January 2, 1972.

7. See Jacques E. Levy, *Cesar Chavez: Autobiography of La Causa* (Minneapolis: University of Minnesota Press, 2007), chap. 1, "Assassination Plot," in book 7, "Target for Destruction 1971–May 1975," 443–46, for these details.

8. Clayborne Carson's *Malcolm X: The FBI File* (New York: Carroll and Graf, 1991), on pages 49, 53, 54, 55, 58, 59, 395, and 404, provides transcribed files of written and telephone messages about the impending murder. Carson, twenty-eight, claims the FBI had over 3,000 black informants across the U.S. under the BlackPro operation. Karl Evanzz's *The Judas Factor: The Plot to Kill Malcolm X* (New York: Thunder's Mouth Press, 1992), beginning with chapter 14, "Good Guys Were White," 197, to end of chapter 19, "The Final Days," 299, describes the events and includes names of FBI agents, New York City police agents, and other informants aware of the assassination plots and harm directed toward Malcolm X.

9. Carson, *Malcolm X*, 444.

10. Ibid., 445.

11. Ibid., 445.

12. Ibid., 446.

13. Richard Hack, *Puppetmaster: The Secret Life of J. Edgar Hoover* (Beverly Hills, CA: New Millennium Press, 2004).

14. Ibid., 393-94.

15. Ibid., 394-96.

16. Ibid., 446.

Chapter 5. The Price of Leadership

1. U.S. Commission on Civil Rights, *Summary*, 15. The reference to the U.S. Code is specifically the statute that prohibits anyone operating under the color of law (meaning working for or acting on behalf of the government) from depriving another of their civil rights. In 1967 the fine for such conduct was up to $5,000 and has now been amended to $10,000 per violation and incident.

2. Ibid., 14.

3. See appendix 3 for list of presidents, U.S. attorney generals, and FBI directors, acting and permanent, from 1930 to 2014. Hoover died May 1972 and President Nixon appointed L. Patrick Gray III to head the Bureau. He resigned, and William Ruckelshaus was appointed interim director, April to July 1973, when Clarence Kelley was appointed and served until 1978.

4. See letter dated June 27, 2017, from David M. Hardy, Section Chief, Record/Information Dissemination Section, Records Management Division, Federal Bureau of Investigation, Department of Justice to me. The letter's second paragraph is disturbing: "Records which may have been responsive to your

request were destroyed November 1977." The third paragraph's last sentence offers some hope of finding additional documents: "If you wish to review these potentially responsive records, send your request to NARA at the following address using these file numbers 105-HQ-157123, 161-HQ-51593, 100-SC-1120, 100-PH-52280, 100-AX-150, 100-AX-619 as a reference." The address for the National Archives followed. Letter is archived under my name for files on Cesar E. Chavez at Special Collections, Michigan State University Library.

5. "C" is added to this case file and it can mean one of several things. One, it could be for "Communist," since this is one of the designations given to Chavez in the early years. Two, it could be for "Confidential," but not likely in the context of this case. Third, it could be for "Criminal," and this would make sense because the FBI labeled this Extortion. Fourth, it could mean "Case closed," and most likely this is the intent. See Ann Mari Buitrago and Leon Andrew Immerman, *Are You Now or Have You Ever Been in the FBI Files? How to Secure and Interpret Your FBI Files* (New York: Grove Press, 1981) for their explanations of "C."

Chapter 6. The Six-Year War with Teamsters

1. Steven Brill, *The Teamsters* (New York: Simon and Schuster, 1978), 94, 134, and 366. It is an exhaustive account of the Teamster years under Fitzsimmons and covers somewhat the foray into Chavez's jurisdiction of farm labor organizing in California. See also Anthony Summers, *The Arrogance of Power: The Secret World of Richard Nixon* (New York: Penguin Books, 2000), 54, 213, 221, 399.

2. Summers, *Arrogance of Power,* 374-76.

3. Brill, *The Teamsters,* 371-76.

4. Ronald B. Taylor, *Chavez and the Farm Workers* (Boston: Beacon Press, 1975), 251-59.

5. Miriam Pawel, *The Crusades of Cesar Chavez: A Biography* (New York: Bloomsbury Press, 2014), 219.

6. Taylor, *Chavez and the Farm Workers,* 259-60.

7. Ibid., 94-95.

8. Matt Garcia, *From the Jaws of Victory: The Triumph and Tragedy of Cesar Chavez and the Farm Worker Movement* (Berkeley: University of California Press, 2014), 135.

9. Ibid., 370-72.

10. Randy Shaw, *Beyond the Fields: Cesar Chavez, the UFW, and the Struggle for Justice in the 21st Century* (Berkeley: University of California Press, 2008), 44.

11. Tom Kuntz and Phil Kuntz, *The Sinatra Files: The Secret FBI Dossier* (New York: Three Rivers Press, 2000).

12. Jack Mitchell, *Executive Privilege: Two Centuries of White House Scandals* (New York: Hippocrene Books, 1992), 311.

13. Pawel, *Crusades*, 433.

14. Alston Purvis, *The Vendetta: FBI Hero Melvin Purvis's War against Crime, and J. Edgar Hoover's War against Him* (New York: PublicAffairs, 2005).

15. Richard Hack, *Puppetmaster: The Secret Life of J. Edgar Hoover* (Beverly Hills, CA: New Millennium Press, 2004), 302.

16. William Sullivan, with Bill Brown, *The Bureau: My Thirty Years in Hoover's FBI* (New York: W.W. Norton & Co., 1979), 117-18.

17. Pawel, *Crusades*, 221.

18. A key figure in the Kennedy administration with ties to Chavez was Jack T. Conway, who in turn worked with McGeorge Bundy and Mitchell "Mike" Sviridoff in the JFK and LBJ administrations. Conway, born in Detroit, was a UAW man up to 1961 when he went from working in California (where he met Chavez, then with the CSO) to elect Kennedy, to helping as part of the administration to create the new Cabinet position, Housing and Urban Development. Conway went on to head the Community Action Program, part of the War on Poverty, and by 1968 founded the Center for Community Change (CCC), based in Washington, DC. The first major funding for the CCC came from the Ford Foundation. The archives of the Center for Community Change during most of the Conway tenure can be found at www.reuther.walter.edu/files/UR000516.pdf. McGeorge Bundy has a similar trajectory: working for the election of John Kennedy, becoming national security advisor to him and later Johnson. Then he became the head of the Ford Foundation in 1964. Sviridoff was also in the labor movement as a young adult, rising to head a state division of the AFL-CIO. He also joined the John Kennedy administration and worked in the State Department directing international aid programs to Latin America. He then became the vice president of the Ford Foundation for national affairs.

19. Pawel, *Crusades*, 221-27.

20. Ibid., 220.

21. Mark Felt and John O'Connor, *A G-Man's Life: The FBI, Being "Deep Throat," and the Struggle for Honor in Washington* (New York: PublicAffairs, 2006), 77-78.

22. Bob Woodward, *The Secret Man: The Story of Watergate's Deep Throat* (New York:

Simon and Schuster, 2005), 35.

23. Ibid., 126–27.

24. Felt, *A G-Man's Life*, 278.

25. This document is "fruit from the sky" in that it does not seem to have any bearing on Chavez or the Texas farm worker affiliation with Chavez. The document does provide new information on the surveillance by the San Antonio FBI office into the activities of Efrain Fernandez and perhaps other persons, organizations, and events that may have been redacted. The file number provided is useful for those interested in further research on Efrain Fernandez, the Pharr Police, and whatever else the file may contain. By referencing the file number and subject matter, those interested can request the documents from both Washington, DC, and San Antonio FBI offices. I have personal knowledge of the activities of Efrain Fernandez, and he was centrally involved with MAYO and later the Raza Unida Party, not the UFWOC or the Texas affiliate of same. At MAYO we all (I was a cofounder of the organization) were supportive of Chavez's efforts, the Texas farm workers in the RGV, and workers' rights in general.

26. Summers, *Arrogance of Power*, 356.

27. He served three presidents, Nixon, Ford, and Carter, in various capacities involving civil rights. At HEW he was the head of the Office of Civil Rights, then served in the capacity mentioned in the narrative 1973 to 1977. During the Watergate hearings, in his official capacity he prevented Mark Felt of the FBI from being asked if he was Deep Throat. He then became an investment banker in New York and wrote novels in his spare time. His archival material is found within the Gerald R. Ford Library and Museum, primarily the library at Ann Arbor, Michigan. See www.fordlibrarymuseum.gov.

28. This U.S. treasurer was the first Mexican American to occupy the office, which has become a "Latina" position in national political appointments. In 2001 President George W. Bush nominated Rosario Marin as the 41st treasurer for the nation; Anna Escobedo Cabral became the 42nd; and Rosa Gumataotao Rios, nominated by President B. Obama, was the 43rd U.S. treasurer. There have been three consecutive Latinas in that office.

Chapter 7. End of Hoover and Nixon

1. Randy Shaw, *Beyond the Fields: Cesar Chavez, the UFW, and the Struggle for Justice in the 21st Century* (Berkeley: University of California Press, 2008), 146–47.

2. Ibid., 148–49.

3. See March 17, 1972, teletype URGENT 3:45 p.m. from San Diego to Director.

4. See Nitel dated April 6, 1972, from Phoenix to Director, two pages.

5. See Nitel teletype dated April 12, 1972, 1:45 a.m. from Phoenix to Director, one page.

6. See Nitel teletype dated May 12, 1972, 11:33 p.m. from Phoenix to Acting Director. Hoover had died May 2, 1972.

7. Jacques Levy, *Cesar Chavez: Autobiography of La Causa* (Minneapolis: University of Minnesota Press, 2007), 464.

8. Shaw, *Beyond the Fields*, 92, 149-50.

9. See Ignacio Garcia, "Chicanos and Mexicanos under Surveillance: 1940 to 1980," in *Renato Rosaldo Lecture Series Monograph*, Mexican American Studies & Research Center, University of Arizona, Tucson, vol. 2 (Spring 1986): 39-43.

10. Shaw, *Beyond the Fields*, 251.

11. Ibid., 250-51.

12. Matt Garcia, *From the Jaws of Victory: The Triumph and Tragedy of Cesar Chavez and the Farm Worker Movement* (Berkeley: University of California Press, 2012), 183.

13. This number, 62, refers to miscellaneous files having to do with other matters but sometimes used for security cases. See Buitrago and Immerman, *Are You Now*, 26.

14. The Young Chicanos for Community Action is the original name of the Brown Berets formed in Los Angeles. The proclamation was a separatist call for creating a Chicano Nation in the Southwest. Chavez was not a separatist, much less a nationalist, as revealed in the literature on the man; he was a labor leader. Carlos Montes, a cofounder of the Brown Berets, donated his papers to California State University-Los Angeles, and these are being indexed under the holdings and title of East Los Angeles Archive.

15. Ralph de Toledano wrote a critical monograph, *Little Cesar*, on Chavez (Washington, DC: Anthem, 1971). He was an archconservative from the 1940s to his death, with an interesting background. He was born in Tangiers, Morocco, to U.S. citizens who were Sephardic Jews, and he was educated in the United States. In adulthood he became friends with Richard Nixon during the Alger Hiss trial, which he covered for *Newsweek*, and was a founding member of *National Review*. He sued Mark Felt over royalties from *The FBI Pyramid*, which he allegedly cowrote before Felt admitted to being Deep Throat. He died on February 2, 2003, at age ninety. This Toledano is not to be confused with Mexican Communist Vicente Lombardo Toledano.

16. Darwin Porter, *J. Edgar Hoover and Clyde Tolson: Investigating the Sexual Secrets of America's Most Famous Men and Women* (New York: Blood Moon Productions, Ltd., 2012), 84.

17. Henry Ramirez, *A Chicano in the White House: The Nixon No One Knew* (self-published, 2013; ISBN 13: 9781497545823), 394.

18. Manuel Chavez was Cesar's tough guy, his muscle. Miriam Pawel in *The Crusades of Cesar Chavez: A Biography* (New York: Bloomsbury, 2014) recounts how Manuel used violence, bribery, and deception, perhaps even pocketing union money to stop Mexican workers from crossing into the U.S. at Arizona. Manuel's budget for keeping Mexicans out of the U.S. was $80,000 a week. He called the setting up of a private vigilante patrol along the border the "wetline." According to Pawel, Cesar was always aware and supportive of Manuel's actions; see 288–95.

19. Levy has the account of this trip and rushed journey to see the pope in his book *Cesar Chavez*, 522–26.

20. Ibid., 525.

21. Ibid.

22. The Riesel articles are in the file, in my estimation, because he was one of Hoover's friendly pressmen. He wrote for Hoover what the Director could not say in public. Thomas Bishop, FBI head of the Crime Records Division, kept the file for Hoover in his desk. Riesel continued in his role as FBI mouthpiece for decades, and post-Hoover with Kelley and Mueller. The papers of Victor Riesel are on deposit at New York University in the Robert L. Wagner Labor Archives. These articles were published by Hill Newspaper Syndicate of Chicago, Illinois.

23. Alan J. Watt, *Farm Workers and the Churches: The Movement in California and Texas* (College Station: Texas A&M University Press, 2010), does a good job of revealing the underpinnings of relations among the various Christian denominations and farm workers, primarily César Chávez's UFW.

24. This mention of a "1,000-mile walk" is the only other entry anywhere about the *caminata* Chavez had supposedly taken during the ALRA struggles.

25. Stuart A. Kallen, *We Are Not Beasts of Burden: Cesar Chavez and the Delano Grape Strike, California, 1965–1970* (Minneapolis: Twenty-First Century Books, 2011), 129.

26. Marshall Ganz, *Why David Sometimes Wins: Leadership, Organization, and Strategy in the California Farm Worker Movement* (New York: Oxford University Press,

2009), 246. Marshall Ganz resigned from the UFW board and union in 1981.

27. Caitlin Flanagan, "The Madness of Cesar Chavez," *The Atlantic*, July/August 2011.

28. Kevin Hile, *Cesar Chavez: UFW Labor Leader* (Farmington, MI: Gale, Cengage Learning, 2008), 74-75.

29. Frank Bardacke, *Trampling Out the Vintage: Cesar Chavez and the Two Souls of the United Farm Workers* (Brooklyn: Verso, 2012), 541-42.

30. Garcia, *From the Jaws of Victory*, 244.

31. Friedly and Gallen, *Martin Luther King, Jr.: The FBI File*, 680. Subsequent pages (682-85) list all hotel rooms used by Dr. King that were bugged by the FBI, by date from 1964 to 1966, hotel name, and city. See also Kenneth O'Reilly, "*Racial Matters": The FBI's Secret Files on Black America, 1960-1972* (New York: Free Press, 1989), 125-55; and William Sullivan's *The Bureau: My Thirty Years in Hoover's FBI* (New York: W.W. Norton & Co., 1979), 135-46.

32. Marc Aronson, *Master of Deceit: J. Edgar Hoover and America in the Age of Lies* (Somerville, MA: Candlewick Press, 2012), 174-75, which contains an actual copy of the purloined letter.

33. Curt Gentry, *J. Edgar Hoover: The Man and His Secrets* (New York: W.W. Norton & Co. 1991), 567-76.

34. Pawel, *Crusades*, 348-97, for a lengthy narrative on Chavez's turn towards destruction.

35. For titles to accompany the names of those departing the Chavez union, see Richard J. Jensen and John C. Hammerback, eds., *The Words of Cesar Chavez* (College Station: Texas A&M University Press, 2002), 89.

36. Nathan Heller, "Hunger Artist," *New Yorker*, April 14, 2014.

37. Shaw, *Beyond the Fields*, 250-67.

38. See letter from David M. Hardy, dated June 27, 2017, to me. The second paragraph states what is mentioned in the narrative. This letter is with the Chavez file at Special Collections, Michigan State University Library.

39. Number 9 is the FBI's classification number for Extortion; 1191 is the case sequence (i.e., the 1,191th file opened under Extortion in that office). And the last number, 1A, means it is the first document in this specific file. The A means it is a subfile; it was handwritten, therefore not the main document but a subfile.

40. Oddly, the word *incar* means to kneel, but they use it as an acronym for their organizational name.

41. See "Onomasticon" at beginning of this book for explanations of numbers and names and abbreviations, etc.; and also see Buitrago and Immerman, *Are You Now,* appendix B: "Material Found in Field Office Files but Usually Not in Headquarters Files," 23.

42. Jennifer Medina, "Family Quarrel Imperils a Labor Hero's Legacy," *New York Times,* May 14, 2011, A1.

Chapter 8. The Unraveling of Chávez

1. There were many other influential groups who joined in opposition, such as the Jewish Board of Rabbis, Southern California Council of Churches, black ministers organized under Inter-Faith Council, and scores of Catholic bishops and major state and federal political figures. See *Southern California Teamster* newsletter and campaign pamphlet 32, no. 43 (October 4, 1972).

2. Randy Shaw, *Beyond the Fields: Cesar Chavez, the UFW, and the Struggle for Justice in the 21st Century* (Berkeley: University of California Press, 2008), 156–57.

3. Ibid., 157.

4. Ibid., 250–51.

5. See www.biography.com/people/jane-fonda-9298034 and Mary Herschberger, *Jane Fonda: A Political Biography of an Antiwar Icon* (New York: New Press, 2005); both have personal and political data on the Hollywood actress.

6. Miriam Pawel, *The Crusades of Cesar Chavez: A Biography* (New York: Bloomsbury, 2014), 360.

7. See U.S. v. Dellinger, 472 F.2d. 340 (7th Cir.), 410 US 970, cert. denied, 410 U.S. 970, 935 S. Ct. 1443, 35 Ed. 2d. 706 (1973).

8. Pawel, *Crusades,* 313.

9. Ibid., 339.

10. Ibid., 341.

11. Ibid., 344.

12. Ibid., 345–46.

13. Matt Garcia, *From the Jaws of Victory: The Triumph and Tragedy of Cesar Chavez and the Farm Worker Movement* (Berkeley: University of California Press, 2012), 125.

14. Pawel, *Crusades,* 361.

15. Garcia, *From the Jaws,* 126–27.

16. Ronald B. Taylor, *Chavez and the Farm Workers* (Boston: Beacon Press, 1975), 181.

17. Jacques Levy, *Cesar Chavez: Autobiography of La Causa* (Minneapolis: University of Minnesota Press, 2007), 490-96.

18. Shaw, *Beyond the Fields*, 259-60.

19. Marshall Ganz, *Why David Sometimes Wins: Leadership, Organization, and Strategy in the California Farm Worker Movement* (New York: Oxford University Press, 2009), 116.

20. Garcia, *From the Jaws*, 221, 222, 238.

21. Ibid., 253.

22. Frank Bardacke, *Trampling Out the Vintage: Cesar Chavez and the Two Souls of the United Farm Workers* (Brooklyn: Verso, 2012), 679-81.

23. See undated and without sources, seven-page document, "1967" file, for this quote on page 6.

24. Bardacke, *Trampling Out the Vintage*, 681-82. This same version, page 6, is in the "1967" file, a seven-page document that is undated and without sources.

25. *El Malcriado*, no. 11, May 1965, 2.

26. David Bacon, *Illegal People: How Globalization Creates Migration and Criminalizes Immigrants* (Boston: Beacon Press, 2008), 207. Bacon discusses the role of Filipino farm laborers in California during the Ernesto Galarza and César Chávez years of organizing (200-231).

27. Ganz, *Why David Sometimes Wins*, 111.

28. Dick Meister and Anne Loftis, *A Long Time Coming: The Struggle to Unionize America's Farm Workers* (New York: Macmillan, 1977), 127-28.

29. Ganz, *Why David Sometimes Wins*, 99.

30. Ibid., 123-24.

31. Ibid., 204.

32. Susan Ferris and Ricardo Sandoval, *The Fight in the Fields: Cesar Chavez and the Farmworkers Movement*, ed. Diana Hembree (New York: Harcourt Brace & Co., 1997), 211.

33. Ibid., 212.

34. Bardacke, *Trampling Out the Vintage*, 404-5.

35. Ibid., 405.

36. Ibid., 568.

37. Shaw, *Beyond the Fields*, 253-54.

38. Bardacke, *Trampling Out the Vintage*, 573.

39. Ibid., 570-71.

40. Bacon, *Illegal People*, vi.

41. Glenn Anthony May, *Sonny Montes and Mexican American Activism in Oregon* (Corvallis: Oregon State University Press, 2011), 171, 206, and 265.

42. See Carlos Saldivar Maldonado, "Testimonio de un Tejano en Oregon: Contratista, Julian Ruiz," in Jerry Garcia and Gilberto Garcia, eds., *Memory, Community, and Activism* (East Lansing: Michigan State University Press), 205-32, for a personal testimony of a labor contractor from Asherton, Texas, and his trek to Oregon and becoming an *empresario* over many contracts with growers, a labor camp owner, a trucker, and a labor crew operator.

43. In the early 1970s, many an unemployed activist from South Texas could find a job in Milwaukee with the War on Poverty programs being headed by activists of the Raza Unida Party. Jesus Salas, Francisco Rodriguez, Esequiel Guzman, and Mario Compean, to name a few, at one time or another worked in these programs and at the state government in Madison, Wisconsin. Jesus Salas was appointed a regent of the University of Wisconsin System of Higher Education in the late 1990s.

44. W. K. Barger and Ernesto M. Reza, *The Farm Labor Movement in the Midwest: Social Change and Adaptation among Farmworkers* (Austin: University of Texas Press, 1993), 54-97. See also the works of Dennis Nodin Valdes, particularly the article "From Following the Crops to Chasing the Corporations: The Farm Labor Organizing Committee, 1967-1983," in Guadalupe Luna, ed., *The Chicano Struggle* (Tucson: Bilingual Press, 1984); and his 1991 book *Al Norte: Agricultural Workers in the Great Lakes Region, 1917-1970* (Austin: University of Texas Press).

45. Barger and Reza, *The Farm Labor Movement in the Midwest*, 63.

46. Ibid., 70.

47. Ibid., 84-85, 96.

48. We shared a speaker's platform in Mexico City at the invitation of the Mexican Senate on Migrant Labor and Immigration, and I asked him for his file if he had it. He was not eager or interested in having that conversation at that time. I am sure he had his reasons, because we had an ongoing collaborative relationship in that many migrants he sought to organize and bring into his fold were residents of my hometown. In the 1970s and 1980s I also supported his efforts publicly and made it a point to provide resources for him to meet with migrants before they could leave Crystal City for Ohio and inadvertently break his strike.

49. Bardacke, *Trampling Out the Vintage*, 319–20. See also p. 320 for the "For Your Eyes Only" memo prepared by Fred Hirsch on his and his wife's opposition to some of the same things as Orendain.

50. Pawel, *Crusades*, 419. Levy in *La Causa* completely ignores all other unionizing efforts elsewhere. The biography does end in 1976, well before many other catastrophes beset Chavez. He does not cite any names of leaders associated with farm worker organizing for Chavez in other states in his index. I assume he never asked Chavez about Orendain, Gustavo Gutierrez in Arizona, or Baldemar Velasquez in Ohio, and Chavez did not mention them on his own. On pp. 277 and 282, the only mention of Orendain is to portray him as a bigot regarding religion and Chavez's adherence to his faith.

51. Athan Theoharis, *Spying on Americans: Political Surveillance from Hoover to the Huston Plan* (Philadelphia: Temple University Press, 1978), 136.

52. William Turner, *Hoover's FBI* (New York: Thunder's Mouth Press, 1993), 189.

53. Ibid., 189.

54. Pawel, *Crusades*, 86, 88.

55. Bardacke, *Trampling Out the Vintage*, 160.

56. Taylor, *Chavez and the Farm Workers*, 115.

57. The affidavit is on FBI form FD-302 with "date of transcription 10/10/75" and taken in San Juan, Texas, by SA (name redacted) on the same day and placed in "File # SA 44-2889." This notarized document has two sets of page numbers. The first is at bottom, "17," and the other is bottom right, "211." The copy used here is in the Chavez file under "Chavez 1975."

58. The reference to UFW in this message is erroneous. Antonio Orendain had formed the Texas Farm Workers Union in August 1975 and subsequently broke all relations with the UFW and Cesar Chavez. The TFWU continued its existence until 1986. On the other hand, it could have been the FBI's ploy to make the threat of the UFW seem bigger than reality and combine all farm worker incidents nationwide as part of the Chavez unionization efforts.

59. The letter to the U.S. AG Levi from Orendain dated July 25, 1975, can be found in the Chavez file, folder Chavez 1975.

60. Pawel, *Crusades*, 475.

61. Ibid., 419–22.

62. Ann Mari Buitrago and Leon Andrew Immerman, *Are You Now or Have You Ever Been in the FBI Files? How to Secure and Interpret Your FBI Files* (New York: Grove Press, 1981), 181.

63. Chavez and Helen F. Chavez were both tried and convicted of criminal contempt for violating the court order. An appeal of the injunction was untimely filed and therefore dismissed. It is unfortunate because apparently the injunction was issued *ex parte* without a hearing on the merits. The Chavezes could have prevailed just on those grounds. It is also unfortunate that the appeal of their convictions did move forward but was also dismissed. The appellate court sided with the state in holding the Chavezes should have appealed the injunction, and not having done so waived any right to argue their convictions under the injunction as unconstitutional. See State of Arizona v. Cesar E. Chavez and Helen F. Chavez, 601 P.2d 301 (Ariz. Ct. App. 1979).

64. See Mark North, *Act of Treason: The Role of J. Edgar Hoover in the Assassination of President Kennedy* (New York: Carroll & Graf Publishers, 1991), 37–42, for additional insight into the FBI's system of record keeping, and policy manuals in place during the 1960s to the end of Hoover's years as Director.

65. Over the years that I have been submitting and receiving documents based on FOIA requests, an occasional document unrelated to a specific request was released either by mistake, inadvertently, or purposely by a conscientious employee. This was the case in obtaining a page on the Border Coverage Program COINTELPRO as part of another unrelated FOIA request, which led to my making further requests on this heretofore unknown and hidden FBI program. The same scenario occurred with documents on "Mexican American Militancy" included in response to a request not utilizing that subject or title or program name. Mexican American Militancy probably is another COINTELPRO operation in addition to other existing ones in which files on Mexican Americans, Chicanos, Puerto Ricans are kept such as Internal Security-Communists or Internal Security-Spanish. This 1982 document released as unclassified in the Chavez file clearly indicates there are more files on Chavez and the UFW not being released despite appeals for more. The FBI continues to hide and withhold information on the surveillance of Chavez that surely continued for at least four more years from 1978 to 1982 as this lone page indicates—perhaps fifteen more years from 1978 until he died in 1993. Other scholars in this field have also encountered "jewels" among other documents, such as Athan Theoharis finding reference to a program on "Sexual Deviates" (former FBI file #105-34074-104), which led to finding over 330,000 pages that later were destroyed between 1977 and 1978. For more information, see Douglas Charles's work in *Hoover's War on Gays: Exposing the FBI's "Sex Deviates" Program* (Lawrence: University Press of Kansas, 2015), xi, xiv, 31–33, 67–72. Similarly, and inadvertently, Charles also found a new

classification, "SM-C (Key Activist)," for an FBI program, perhaps another COINTELPRO, by the name "Key Activist Program." See p. 322 in *Hoover's War on Gays* and the FBI source cited in 418 n. 64.

The entire existence of the FBI's COINTELPRO operations was discovered by a serendipitous glance at those words on a file atop a staffers desk while NBC newsman Carl Stern was covering the Senate Judiciary Committee hearings early in 1972. Nobody knew what that was or referred to, so Stern wrote to then deputy attorney general Richard Kleindienst on March 20, 1972, requesting information under FOIA on the creation, existence, duration, and purposes of COINTELPRO at the FBI. He was consistently denied by others, including the new acting director of the FBI, L. Patrick Gray III. He sued in early 1973 and obtained the first of two documents. On December 7, 1972, Stern sent a new FOIA to FBI Director Clarence Kelley for more documents and was again refused. Finally, on March 6, 1974, he was able to obtain the first set of documents that began to expose the entire range of programs that were implemented based on FBI COINTELPRO targets. See James Kirkpatrick Davis, *Spying on America: The FBI's Domestic Counterintelligence Program* (Westport, CT: Praeger Publishers, 1992), 161–65, for greater details on this chain of events.

Epilogue. Chávez and the FBI Surveillance

1. 29 USC 152 (3) is the federal law the National Labor Relations Act (NLRA), which specifically excludes agricultural employees from its coverage. Ten states have granted agricultural employees the right to enter into collective bargaining agreements. California is one of these states as of 1975 under the California Agricultural Labor Relations Act; Arizona is another as of 1972, Oregon as of 1963, and Wisconsin also. These are states in which the UFW or some group who sought to affiliate with the UFW began to organize farm workers. Only Texas does not have such a right to collective bargaining, and the UFW was involved in organizing in that state since 1966.

2. Jack Mitchell, *Executive Privilege: Two Centuries of White House Scandals* (New York: Hippocrene Books, 1992).

3. See Jane Mayer, *Dark Money: The Hidden History of the Billionaires behind the Rise of the Radical Right* (New York: Doubleday, 2016). Mayer in *Dark Money* lists on 381–82 n. 9 those worth $1 billion or more, and collectively worth $222 billion, who belong to the "Investors Group" led by Charles Koch. Charles and brother David Koch own the second largest private company in the United States, Koch Industries. Their father, Fred, was one of the founders and funders of the John Birch Society. These investors are reactionary conservatives to the

point of being libertarians, and some are members of the political party. They were the heirs to conduit capitalism of the New Deal and War on Poverty and implemented the politics of neoliberalism. Now they seek to privatize the operations of government to make it their parallel structure, privatized statism: a structure of two conjoined bodies with one head.

4. Quote is taken from Derek S. Reverson and Kathleen A. Mahoney-Norris, *Human Security in a Borderless World* (Boulder, CO: Westview Press, 2011), 1.

5. Miriam Pawel, *The Crusades of Cesar Chavez: A Biography* (New York: Bloomsbury, 2014), 444.

6. Ibid., 445.

7. Ibid., 449.

8. Ibid., 450.

9. Ibid.

10. Ibid.

11. Ibid., 448-54.

12. See the ACLU's "Mapping the FBI" initiative at www.aclu.org/mapping-FBI/.

13. See "Facial Recognition Database Used by FBI Is Out of Control," *The Guardian*, March 27, 2017. See also U.S. Government Accountability Office, "Face Recognition Technology: FBI Should Better Ensure Privacy and Accuracy," www.gao.gov/assets/680/677098.pdf.

14. See Mayer's earlier work *The Dark Side* (New York: Doubleday, 2008).

15. See Daniel Kreiss, *Prototype Politics: Technology-Intensive Campaigning and the Data of Democracy* (New York: Oxford University Press, 2016), 204 and 260 n. 2.

16. See Jeremy Scahill, *Blackwater: The Rise of the World's Most Powerful Mercenary Army* (New York: Nation Books, 2007) for an illuminating history of how one contractor has now made the Department of Defense its subsidiary for all practical purposes.

17. Ibid., xix.

18. See Rumsfeld's plan to corporatize the military in "Transforming the Military," *Foreign Affairs*, May/June 2002.

19. Scahill, *Blackwater*, xviii-xix.

20. Ibid., 343.

21. *USA Today* special edition, *Transportation Today*, April 1, 2017, 51.

22. *The Economist*, "Secrets, Lies and America's Spies," and "Look Who Is

Listening," June 15, 2013, pp. 11 and 23–26, respectively.

23. Richard Wolf, "Supreme Court Limits Phone Searches," *USA Today*, June 26, 2014, 2A.

24. *United States v. Quartavious Davis*, docket number 12-12928 (11th Cir. 2017) was heard by a three-judge panel on June 11, 2014.

25. Jessica Guynn, "The Face of Facebook is Male, White," *USA Today*, June 26, 2014, B1.

26. *The Atlantic*, June 2014. The lead article is on pp. 54–71. Photographs utilized in the article were credited to Carlos Javier Ortiz.

27. Sue Halpern, "How He Used Facebook to Win," *New York Review of Books*, June 8, 2017, 59–61.

28. Jim Hightower, "'Thinking Robots' Will Soon Shake Our Definition of Human Worth," *Hightower Lowdown* 19, no. 9 (September 2017): 2.

29. See George Dvorsky, "Robots Are Already Replacing Human Workers at an Alarming Rate," Gizmodo, March 28, 2017, http://www.gizmodo.com. Another economist, James Surowiecki, concerns himself with the pace of substitution, arguing that robots will come, but slowly, while MIT's Andrew McAfee argues that net job loss is not the issue, but what is are the kinds of jobs that will be available. See https://www.wired.com/2017/08/robots-will-not-take-your-job/.

30. Peter Lance, *1000 Years for Revenge: International Terrorism and the FBI: The Untold Story* (New York: William Morrow, 2003), 4.

31. Mayer, *The Dark Side*.

32. Paul Szoldra, "These 17 Agencies Make Up the Most Sophisticated Spy Network in the World," *Business Insider*, May 11, 2013, http://businessinsider.com.

33. Sally Kane, "The FBI Today," The Balance, https://www.thebalance.com/company-profile-federal-bureau-of-investigation-2164427.

34. Joseph (Joe) Franco with Richard Hammer, *Hoffa's Man: The Rise and Fall of Jimmy Hoffa as Witnessed by his Strongest Arm* (New York: Prentice-Hall, 1987).

35. See *Consumer Reports* for a series of articles on the subject: "Your Secrets Aren't Safe," "Your Info: At Risk Everywhere," and "7 Security Disasters," July 2014, 15–19.

36. See www.gettingacreditcard.com.

37. Dave Lindorff, "How Badly Did Equifax Breach Damage the Social Security System?," *Salon*, September 15, 2017, https://www.salon.com/2017/09/15/how-badly-did-equifax-breach-damage-the-social-security-system/. Also Gretchen

Morgenson, "Consumers, but Not Executives, May Pay for Equifax Failings," *New York Times*, September 13, 2017.

38. See original disclosure leak by the International Consortium of Investigative Journalists, "Giant Leak of Offshore Financial Records Exposes Global Array of Crime and Corruption," www.occrp.org/en/panamapapers/overview/intro/, April 3, 2016.

39. David Streitfeld, "Court Says Privacy Case Can Proceed vs. Google," *New York Times*, September 10, 2013.

40. Gordon M. Goldstein, a participant as U.S. representative to the UN conference on telecommunication, has written an incisive article on global developments in this area of concern. See his "The End of the Internet?" in *The Atlantic*, July/August 2014, 24–26.

41. Katherine Albrecht and Liz McIntyre, *Spychips: How Major Corporations and Government Plan to Track Your Every Move with RFID* (Nashville, TN: Nelson Current, 2005).

42. See "Tiny Package, Big Impact," *UT Arlington* magazine (Spring 2014): 6.

43. While she was head of the Senate Intelligence Committee investigating the CIA.

44. See David C. Kent, "Civil Liability for Commercial Use of Drone Aircraft in Texas," *Headnotes* (Dallas Bar Association), July 2014, 7. The Texas law made effective September 1, 2013, can be found at 4 Tex. Gov. Code, Ch. 423 (Vernon Supp. 2013). The *Smithsonian*, June 2014, carried an article on p. 23, "Friendly Skies," that suggested that the public does not feel insecure or threatened by drones, and notes that the FAA is preparing to permit drones to fly in U.S. airspace.

45. See Jack Gillum, Eileen Sullivan, and Eric Tucker, "FBI Is Operating Fleet of Spy Planes over U.S.," *Fort Worth Star-Telegram*, June 3, 2015, 1A, 19A. The article also makes mention that a 2010 federal budget document does reveal an allocation for 115 planes.

Appendix 1. Methodology and Research Note

1. Richard Steven Street ("The FBI's Secret File on Cesar Chavez," *Southern California Quarterly* 78, no. 4 (Winter 1996): 347–84) was the first person to request the Chavez file from the FBI and he was able to obtain "over 1,500 pages, with new documents being disclosed regularly." See his article, p.348. I have requested via FOIA appeal more files post-1975, specifically from August 2, 1975, to April 30, 1993, the date of his death.

2. Douglas M. Charles, *Hoover's War on Gays: Exposing the FBI's "Sex Deviates" Program* (Lawrence: University Press of Kansas, 2015), 33. Another companion file opened was the Obscene File to track interstate pornography and white slavery (Mann Act), which was the transporting of white women across state lines for prostitution.

Bibliography

Ackerman, Kenneth. *Young J. Edgar: Hoover and the Red Scare, 1919–1920.* Washington, DC: Viral History Press, 2011.

Acuña, Rodolfo. *Occupied America: The Chicano Struggle toward Liberation.* 1st ed. San Francisco: Canfield Press, 1972.

Allee, Sheila. *Texas Mutiny: Bullets, Ballots, and Boss Rule.* Victoria, TX: Redbud Publishing Co., 2003.

Alvarez, Luis. *The Power of the Zoot Suit: Youth, Culture, and Resistance during World War II.* Berkeley: University of California Press, 2008.

Arkin, William M. *Code Names: Deciphering U.S. Military Plans, Programs, and Operations in the 9/11 World.* Hanover, NH: Steerforth Press, 2005.

Aronson, Marc. *Master of Deceit: J. Edgar Hoover and America in the Age of Lies.* Somerville, MA: Candlewick Press, 2012.

Arundhati, Roy, and John Cusack. *Things That Can and Cannot Be Said.* Chicago:

Haymarket Books, 2016.

Bacon, David. *Illegal People: How Globalization Creates Migration and Criminalizes Immigrants.* Boston: Beacon Press, 2008.

Bamford, James. *Body of Secrets: Anatomy of the Ultra-Secret National Security Agency from the Cold War through the Dawn of a New Century.* New York: Doubleday, 2001.

———. *The Puzzle Palace: A Report on NSA, America's Most Secret Agency.* Boston: Houghton Mifflin, 1982.

Bardacke, Frank. *Trampling Out the Vintage: Cesar Chavez and the Two Souls of the United Farm Workers.* Brooklyn, NY: Verso, 2012.

Barger, W. K., and Ernesto M. Reza. *The Farm Labor Movement in the Midwest: Social Change and Adaptation among Farmworkers.* Austin: University of Texas Press, 1993.

Bedolla, Lisa Garcia. *Latino Politics.* 2nd ed. Malden, MA: Polity Press, 2014.

Bender, Steven W. *One Night in America: Robert Kennedy, Cesar Chavez, and the Dream of Dignity.* Boulder, CO: Paradigm Publishers, 2008.

Blackstock, Nelson. *COINTELPRO: The FBI's Secret War on Political Freedom.* New York: Pathfinder Press, 1988.

Boykoff, Jules. *Beyond Bullets: The Suppression of Dissent in the United States.* Oakland, CA: AK Press, 2007.

Brill, Steven. *The Teamsters.* New York: Simon & Schuster, 1978.

Buitrago, Ann Mari, and Leon Andrew Immerman. *Are You Now or Have You Ever Been in the FBI Files? How to Secure and Interpret Your FBI Files.* New York: Grove Press, 1981.

Burnham, David. *A Law unto Itself: Power, Politics, and the IRS.* New York: Random House, 1989.

Burton, Bob. *Top Secret: The Dictionary of Espionage and Intelligence.* New York: Citadel Press, 2005.

Cannon, Lou. *President Reagan: A Role of a Lifetime.* New York: Simon & Schuster, 1991.

Carrigan, William D. *The Making of a Lynching Culture: Violence and Vigilantism in Central Texas, 1836–1916.* Chicago: University of Illinois Press, 2006.

Carrigan, William D., and Clive Webb. *Forgotten Dead: Mob Violence against Mexicans in the United States, 1848–1928.* New York: Oxford University Press, 2013.

Carson, Clayborne. *Malcolm X: The FBI File.* Edited by David Gallen. New York: Skyhorse Publishing, 1991.

Cecil, Matthew. *Branding Hoover's FBI: How the Boss's PR Men Sold the Bureau to*

America. Lawrence: University Press of Kansas, 2016.

Charles, Douglas M. *The FBI's Obscene File: J. Edgar Hoover and the Bureau's Crusade against Smut.* Lawrence: University Press of Kansas, 2012.

———. *Hoover's War on Gays: Exposing the FBI's "Sex Deviates" Program.* Lawrence: University Press of Kansas, 2015.

———. *J. Edgar Hoover and the Anti-interventionists: FBI Political Surveillance and the Rise of the Domestic Security State, 1939–1945.* Columbus: Ohio State University Press, 2007.

Chavez, John R. *The Lost Land: The Chicano Image of the Southwest.* Albuquerque: University of New Mexico Press, 1984.

Churchill, Ward, and Jim Vander Wall. *The COINTELPRO Papers: Documents from the FBI's Secret Wars against Dissent in the United States.* Boston: South End Press, 1990.

Cinotto, Simone. *Soft Soil, Black Grapes: The Birth of Italian Winemaking in California.* New York: NYU Press, 2012.

Cohen, Deborah. *Braceros: Migrant Citizens and Transnational Subjects in the Postwar United States and Mexico.* Chapel Hill: University of North Carolina Press, 2011.

Cooper, Phillip J. *By Order of the President: The Use and Abuse of Executive Direct Action.* Lawrence: University Press of Kansas, 2012.

Dalton, Frederick John. *The Moral Vision of Cesar Chavez.* Ossining, NY: Orbis Books, 2003.

Davenport, B. T. *Soldiering at Marfa, Texas, 1911–1945.* Kearney, NE: Morris Publishing, 1997.

Davis, James Kirkpatrick. *Spying on America: The FBI's Domestic Counterintelligence Program.* Westport, CT: Praeger Publishers, 1992.

De León, Arnoldo. *They Called Them Greasers: Anglo Attitudes toward Mexicans in Texas, 1821–1900.* Austin: University of Texas Press, 1983.

Delgado, Richard. "The Law of the Noose: A History of Latino Lynching." *Harvard Civil Rights–Civil Liberties Law Review* 44 (2009): 291–312.

Donner, Frank. *Protectors of Privilege: Red Squads and Police Repression in Urban America.* Berkeley: University of California Press, 1990.

Dunn, Timothy J. *The Militarization of the U.S.-Mexico Border, 1978–1992: Low-Intensity Conflict Doctrine Comes Home.* Austin: University of Texas Press, 1996.

Ehrlichman, John. *Witness to Power: The Nixon Years.* New York: Simon & Schuster, 1982.

Escobar, Edward. *Race, Police, and the Making of a Political Identity: Mexican Americans and the Los Angeles Police Department, 1900–1945.* Berkeley: University of California Press, 1999.

Etulain, Richard W., ed. *Cesar Chavez: A Brief Biography with Documents.* Boston: Bedford/St. Martin's Press, 2002.

Evanzz, Karl. *The Judas Factor: The Plot to Kill Malcolm X.* New York: Thunder's Mouth Press, 1992.

Farren, Mick, and John Gibb. *Who's Watching You? The Chilling Truth about the State, Surveillance, and Personal Freedom.* New York: Disinformation Co., 2007.

Felt, Mark, and John O'Connor. *A G-Man's Life: The FBI, Being "Deep Throat," and the Struggle for Honor in Washington.* New York: PublicAffairs, 2006.

Ferris, Susan, and Ricardo Sandoval. *The Fight in the Fields: Cesar Chavez and the Farmworkers Movement.* Edited by Diana Hembree. New York: Harcourt Brace & Co., 1997.

Feuerlicht, Roberta Strauss. *America's Reign of Terror: World War I, the Red Scare, and the Palmer Raids.* New York: Random House, 1971.

Flanagan, Caitlin. "The Madness of Cesar Chavez." *The Atlantic*, July/August 2011.

Flynn, Michael T., with Michael Ledeen. *Summary of the Field of Fight.* Lexington, KY: Instaread, 2016.

Friedly, Michael, and David Gallen, eds. *Martin Luther King, Jr.: The FBI File.* New York: Carroll & Graf Publishers, 1993.

Galarza, Ernesto. *Merchants of Labor: The Mexican Bracero Story.* Charlotte, NC: McNally and Loftin, 1964.

———. *Spiders in the House and Workers in the Field.* Notre Dame, IN: University of Notre Dame Press, 1970.

Ganz, Marshall. *Why David Sometimes Wins: Leadership, Organization, and Strategy in the California Farm Worker Movement.* New York: Oxford University Press, 2009.

Garcia, Ignacio, ed. "Chicanos and Mexicanos under Surveillance, 1940-1980." Renato Rosaldo Lecture Series Monograph. Tucson: Mexican American Studies and Research Center, University of Arizona, 1986.

———. *Viva Kennedy: Mexican Americans in Search of Camelot.* College Station: Texas A&M University Press, 2000.

———. *White But Not Equal: Mexican Americans, Jury Discrimination, and the Supreme Court.* Tucson: University of Arizona Press, 2008.

Garcia, Juan Ramon. *Operation Wetback: The Mass Deportation of Mexican*

Undocumented Workers in 1954. Westport, CT: Greenwood Press, 1980.

Garcia, Matt. *From the Jaws of Victory: The Triumph and Tragedy of Cesar Chavez and the Farm Worker Movement.* Berkeley: University of California Press, 2012.

———. "What the New Cesar Chavez Film Gets Wrong about the Labor Activist." *Smithsonian,* April 2, 2014.

Gentry, Curt. *J. Edgar Hoover: The Man and His Secrets.* New York: W.W. Norton & Co., 1991.

Goldfinch, Charles, and José T. Canales. *Juan N. Cortina: Two Interpretations.* New York: Arno Press, 1974.

Graham, Thomas, Jr., and Keith A. Hansen. *Spy Satellites and Other Intelligence Technologies That Changed History.* Seattle: University of Washington Press, 2007.

Gutierrez, Jose Angel. "Cesar Chavez Estrada: The First and Last of the Chicano Leaders." *San Jose Studies* (Spring 1994): 32–44. Special Issue in Memory of Cesar Chavez, 1927–1993.

Hack, Richard. *Puppetmaster: The Secret Life of J. Edgar Hoover.* Beverly Hills, CA: New Millennium Press, 2004.

Hagedorn, Ann. *The Invisible Soldiers: How America Outsourced Our Security.* New York: Simon and Schuster, 2014.

Hall, Thomas D. *Social Change in the Southwest, 1350–1880.* Lawrence: University of Kansas Press, 1989.

Halperin, Morton H., Jerry J. Berman, Robert L. Borosage, and Christine M. Marwick. *The Lawless State: The Crimes of the U.S. Intelligence Agencies.* New York: Penguin Books, 1976.

Haro, Juan. *The Ultimate Betrayal: An Autobiography.* Pittsburg, PA: Dorrance Publishing Co., 1998.

Heller, Nathan. "Hunger Artist." *New Yorker,* April 14, 2014.

Hile, Kevin. *Cesar Chavez: UFW Labor Leader.* Farmington, MI: Gale, Cengage Learning, 2008.

Jeffery-Jones, Rhodri. *The FBI: A History.* New Haven, CT: Yale University Press, 2007.

Jensen, Joan M. *Army Surveillance in America, 1775–1980.* New Haven, CT: Yale University Press, 1991.

Jensen, Richard J., and John C. Hammerback, eds. *The Words of Cesar Chavez.* College Station: Texas A&M University Press, 2002.

Johnson, David K. *The Lavender Scare: The Cold War Persecution of Gays and Lesbians in the Federal Government.* Chicago: University of Chicago Press, 2004.

Kallen, Stuart A. *We Are Not Beasts of Burden: Cesar Chavez and the Delano Grape Strike, California, 1965–1970.* Minneapolis: Twenty-First Century Books, 2011.

Kessler, Ronald. *The Bureau: The Secret History of the FBI.* New York: St. Martins, 2003.

———. *The FBI: Inside the World's Most Powerful Law Enforcement Agency.* New York: Pocket Books, 1993.

——— *In the President's Secret Service.* New York: Three Rivers Press, 2010.

———. *The Secrets of the FBI.* New York: Broadway Paperbacks, 2012.

Kushner, Sam. *Long Road to Delano.* New York: International Publishers, 1975.

Lance, Peter. *1000 Years for Revenge: International Terrorism and the FBI: The Untold Story.* New York: William Morrow, 2003.

Leon, Luis D. *The Political Spirituality of Cesar Chavez: Crossing Religious Borders.* Los Angeles: University of California Press, 2015.

Levario, Miguel Antonio. *Militarizing the Border: When Mexicans Became the Enemy.* College Station: Texas A&M University Press, 2012.

Levy, Jacques E. *Cesar Chavez: Autobiography of La Causa.* Minneapolis: University of Minnesota Press, 2007.

Lindsey, Lawrence B. *Conspiracies of the Ruling Class: How to Break Their Grip Forever.* New York: Simon and Schuster, 2016.

"Look Who's Listening." *The Economist,* June 15, 2013, 23-26.

Marquez, Benjamin. *Democratizing Texas Politics: Race, Identity, and Mexican American Empowerment, 1945–2002.* Austin: University of Texas Press, 2014.

Martin, Gail Z. *30 Days to Social Media Success: The 30 Day Results Guide to Making the Most of Twitter, Blogging, LinkedIn, and Facebook.* Pompton, NJ: Career Press, 2010.

Martin, Philip. *Promises Unfulfilled: Unions, Immigration, and Farm Workers.* Ithaca, NY: Cornell University Press, 2003.

Matthiessen, Peter. *Sal Si Puedes: Cesar Chavez and the New American Revolution.* New York: Dell Publishing Co., 1969.

May, Glenn Anthony. *Sonny Montes and Mexican American Activism in Oregon.* Corvallis: Oregon State University Press, 2011.

Mayer, Jane. *Dark Money: The Hidden History of the Billionaires behind the Rise of the Radical Right.* New York: Doubleday, 2016.

———. *The Dark Side: The Inside Story of How the War on Terror Turned into a War on American Ideals.* New York: Doubleday, 2008.

Mazon, Mauricio. *The Zoot Suit Riots: The Psychology of Symbolic Annihilation.* Austin: University of Texas Press, 1984.

Medina, Jennifer. "Family Quarrel Imperils a Labor Hero's Legacy." *New York Times,* May 14, 2011, A1.

Meier, Matt S., and Feliciano Rivera. *The Chicanos: A History of Mexican Americans.* New York: Hill and Wang, 1972.

Meister, Dick, and Anne Loftis. *A Long Time Coming: The Struggle to Unionize America's Farm Workers.* New York: Macmillan, 1977.

Melanson, Philip, and Peter E. Stevens. *The Secret Service: The Hidden History of an Enigmatic Agency.* New York: MJF Books, 2002.

Miles, Elton. *More Tales of the Big Bend.* College Station: Texas A&M University Press, 1988.

Mink, Patsy T. "The Cannikin Papers: A Case Study in Freedom of Information." In *Secrecy and Foreign Policy,* ed. Thomas M. Franck and Edward Weisband, 114–31. New York: Oxford University Press, 1974.

Mitchell, Jack. *Executive Privilege: Two Centuries of White House Scandals.* New York: Hippocrene Books, 1992.

Moquin, Wayne, and Charles Van Doren. *A Documentary History of the Mexican Americans.* New York: Praeger, 1971.

Murray, Douglas L. "The Abolition of El Cortito, the Short-handled Hoe: A Case Study in Social Conflict and State Policy in California Agriculture." *Social Problems* 30, no. 1 (1982): 26–39.

Navarro, Armando. *La Raza Unida Party: A Chicano Challenge to the U.S. Two-Party Dictatorship.* Philadelphia: Temple University Press, 2000.

Nelson, Eugene. *Huelga: The First Hundred Days of the Great Delano Grape Strike.* Delano, CA: Farm Worker Press, 1966.

Nevins, Joseph. *Operation Gatekeeper: The Rise of the "Illegal Alien" and the Making of the U.S.-Mexico Boundary.* New York: Routledge, 2002.

North, Mark. *Act of Treason: The Role of J. Edgar Hoover in the Assassination of President Kennedy.* New York: Carroll & Graf Publishers, 1991.

O'Reilly, Kenneth. *Black Americans: The FBI Files.* Edited by David Gallen. New York: Carroll & Graf, 1994.

——— . *"Racial Matters": The FBI's Secret Files on Black America, 1960–1972.* New York: Free Press, 1989.

Pagan, Eduardo. *Murder at the Sleepy Lagoon: Zoot Suits, Race, and Riot in Wartime L.A.*

Chapel Hill: University of North Carolina Press, 2006.

Pawel, Miriam. *The Crusades of Cesar Chavez: A Biography.* New York: Bloomsbury, 2014.

Paz, Maria Emilia. *Strategy, Security, and Spies: Mexico and the U.S. as Allies in World War II.* University Park, PA: Penn State University Press, 1997.

Perkins, Clifford Alan. *Border Patrol: With the U.S. Immigration Service on the Mexican Boundary, 1910–1954.* El Paso: Texas Western Press, 1978.

Pitrone, Jean Maddern. *Chavez, Man of the Migrants: A Plea for Social Justice.* New York: Alba House, 1972.

Porter, Darwin. *J. Edgar Hoover and Clyde Tolson: Investigating the Sexual Secrets of America's Most Famous Men and Women.* New York: Blood Moon Productions, Ltd., 2012.

Powers, Richard Gid. *G-Men: The FBI in American Popular Culture.* Carbondale: Southern Illinois University Press, 1983.

———. *Secrecy and Power: The Life of J. Edgar Hoover.* New York: Free Press, 1987.

Priess, David. *The President's Book of Secrets: The Untold Story of Intelligence Briefings to America's Presidents from Kennedy to Obama.* New York: Public Affairs, 2016.

Priest, Dana, and William M. Arkin. *Top Secret America: The Rise of the New American Security State.* New York: Little, Brown and Co., 2011.

Prouty, Marco G. *Cesar Chavez, the Catholic Bishops, and the Farm Workers' Struggle for Social Justice.* Tucson: University of Arizona Press, 2006.

Pycior, Julie Leininger. *LBJ and Mexican Americans: The Paradox of Power.* Austin: University of Texas Press, 1997.

Ramirez, Catherine S. *The Zoot Suit Women: Gender, Nationalism, and the Culture Politics of Memory.* Durham, NC: Duke University Press, 2009.

Ramirez, Dr. Henry M. *A Chicano in the White House: The Nixon No One Knew.* Self-published, 2013. ISBN 9780615821931.

———. *The Wizards of Langley: Inside the CIA's Directorate of Science and Technology.* Boulder, CO: Westview Press, 2002.

Reveron, Derek S., and Kathleen A. Mahoney-Norris. *Human Security in a Borderless World.* New York: Routledge, 2011.

Rosenbaum, Robert J. *Mexicano Resistance in the Southwest: The Sacred Right of Self-Preservation.* Austin: University of Texas Press, 1981.

Ross, Fred. *Conquering Goliath: Cesar Chavez at the Beginning.* Keene, CA: Taller Grafico Press, 1989.

Rosswurm, Steve. *The FBI and the Catholic Church, 1935–1962.* Amherst: University of Massachusetts Press, 2009.

Rothkopf, David. *National Insecurity: American Leadership in an Age of Fear.* New York: PublicAffairs, 2014.

Samora, Julian. *Los Mojados: The Wetback Story.* Notre Dame, IN: University of Notre Dame Press, 1971.

San Miguel, Guadalupe. *Let All of Them Take Heed: Mexican Americans and the Campaign for Educational Equity in Texas, 1910–1981.* College Station: Texas A&M University Press, 2000.

Scarborough, Mike. *Trespassers on Our Own Land: Structured as an Oral History of the Juan P. Valdez Family and of the Land Grants of Northern New Mexico.* Indianapolis, IN: Dog Ear Publishing, 2011.

Scharlin, Craig, and Lilia Villanueva. *Philip Vera Cruz: A Personal History of Filipino Immigrants and the Farmworkers Movement.* 3rd ed. Seattle: University of Washington Press, 2000.

"Secrets, Lies and America's Spies." *The Economist*, June 15, 2013, 11.

Shaw, Randy. *Beyond the Fields: Cesar Chavez, the UFW, and the Struggle for Justice in the 21st Century.* Berkeley: University of California Press, 2008.

Shockley, John. *Chicano Revolt in a Texas Town.* Notre Dame, IN: University of Notre Dame Press, 1974.

Stout, Joseph A., Jr. *Spies, Politics, and Power: El Departamento Confidencial en Mexico, 1922–1946.* Fort Worth, TX: TCU Press, 2012.

Street, Richard Steven. "The FBI's Secret File on Cesar Chavez." *Southern California Quarterly* 78, no. 4 (Winter 1996): 347–84.

Sullivan, William C., with Bill Brown. *The Bureau: My Thirty Years in Hoover's FBI.* New York: W.W. Norton & Co., 1979.

Summers, Anthony. *The Arrogance of Power: The Secret World of Richard Nixon.* New York: Penguin Books, 2000.

———. *Official and Confidential: The Secret Life of J. Edgar Hoover.* New York: G.P. Putnam's Sons, 1993.

Taylor, Ronald B. *Chavez and the Farm Workers.* Boston: Beacon Press, 1975.

Theoharis, Athan. *Abuse of Power: How Cold War Surveillance and Secrecy Policy Shaped the Response to 9/11.* Philadelphia: Temple University Press, 2011.

———. *The FBI and American Democracy: A Brief Critical History.* Lawrence: University Press of Kansas, 2004.

———. *From the Secret Files of J. Edgar Hoover.* Chicago: Ivan R. Dee, 1992.

———. *Spying on Americans: Political Surveillance from Hoover to the Huston Plan.* Philadelphia: Temple University Press, 1978.

Toledano, Ralph de. *J. Edgar Hoover: The Man in His Time.* New Rochelle, NY: Arlington House, 1973.

———. *Little Cesar.* Washington, DC: Anthem, 1971.

———. *Spies, Dupes, and Diplomats.* New Rochelle, NY: Arlington House, 1967.

Turner, William W. *Hoover's FBI.* New York: Thunder's Mouth Press, 1993.

Utley, Robert M. *Lone Star Lawmen: The Second Century of the Texas Rangers.* New York: Berkley Books, 2007.

Valdes, Dennis Nodin. *Al Norte: Agricultural Workers in the Great Lakes Region, 1917-1970.* Austin: University of Texas Press.

———. "From Following the Crops to Chasing the Corporations: The Farm Labor Organizing Committee, 1967-1983." In *The Chicano Struggle*, ed. Guadalupe Luna. Tucson: Bilingual Press, 1984.

———. *Materials on the History of Latinos in Michigan and the Midwest: An Annotated Bibliography.* Detroit: Wayne State University, 1982.

Vigil, Ernesto B. *The Crusade for Justice: Chicano Militancy and the Government's War on Dissent.* Madison: University of Wisconsin Press, 1999.

Watt, Alan J. *Farm Workers and the Churches: The Movement in California and Texas.* College Station: Texas A&M University Press, 2010.

Weber, Devra Anne. *The Organizing of Mexicano Agricultural Workers: Imperial Valley and Los Angeles, 1925-1934: An Oral History Approach.* Los Angeles: Aztlan Publications, 1973.

Weitz, Mark A. *The Sleepy Lagoon Murder Case: Race Discrimination and Mexican-American Rights.* Lawrence: University Press of Kansas, 2010.

"Zoot Suit Riots." *The American Experience.* Video. PBS, 2002.

Index

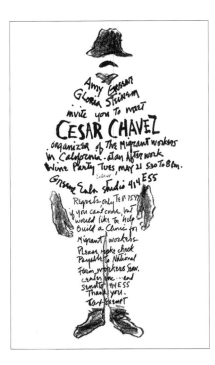